W9-CHV-648

Managing World Debt

Managing World Debt

Edited by
Stephany Griffith-Jones
Reader at the Institute of Development Studies
University of Sussex

HARVESTER • WHEATSHEAF
ST. MARTIN'S PRESS • NEW YORK

AGU 4954- 0/3

First published 1988 by
Harvester · Wheatsheaf
66 Wood Lane End, Hemel Hempstead
Hertfordshire HP2 4RG
A division of
Simon & Schuster International Group

and in the USA by
St. Martin's Press, Inc.
175 Fifth Avenue, New York, NY10010

© 1988 Stephany Griffith-Jones

Printed and bound in Great Britain by
Billing & Sons Ltd, Worcester

British Library Cataloguing in Publication Data
Managing world debt.
1. Latin America. Governments. Debts.
Financing
I. Griffith-Jones, Stephany
336.3′6′098
ISBN 0–7450–0327–3

Library of Congress Cataloging-in-Publication Data
Managing world debt.
Includes index.
1. Debts, External—Latin America—Case studies.
2. Loans, Foreign—Latin America—Case studies.
3. Debt relief—Latin America—Case studies.
4. Debts, External.   5. Loans, Foreign.
I. Griffith-Jones, Stephany.
HJ8514.5.M35   1988   336.3′435′098   88–4678
ISBN 0–312–01986–6 (St. Martin's)

1 2 3 4 5   92 91 90 89 88

To Robert, Edward and David

You tell me what is, and you ask why?
I tell you what could be, and ask why not?

George Bernard Shaw

Contents

List of figures

List of tables

List of Contributors

S. Griffith-Jones is a Reader at the Institute of Development Studies, University of Sussex

R. Villarreal is a former Under-Secretary of Trade and Industrial Planning, Mexico

A. Gurria Trevino is Head of the External Credit Department of the Mexican Ministry of Finance and Chief Negotiator for Mexico on foreign debt since 1982

R. Ffrench-Davis is Vice-president of CIEPLAN and a former Head of the Studies Department of the Central Bank

D. Dias Carneiro is Head of Economics at the Catholic University, Brazil

O. Ugarteche of IEP, Peru is also an Adviser on External Debt for UNCTAD

E. Rodriguez is a former Minister of Debt and Foreign Finance for Costa Rica

Ana Maria Alvarez De Stella works for the Central Bank of Venezuela

R.S. Green is a Fellow of the Institute of Development Studies

Diana Tussie is Head of the Foreign Trade Department, Ministry of Planning, Argentina

C. Fortin is a Reader at the Institute of Development Studies

Preface

This book deals with how the debt crisis has been managed since 1982, taking as point of entry the point of view of debtor governments. It starts from the following questions; why have the debtors on the whole got such bad deals, and why have the debtor governments—and their peoples—been so patient for so long in accepting a blueprint roughly imposed by creditors?

To understand the outcome of the negotiation, we have looked in some detail at the process of bargaining, incorporating where appropriate some elements from bargaining theory when these were helpful to our analysis. As a part of our evaluation of the past experience of debt rescheduling and adjustment, we suggest better more 'positive sum' ways of handling the problem in the future. As so much of our analysis is on analysing the bargaining from the point of view of the debtors, we finish with some recommendations on bargaining tactics and strategy.

The book is thus basically about the process of managing debt crises, particularly since 1982, in different Latin American countries and or Africa. It is *not* about the social origins or causes of the debt crises, a subject which has already been vastly explored in the literature, and on which several of us have written articles or even books. The book does, however, examine the specific ways in which debt crises arose in the different countries' studies; again in our analysis of bargaining and debt management, we have emphasised the specific economic and political features of individual countries. Again, here we hope to differ from much of the literature, which deals with Latin America's or the 'Third World's' debt as a whole.

Though we believe these countries clearly share many common problems, and indeed should collaborate far more closely in the search for common solutions than they have until now, we also believe it useful to understand the differences—in both economic and political aspects—amongst them.

This book is the result of a collective project carried out by a group of researchers and senior government officials in Latin America and Great Britain. First of all, I wish to thank all of them very warmly for their contribution. In particular, I wish to thank Rene Villarreal not just for his valuable input, but also for his excellent organisation of our third workshop in Mexico City; in that meeting, our group benefited also from the extremely interesting comments made by Angel Gurria and the excellent contributions made by Rocio Villarreal. I also wish to thank Diana Tussie for her support in the initial stages of setting up the project and the research team.

The project, and this book, became feasible due to the financial support of the Canadian agency, IDRC and the British agency, ESRC. I particularly wish to thank David Glover from IDRC, who was not only concerned with providing financial and administrative support to the project but also gave our group valuable comments in our meetings at Brighton, England and in Mexico City.

I would also wish to thank very warmly the British and other European parliamentarians, bankers, journalists, academics and officials of international institutions, who gave us valuable comments during the meetings held in the British House of Commons. I am particularly grateful to the two British Members of Parliament, Bowen Wells and Dame Judith Hart, who kindly chaired those meetings.

Many colleagues have contributed to the organisation and discussion of this project, I would particularly like to thank Susan Strange, Professor at the London School of Economics; David Suratgar, Director of Morgan Grenfell; Mike Faber, at the time Director of the Institute of Development Studies; Ricardo Carciofi, Under-Secretary of Finance in Argentina; Jorge Navarrete, Mexican Ambassador in Great Britain; Mike Anderson, G. Landau and Rodolfo Silva at the Inter-American Development Bank; Frances Stewart from Queen Elizabeth House; Sheila Page and Adrian Hewitt, from ODI;

and Steven Treagust at the Institute of Development Studies for preparing the index.

Last, but certainly not least, my very warm thanks go to Colette Nurse who not only typed so much of this book, but also provided essential administrative and secretarial backing to the project.

1 Debt Crisis Management, an Analytical Framework

S. Griffith-Jones[1]

INTRODUCTION

This chapter is intended as a framework for analysing and evaluating debt crisis management in Latin America and Africa, for the 1982–6 period with emphasis on the experience of Latin American debtors.

The paper consists of two parts. The first part will outline the major features of debt crisis management since 1982. The second part will draw on elements of bargaining and political science theory as well as on other elements in an attempt to explain the main features of the debt rescheduling/adjustment deals, as well as the differences between deals reached by different countries.

1. MAIN FEATURES OF DEBT RESCHEDULING AND MANAGEMENT DEALS

Since August 1982, debt crises and reschedulings became very widespread both in Latin America and Africa. This is in sharp contrast with previous periods when only a very limited number of fairly small debtors undertook multilateral debt negotiations (most of which were renegotiations of official debt).

The existence of clearly established procedures for dealing particularly in the case of official debt through the *Paris Club*—with a few 'problem' debtors may have had a significance for the post–1982 deals, not sufficiently highlighted in the literature. *A sort of blueprint thus existed, which had been designed by a collective of creditors*, for dealing most appropriately—from the creditors' point of view—with a few 'problem' debtors, whose debt crises could, to a large extent, be attributed either to specific ill fortune affecting that country (e.g. drought, weak price of its' main exports) or to mismanagement. These 'problem' debtors had little bargaining power, given the small size of their debts and their economies; as much of the debt affected was official, their debt crises did not pose any threat to the stability of the private banks.

As a result, precedent and initiative—both important elements in negotiations, as bargaining theory rightly tells us—were heavily biased towards the interests of the creditors, at the time when the major and widespread debt crises erupted in 1982. As the IMF document[2] sees it:

A multilateral approach to debt restructuring permitted the negotiations to proceed according to practices and policies that—at least for official debt—were well established. This was advantageous to the parties concerned because it helped to ensure that broadly comparable treatment was accorded to all creditors within a particular multilateral framework, as well as to different debtor countries over time.

The emphasis is clearly on equity *between* creditors and *between* debtors; there is no concern over equitable sharing *between debtor and creditor countries*.

Even though precedents and blueprints existed, there was no framework in 1982 for managing widespread and major debt crises for most of the large bank debtors simultaneously and in a situation where the origins of debt crises was determined largely by factors outside the control and responsibility of the debtor governments.

The framework adopted and operated since 1982 has the following general features:

1. Crisis management of bank debt brought back to the *centre of the stage* official international organisations as well as central banks of the major industrial governments. This was in sharp contrast with the seventies when industrial countries' governments and international institutions had almost abandoned the

field of private international lending and borrowing to their private banks.

The IMF has played a key role in assembling 'rescue packages' which have simultaneously included an upper credit *tranche* (high conditionality) adjustment programme between the debtor country and the IMF, rescheduling of maturing debts and arrangements of new finance by all the creditor banks. The Fund's influence became crucial; for the first time, adjustment financing provided by the IMF (which would bless the whole rescheduling package) was not only conditional upon adjustment following IMF 'advice' in the debtor country, but also upon the extension of new credit by the creditor banks.

2. An important new characteristic of the post–1982 rescheduling deals has been 'involuntary lending by creditor private banks, the level of which was not determined by individual banks' management but more or less imposed through pressure by the IMF, the industrial countries' central banks and, to a certain extent, by the major creditor banks.

Since 1982 the magnitude of 'involuntary lending' was in all cases involving Latin American countries with debt-servicing difficulties significantly less than interest and amortization payments being made on the debt, thus leading to a negative net transfer of financial resources from the debtor countries to creditor banks. 'Involuntary lending' was in the interest of the *collective of creditors*, because it avoided default, at least temporarily and possibly for always, and the additional funds lent were significantly less than the country was paying in debt service.[3]

Though the creditors had a 'collective' interest in new lending to avoid default, this was less clear at an *individual* level, as individual banks could have tried to 'free-ride' by refusing to lend any new money or indeed by reducing their total exposure. The problem was made more difficult by the involvement of two types of banks: a) banks whose loans to the major debtors formed a high proportion of their total assets, often exceeding their capital; their fundamental target was default avoidance of major debtors, and they were willing to increase their exposure for this purpose; b) banks whose loans were smaller in relation to their assets and capital had less incentive to increase lending for default avoidance and more preference to withdraw loans. It was to deal with the problems of 'free-riders' and different categories of creditor banks that the IMF 'imposed' involuntary lending, whereby *all creditor banks were forced to increase* their exposure by a certain percentage.

Since 1982, the IMF (with the help of central banks from industrial countries) to a certain extent 'created' a market, by pressing all and each creditor bank to lend where they did not necessarily wish to do so. The BIS in its Annual Reports talks about 'a split market, with no spontaneous lending to Latin America since late 1982'. I would like to go beyond this and argue that 'a non-spontaneous market' is, in fact, not a market at all in the sense conventionally adopted by economic theory, and that *de facto* in the period after late 1982 a proper market of international private lending to Latin America largely ceased to exist.

It should be stressed that 'involuntary lending' merely prevented a greater fall of net new lending (probably becoming even negative) than would have occurred if

Table 1.1:   New net flows from private banks to Latin America and Africa, 1980–6 (US $ billion)

	1980	1981	1982	1983	1984	1985	1st half 1986
Latin America	27.3	30.5	12.1	7.8	5.7	1.3	-1.6
Africa	2.0	2.2	1.7	0.3	0.1	0.4	-0.1
Asia and Middle East	9.7	7.4	5.9	3.5	4.6	6.8	-2.1
Total non-OPEC LDCs	39.0	39.9	19.8	12.2	10.4	8.5	-3.8

Source: BIS, *1986 Annual Report*, p 95. Coverage of information has been slightly enlarged for 1984. For 1986 (first half), BIS, *The maturity distribution of international bank lending, first half 1986*. December 1986; the figures exclude valuation effects.

markets had operated spontaneously since 1982. As can be seen in Table 1.1, net new lending to Latin America declined significantly (from US $30.5 billion in 1981 to US $3.6 billion in 1985 and even became negative during the first half of 1986) even though 'involuntary lending' was introduced. It is noteworthy that, for example, the US $5.7 billion in net new lending in 1984 to Latin America *was significantly less than the US $10.5 billion* of new funds obtained by these countries from banks under IMF-sponsored packages, which implies that there were important offsetting reductions of other bank credits.

The fact that a market for private international lending to Latin America has practically ceased to exist, and has been replaced by administered decisions, in which governments (of both creditor and debtor countries) as well as official international institutions, determine credit flows and net transfers of financial resources involving private agents implies that bargaining theory (as well as analysis of relative power positions of the actors involved) can throw useful light in explaining the types of deals reached.

3. A third feature of debt crisis management has been the formation of steering committees by the private banks for the purpose of negotiating with the debtor governments; the private banks represented in these committees are those holding the largest debts of a particular country; they tend also to be the largest banks in the industrial countries.

The steering committee has performed a positive role in coordinating hundreds of banks and representing them in negotiations, thus facilitating the negotiations. The steering committees have been successful in assuring some 'new money' was granted to Latin American countries and that debt was rescheduled; however, as the 'new money' that the collective of banks are willing to contribute declines significantly (and as new lending is near zero) their function is increasingly reduced to ensure maximum debt service repayment from debtor governments.

The existence and operation of the steering committee has been clearly functional to the interests of the big banks, mainly because it has implied *cohesion amongst themselves on the negotiating front with the debtors*, and subordination of the smaller banks' actions and interests to their own. An interesting difference arises here with the thirties, when creditors, particularly in the US, were much less able than in the eighties to organise themselves to represent their interests collectively; another significant difference is that—linked to the nature of the finance provided, via bonds— negotiations and the attempted organisation of creditors occurred in the thirties only *after default* was declared, with important implications for the relative bargaining positions of debtors and creditors.[4]

There are a number of indications that in 1987 the unity of banks in the steering committees is less ironcast than in the past. For example, tensions between large and small banks, as well as between banks of different nationalities surfaced particularly clearly in relation to the 1986–7 Mexican deal. Furthermore, banking sources report that the leader of the steering committee for Peru (Citibank) favours actually dissolving the committee.

4. The intimate cohesion amongst creditor banks—and their close links with the IMF and other international financial institutions—has been in sharp contrast to the the way that debtors have accepted or been forced to conduct negotiations, on an individual 'case-by-case' basis. Since 1982, the governments of industrial countries and the IMF have extolled the virtues and successes of the 'case-by-case' approach and rejected 'global plans' for dealing with the debt problem.

Although since early 1984, Latin American debtor government representatives at the most senior level have jointly discussed the debt problem in a series of meetings (see chapter by Diana Tussie), they have not broken the pattern of the actual financial negotiations, whereby creditors negotiate *en bloc* while debtors negotiate individually.

This structure of the negotiation gives creditors an advantage on two different fronts. Their collective and closely coordinated stance confronts each country separately, by which the countries are forfeiting the potential gains of a collective common bargaining stance. Less obviously, this procedure gives the creditors the advantage known in bargaining theory, as that of intersecting negotiations. As Schelling[5] points out, 'the advantage goes to the party that can precisely point to an array of other negotiations in which its own position would be prejudiced if it made a concession in this one'. Steering committees have used the argument of 'precedent' successfully as a bargaining tactic, to avoid concessions for which individual debtors have been pressing for on grounds that—if granted to that particular debtor, which could be feasible—they would be obliged in their simultaneous or future negotiations to grant them to other debtors. For example, M. Castillo, ex-Governor of the Costa Rican Central Bank has reported that the creditor banks took a tougher position *vis-à-vis* his government after the debt crisis became widespread, due, obviously, to the fear of precedent (see also chapter by E. Rodriguez).

Krugman, *op. cit.* makes a similar point in evaluating the potential effects of individual or collective default; he argues that 'if creditors believe that leniency with one debtor will result in demands from others, the additional cost may make creditors unwilling to be lenient. Recognition of this unwillingness may make debtors pay; and the result will be a *self-sustaining set of beliefs*. This explanation should provide an incentive for debtors' collective positions, as creditors willing to discipline one debtor as an example to others, might not be able to make credible the threat to discipline several at once.

5. A crucial feature in debtors' initial attitudes (particularly till mid-1985) was their broad commitment—to multilaterally-agreed, cooperative solutions negotiated with the banks, their host governments and international financial institutions. The option of

unilateral action (leading to default or extended
moratoria) has not been officially adopted by any major
debtor since 1982. (However, several of the major
debtors have unilaterally declared *temporary* moratoria;
two medium-sized debtors, *Peru and Nigeria, in 1985
unilaterally put a limit on debt service payments*, which,
in the Peruvian case, implied very little debt service
payments to private banks; in February 1987, the
Brazilian Government declared a moratorium on
interest payment for a period that was not clearly
defined at the time; many small debtors, for example
Bolivia, as well as several African countries, have had
prolonged moratoria or arrears (see chapter by Reg
Green)).

The large debtors' 1982–6 approach had implied
basically a request to their creditors for debt
restructuring and new loans, rather than a *unilateral
initiative*, either on an absolute debt default, a
temporary one (moratoria) or a limit on their debt
service payment. Though the threat of potential default
and its damaging impact on the international banking
system has lurked in the background of negotiations,
actual defaults did not occur. This situation contrasts
with the 1930s, when negotiations *followed* outright
default. In the thirties, financial institutions were not
willing to extend new loans as debt crises broke out, as it
was their customers' rather than their own assets which
were at stake; public international financial institutions
and cooperation were either non-existent or far weaker
in the thirties than in the eighties. Default avoidance
mechanisms were, therefore much weaker in the thirties.

In the eighties, the heavy involvement of the
industrial countries' major private banks in the debt
problem as well as the development of important
international *public* financial institutions extremely
competent at 'debt crises management' has contributed
to default avoidance, playing a positive role in
preserving the stability of the international financial
system. The strength and influence of these institutions
and the unwillingness of debtors to take unilateral

action seems to have been an important factor in making the 'solutions negotiated' to deal with debt crisis, till now, one whose *costs were mainly borne by the debtors' economies.*

6. The preservation of the international financial system in its existing form and the mode adopted for debt crisis management have had high costs *not only for debtor countries but also for non-financial actors in the developed world.* The decline in growth (or of output) in Latin American economies, linked to the large negative net transfer of financial resources from the continent, have an important cost to exporters of goods to that continent. It would seem that the interests of agents, such as exporters to Latin America and Africa, and foreign investors in these areas have not been sufficiently considered in debt crisis management.

According to UNCTAD estimates (in the 1985 *Trade and Development Report*), as a result of the contraction of exports from industrial market economies to developing ones (linked to widespread debt crises), between 1982 and 1984, there was a cumulative loss of jobs in the industrial countries of about 8 million men/women years; of these, 7 million men years were lost in Europe and close to one million men years in the United States and Canada.

More broadly, it can be argued that *financial interests, institutions and criteria have been extremely dominant in the way that debt crises have been managed.* The main actors involved in the negotiations have been representatives of the major private banks and the central banks of debtor countries. Broadly absent from the negotiations have been private agents in the industrial countries who benefit from LDC growth (e.g. exporting to LDCs) and public international institutions concerned with development (e.g. World Bank and UNICEF); representations of LDCs have also not included private or government institutions involved in the productive sectors of the economy.

The perspective adopted (or imposed) by the creditors has been a very short-term and an almost exclusively financial one. Debt rescheduling particularly was initially done on a 'short-leash' year by year approach, linked to very short-term stabilisation programmes that placed very strong emphasis on rapid transformation of the trade account into large trade surplus positions (in the case of Latin America), or rapid reductions of trade deficits (in the case of Africa).

Annual negotiations—with the complexities involved — have implied *de facto* almost a continuous process of negotiation. From the point of view of developing countries' governments, the focus and time-intensiveness of recurrent negotiations as imposed by the 'needs' of debt crisis management, has distracted time and energy from *the more long-term concerns of developing countries' governments, those of growth and development.*

The dominance of financial institutions and criteria in debt crisis management has also had a major impact on perceiving the crisis of debt and growth as purely *temporary* phenomena. The implication was that if developing countries adjusted their economies speedily, the crisis both of debt and growth could be dealt with fairly soon, *without* any need to bring about major structural changes either: 1) in the development policies of countries (except those advocated traditionally by institutions like the IMF); 2) in the international financial system or; 3) in the framework of debt renegotiations.

A veritable 'war of forecasts' erupted, particularly between 1982 and 1985, which clearly played a fairly important role in the *bargaining process* of how debts should be rescheduled and how much debtor economies should adjust. The optimistic scenarios produced initially by institutions such as the IMF and for example by Cline's 1983 and 1984 studies contributed to the acceptance (even by the debtor governments) of the crisis as conjunctural phenomena to be dealt with by short-term adjustment. The far less optimistic, or more pessimistic projections developed as a response to the optimistic ones[6] contributed to the fact that debtor governments increasingly challenged the approach supported by the IMF and the private banks. Furthermore, around mid–1985, it became evident that whatever the evolution of international economic variables, the debt overhang would continue to act as a major constraint for development of debtor nations, dragging down world economic growth.

A final caveat seems relevant. In a world economy with very sharp fluctuations in key international variables and with great uncertainty about their future evolution, *the diagnosis of the nature of the debt problem and the design of optimal (or appropriate) solutions is linked to forecasts of a very uncertain future*, relating both to the actions of the agents involved directly in the problem but also to trends in the world economy, which some of these agents influence to a varied degree, but which they are unable to determine or even predict.

This implies the need of searching for solutions that not only accommodate the conflicting interests of the different agents involved but also—given uncertainty about the future—do so satisfactorily under *different* scenarios. This should imply the appropriateness in the future search for solutions of establishing contingency clauses and compensatory mechanisms on the one hand, and general principles on the other (such as no negative financial transfers, minimum growth) rather than the precise numerical performance targets that have characterised debt crises management and adjustment monitoring in recent years. The recent (1986) agreement between Mexico and the IMF seems to point to the beginning of acceptance of these principles.

Evaluation of debt crises management and adjustment, 1982–5

An evaluation of 'debt crises management' for Latin America as practised between 1982 and 1985 must stress that in spite of 'debt restructuring and involuntary new lending package deals', the region as a whole made a very significant negative net transfer of financial resources to the industrialised countries and particularly the US. This transfer has averaged around US \$25 billion a year between 1982 and 1985, and has been equivalent to around 25 per cent of the region's total exports of goods and services.

Table 1.2: Latin America—net inflow of capital and net transfer of resources (US) $ billion and percentages

Year/s	Net inflow of capital	Net pay-ment of profits and interests	Net transfer of resources	Exports of goods and services	Net transfer/ Export
	(1)	(2)	(3)=(1)-(2)	(4)	(5)=(3)/ (4)
1973–81	21.2	11.0	*10.1*	64.4	+15.8
1982	19.8	38.7	*-18.9*	103.2	-18.3
1983	3.2	34.3	*-13.2*	102.4	-30.5
1984	19.2	36.2	*-27.0*	114.1	-23.7
1985	2.47	35.3	*-32.9*	109.0	-30.2
1986	8.6	30.7	*-22.1*	95.2	-23.2

Source: CEPAL, *Balance preliminar de la economia latinoamericana durante 1986,* December 1986.

Negative net transfers for Latin America on the scale indicated had two types of effects. Together with the large deterioration of the terms of trade, they contributed to the decline of output that occurred in the region, which implied that in 1985, GDP per capita was on average almost 10 per cent below its 1980 level. Furthermore, even the most optimistic forecasters do not expect 1980 per capita GDP to be recovered before 1990, and ECLA as well as others talk of a 'lost decade' for Latin America. Thus *'debt crises management' has been functional to the needs of preserving the survival and stability of the private banks but disfunctional to growth and development in Latin America*; it has also been disfunctional to those agents in industrial countries which benefit from growth in the region.

The magnitude and persistence of the negative net transfer of financial resources had a second type of effect, whose implications have been not fully perceived. This relates to its impact on strengthening the bargaining position of Latin American countries (both collectively and individually *vis-à-vis* creditor banks). When net transfers of financial resources flow towards a developing country, the greater bargaining strength lies in the lenders, as it is they who must ultimately decide to make the new loans and transfer the funds. This implies that the lender can easily impose all types of conditions. When the net transfers are negative, the greater bargaining strength has potentially shifted to the debtor government, as *it might decide not to repay and ultimately not to make the transfer of funds.* Consequently, the debtor is in this case not only in a position to resist the conditions of the lender, but even more fundamentally to impose his own.

The problem of negative net transfers and its importance was initially not properly highlighted. Debt crises management was initially evaluated (and still largely is, though decreasingly so) by conventional indicators used in the past to evaluate debt restructuring, for example amounts of debt restructured as a proportion of different economic variables. Successive rescheduling deals were evaluated even by the debtor governments on a comparative basis (in relation to deals attained by the country in previous years or to similar deals arranged by other countries during the same year), with emphasis on improvements such as reductions of spreads, refinancing fees, etc, which—though significant—have only a marginal impact on the value of present and future negative net transfers; this clearly implied accepting the basic parameters of the 'debt rescheduling–adjustment' solution and negotiating only details on the margin. The problem of major negative net transfers and how to avoid them does not seem to have been part of the explicitly negotiated issues at all until 1984, and began to emerge only in 1985. It had not been clear in 1982 that the 'package deals' agreed would imply negative net transfers which would be *both so large and particularly so pervasive*, given that expectations that interest rates would come down quicker and especially that voluntary lending would be resumed after countries adjusted and again became 'creditworthy'. Furthermore, it was considered unacceptable in orthodox circles to add together items of the capital account (net flows of capital) with items from the current account (mainly interest payments) to determine net transfers, a concept that has only recently been accepted as valuable by international financial organisations.

Concern with the issue of negative net transfers, and acceptance of the concept's key relevance, has become far more widespread. For example, the World Bank, in its '1986 and 1987 *World Debt Tables'* analysis attaches great importance to this variable and its impact; similarly, the April 1987 IMF's *World Economic Outlook* points to resource transfers from developing countries as a major source of strain for their development.

2. ELEMENTS FOR UNDERSTANDING DEBT CRISES MANAGEMENT

A. The key questions

The description above of how the debt crisis has been 'managed' seems to pose a number of fundamental questions:

1. The first—and perhaps most fundamental—question is: why were the debt rescheduling/adjustment deals agreed and implemented, particularly, but not only, during the 1982 to mid–1985 period so much closer to the interests and the aims of creditors than of debtors? This question can—for analytical purposes—be divided into three sub-questions: i) Why were the types of deals hammered out in 1982—as an initial response to the debt crisis—so biased towards creditors' interests? ii) Why was the approach to debt rescheduling/adjustment not changed more than marginally during the following three years? iii) Why, once in mid–1985, a broad consensus emerged that debt crisis management as practised until then was unsatisfactory, for all parties involved, but particularly for debtor nations, was not a new way of dealing with the problem implemented multilaterally?

    Two related issues arise here. Why were not more positive-sum elements introduced in the solutions adopted? Why have debtor governments been so patient during such a long period of large negative net transfers, and did not pursue unilateral actions earlier and in a more generalised manner?

2. The second question is: what are the reasons for the differences amongst the debt/adjustment deals reached by individual countries? Indeed, did large differences exist between deals obtained by different countries?

3. The third question relates to how the debt rescheduling/new money/adjustment deals varied from year to year during the period studied for all countries? To what extent was there a common pattern of evolution in the 1982-5 period, implying an improvement of some fairly marginal conditions (e.g. reduction or elimination of rescheduling fee; reduction of spreads), accompanied by a reduction of the level of new credits flowing from the private banks? To what extent after 1985 have some of the deals agreed multilaterally (particularly the Mexican one) implied a qualitative improvement?

Questions 2 and 3 pose the problem of measurement of different deals.

B. Common measures

It is necessary to design common measures for two aspects, which are clearly interconnected but analytically can be separated: the debt bargains themselves and the adjustment. In both cases, the comparison will basically be for each country studied between what would have occurred if the deal had not been struck and what was agreed as part of the actual deal.

(1) Common measures for debt rescheduling deals The most fundamental indicator of how much a debt rescheduling deal has implied an improvement in the foreign exchange situation of a country is the change that it has implied (in relation to the pre-scheduling situation) on the net transfer of financial resources from (or to) the country for the current year in which the deal was agreed and for the next few years (e.g. next four years) duly discounted; to establish a comparative base amongst the countries studied it will be necessary to compare the value of this change in the corresponding year(s) to indicators reflecting the size of the economy, such as the level of the country's exports and imports, its current account deficit, its GDP and its level of gross domestic investment. (The exchange rate for conversion would be the average one for the corresponding year). A further important indicator of the 'goodness' of the deal, as well as of the further bargaining potential of the country, is whether after the rescheduling deal was struck the net transfer of financial resources is negative

and if so, at what normalised scale again as proportion of the country's exports and imports, current account deficit, GDP and level of domestic investment. The advantage of using this indicator is that it takes into account not only the changes in debt servicing flows attained but also the new credit flows obtained.

A second indicator—somewhat more complex to calculate and more relevant for the medium- and long-term— is the extent to which a particular deal affects the change in the net present value of debt; this can be calculated as the change in the stream of payments of interest and amortization (before and after the rescheduling). As in the case of the previous indicator it is necessary to normalise the change in the net present value of debt (NPVD) by comparing it with the size of the NPVD before rescheduling. This indicator has the problematic aspect of requiring a long-term forecast for interest rates.

A third indicator for evaluating debt rescheduling deals[7] refers to the evolution financial aspects, that been stressed in negotiations and their evaluation during the 1982-5 period. Though such an indicator is possibly the easiest to calculate its significance, though clear, is somewhat secondary to variables such as the change in the total net financial resource flows referred to above.

A useful composite indicator has been developed in the ECLAC studies, to reflect the *change in the financial conditions of debt after rescheduling*, where C refers to rescheduling commission or fees, P refers to total period of amortization and M refers to 'spread' over LIBOR; the values are calculated comparing after (1), and before (0), the rescheduling deals, and weighed by the values of the credit involved.

The indicator used is
$$\frac{\dfrac{C_1 + M_1}{P_1}}{\dfrac{C_0 + M_0}{P_0}} - 1$$

A problem with this indicator is that it accepts a 'trade-off' between larger maturities and higher costs.

(2) Common measures of adjustment Perhaps even more complex is the search for common and comparable measures of adjustment required as a condition of the rescheduling/new money deals.

A first qualitative indicator distinguishes between those countries required to sign an upper credit *tranche* agreement with the IMF as a pre-condition for the rescheduling and new money package(s) and those who were not. Within the former group of countries, a distinction could be made between those countries which have signed an Extended Fund Facility (EFF) and those which have operated with repeated stand-bys, given that there is evidence that the EFF has been relatively more successful in protecting growth than the stand-by.[8]

Following Williamson[9] the fundamental indicator would compare the economic performance of the country as agreed in the context of the IMF programme with what would have occurred without Fund involvement. (A good indicator of the latter could be the targets of the government's macro-economic programme at the beginning of—or previous to—the negotiations.) There is a clear link here with the previous indicator on gains from debt rescheduling/new money obtained, as the relatively greater availability of foreign exchange (or the smaller negative net outflow as is the case in most Latin American economies since 1982) should at least potentially enable the economy's adjustment to be less painful than it would have been without rescheduling and new money. Where feasible, it is interesting—though difficult—to compare the economic targets and performance under the Fund supported adjustment (agreed and actual outcome) with the 'best potentially feasible outcome'.[10]

These comparisons must not primarily be focussed on the somewhat narrow and financially biased 'performance criteria' of the IMF itself; instead, they would focus on key economic variables: variation in level of GDP and in level of employment; ratio of investment to GDP; level of income of the poorest 20 per cent (40 per cent) of the population, as well as its share in total income. Other indicators (of a more financial nature) but which clearly link with the medium-term substantiability of the programme would be measured by: the current account of the balance of payments and the rate of inflation. The speed and level of the orthodoxy of adjustment is not mechanically linked to the existence of an upper credit *tranche* agreement with the Fund. For example, some countries do not have such an IMF agreement, and yet pursue fairly orthodox policies (see chapter by A. M. Alvarez); on the other hand, increasingly some countries seem able to include somewhat higher growth targets and some unorthodox elements in their IMF agreements (see, for example, chapters by R. Villarreal and E. Rodriguez)

(3) Other variables involved in rescheduling/new money adjustment deals   There are certain variables in the rescheduling/new money adjustment deals which are difficult to quantify, but are meaningful to the parties concerned.

A very important item is the treatment of loans originally made to the private sector in the debtor country, and particularly the extent to which *ex post* the debtor country government has guaranteed loans originally made to the private sector without guarantee or has made other small concessions in this area.[11]

Other aspects which are part of the 'package deals' but are difficult to quantify relate to aspects such as trade preferences or large contracts specifically linked to a 'financial package', such as the US–Mexico deal on oil in 1982.

C. Relevant theoretical elements
In this section I will attempt to draw on relevant theoretical literature for its potential contribution as a reply to the questions outlined above.

The contribution of bargaining theory   We are assuming that the study of the *process* of bargaining and negotiation can make a contribution to an understanding of the *outcomes* of debt rescheduling/new money adjustment. Most studies on debt restructuring and adjustment approach these issues as purely analytical ones (and search for analytically 'optimum' solutions). A purely analytical approach is more relevant when the actors involved agree fundamentally about the values, principles and criteria for decision.[12] Attaching importance to the *process* of negotiation of debt rescheduling and adjustment seems particularly relevant in a context where there are major conflicts of interests and perceptions between the parties involved. Emphasis on negotiations and bargaining is appropriate in a context where the traditional market mechanisms (e.g. for determining levels of private international lending or their price) are clearly not operating, so that there is no fixed outcome, resulting from mechanisms such as supply and demand, but one resulting from complex negotiations between the parties.

Broadly, we will follow Zartman's[13] definition of negotiation as a process of two (or more) parties combining their conflicting points of view into a single decision; according to Zartman 'a decision is made by changing the parties' evaluation of their values so as to be able to combine them into a single package, by persuasion, coercion or force'. Negotiation is seen as a joint decision-making process in which parties are necessary to the decision which implies that each party has veto power.

1. Stages of debt crises management and their main features The insights of bargaining theory seem useful, in the first place, for distinguishing the stages within debt crises management as it has occurred since 1982.

Zartman *op. cit.* describes three types of negotiations. The first he calls the formula/detail approach, where negotiators first search for a solution and then haggle over and implement detail. In this context, 'negotiations seek a general definition of the items under discussion, conceived and grouped in such a way as to be susceptible of joint agreement under a common notion of justice. Once agreement on a formula is achieved, it is possible to turn to the specifics of items and to exchange proposals, concessions and agreements.' The formula/detail approach stresses that at the time of the search for formula *the very list of items under negotiation is a matter of negotiation.*

The second type of negotiating style is that of concession/convergence, where both sides inch toward a mutually acceptable outcome through offers, counter offers, threats and promises. As Zartman points out, different negotiating modes can coexist. Thus, concession/convergence negotiations often follow the formula/detail approach after a formula has been identified. Indeed, once the *items under discussion are well enough established through prior agreement* this enables concession convergence bargaining to take place.

A third type of negotiating style identified by Zartman is called progressive construction, in which parties deal with related subjects in sequential talks over a long time span.

Using the first two categories of negotiations, it is possible to clearly distinguish three separate phases within the debt rescheduling/new money adjustment negotiations.

Phase 1 During the first phase, the 'formula' for dealing with debt crises of major bank debtors was hammered out. The formula was initially worked out for Mexico in 1982 and then applied in a very similar fashion to a number of major Latin American debtors facing a debt crises.

Senior government officials as well as creditor banks were at the time in broadly 'unchartered waters'. The precedents that existed were either unilateral default or moratoria (as in the thirties) or conventional rescheduling, as applied in the context mainly of the Paris Club. Debtors ruled out unilateral action. The formula adopted was in fact fairly close to the procedures already established in previous debt reschedulings, even though the nature and the discussion of the problem were qualitatively very different (see above); innovative elements were introduced, of which perhaps the most widely emphasised (particularly by the creditors) was the creation of 'involuntary lending'. Intermediate options including *some* agreed debt forgiveness or *some* agreed interest forgiveness were possibly even not considered at the time or were not negotiated by debtors with sufficient strength. The parameters of negotiations were, thus, fairly narrowly defined in relation to amount of new money, spreads, grace periods, total repayment periods, and even the size of rescheduling fees; the amount of new money involved in 'involuntary lending' was clearly to be less than total debt service payments, thus, leading to negative net transfers; debtor governments did not seem to challenge negative net transfers and its absurdity at the time, nor its negative impact on their economies' growth.

By accepting the basic parameters suggested by creditors as a formula, debtors were to a large extent trapped in the next three years to haggle with creditors over variables which were fairly narrowly defined and, thus, fairly marginal to the outcome, and which did not change the fundamental fact that debt crisis management was being carried out in such a way as to be much more functional to the interests of creditor institutions than of debtor economies (and more broadly of those who benefit from their growth).

The fundamental questions as regards phase 1, are therefore: i) why was the 'formula' hammered out so much closer to the interests of creditor institutions than of debtor economies (distributive aspect); furthermore ii) why did the 'formula' hammered out not have more 'positive sum elements', that is why it did not include more elements of mutual interest and benefit to both sides. The only such positive sum element— albeit a very crucial one—was the preservation of the stability of the financial system; other elements such as assuring minimum levels of growth in debtor economies and/or guaranteeing minimum levels of income and welfare for the poorest strata, were not actively pursued in the 'formula' arrived at.

In what follows, I will attempt to draw up some hypotheses to explain why the 'formula' arrived at for debt crisis management in 1982 was not closer to 'the optimum combination of interests of both parties' but was so much closer to the interests of creditors than of debtors.

(i)   A first element in explaining the nature of the 'solution' for debt crises management is relative power relations, as well as their basic perception by the actors involved. Debtor governments probably perceived that unilateral action (or tough bargaining on debt) would provoke the wrath of creditor banks' host governments, as well as endanger the stability of the international financial system. Debtor governments perceived that the costs of unilateral action (or very tough bargaining) would greatly exceed the benefits of such action. The potential leverage that large negative net transfers could give particularly to large debtors was not fully perceived, partly because the magnitude of those transfers and their pervasiveness was not known at the time.

(ii) The perception of costs and benefits of tough bargaining and/or the possibility of unilateral action were clearly linked to the fact that Latin American economies had become very closely integrated into the world economy during the post-war period and that the governments in power at the time the debt crises broke out saw this continued integration as positive and valuable.

To the extent that the costs of debt crises management to the debtor economies were seen as temporary, they were perceived as a short-term sacrifice, worthwhile in the context of the long-run advantages that unchanged integration into the system provided. It is in this context clearly that 'optimistic' forecasting of international economic trends (as discussed above) played an important role in perceiving the problem as 'temporary'. The great fashion for belief in the absolute efficiency of the private market reinforced the perception that the interruption of private 'voluntary' international lending was brief, and would be rapidly overcome.

As the costs of debt crises management are increasingly seen as too high and pervasive, a shift is clearly occurring within debtor countries and governments towards increased influence of political forces that value less the benefits of close integration into the world economy and are less fearful of the cost of cutting or restructuring some of the links.

(iii) As the debt crises broke out, the interests of the bank creditors were clearly based on their commercial aims; their target was clearly after 1982 to minimise current losses (if possible to maximise current profits) and minimise future losses. (Previously to 1982, it would be argued that the banks pursued more complex targets such as expansion of their operations with developing countries, overall expansion of assets, etc.) The interests of debtor governments were much more complex and more difficult to articulate in terms of clear objectives. If the state is defined not as a unitary actor but as a complex social collectivity, with both foreign and domestic interests, each with its provisional conception of the overall national interest related ideologically to its own special interest, the process of defining targets becomes fairly complex. Initially, debtor governments did not perhaps have a very clear purpose and a very clear strategy of how to deal with the debt crisis, responding, therefore, mainly to the initiatives of the creditors.

(iv) The creditors also have previously developed in quite a different context (see above) a formula and a procedure which implied basically safeguarding their interests and assured equitable treatment amongst creditors. Precedent was on the side of the creditors!

Schelling *op cit.* emphasizes both the importance of precedent and initiative as significant advantages in bargaining. Schelling argues that 'the object is to be the first with a firm offer. Complete responsibility for the outcome then rests with the other, who can take it or leave it as he chooses (and, thus, has a strong incentive to take it). Bargaining is all over; the commitment (i.e., the first offer) wins'.

A clear difference emerges here with the 1985 phase in which the debtors are increasingly making their own proposals for solution and even taking unilateral action which radically re-defines the parameters of the 'solution'.

(v) It seems that on the whole creditors were able during this stage to use bargaining tactics better than debtors, not only in the negotiations over the specific items on the agenda, for example, spreads, but far more importantly on keeping the items of the

bargaining within these narrow issues. It is noteworthy that while issues such as 'interest capping'
even of a concessional nature were widely discussed
in industrial countries, at the concrete discussions
between creditors, IMF and individual debtor
countries such options were not even discussed. The
standard bargaining techniques of threats and
promises were more convincingly used by creditors
than debtors, partly perhaps because the former has a
larger array of 'procedural' constraints (e.g. regulating and accounting conventions for treatment of non-
accrual of interest and amortization of bank loans,
'performance criteria' of the IMF, etc).

Whether consciously or not, creditors were able to
use brilliantly the principle (presented for example in
Schelling *op cit.*) of making threats more effective by
de-composing it into a series of consecutive smaller
threats, which gave the creditors opportunity to
declare, or threaten to declare, loans in arrears or
even value impaired (after certain crucial deadlines
were or would be overcome) *without forcing them to
declare overall default*, declaration which would have
been probably more damaging to them than to the
debtors. Great focus was thus placed on meeting
certain deadlines (e.g. no more than ninety days
interest arrears) which led the negotiations into
brinkmanship exercises that clearly distracted attention from the option of changing the rules of the
game and ultimately forced most debtors to fall into
line with the procedures basically determined by the
creditors. This seems well exemplified by the
negotiations between Argentina, its bank creditors
and the IMF during 1984. The creditors, thus, were
able to transform, 'a dangerous once-for-all-threat
into a less continuous one'. The debtors could have
used de-composition of threats in a similar way, for
example by reducing debt service payments while
negative net transfer payments persist or while their
exports grew below minimum levels, while committing themselves in the long term to debt servicing

once those conditions were overcome, thus, shifting the responsibility of action for short-term arrear/long-term default avoidance much more to creditors' banks and their governments. Since 1985 some debtor governments, for example, Peru, have begun to use such tactics. The search in developing countries (and amongst those sympathetic to their growth and development) for proposals that would allow for a reduction in debt service payments *without* leading to problematic developments for the creditor banks (e.g. by changing regulations, by contributions from official institutions) can be also seen as weakening the threat of collapse of the banking system as a mechanism for pressing for high debt service payments; such measures became more feasible as the private banks have built up their loan loss provisions, their capital and have improved their capital asset ratios fairly significantly, since 1982 (see also conclusions chapter).

Debtor governments have been closely monitored in the short term in their commitments on the adjustment of their economics (usually by the rigorous performance criteria of upper credit *tranche* IMF conditionality) while the commitments of creditors were mainly for restoring significant flows *in the future.* Interestingly, though the IMF demanded a commitment of 'involuntary lending' from creditor banks, it did not monitor total new lending, which as was shown in Table 1.1 above, was well below 'involuntary lending', as other items were drastically reduced. Regular monitoring of creditor 'performance' by debtor governments could perhaps be institutionalised.

A related feature of the bargaining between debtors and creditors was the extent to which the banks were able to actually use differences in their aims and positions to their advantage. The amount of new lending by all banks was severely constrained by the small banks' unwillingness to lend at all, and by *the need* to reach a figure of increased lending that would *be also acceptable to the more reluctant amongst the creditors*, thus, the steering committee was bound or constrained in the amount of new lending it would deliver by the least cooperative of its members!

(vi) One of the reasons why the issues negotiated were so narrow seems to have been that several of the key variables affecting net transfers of financial resources *were beyond the competence and responsibility* of the *negotiating agents, the commercial banks and the debtor governments.*[14] Thus, negotiations with the banks could affect the payments to banks on spreads (over the market interest rate), as well as the fees and commissions charged by the banks, elements which, had a fairly marginal impact on total debt service incurred; however, the banks could *do practically nothing* to influence the general level of interest rates, as this is determined by government policies in industrial countries; not only was the level of interest rate far more important than the elements dependent on the banks' discretion, but furthermore, it was by far the most important single factor in determining the overall magnitude of debt service obligations. Neither could banks, and particularly those of the US, allow interest payments to be overdue, without having to exclude them from accrued income, unless the government regulatory authorities allowed such a procedure; thus, any form of capping interest, for US banks would have implied profits, which banks clearly tried to avoid.

As Dell *op. cit.* points out it is the limited nature of the forum where debt rescheduling/new money packages were negotiated, which led the signatories of the Cartagena Consensus to call in April 1985 for 'a political dialogue between the creditor and debtor countries, a dialogue which must be structured and pursued in an *appropriate forum*' (my italics). Among the concrete proposals of the Cartagena Consensus, several were clearly related to the crucial variables determining net transfers; for example, the first proposal urged 'the adoption of measures leading to the immediate and drastic reduction of nominal and real interest rates in international markets as ... a fundamental objective towards which the governments of industrialised nations ought to direct their best efforts'. However, particularly until late–1985, these calls did not seem to have a very large impact on the main issues being negotiated.

(vii) Thus, a final element (last but clearly *not* least) explaining the relative weakness of debtors in relation to creditors is that the latter rapidly developed institutions to coordinate their strategies, overcome or use their differences and negotiate jointly whereas the institutions to coordinate debtors' interests were much slower to emerge and were far less effective in the bargaining context, as the crucial financial negotiations were conducted on an individual basis (for the debtors) and without jointly-established terms of reference or minimum bargaining positions.

Phase 2 This phase of debt crises management broadly covers the period from late–1982 to the second quarter of 1985, during which negotiations approximately followed the concession/convergence approach; as discussed above, the agenda for debt restructuring/new money negotiations was fairly narrowly defined in relation to discussions on spreads, grace periods, total repayment periods, size of rescheduling fees and the amount of new credit (the latter again within rather constrained limits). As regards adjustment, in a majority of cases, the creditor banks insisted as a pre-condition for negotiating on debt restructuring/new flows that countries agree an upper *tranche* credit with the IMF, which implied again that the process of policy options in adjustment was severely constrained by the type of package preferred by the IMF and by periodic and rigorous monitoring of 'performance criteria' that such an agreement entails.

Commitment on all sides to the broad 'formula' was strengthened, particularly during 1984, by the significant recovery of industrial countries, spearheaded by the US.

Some initial emphasis by the debtors on the reduction of financial costs charged by the banks (e.g. high rescheduling fees, high spreads) was clearly justified as these costs had been severely increased during the first round of debt renegotiations in 1982–3. Indeed, according to ECLAC estimates,[15] the majority of debtors suffered a deterioration in terms (which include: change in commission, change in spreads, and in amortization periods) of between 100–250 per cent, which implied an increase of around 20 per cent in the real financial cost of credit.

Because debtors had suffered a large deterioration in the financial conditions of their loans and because the parameters of the negotiation had been already limited so as to give priority to these issues, most debtors focussed on achieving an improvement in those terms during successive rounds; there also was quite a high priority attached to this issue in the collective positions of debtor governments as reflected, for example, in the proposal made in the June 1984 Cartagena Consensus 'that intermediation margins and other related costs should be reduced to a minimum and fees and commissions eliminated'. As a result of pressure from debtors in the negotiations on this issue, during 1983–4 and particularly during 1984–5, a fairly meaningful improvement was achieved in the *negotiated* cost of credit; spreads declined, rescheduling commissions were drastically reduced—falling to zero in several cases—and amortization periods increased significantly.

On the other hand, the deals in 1983–4 and particularly 1984–5 were characterised by a *significant decline in 'new money' lent by the banks*, as part of the rescheduling packages.

Phase 3   Since mid–1985, Latin American and African debtor governments increasingly not only perceived that debt crises management as had been practised since 1982 was excessively costly to their economies, but were increasingly willing (individually and collectively) to go beyond criticism of current practice and make their own proposals on how the crises should be managed and even were willing to take unilateral actions. The US Government responded—through the so-called Baker initiative—by making a proposal which reflected some of the concerns by debtor governments and others, on the perceived limitations of previous debt crises management.

Phase 3 similarly to phase 1 outlined above, can be broadly put in Zartman's category of search for a 'new solution' as opposed to the far more narrow concession/convergence negotiations on details of an accepted 'formula' that had been occurring in the past three years; however, it differs from phase 1 in that debtor governments are more actively making proposals and even in some cases interrupting negotiations on the 'new solution', by taking unilateral action.

Particularly clear in the Peruvian and Brazilian actions, but also implicit in the counter-proposals to the Baker plan made by the Cartagena group of debtors in December 1985, is a significant change of emphasis. Until mid–1985, as the initiative was in the hands of the creditors, the main aim of debt crises management was to *ensure debt service payments*, either according to the original schedule or—if and to the extent that creditors accepted to grant rescheduling—within a jointly agreed modified schedule of repayments; the debtor government then had to attempt to 'adjust' its country's economy so as to be able to service the debts in the original or modified schedule. In the Peruvian Government's action, since 1985, similar actions by African governments, and also in the Brazilian Government's unilateral action in February 1987, the main aim is to ensure a minimum of economic growth for their economies, which determines the maximum of debt servicing that those countries are willing or able to make. If such an approach were effectively to be followed, it would imply that it is the international financial system which would have to 'adjust' to the minimum growth targets of debtor economies.

The need to search for a 'new solution/s' to the crises of debt and growth arose for a number of reasons, which seem to mutually reinforce each other:

(i)   First, in 1985 there was a deterioration in the international economic environment, particularly in crucial aspects which affected negatively the external constraints for debtor economies' growth. Amongst these features were the slowdown of the volume of world trade growth and, even more importantly, the sharp further decline in commodity prices; this was accompanied by a further slowing down of net new lending by banks to debtor economies, particularly those of Latin America.

Thus, two of the crucial economic assumptions on which the post–1982 debt crises strategy was based were being undermined. The first had been that rapid growth in industrial countries would generate a potential for rapid growth in debtor economies. The second assumption was that 'involuntary bank lending' would be quickly transformed into 'voluntary bank lending' as debtor economies adjusted and their 'creditworthiness' was restored. Debtor countries' willingness to service their debts was initially stimulated by the promise of enhanced future new private lending. Private banks' willingness to make at least 'involuntary lending' was initially sustained by their expectation that countries' debt servicing would continue. Both these attitudes were increasingly undermined by mid–1985; on the one hand, Latin American governments were increasingly concerned that new flows had not materialised in spite of their large sacrifices in terms of national adjustment; on the other hand, banks became interestingly reluctant since early 1985 to increase their exposure to Latin America, whether 'voluntary' or 'involuntary'. As a result mainly of the sharp decline in new private lending to the region, negative net transfers from Latin America actually increased in 1985, in absolute values and even more as a proportion of total exports!

Unfortunately, world economic trends in 1986 confirmed the diagnosis made in mid–1985. Though total world trade expanded slightly faster than in 1985, commodity prices continued to decline in real terms; according to World Bank figures, received against the prices of manufactured exports, non-oil commodity prices fell by 10 per cent in 1986 to their *lowest level in at least* fifty years. As described above, (see Table 1.1) new net private bank flows not only continued this decline, but during the first half of 1986 became negative.

(ii) The tolerance of continued very slow growth or stagnation in most Latin American countries and pervasive negative net transfers was diminished further due to the transition in several countries of the region (including two of the major debtors) to far more democratic forms of government. These new governments had greater international legitimacy and respectability, and, thus, their demands are listened to more seriously by industrial governments and the international community. Perhaps more importantly, democratic governments obviously have to respond far more directly than authoritarian ones to public opinion in their countries. As a result, such governments can genuinely say to their creditors that their ability to service debts is constrained not only by their own willingness to do so, but by the willingness of the legislative branch, and is conditioned by pressures from trade unions, associations of industrial entrepreneurs, etc. As there is in practically all of Latin America a groundswell of support for giving greater priority to growth and development than to debt servicing, then the pressure of public opinion, from organised groups and/or from parliaments tends to bind the 'ability' of debtor governments to service debt beyond certain limits. As is well established in bargaining theory (see Schelling *op. cit.*), 'the power of a negotiator often rests on a manifest inability to make concessions and meet demands, so that the ability of a democratic government to get itself tied by public opinion may be different from the ability of a totalitarian government to incur such a commitment'.

Linked importantly to the changes in political regime, but also to the unexpected pervasiveness of the economic sacrifices required to continue servicing the debt, debtor governments have increasingly attached greater importance to the views and needs of their people in relation to those of their creditors. The magnitude of the costs of adjustment borne by Latin American and African economies, and particularly by the poorest and more vulnerable groups within those countries,[16] has become more widely perceived and has had an interesting impact on policy-makers in developing and developed countries. This was perhaps most clearly articulated by President Alan Garcia's statement that 'The main creditor of Peru is its people'.

At the level of bargaining theory, Druckman[17] has made a useful distinction, which throws light on this shift of debtor governments' position; he suggests that the international negotiator is primarily a problem solver who responds *simultaneously* to his opposite-number negotiators *and* to his constituents. Druckman further argues that 'the *extent* to which the negotiator is responsive to one *or* the other affects the course of a negotiation'. In this context, theory confirms the point that as debtor governments become more responsive to their own constituents rather than to their creditors, they will be able to obtain deals that are closer to the interests of their constituents.

According to Druckman, major changes in negotiating posture are likely to occur when—in an assessment of the negotiating postures and concessions made both sides—it is found that there was 'unfair advantage'; the change in negotiating position assumed as a result of this evaluation is related to how closely the negotiator responds to his own constituents. Druckman states that 'direct responsiveness between bargainers is likely to characterise early bargaining while own responsiveness (to its own constituents) occurs as they develop a concession-making history'. The greater focus of debtor governments on the needs of their main constituents, thus, does not only respond to moral justification, or follow certain political and economic trends outlined above, but also seems to be responding to the logic of the bargaining process.

2. *Explanation for differences amongst debt/adjustment deals*   Bargaining theory can also contribute some elements to explaining differences *between* deals reached by individual countries, although several of the hypotheses outlined below

are not in the realm of bargaining theory.

In attempting to explain the differences in the terms obtained by the different countries in their debt/new money rescheduling deals, the following working hypotheses are suggested:

1. The range of manoeuvre for obtaining a relatively more favourable deal is influenced by factors inherited by the debtor governments. Perhaps the most important one is the size of the debt owed to large private banks; the argument commonly made that, the bigger the debt to private banks, the greater the bargaining strength of the debtor government and, thus, the better the deal, seems only partially correct.

It would seem broadly true that the larger is the size of the debt owed by a country to large private banks in relation to those banks' capital, the stronger is the debtor government's *potential* bargaining strength to obtain favourable terms from these banks, *both* as regards *agreed* magnitude and terms of rescheduling of debts, and magnitude of new private flows; potentially they could also be able to agree more favourable terms in the type of adjustment required, in their negotiations, with the IMF or otherwise, as creditor banks' governments will be unwilling to risk breakdowns of negotiations.

On the other hand, countries with relatively small debts (in relation to banks' capital) may be able to obtain informally or *de facto* better terms, (via mechanisms such as long arrears, or refinancing of interest) on the servicing of their past debt, precisely because the impact of such arrears on creditor banks' profits and capital will be fairly marginal; those countries' likelihood to get significant 'involuntary new lending' from banks would, however, be low, precisely because the potential cost of default or arrears to the creditor banks could be fairly easily absorbed. Small bank debtors may get proportionally larger official flows than large bank debtors, partly because small bank debtors tend to have relatively lower incomes (and, thus, be eligible for special facilities, e.g, IDA flows) and partly because official flows programmes may tend to start at a minimum level, which may imply a relatively bigger contribution to small debtor countries' net transfer of resources.

2. A similarly complex relationship (where great financial weakness may also in some situations be a source of relative strength) emerges between the level of foreign exchange reserves and the type of deal which a debtor country can obtain. Again, two extreme positions would seem to enhance a debtor government's bargaining position. On the one hand, very low or negative net foreign exchange reserves may *de facto* strengthen countries' 'bargaining power' for obtaining better terms on debt servicing, as the country can effectively only afford to pay a limited amount of debt service done, quoting Schelling *op. cit.* again, 'when a country has lost the power to help itself, or the power to avert mutual damage, the other interested party has no choice but to accept the cost or responsibility'. While low foreign exchange reserves are very undesirable they can be turned, to a limited extent, into a bargaining factor for a better debt rescheduling deal, or for acceptance by creditors of debtors' unilateral actions; it will, however, be clearly a negative factor for obtaining new private credit flows and may imply greater and more effective pressure applied by creditors on the type of adjustment which they prefer. On the other hand, clearly a high level of foreign exchange reserves in relation to the level of imports gives the debtor government the option of trading on a cash basis, decreasing the cost of possible curtailment of trade credit lines should the debtor government not reach agreement with the creditor banks. By reducing the urgency for the debtor government of reaching an agreement, high reserves, thus, clearly enhance its bargaining power. This is much more true in cases where debtors take the initiative as in the unilateral action of Peru. On the contrary, where deals are negotiated, a high level of reserves may increase

creditors' pressure for larger debt service.[18]

More broadly, the less dependent the country is on commercial trade credit to fund its essential imports, the more its bargaining power is increased *vis-à-vis* its creditors, who also are the providers of this short-term credit; this relative independence from trade credit can be enhanced not only by higher foreign exchange reserves, but also by successful import substitution policies, increased bilateral (or counter-trade) arrangements between debtor nations and even by the accumulation or existence of inventories of basic imports.

3. An important factor that will increase the bargaining potential of debtor governments to obtain a relatively more favourable deal is the existence at present and the projection in the medium-term of very large negative net transfers of financial flows from the country, as its incentive is greater not to meet debt service *unless* a favourable deal (on new money, rescheduling of existing debt and even on adjustment) is obtained. Also of relevance is whether the negative net transfers is being— and is likely in the future to be—attained: i) mainly by some large improvement in the country's terms of trade; ii) mainly by export-led adjustment or import substitution which though requiring transfers of real internal resources abroad so as to service the debt does so in the context of general economic growth or; iii) is mainly achieved by drastic import compression and related recession. In option i) and to a lesser extent, in option ii), the cost of and resistance to, the negative net transfers, is smaller than in option iii). This point brings us to the significance of political factors and their potential impact on effective or potential bargaining strength.

4. Based on the principle of bargaining theory discussed above, that 'the power of a negotiator often rests on a manifest inability to make concessions and meet demands', it would seem that greater bargaining strength exists potentially for those governments that need to be particularly responsive to their populations,

as the deals negotiated have to be defensible *vis-a-vis* their constituencies. Everything else being equal, the more democratic and open the political process, in terms of genuinely free elections and more broadly in terms of freedom of expression and political activity, and the more differentiated and organised the political actors, in terms of interest groups and parties, the greater the bargaining power of the government in relation to the creditors and international financial institutions. For similar reasons, the more differentiated the decision-making apparatus of the government, and the more the powers of the executive branch are checked and balanced by the legislative and the judiciary, the greater the bargaining power of the government.

5　The 'inability to make concessions' of governments is also linked to the extent to which 'public opinion' (and/or influential groups and parties) exists and attaches priority in each country to the issues of debt and adjustment. The government may either genuinely be 'bound' by interest groups or political parties that are more radical on debt and adjustment issues than it is, or it may have explicitly 'cultivated' such a public opinion, by public statements, promises during electoral campaigns, etc. Once publicly committed nationally to a particular line of action or principle, governments are 'unable' to change such positions in international negotiations. By making promises, or public statements to their constituents or electorates, some debtor governments may reduce the scope of their own authority in negotiations, which would tend to strengthen the debtor government's position. On the contrary, the ruling out of any unilateral action, and extreme willingness to cooperate with creditors and the IMF on drastic adjustment will on the whole weaken that particular government's bargaining position, as it would clearly decrease the likelihood of default and, thus, the incentive of creditors to make concessions for default avoidance.

6.　Governments with a greater level of stability on the

whole have greater bargaining power. In cases of regimes that are broadly seen as well established, including the operation of orderly procedures for succession, creditors can expect the commitments that the government does make to be fulfilled.

7. Not only can more stable regimes obtain a better deal, but this is also true for governments which have a commitment—once an acceptable deal has been reached—to implement economic policies that will make future debt servicing more likely. By increasing the likelihood of future default or moratoria avoidance, a feasible adjustment and development programme would tend to increase creditors' willingness to make concessions so that a mutually acceptable deal can be reached.

The existence of a clear and consistent alternative adjustment package to that preferred by international financial institutions may enhance the prospects for the debtor government to reduce the cost of adjustment, and distribute according to its own priorities. If successfully negotiated, an alternative adjustment package has the virtue that the government's commitment to it will be stronger than to an adjustment package which it broadly sees was 'imposed' on it.

8. Finally, the greater the geo-political importance of the debtor country to the government(s) of the country where most of the creditor banks have headquarters, the larger leverage debtor governments have to extract favourable deals. Similarly, if the debtor economy is an important market for the industrial countries' exports or host to their investors it could be expected that it could ensure a more 'growth oriented' (and, thus, more favourable) deal, though this does not seem to have been the case in the 1982–5 period.

NOTES

1. This chapter was initially prepared for discussion at a workshop in Montevideo in April 1986, funded by IDRC. Research assistance and

very useful discussions with Lucy Nichols are acknowledged. I am grateful to the participants of the workshop at Montevideo for valuable comments. Very useful and stimulating comments were also received at a seminar given in Santiago at CIEPLAN in April 1985. The paper was updated in April 1987, in preparation for the IDRC funded workshop there.

2. IMF: *Recent Multilateral Debt Restructurings with official and Bank Creditors,* IMF Occasional Paper no. 25, December 1983.

3. See Krugman, P. 'International Debt strategies in an Uncertain World' in J. Cuddington and G. Smith *International Debt and the Developing Countries,* World Bank, 1985, for a clear analysis.

4. See Eichengreen, B. and Portes, R. *Debt and Default in the 1930s: Causes and Consquences.* CEPR Discussion Paper no. 75, London, 1985.

5. Schelling, T. C. *The Strategy of Conflict,* Oxford University Press, 1963, Chapter 2.

6. More pessimistic approaches appeared, for example, in the Commonwealth Secretariat 1984 report, *The Debt Crises and the World Economy,* in UNCTAD, *Trade and Development Reports* and in articles such as Ffrench-Davis, R. and Molina, S. 'Proposals for bank lending to LDCs in the remainder of the decade' in *Journal of Development Planning* no. 16, 1985. See also, Griffith-Jones, S. and Sunkel, O. *The Crisis of National Development and International Debt,* Oxford University Press, 1986.

7. Source: CEPAL Cuaderno 47. *La economica de America Latina en 1982. Evolucion general, politica cambiaria y renegociacion de la deuda externa.* Santiago de Chile, 1984, and for recent data Devlin, R. *La deuda externa vs el desarrollo economica: America Latina en la encrucijada, CEPAL Review* no. 27, December 1985.

8. Killick, T. (ed.) *The Quest for Economic Stabilisation: the IMF and the Third World,* Heinemann, 1984.

9. Williamson, J. 'On judging the Success of IMF Policy Advice' in Williamson, J. (ed.) *IMF Conditionality.* Institute of International Economics, Washington DC, 1983.

10. See Williamson, *op. cit.*

11. For a detailed discussion of ex-post government guarantees for private debts in the Chilean case, see Ffrench-Davis, R. and de Gregoria, J. *La renegociacion de la deuda externa de Chile en 1985: Antecedentes y Commentarios.* Coleccion Estuidos CIEPLAN no. 17.

12. See Cox, R. W. and Jacobson, H. K. *The Anatomy of Influence Decision Making in International Institutions.* Yale University Press, 1973.

13. See Zartman, W. 'Negotiation as a Joint Decision-Making Process' in W. Zartman (ed.) *The Negotiation Process: Theories and Applications.* London: Sage Publications, 1978, and Zartman, W. 'Global negotiations: path to the future or dead-end street' *Third World Quarterly,* April 1984.

14. See Dell, S. 'Crisis management and the debt problem' *International*

Journal, Autumn 1985.

15. ECLAC: *External Debt in Latin America, Adjustment Policies and Renegotiation*, Colorado, US, Lynne Rienner Publishers, 1985. Study prepared by A. Bianchi, R. Devlin and J. Ramos; see also Devlin, R. *opt. cit.*, above.

16. For a detailed discussion of the evidence, see Cornia, A. Jolly, R., Stewart, F. (eds) *Adjustment with a Human Face*, Oxford University Press, 1987.

17. Druckman, D. 'Boundary Role Conflict, negotiation as dual responsiveness' in Zartman (ed.) *op. cit.*

18. I thank R. Ffrench-Davis for making this point.

2 External Debt and Adjustment Policies: The Case of Mexico 1982–6

Rene Villarreal

INTRODUCTION

In 1982 Mexico had to face a very severe crisis, after having grown at an average rate of 6.5 per cent for over forty years (1940–81).

The Mexican economic cycles have traditionally been shorter and smoother than those in countries with a similar economic structure. The stages of decline and recovery of activity took place as a result of the restrictions imposed by the result in the current account of the balance of payments.

The external deficit of the manufacturing sector was financed in the 1950s and 1960s with agricultural exports and tourism; and in the 1970s with oil exports and increased borrowing on the international capital markets.

The size of the 1982 crisis led the government to adopt an emergency economic programme and to devise a new development strategy that allowed important changes in the economic structure. The external debt, already over US $80 billion, had become one of the main determinants of the current account deficit, as interest payments were greater than the combined surplus of the trade account and non-factor services.

Thus, the adjustment problem of the Mexican economy became tied to the conditions for debt servicing and repayment. The fall in imports and the growth and diversification of exports were not enough to correct the external imbalance. The debt service is now a structural element of both the external imbalance and the gap between savings and investment.

Towards the end of 1982 the Mexican Government designed the programmes of adjustment and structural change and, within this framework, it agreed a three year stabilisation programme with the IMF under the extended fund facility.

As regards structural change, Mexico has made significant progress. The rationalisation of the structure of protection has meant that more than 90 per cent of import items—that account for over 70 per cent of import value—are currently exempted from the prior licence requirement. Reducing the size of the public sector has meant a fall in the number of public industrial enterprises from 412 to 151, and a concentration in just thirteen industrial activities, compared with twenty-eight in 1982. The reorganisation of public sector activity in the industrial sector will enable increased efficiency and international competitiveness, as well as substantially reducing the burden on the federal budget.

The internal adjustment efforts were significant, as shown by the reduction of the economic public sector deficit from the equivalent of 16.8 per cent of GDP in 1982 to 10.7 per cent in 1983. However, there was a high cost involved and GDP fell sharply in 1983. This internal adjustment and the relative improvement in the external environment allowed a moderate rate of growth in 1984–5. The external shock brought about by the collapse in oil prices in 1986 caused a loss of foreign exchange earnings in the region of US $8.5 billion.

In February 1986 the Mexican Government expressed the need for the cost of the new adjustments to be more evenly shared with the international financial community. Since then the negotiations with the IMF were based on a new approach of adjustment with growth and structural change that tried to ensure: 1) the availability of fresh resources to secure moderate but steady increases in the level of activity; 2) the relative isolation of the domestic economy from unforeseen fluctuations in the world markets; and 3) the evaluation of public sector performance from the operational rather than the financial side.

Within this framework the country started negotiations with the international financial community to obtain a new US $12 billion credit to balance the external accounts through 1988. This agreement is the basis to launch the Programme of

Stimulus and Growth (PAC—Programa de Aliento y Crecimiento) which will ensure moderate economic growth and progress in the structural change process, particularly in the areas related to industrial reorganisation, the reduction in the size of the public sector and the consolidation of the new structure of protection.

Between 1983 and 1986 the adjustment was made via the contraction of investment, which fell from 28 per cent to 18.4 per cent of GDP, while savings remained at around 24 per cent. Faced with the lack of external credits in 1986 the country had to absorb the cost of the adjustment, implying a 3.8 per cent drop in real GDP, inflation at 105.7 per cent, a 8.1 per cent loss in purchasing power at the minimum wage level, and a 150 per cent appreciation of the dollar *vis-à-vis* the peso on the official controlled market.

Despite the important progress made in the debt negotiations, particularly regarding the adjustment with growth and the use of the operational public sector result criterion, the debt crisis in Mexico—as in other countries—is far from having been solved. This is why creative and innovative negotiation schemes need to be devised that would ensure long-term growth, which will enable the consolidation of structural change, increase employment generation and the satisfaction of the basic needs of the population. This entails to keep adjusting the foreign debt service to the real payment capacity of the economy and to get the international financial community to share more evenly the costs of an adjustment process derived from a high level of indebtedness of which it was also partly responsible.

1. THE MEXICAN ECONOMY BEFORE THE 1982 CRISIS

The Mexican economic growth process is one of the most successful in the postwar era. This process became evident in the 1950s and developed at a steady pace since 1954.

Between then and the beginning of the 1970s, following protectionist policies, there were profound changes in the country's productive structure, within a framework of moderate inflation and great stability of the nominal exchange rate, which was fixed for over twenty-two years.

During the most part of this period the external restriction did not represent a serious obstacle to the growth process. Until the mid-1960s there were important agricultural surpluses to satisfy a large part of the financing requirements of the industrialisation process. These resources were complemented with increased manufactured exports and moderate foreign indebtedness.

Since the mid-1960s the stagnation of agricultural output, that led to the decrease in exportable surpluses, and the loss of the advantages associated with the dynamic import substitution process, made the external restriction more evident. This was shown in the increased current account deficit and growing need for foreign indebtedness.

The situation went out of control in 1976 when substantial capital flight took place, fuelled by a high public sector deficit and an overvalued exchange rate resulting from the fixed parity policy in the presence of an acceleration of domestic inflation since 1973.

Under these circumstances the Government proposed a stabilisation programme that included an accord with the International Monetary Fund. It involved a devaluation of the peso in August 1976, fiscal adjustment for 1977 and the intention to liberalise international trade. Originally, the programme was to cover three years, from 1976 to 1978, but the discovery of oil and the massive exports that followed offered a sudden relief to the external restriction, and the adjustment programme was swiftly abandoned.

The improvement in external earnings made it possible that economic recession only affected 1976 and 1977, when output grew at an average rate of 3.8 per cent per annum, well below the historic average. The greater freedom in the balance of payments position allowed the country to rejoin the path of steady economic growth from 1978 to 1981, at an average annual rate of 8.4 per cent. The sizeable amounts of external finance were at the base of this impressive performance. The rising trend in oil prices not only contributed to raise export earnings but converted them in the best guarantee for the international banks which, faced with high liquidity, were in a position to extend creditors to Mexico. Between 1977 and 1982 export earnings coming from oil grew at an average annual rate of 73.9 per cent US$30 billion in 1977 to US$87.6 billion at the end of 1982.

These resources made possible an above average increase in public and private investment compared to the 1970–5 period (see Table 2.1). However, the structure of this resource flow favoured more the expansion of oil-related activities than the development of the manufacturing sector.

The growing importance of oil exports in the total foreign exchange earnings, combined with the increase in external debt, contracted basically over the short term, had an impact over the vulnerability of the domestic economy and the growth capacity, which depended heavily upon two variables that were outside domestic policy control: the international interest rates and the price of oil.

Table 2.1: *Gross fixed capital formation, 1970–81—Mexico*

	AGR[1]	Yearly growth rate			
	1970–5	1978	1979	1980	1981
TOTAL	8.3	15.2	20.2	14.9	14.7
Public	13.4	31.6	17.1	16.7	15.8
Private	5.5	5.1	22.7	13.7	13.9

Source: The author's own figures based on data from the Sistema de Cuentas Nacionales 1970–81.
Note: 1. Annual average rate of growth.

The policy followed was based on expectations—shared by both policymakers and international creditors—that the evolution of the above-mentioned variables would yield a net positive result for Mexico.

From 1981 onwards international interest rates started to rise and at the same time oil prices began to decline. In this context, with the exchange rate becoming overvalued given the rise in domestic inflation and the maintenance of a free convertibility regime, capital flight accelerated. In 1981–2 unexplained foreign exchange outflows amounted to US$16 **billion.**

In February 1982 the peso was devalued and a set of measures was adopted to limit public expenditure. These measures caused a recession and achieved some improvement in the current account; however, capital flight, and reserves drain, persisted, leading Mexico to declare a suspension of payments in August 1982. This marked the beginning of the international debt crisis.

2. ADJUSTMENT POLICY AND STRUCTURAL CHANGE: 1983-5

The crisis that hit the Mexican economy in 1982 caused imbalances at the internal—98.8 per cent inflation, 0.5 per cent fall in real GDP—as well as external level—US$6.2 billion current account deficit (see Table 2.2).

However, it was the external imbalance that was at the origin of it: in 1981 the current account deficit exceeded US$12.5 billion, leading to the 1982 devaluation that took the exchange rate from 25 to 150 pesos to the dollar.

Together, with this external imbalance, public finances were also in the red, the economic deficit of the public sector representing 16.8 per cent of GDP in 1982. The external imbalance had its structural origins in both, the manufacturing trade deficit—which amounted to US$4.7 billion between 1977 and 1981—and the high interest payments on the external debt—US$12.2 billion in 1982.

Adjustment policy and structural change

This is characterised by the following elements:

1. Contraction of demand. Fiscal policy squeezed public consumption and investment, and credit policy reduced private demand by raising interest rates and restricting credit.
2. The policy of relative prices, covering the exchange rate as well as prices and public utilities tariffs, was an important element of the adjustment policy.
3. Trade policy. Given the contraction in demand and the high level of corporate indebtedness, a programme was

Table 2.2: Mexico: Some important economic indicators, 1981–8

	1981	1982	1983	1984	1985	1986	1987	1988
Inflation (CPI annual %)	27.7	98.8	80.8	59.2	63.7	105.7	70–80	50–60
GDP (annual % change)	7.9	- 0.5	- 5.3	3.7	2.8	- 3.8	2–3	4
Economic public deficit/GDP (%)	-12.5	-16.8	-10.7	- 6.3	- 6.0	-15.2	-12.6	–
Operational public deficit/GDP (%)	- 4.2	- 3.4	1.8	0.3	- 0.9	- 2.0	- 0.5	- 0.2
Current account (US$ bn)	-12.5	- 6.2	5.4	4.2	1.2	- 1.3	- 2.9	- 2.7
Trade balance (US$ bn)	- 4.5	6.8	13.8	12.9	8.4	4.6	1.4	1.6
Merchandise exports (US$ bn)	19.4	21.2	22.3	24.2	21.9	16.0	15.7	17.4
oil (US$ bn)	14.6	16.5	16.0	16.6	14.8	6.3	6.0	6.3
non-oil (US$ bn)	4.8	4.7	6.3	7.6	6.9	9.7	9.7	11.1
Merchandise imports (US$ bn)	23.9	14.4	8.6	11.3	13.2	11.4	14.3	15.8
Exchange rate (annual aver % ch)								
controlled market (nominal)	–	–	109.2	39.6	53.2	137.9	90.0	50.4
(real)	–	–	2.1	-16.1	- 0.7	23.0	0.0	0.0
free market (nominal)	6.8	133.3	162.8	23.2	67.5	105.6	–	–
(real)	- 6.3	52.4	28.4	-26.0	8.6	6.4	–	–
Open unemployment rate (%)	4.0	8.0	10.1	9.7	9.7	–	–	–
Real minimum wage (annual % ch)	1.7	-11.6	-16.9	- 6.8	- 1.2	- 8.1	–	–

Source: The author's own figures based on data from Secretaria de Programacion y Presupuesto, Secretaria de Hacienda y Credito Publico and Banxico.

implemented to defend production and employment. Thus, initially all imports were subject to tight quantitative controls and later they were gradually changed to the tariff system. Additionally, fiscal and credit support to the productive plant was established in order to prevent bankruptcies and massive unemployment. With this in mind a Keynesian type emergency programme of employment was launched at federal and municipal level. Nevertheless, basic popular consumption was protected through imports of foodstuffs by the state entity CONASUPO when deemed necessary.

4. The structural change proposed involved a reduction in the size of the public sector, rationalisation of excessive protectionism, streamlining of public enterprises and industrial reorganisation including the public sector.

Development of the internal and external adjustment process
The adjustment policy had positive results in 1983–5 but the

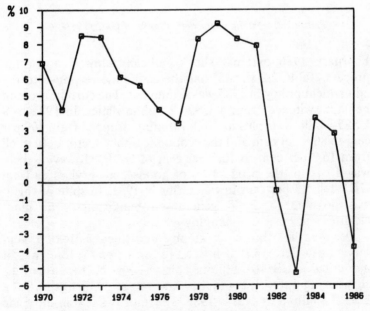

Figure 2.1:   Real GDP (% change) 1970–86

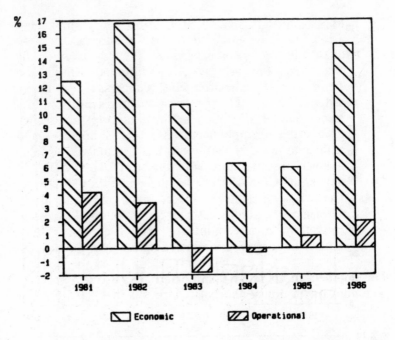

Figure 2.2:   Public sector deficit (as % of GDP) 1981–86

February 1986 external shock radically slowed down the process. Table 2.2 shows that the economic response to the adjustment policy in 1983 was significant. The current account balance switched from a US$6.2 billion deficit in 1982 to a US$5.4 billion surplus in 1983. Inflation dropped from 100 per cent to 80.8 per cent and the economic public sector deficit fell from 16.8 per cent to 10.7 per cent of GDP. However, there was a cost in the production of goods and services as total GDP fell 5.3 per cent in real terms in 1983. In spite of this it was possible to avoid generalised bankruptcies or plant closures and massive unemployment.

Despite the drastic economic adjustment, Mexico kept servicing its debt; in 1983 interest payments on the foreign debt amounted to US$10.1 billion. This was possible because of the significant improvement in the trade balance, which recorded a US$13.8 billion surplus in 1983. The improvement in the trade accounts was in turn a result of a sharp reduction in

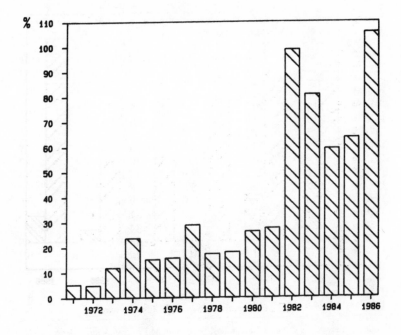

Figure 2.3: Consumer price index (% change) 1971–86

merchandise imports from US$23.9 billion in 1981 to US$8.6 billion in 1983, while exports increased from US$19.4 billion to US$22.4 billion in the same period.

Open unemployment increased from 8 per cent in 1982 to 10.1 per cent in 1983; it did not grow more due both to the programmes of defence of production and employment and to the regional employment protection emergency programmes. However, the unemployment rate had been only 4.0 per cent in 1981.

During 1984–5 the adjustment policy allowed some reactivation of the economy, with real GDP growing at 3.7 per cent in 1984 and 2.8 per cent in 1985. Inflation was reduced further and stabilised at 60 per cent. The current account surplus of US $4.2 billion in 1984 was nearly wiped out in 1985 due to the debt service burden. In 1984 the trade surplus reached US $12.9 billion while interest payments on the foreign debt amounted to US $11.7 billion, but in 1985 the

Table 2.3: Evolution of the components of internal and external adjustment 1970–86 (% share in GDP)

	Savings –	Investment =	Exports	– Imports	= Trade Balance[1]
1970	20.8	22.7	7.7	9.6	-1.9
1971	19.6	20.7	7.7	8.8	-1.1
1972	20.5	21.1	8.3	8.9	-0.6
1973	21.5	22.5	8.7	9.7	-1.0
1974	22.2	24.9	8.2	10.9	-2.7
1975	21.4	24.7	7.1	10.4	-3.3
1976	21.0	23.2	7.9	10.1	-2.2
1977	22.3	22.3	8.8	8.8	0.0
1978	22.2	23.1	9.0	9.9	-0.9
1979	22.6	25.0	9.3	11.7	-2.4
1980	22.8	28.0	9.1	14.3	-5.2
1981	23.1	30.0	9.0	13.9	-6.9
1982	21.7	21.5	10.2	10.0	0.2
1983	22.8	17.0	12.0	6.2	5.8
1984	23.4	17.7	12.9	7.2	5.7
1985	23.9	19.6	12.1	7.8	4.3
1986[2]	24.6	18.4	13.3	7.1	6.2

Source: Sistema de Cuentas Nacionales, Secretaria de Programacion y Presupuesto.
Notes: 1. Excluding factor services
2. Preliminary figures

trade balance was US $1.8 billion lower than interest payments (trade surplus: US $8.4 billion; interest payments: US $10.2 billion). The economy grew at 2.8 per cent in 1985 and the open unemployment rate declined slightly and remained at 9.7 per cent in 1984 and 1985.

The adjustment process was already showing in 1985 the high vulnerability of the economy to reductions in export earnings (both oil or non-oil), given the high debt service burden. It is important to analyse the development of the different parts of the internal and external adjustment process (see Table 2.3 and Figure 2.4). In doing so we must stress the fact that the Mexican economy has the highest savings ratio in Latin America, which remained around 23 per cent of GDP from 1981 to 1986. In 1981 the savings ratios to GDP was 23.1 per cent, while investment was 30 per cent of GDP (Table 2.3), implying a net transfer of resources into the Mexican economy

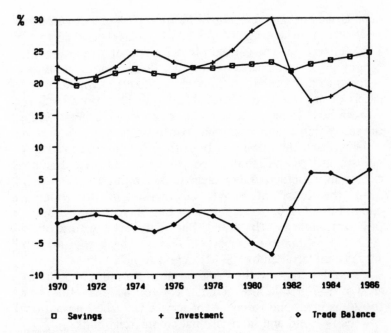

Figure 2.4: Evolution of the external and internal adjustment (% share of GDP) 1970–86

of 6.9 per cent of GDP. However, in 1986 the savings ratio rose to 24.6 per cent and the investment coefficient fell to 18.4 per cent of GDP, more than eleven percentual points since the beginning of the decade, implying a net transfer of resources abroad of 6.2 per cent of GDP. This marked change in the net resource transfer relied both on increases in exports and reductions in imports. The first rose from the equivalent of 9 per cent of GDP in 1981 to 13.3 per cent in 1986, while imports fell from 15.9 per cent to 7.1 per cent of GDP in the same period. Therefore, it can be stated that the core problem for Mexico did not reside in a low savings rate but in the channelling of these resources towards productive investment, which was jeopardised by the high transfers abroad tied to servicing the foreign debt.

The 1986 oil shock The external vulnerability of the Mexican economy and its dependence on oil income and on the high debt service became evident in February 1986. The fall in oil prices from an average of US $25.4 a barrel in 1985 to US $11.8 a barrel in 1986 caused Mexico a loss of around US $8.5 billion in exports; as a result the 1986 trade surplus was reduced to just US $4.6 billion while interest payments on the external debt totalled US$8.4 billion. This prompted the Government to devise a new debt negotiation scheme and at the same time a new economic growth strategy.

This raised the question about the need for the cost of the adjustment to be shared by the international financial community. In fact, in a message to the nation on 21 February 1986, the President urged the revision of the financial conditions of debt servicing, adjusting them to the country's payment capacity. He stated that 'it is now the turn of our creditors to make an effort similar to the great task and sacrifice undertaken by the Mexican people'.

From this emerged the Programme of Stimulus and Growth (PAC), 1987–8, that has been the basis for the renegotiations of the adjustment and foreign debt service with the International Monetary Fund and international commercial banks.

3. PROGRESS IN THE PROCESS OF STRUCTURAL CHANGE, 1983–6

The structural change process that started in 1983 shows marked progress in different areas, the most important of them being the correction in the structure of the main relative prices of the economy, the streamlining of public finances, the reduction in size and the reorganisation of the public corporate sector and the rationalisation of protection of the domestic market.

Adjustments in the structure of relative prices
As to the structure of relative prices, the prices of goods and services provided by the public sector have been brought into line with the general price level and at the same time depositors have been assured a positive real interest rate on their savings. It can be said that in this field the main targets of structural change have been achieved.

Streamlining of public finances

There has been important progress in this area, shown clearly by the fact that the primary economic balance of the public sector (defined as total less income expenditure excluding interest payments) relative to GDP has moved from a 6.4 per cent deficit in 1981 to a 2.0 per cent surplus in 1986. The elimination of adjustment lags in the prices of goods and services offered by the public sector, the reduction in current expenditure and investment and the increase in tax revenue have been important factors in this process. In the coming years the continuation of this process will rely on a real increase in tax collection derived from the fiscal reform that has been proposed to congress by the federal government. One of the main mechanisms in this reform is the gradual elimination of selected tax exemptions accorded to enterprises.

As to the reduction of public expenditure it is worth mentioning that the programmed outlays relative to GDP fell nearly three percentual points between 1982 and 1986, passing from 28.1 per cent to 25.2 per cent. The main factor behind this reduction was the cut in investment by 3.1 percentual points. The main rigidities in public expenditure can be found in the non-programmable outlays, particularly in the item of interest payments, which had remained at a stable 12–13 per cent of GDP in 1982–5, rising to 17.4 per cent in 1986. As a comparison, total revenue represented 30 per cent of GDP in 1986.

Contraction and reorganisation of the public sector

The structural change process implied the concentration of public sector efforts on strategic and priority activities, de-investing in enterprises and agencies in other non-priority areas. A decision to release from public control 702 out of the 1,155 existing enterprises was made in December 1982.

The most important adjustments took place in the energy, mining and manufacturing sectors. In the latter the number of firms shrank from 412 at the beginning of the current administration to 151 at the end of 1986. This implied the withdrawal of the public sector from fifteen out of the forty-nine activities that make up the Mexican manufacturing industry. Among them we have the manufacturing of cars, cement, china and pottery, textiles, beverages, bicycles, chemicals and secondary petrochemicals. The de-investment process had already been completed in 1986 in 40 per cent of the entities whose separation from the public sector had been decided.

The concentration of state efforts and resources in a set of core activities (petroleum, mining, electricity, steel, fertilisers and transport equipment) has helped to inject dynamism to the industrial reorganisation process in the more mature or traditional branches within those activities. The process of industrial reorganisation goes hand in hand with a process of modernisation in the public corporate sector in the areas of production techniques, trading, finances and human resources. The reduction in the size and the reorganisation of state-owned industry are two processes of structural change that have been complemented and reinforced mutually.

Rationalisation of protection

From the beginning of the de la Madrid administration, one of the main objectives of structural change was to make protection more rational, to improve resource allocation and increase efficiency and non-oil exports.

During 1983–6 there were remarkable achievements in export promotion and the gradual liberalisation of imports. The rationalisation of protection was to be done via: a) the replacement of quantitative import controls—prior licence—by tariffs; b) changes to the tariff structure to reduce its general level and its dispersion; and c) access to GATT and the adoption of internationally accepted commercial practices.

It has to be pointed out that the decision to join GATT was made in November 1985, and it is presumed that it did not arise from external pressures, being instead a corollary of the trade liberalisation measures adopted in July 1985.

According to SECOFI, in 1982 all import items were subject to a prior licence. By December 1985, 7,252 items had been exempted from this requirement, representing 89.5 per cent of all importable items and 65 per cent of the total value of imports in 1985. The average tariff declined from 27 per cent in 1982 to 25.5 per cent in 1985. Additionally, the weighted average tariff fell from 16.3 per cent to 13.3 per cent. The process of rationalisation of protection continued in 1986. As to the impact of trade policy measures on the behaviour of merchandise imports, it must be stressed that the latter fell in 1982 and 1983 due to the existence of quantitative controls, the peso devaluation and the decline in economic activity. During 1984 and the first half of 1985 the gradual phasing out of prior licensing, the real appreciation of the peso and economic recovery explain the increase in purchases abroad. From mid–1985 onwards imports started to lose dynamism despite the lifting—that July—of the prior licence requirement for 3,604 import items (45 per cent of the total). This can be explained by: a) a substantial devaluation of the peso; b) reduced economic activity; c) increased tariff levels; and d) cuts in public expenditure. During 1986, and despite the tariff reduction programme already in place, the pre-eminence of a), b) and d) help to explain the fall in merchandise imports that year.

In summary, notwithstanding the negative impact of the 1986 oil shock, the Mexican government's structural change strategy shows important progress in the area of external trade. Non-oil exports rose from US $4.8 billion in 1981 to US $9.7 billion in 1986, representing 70 per cent of imports, while in the period 1977–81 they were only enough to cover 33 per cent of imports.

4. THE 1986 EXTERNAL SHOCK: ADJUSTMENT STRATEGY AND RENEGOTIATION POLICY

4 The Program of Stimulus and Growth (PAC)

Once it had assessed the extent of the damage to foreign exchange income caused by the oil price fall, the Mexican government set itself the task of devising a new strategy to face its foreign debt service in a context of moderate but steady growth. It was within this framework that the Program of Stimulus and Growth (PAC) was conceived, which was used as a basis for the negotiation of a 18–month stand-by agreement with the International Monetary Fund, finally signed in July 1986.

The 1987–8 programme sets the growth target for 1987 at

around 2 per cent to make up, at least partly, for the 3.8 per cent output fall recorded in 1986. This programme was first embodied in the 1987 general criteria for economic policy which put forward the following goals:

1. To foster moderate economic growth with high generation of employment.
2. To renew and reinforce the fight against inflation.
3. To consolidate and widen the scope of the ongoing processes of structural change and reorganisation of the public corporate sector.
4. To urge decentralisation at the national level.

In order to attain these objectives, the Government is using specific policies directed to incomes, public expenditure, interest and exchange rates, credit and foreign trade.

In the fiscal area the Government is aiming at a reduction in the operational public sector deficit of 1.5 per cent of GDP, to be achieved via increase in tax revenue (1.3 per cent), adjustment in prices of goods and services (0.6 per cent) and the reduction in programmable expenditure (0.5 per cent). The latter should come as a result of an increase in investment (0.5 per cent) accompanied by a higher reduction in current expenditure (1.0 per cent). The plan envisages a 15 per cent real growth of public expenditure.

In this sense, there is a change in the type of adjustment since, in giving priority to growth, public expenditure is reassigned rather than cut indiscriminately. A great share of the effort is made on the fiscal revenue side, without concentrating the pressure on the expenditure side, a feature of the 1982 accord.

Exchange rate and credit policy aims at the gradual reduction of inflation and nominal interest rates and the maintenance of the real exchange rate. The process of rationalisation of protection will be maintained.

Negotiations with the International Monetary Fund (IMF)
In order to make the PAC attractive in terms of external finance, the Government went on to make an agreement with the IMF that stands out for its originality, compared with the traditional practices of this organisation.

The agreement explicitly acknowledged the need to ensure economic growth in the range of 3 to 4 per cent a year for 1987–8, that was to be achieved independently of potential unfavourable fluctuations on the international oil market, by means of an automatic compensatory financing mechanism which would be triggered if the average export price per barrel of Mexican oil falls below US $9. Also the agreement involved some changes in the methodology generally used by the Fund in the definition of the evaluation mechanisms. A new technical concept of fiscal deficit was accepted for monitoring purposes, that acknowledged the distorting impact of inflation on the traditional concept of financial deficit. It excluded interest payments on debt that accrued because of inflation; the concept of operational deficit, therefore, included only 'real' interest payments.

In terms of finance, the negotiation of new resources consisted in obtaining US $12 billion in 'new money' for 1986 and 1987. Also a novel contingency fund was established to be used in the case of further deterioration to oil prices or if the economy did not have a positive response in the first months of 1987.

A summary of the main features of the new stand-by credit agreement are included below:

Table 2.4: IMF stand-by credit agreement

Variable	Description
Length	18 months (July 1986 – December 1987).
Amount requested.	SDR 1,400 million.
Structural reform of the tax system	To widen the taxable base of global corporate tax. To adjust to delays between tax generation and collection dates. The fiscal effort is estimated at 1.3 per cent of GDP.
Adjustment in prices of public sector goods and services.	To increase revenues by 1.2 per cent of GDP in the 18 months of the accord.

Table 2.4: continued

Variable	Description
Public expenditure.	Total expenditure in goods and services fell to 26.5 per cent of GDP in 1985 and around 25 per cent in 1986, with a further reduction of 0.5 per cent of GDP targeted for 1987.
Public sector de-investment	The number of state-owned entities has fallen from 1,155 in 1982 to just 697 and will reduce further in the following months.
Monetary and credit policy.	To aim at reducing the inflation rate, meeting balance of payments targets and supporting productive capacity. To maintain private sector credit according to the availability of resources.
Exchange rate policy.	To be flexible in order to maintain Mexico's external competitiveness, strengthen its international reserve position and ease the trade liberalisation policy.
External indebtedness.	To amount to around US $12 billion in 1986–7 to cover the financing gap and restart economic growth and the feasibility of external payments.
Trade policy	Prior import licence requirement has been lifted for further 3,604 import items, which represent about 36 per cent of the value of 1984 imports. Mexico joined GATT's multilateral trade negotiations in September as an official member.
Foreign direct investment	A selective policy to promote investment in areas related to non-oil exports and technology transfer

Source: Secretaria de Hacienda y Credito Publico.

Renegotiation with commercial banks.

Once the accord with the IMF was signed, the Government proceeded to start negotiations with 360 foreign banks in order to reschedule public and private obligations and at the same time obtain new credits (for more details, see Gurria's chapter in this book).

Table 2.5: *Scenarios agreed with the IMF and the International Financial Community to protect the Mexican economy from drastic fluctuations in oil prices*

Scenarios	Action
Basic scenario.	If average export price of oil remains in the US $9–14/barrel range, the financing programme remains unchanged. If price fluctuations exceed such range the relevant targets in the programme will be modified accordingly
Low-case scenario.	If prices fall below US $9/barrel, the programme would be protected in the first nine months by additional finance on a 1:1 basis. The additional potential financing coming from all sources should not exceed US $2.5 billion over eighteen months.
High-case scenario.	If prices increases above US $14/barrel, the external financing could be reduced in accordance with the additional income.

Source: Secretaria de Hacienda y Credito Publico.

An accord was finally signed on 20 March 1987, giving Mexico access to new resources, but not without strong reluctance on the part of the smaller banks to participate in the financial package. The portion of the debt that had been rescheduled in 1982 and on which repayments were due to start in 1987 was rescheduled again, over twenty years with seven years grace. In addition, the negotiations included the rescheduling of debt owed to Paris Club governments.

1986 results: costs and benefits of the adjustment

In face of the lack of external credit in 1986, the adjustment had to be absorbed internally through contraction in aggregate demand, increased depreciation of the currency and higher interest rates that attracted capital held abroad.

Aggregate demand fell by 4.4 per cent in 1986. Total consumption declined by 4.6 per cent and exports increased by 5.2 per cent, while gross fixed public and private investment shrank by 16.8 per cent and 8.8 per cent respectively. This was reflected in a 3.8 per cent fall in Gross Domestic Product. Inflation was slightly above 105 per cent, while the price of the dollar on the controlled market rose by 150 per cent, implying an increased depreciation of the peso *vis-à-vis* the dollar. Interest rates were high throughout 1986, standing at around twenty-five percentual points above those in 1985 for fixed term deposits. This favoured capital inflows estimated at about US $700 million. The costs of the adjustment that year were the fall in demand, that was translated into a fall in investment and output, an increase in unemployment and a 8.1 per cent contraction of real wages.

Not all the adjustment was of a negative sort. The adjustment was carried out in an orderly manner and the increases in international reserves held by Banco de Mexico and in foreign exchange earnings from higher exports enabled the country to widen its bargaining capacity.

However, the real problem remains: servicing the external debt exceeds the real payment capacity of the country. This is reflected in the fact that, having had investment/GDP ratios of around 28 per cent before 1982, this ratio was only 18 per cent in 1986, at a time when the challenge is not just to raise the economic efficiency of its productive system substantially but, more importantly, to accelerate the capital accumulation process in order to change the productive structure and reorganise industry. Such a process is jeopardised by the size of the external debt service that has caused the historical investment ratio to fall by one-quarter, having also compressed real wages and the expansion of employment.

FINAL REMARKS

In recent years the Latin American countries have made substantial efforts to try to correct the structural imbalances affecting their economies, but this process has been jeopardised by the high burden of the external debt service. As is widely known, the major problem facing Latin American countries is to service their external debt, which amounted to US $383,080 million at the end of 1986. In 1986 interest payments on their debt totalled US $28,400 million, or 35.1 per cent of total export earnings.

In the case of Mexico, the US $8.5 billion fall in oil export earnings in 1986 and the limited availability of external credit forced an internal adjustment at a very high cost. The operational fiscal balance has been almost in equilibrium since 1984. This has had an important effect in reducing the investment/GDP ratio to the current 18 per cent. This investment level is not due to low generation of domestic savings. Mexico's savings ratio, at 24 per cent of GDP, is one of the highest of the semi-industrialised countries. The reduction in investment, particularly from the public sector, was made to curb internal absorption and release funds for a net transfer of resources abroad equivalent to 6.2 per cent of GDP in 1986. The costs of the adjustment can be seen in the 1986 economic results: decline in GDP, rise in urban unemployment, fall of minimum wage in real terms, higher inflation. It must be said however that the adjustment process took place in an orderly manner.

In spite of the high cost incurred, the efforts made in the areas of rationalisation of protection, reduction in the size of the public sector, industrial reorganisation and export promotion, laid the foundations for consolidation of these changes in the medium and long term.

Developing countries have become net exporters of financial resources via the debt service and other foreign exchange outflows. What strikes as paradoxical is that the poorer countries, traditionally insufficient in capital, are exporting it to the richer ones, where presumably it is abundant. Under these circumstances, it is necessary to recognise that, in the particular case of Mexico, any renegotiation mechanisms to be established will have to consider, firstly, that the market value of debt is around 60 cents for every dollar and, secondly, that it is essential to secure steady GDP growth in the region of 5 to 6 per cent per year. Only then it will be possible to look for likely solutions to the challenges of generating 900,000 new jobs annually and of producing basic goods for additional 1.6 million people every year.

In summary, there is a need for continued progress in the handling of the external debt issue under the joint responsibility approach between debtors and creditors. Precedents from earlier arrangements should not prevent that future renegotiations take more into account a country's real payment capacity. Any scheme of debt servicing and repayment that is based on stagnation and the reduction of investment will only serve to postpone and enlarge the scope of the debt crisis. The only solution lies in economic growth and the increase in exports. Stagnation in developing countries and protectionism in the developed ones leads nowhere near a solution: the international financial system will not be stabilised and the chances of a radical breaking off with the system, which we all want to avoid, will remain.

BIBLIOGRAPHY

Arida, P. and Taylor L. 'Development Macroeconomics', chapter prepared for *The Handbook of Development Economics*, edited by Chenery and Srinivasan, mimeo (1985).

Banco de Mexico, *Informe Anual*, several issues.

Ize, A. and Salas, J. 'El Comportamiento Macroeconomico de la Economica Mexicana entre 1961–81', in *La Inflacion en Mexico*, El Colegio de Mexico (1984).

Kaldor, N. (1971), *Conflicts in national economic objectives*.

Khan, M. and Knight, M. Fund-supported adjustment programs and economic growth, Occasional Paper no. 41, International Monetary Fund, Washington, November, 1985.

Meller, P. and Solimano, A. *Reactivation interna ante una severa restriccion externa: analisis de distintas politicas economicas*, CIEPLAN, junio de 1985.

Miller, M. 'Inflation. Adjusting the public sector financial deficit: measurement and implications for policy', in Kay, T. (ed.) *The 1982 Budget*, London, 1982.

Rodriguez, G. 'El comportamiento de los precios agropecuarios', *Economia Mexicana*, no. 1, CIDE, Mexico.

Ros, J. 'Pricing in the Mexican manufacturing sector', *Cambridge Journal of Economics*, Vol. 4, no. 3, September, 1980.

Ros, J. and Vasquez, A. 'Industrializacion y Comercio Exterior,

1950-1977', *Economia Mexicana*, no. 2, CIDE, Mexico, 1980.
Taylor, L. 'The Crisis and thereafter: macroeconomic policy problems in Mexico', mimeo, 1985.
Villarreal, R. *El desequilibrio externo en la industrializacion de Mexico*, Fondo de Cultura Economica, Mexico, 1976.

3 Debt Restructuring: Mexico as a Case Study

Angel Gurria Trevino

INTRODUCTION

In order to fully appreciate the process of debt restructuring, its benefits and limitations, it is imperative to understand the conceptual framework and its underlying causes due to internal or external factors, or both. The behaviour of the Mexican economy in recent years provides an excellent opportunity to analyse, as a case study, the interplay between and relative importance of international circumstances and domestic macroeconomic policies (section 2 of this chapter and in the chapter by Villerreal) which affected the growth and composition of Mexico's external debt. To begin, it is necessary to gather an overview of the external debt processes of developing countries.

THE CONCEPTUAL FRAMEWORK

Mexico, like the majority of developing countries, has traditionally registered an external deficit both in its Trade Balance as well as in its current account. As from World War II it was considered acceptable—and even advisable—for developing countries to run a reasonable balance of payments deficit in their current account based on economic arguments of the greater use of financial and real resources for furthering growth and development. A developing country could generate and sustain external deficits in order to promote economic growth so long as such deficits were kept within a reasonable proportion to its GNP and exports. This pattern of economic thought for developing countries may not hold in the future, but during the postwar period until the early–1980s such was the prevailing economic wisdom.

What is the significance of running continued current account deficits from the external point of view of a developing country? The magnitude of a country's current account deficit in any one year will determine, in a major sense, the extent of such country's new external borrowing needs: in addition to such yearly borrowing for the finance of the current account deficit, an increasing outstanding amount of foreign debt will arise as a function of the accumulated yearly deficits. This outstanding debt will need *refinancing* of the amortizations that fall due during the year to maintain the same original outstanding, apart from the additional financing required for that year's current account deficit incurred.

We, therefore, have two types of external finance needs by a country: On the one hand, in any particular year the net external indebtedness of a country is a function of its external current account deficit for that year: it may be somewhat more (because of, for example, capital flight, negative errors or omissions, net foreign direct disinvestment, or the build-up of Central Bank foreign currency reserves), or somewhat less. This we can call 'net' borrowing, that is, the net amount by which the outstanding amount of a country's foreign debt rises. On the other hand, a country needs to continually *refinance* the amortizations of its debt due during any one year, to maintain the same original outstanding amount. The *vulnerability*—or even in a certain sense the *dependence*—of a country with respect to external indebtedness is a function of these two critical variables. The more current account deficits are reduced, the less are the 'net' requirements of finance from abroad—and, hence, the less external vulnerability; in the case of the other variable, the slower the pace at which the outstanding external debt falls due over time—that is, the more extended the debt 'profile', the less will be the yearly needs for refinancing from abroad, and hence, the lesser vulnerability of that country.

Traditionally, Mexico—like most other developing countries—could refinance amortizations of its external debt largely through international market operations; Mexico could 'pay' the amortizations due on its debt because the international market mechanisms existed to refinance them, and to obtain the additional financial resources needed in relation to the magnitude of its current account deficits.

So long as a country is in current account deficit, its external debt will continue to rise in outstandings even though such a country may be 'paying' amortizations; in effect, it is recontracting the necessary funds abroad in order to re-establish outstandings plus the additional amount of the deficit. We can, therefore, appreciate that for deficit countries the notion of 'paying' debt is an elusive one.

The understanding of this global financial process is vital for a full appreciation of not only the Mexican debt restructuring, but also that of developing countries in general. It is not a simple question of whether the borrowing country 'can pay' or 'cannot pay' its foreign debt; this type of questioning seems misguided if aimed at the reduction and/or disappearance of the external debt outstandings, for it would imply sustained and sizeable current account surpluses by those borrowing countries which would result in reduced or even negative rates of growth. Debt, productively utilised and prudently contracted, yields more room for expansion and growth. What we have here is a question of *management* of external debt.

Until the first oil shock in 1973, the major lenders to developing countries had been official sources. The first oil shock changed all that; official sources began to lag behind private sources, essentially banks. Starting from a relatively low level of exposure to developing countries in relation to their capital base and total assets, international banks had substantial leeway on increment oustandings. The net flow of financing to developing countries, grew very rapidly until the end of 1981. Then, various large borrowers began to experience a series of internal and external problems; private lenders, after a brief period of additional financial support, began to individually react (and in some cases over-react) by drastically cutting new disbursements. By mid-1982 the traditional refinancing mechanisms from international mar-kets had virtually dried up. Amortizations of external debt by various developing countries could no longer be 'rolled over' with private lenders as in the past, and developing countries began to be affected by the 'domino effect' of bank lending cutbacks across the board. A new mechanism for refinancing had to be devised, though the concept remained the same as before. *It was a new formula for an old practice.*

MEXICO: THE HISTORICAL CONTEXT

At the end of 1976, at the time of Presidential change, Mexico was in economic recession, with a large fiscal deficit, a deteriorated current account position of almost US $3.7 billion, and a foreign debt of US $26 billion. The growing Mexican oil reserves, and escalating price of oil seemed an irresistible option to pull the country out of recession and generate foreign currency revenues. The development of the oil industry required an enormous volume of financial resources particularly from abroad, to finance the high import content of the investment programme.

A substantial proportion of the foreign financial resources, mainly from banks, was, therefore, used since 1977 in the expansion of Mexico's oil production and export platform. Between 1977–81, Mexico's GDP grew at an average annual rate of around 8.5 per cent high not only in relation to Mexico's historic average of 6 per cent, but also in relation to other developing countries and particularly in relation to developed economies, then in a period of relative stagnation and increasing unemployment. Investment in Mexico rose from a historic 20 per cent of GDP to a peak of 25 per cent of GDP in 1981; the annual growth of income per capita during the period was over 6 per cent, and the growth of employment was on average 5.4 per cent annually.

This laudable—though temporary—progress was unfortunately achieved at cost of growing internal and external disequilibria. During the period 1977–82, the Mexican economy had been increasingly overheated, even before the fall in the prices of oil in mid–1981. Growing governmental expenditure without its counterpart in adequate fiscal income, generated an increasing fiscal deficit which rose from 7.1 per cent of GDP in 1977 to 7.8 per cent in 1980, to a disquieting

14.7 per cent in 1981 and to an alarming 17.9 per cent in 1982.

The undue expansion in Government expenditure, coupled with a widening fiscal deficit, financed principally with external indebtedness, boosted internal demand well beyond the economy's productive and growth capacity, creating domestic bottlenecks. The excess demand spilled into imports which grew at an inordinately high rate. At the same time, potential non-oil exports were being sucked into the domestic market, making the country increasingly dependent on oil exports. An added boost to this deteriorating trend was provided by the increasing overvaluation of the peso since early 1979. The overheating of the economy was exacerbating inflationary pressures.

In the external sector, the current account deteriorated inexorably from US $1.6 billion in 1977 (2 per cent of GDP), to $4.9 billion in 1979, to $6.8 billion in 1980 (3.5 per cent of GDP) and to a huge 13 billion in 1981 (5.2 per cent of GDP); in this last year, merchandise imports had risen to the extraordinary figure of US $24.4 billion.

In view of this widening current account deficit, the total external debt outstanding of Mexico (public and private) grew from US $29.7 billion in 1977 to US $50.7 billion in 1980, and in the year of 1981 to US $74.9 billion, a leap of US $24.2 billion in one year, comparable to half the entire debt outstanding in 1980. Private sector debt had itself risen from US $5 billion in 1977 to US $18 billion in 1982, both because of its being crowded out of internal financing by the public sector's need of funds, and because of the financial attractiveness of borrowing abroad in view of the more favourable interest levels and the overvaluation of the peso.

The underlying deterioration of Mexico's internal and external finances surfaced severely in 1981, when in the middle of that year the international prices of oil began to fall. As a policy response to this, had the price of Mexican oil been accordingly lowered to maintain the existing volume of sales, had the peso been devalued to correct its overvaluation, and had government expenditure been substantially reduced, it may be estimated that the recorded current account deficit for 1981 would have been of a similar magnitude to that of the previous year, with an increasing correction the ensuing year.

The debt crisis, as it erupted in 1982, could to some extent have been avoided. Instead of these corrective measures, the price of Mexican oil was initially maintained, with the result that in the ensuing months the volume of international sales fell to only a minor fraction of the previous amount; the overvalued peso was sustained until early 1982, notwithstanding the rapid escalation of capital flight which was draining the country's reserves and pressing for even more external indebtedness; government expenditure was continued with only minor adjustments.

In view of the unstable economic situation and inadequate policy response, capital flight in all its forms (leads and lags on foreign trade, contraband, prepayment of private foreign debt and outright speculation) began to accumulate since mid–1981; the 'errors and omissions' in the balance of payments rose in that year to the extraordinary figure of US $8.3 billion, followed by a similar one in 1982. Hence, the inordinate rise in foreign indebtedness in 1981 was well above the high current account deficit of that year. In the last months of 1982, domestic interest rates were lowered in order to ostensibly reduce inflationary pressures and encourage productive activities: this policy response fuelled an even greater flight of capital.

With respect to international factors that have adversely affected the non-oil developing countries, some of them also had an adverse impact upon Mexico: the high and rising real interest rate in the period 1979–82, the slowdown in world trade and the recession of developed economies which caused low export demand, the deteriorating terms of trade for non-oil commodities (and, since mid–1981, oil included); all of these were negative external shocks to the Mexican economy. Nevertheless, in the case of Mexico the quantification of all the external shocks, during the 1977–82 period, taken as a whole, appears to yield a net positive result, essentially because of the improved volume and terms of trade in oil until mid–1981.[1] After that date, the external factors seemed to concentrate in a negative direction for Mexico.

Probably the most fundamental mistake of economic appreciation made not only by Mexico, but also by lenders and observers, was to believe that oil prices would unquestionably remain firm for the foreseeable future; from that starting point, balance of payments projections were over-optimistic, government expenditure was over-expansive, foreign borrowing was excessive, financial controls were lax and exchange rate policy was distortive. A number of internal policy mistakes *after* the onset of the oil crisis in 1981 all added dramatic impetus to the debt crisis that erupted in mid-1982. For the 1977–82 period, a quantitative analysis of external and internal factors (both positive and negative ones) would lead to the conclusion that the deterioration in Mexico's external accounts was essentially due to internal causes; if we take only the 1981–2 period, a substantially larger role in the crisis is assigned to external factors, although admittedly internal factors continued to play a heavy part.

From 1977 to mid-1981, Mexico relied substantially on international banks for its foreign financing needs. Two aspects are worth noting: there was a substantial under-utilisation of official export credits from other countries in relation to the country's imports due to lack of exchange or other controls (in contrast to, for example, Brazil which had exchange controls and a tighter control over this aspect); there was flexibility on maturities offered by the market to maintain competitive margins on bank loans (in contrast to, for example, Brazil, which laid all emphasis upon the required maturities for the maintenance of a debt profile as stretched as possible even if it meant very high borrowing costs). When world liquidity was high and banks eager to lend the equivalent of repayments received plus more, there was a general perception that what mattered most was the amount of 'net' borrowing needs, since 'gross' ones (i.e. repayment profile) would invariably be refinanced. It was usual to see syndicated loans with maturities of seven, five or even three years, at attractive margins on the unmentioned 'under-standing' by all parties concerned, that these would naturally be refinanced at the time of repayment upon agreement of the new tenors and margins.

In the middle of 1982, there is a conceptual cut-off on the external finances of Mexico: first, we needed to continually refinance our heavy foreign debt amortizations abroad as they came due; second, we needed to borrow new additional funds from abroad to finance an already sizeable current account deficit up to the middle of 1981, and a much larger one from then on, due to the heavy temporary fall in oil sales and revenues and the high dollar interest rates; third, we had sizeable and increasing capital flight from the country as from mid–1981, which effectively called for even greater borrowing from abroad to prevent an unduly rapid fall in reserves. These three types of foreign currency requirements had, together, increased the gross borrowing needs of Mexico from abroad, from a monthly volume of up to US $1.5 billion until mid–year to double that figure, around US $3 billion, thereafter.

Although there was some bilateral and multilateral borrowing, the overwhelming majority of such needs had to be satisfied from the international private financial and capital markets. From a variety of international operations, like syndicated credits, bonds, private placements, etc., a country like Mexico working at full steam in those markets could in mid–1981 raise up to US $1 billion a month in gross medium-term funds; but US $2 billion a month or more in medium-term funds was quite out of reach in those markets.

The answer lay in short-term funds from banks; these were obtainable with relative ease and speed of disbursement, and minimum requirements for documentation. From mid–1981 Mexico began to contract a great number of short-term bank credits and refinance them periodically (monthly, three-monthly or six-monthly), so that by mid–1982 the outstanding amount of short-term bank loans by the public sector had risen to around US $10.8 billion. This exceptionally intense quest for short-term funds, together with the US $24.2 billion increasingly eroded the confidence of the international banking community, after a period of accommodating the enormously increased demand for funds. The negative effects of this arose in 1982, as financial entities individually, and then collectively, began to slow down the pace of new lending and, ultimately, to retrench by mid–1982.

The unthinkable was also happening, some banks were by then not even willing to re-lend the repayments received in order to maintain the same exposure.

The drastic insufficiency of funds gathered from financial sources in relation to the monthly global payments of the country was causing a dramatic fall in the reserves of the Bank of Mexico. It was absolutely vital and urgent that we should greatly contract our foreign currency needs through, on the one hand, reducing our current account deficit and, on the other, working out new mechanisms to roll over the maturing debt given that the traditional refinancing mechanisms had at least temporarily vanished.

The devaluation of the peso in February 1982 (the first of many and more sizeable ones) together with the sheer scarcity of foreign exchange began to force a rapid downward trend in imports: But in mid–1982, the most pressing and visible problem was the foreign debt servicing area; the total lack of foreign exchange and foreign financing inevitably raised the spectre of default, without any other choice. The debt refinancing problem had to be tackled with utmost urgency.

THE FIRST RESTRUCTURING OF PUBLIC DEBT

In the first instance, it was necessary to concentrate our attention upon the public sector and, in particular, upon amortizations, because they could no longer be refinanced. An initial communication (by telex) was sent to all lending banks to Mexico on 22 August, 1982, requesting a three-month renewal of all commercial bank debt amortizations (interest continued to be paid) that would come due from all public sector entities during the next three months as from the subsequent day, 23 August, 1982, including short-term credit outstandings. The renewals would be on a PRIME or LIBOR basis, at the option of the lender, with the addition of an established margin for all lenders concerned. Naturally, all Mexican public sector entities were so advised so that internal administrative measures would be taken for renewals to be requested to, and accepted by, the lender prior to the maturity days of obligations to avoid an open default situation.

As a result of this telex, Mexico had halted the outflow of payments from its public sector amortizations, which formed the great majority of Mexico's overall requirements on foreign debt capital servicing. But, although capital payments on foreign debt had effectively stopped, it should be noted that

Mexico had not declared or implemented a moratorium, but had rather requested a renewal of maturing obligations akin to the concept of obtaining a roll-over in the form of short-term credits.

At the very same time, Mexico announced the creation of a Bank Advisory Group composed of thirteen banks (initially fourteen, but the Mexican bank involved withdrew soon thereafter because of the nationalisation of the banks); this group would cooperate with Mexico in order to find the most appropriate path towards the formal and medium-term restructuring of Mexico's public debt. Within the Advisory Group, there were seven commercial banks from the USA and six banks from other major lending countries and such banks would be responsible for communications with other banks within their country and, in some cases, in other countries. The country distribution of banks in the Advisory Group was naturally linked to Mexico's overall geographic distribution of foreign debt and each Advisory Group bank was to be a major lender to Mexico in terms of outstandings.[2]

The creation of this Bank Advisory Group was a factor of crucial importance in the successful search for the most effective path to deal with the complexities of formal debt restructuring on a medium-term basis.

This group of bank advisors had in practice different roles and functions:

1. It was a *coordinating* group with the rest of the banks throughout the world. Mexico had more than 530 lending banks worldwide, and almost 1,000 lending entities if we consider different branches, agencies, subsidiaries and affiliates of banking groups. It was not possible, physically and time-wise, to communicate with each and every one of them for the negotiations; this group, therefore, informally acted on behalf of and as a communications link with all other banks.

2. It was an *advisory* group for Mexico; the various restructuring ideas were discussed by Mexico within that group in order to ensure that the final restructuring proposals would be effected in the most fluid, efficient and effective way possible, taking into account a

multitude of technical factors involved.

3. It was a *support* group with other banks; once we had agreed upon a certain policy, terms or actions, it was important that these leading banks should entice, convince and, if necessary, press other banks into acceptance of such decisions.

4. It was a group for the *transmission of information* of a technical, financial and economic nature, both from the Ministry of Finance to all the banks as well as vice versa.

5. Most importantly, this group acted *de facto* as the *negotiating representative* of the international banking community as a whole with Mexico for the restructuring of its foreign debt.

The Bank Advisory Group and the Mexican Government worked relentlessly at the restructuring proposals. Progress was affected by the nationalisation of the Mexican commercial banks on 1 September, 1982, the imposition of unwieldy exchange controls, the transition towards the new Administration that was to take over on 1 December (together with the problems that such a state of affairs created for the IMF discussions), and temporary imposition of unrealistic exchange and interest rate policies, which were fuelling disintermediation in the banking system and increasing capital flight.

By 8 December, 1982, the Minister of Finance communicated (through a famous 9-foot telex) to the international banking community the restructuring scheme for the Mexican public sector external debt, as formally agreed with the Bank Advisory Group. The restructuring scheme essentially requested that all principal amortizations due to commercial banks (excluding trade lines and certain other loans) maturing with public sector entities from 23 August, 1982 until 31 December, 1984, including the short-term bank credit outstandings, should be restructured (at the high, agreed margins of LIBOR plus $1\frac{7}{8}$ per cent or PRIME plus $1\frac{3}{4}$ per cent, at the option of each lender with a front-end 1 per cent commission) for a period of eight years' grace; the total estimated amount involved was approximately US $23,000 million.[3]

In essence, what we achieved was that the bank amortizations maturing for almost the next two and a half years would be refinanced (i.e. restructured) over the medium-term, to curtail foreign currency payment needs of the country by way of debt capital amortizations; it should be noted that the interest on outstanding debt continued to be paid punctually, and, thus, continued to affect the current account. The effect of the restructuring upon the debt profile of Mexico's public sector is shown in the graph that follows (Figure 3.1).

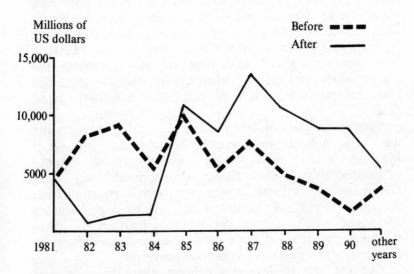

Figure 3.1: Profile of capital amortization payments before and after the first restructuring (August 1982–4 maturities)

As may be appreciated from the graph, the approximately US $23 billion due in repayment up to the end of 1984 had effectively been deferred, through restructuring, to ensuing years between 1987 and 1990. The trough in repayments up to end–1984 was followed, as from the start of the following years, again by enormous requirements of refinancing for repayment of the non-restructured debt and, starting in 1987 of the accumulated effect of the restructured payments. After the restructuring, the repayments due in 1985 were US $10.2 billion, in 1986 US $8.5 billion, in 1987 US $13.7 billion, and in the three years thereafter in the range of US $10 billion annually.

This was clearly like having Damocles' sword hanging over Mexico's future; international lenders and domestic investors alike were aware of such dark clouds in the country's external finances as from 1985; the subsequent debt restructuring—discussed later—addressed itself primarily to that problem.

With respect to the first restructuring scheme it was necessary to exclude certain types of facilities that were by their nature not easily subject to such process. That was, for example, the case of official export credits, World Bank and IADB credits, bonds, private placements, leases, banker's acceptances, trade lines, and other special facilities which were agreed with the banks. Even after 23 August 1982, Mexico's public sector entities continued to pay promptly the amortizations and interest when due on facilities excluded from the restructuring scheme; this policy has continued to date.

Another category of debt not included in the restructuring was the inter-bank borrowings by branches and agencies of Mexican banks—mainly those in the private sector—established abroad. These amounted to approximately US $6 billion and were essentially very short-term borrowings from foreign money markets used to fund loans by those branches and agencies to public and private entities within Mexico (a marginal amount had been used to re-lend internationally particularly to other Latin American countries).

Like the rest of Mexico's debtors, these branches and agencies abroad encountered increasing difficulties, from the second quarter of 1982, in their ability to roll-over outstandings; when this began to occur by mid-1982 because of a lack of voluntary renewals, it added further pressure to the already dwindling reserves of the Bank of Mexico. The Mexican private banks could not be allowed to default abroad in their money-market activities because of a lack of foreign exchange, but the added drain on reserves had to stop. Hence, as part of the communication to banks on 22 August 1982, the Mexican authorities requested the banking community to roll-over such deposits on interest terms to be agreed upon each renewal; interest would be paid, but branches and agencies were not allowed to effect any capital repayment on such facilities.

Although under the critical circumstances the move was a necessary one for sheer lack of foreign exchange, it was highly controversial with the banking community; they argued that the freezing of such deposits was a severe blow to international money market activities and that at least the semblance of normality should be re-established as soon as possible. The medium-term restructuring of such deposits with the rest of the package, thus, became an impossible task; what was achieved was that, in the restructuring loan documentation, such deposits should not fall below US $5.2 billion until the end of 1986. They would, thus, continue to be rolled over until that date, when more normal voluntary roll-overs should in principle be re-established. When private commercial banks were nationalised on 1 September 1982 (for different reasons), the effect was to convert such debts into the responsiblity of the Mexican public sector.

NEW MONEY NEEDS

The restructuring of existing public sector maturities was only one part of the issue. Another vital problem was obtaining further credit support for Mexico's expected current account deficit in 1983: This problem was also tackled in the 8 December 1982 communication by the Minister of Finance. Mexico undertook to abide by an economic programme, supported by the IMF (for details, see chapter by Villarreal).

On the basis of the above economic programme, Mexico requested a new loan of US $5 billion with a tenor of six years and three years' grace, from the international banks equivalent to approximately 7 per cent of the total outstanding exposure in Mexico of each individual banks as at 23 August, 1982. Each bank was requested to calculate its total exposure together with the amount corresponding to 7 per cent of such outstandings, and communicate the amount and acceptance of the terms to the Bank Advisory Group before the end of December 1982. The cost was even more onerous than the restructured amounts: LIBOR plus $2\frac{1}{4}$ per cent or Prime plus

2⅛ per cent, and a front-end fee of 1¼ per cent. The reason given by the banks was that creditors had to be enticed by high spreads to lend new funds.

In turn the IMF had, in a novel form of ensuring bank support for a country, requested the international banking community of early confirmation of their commitment for the 1983 US \$5 billion facility as a pre-requisite for presenting to its Board for approval an Extended Fund Facility for the global amount of approximately US \$3.9 billion, to be drawn quarterly during a total period of three years, upon compliance with quarterly economic targets. An additional source of support for 1983 was to come from the commitment by foreign official agencies to allow the utilisation of at least US \$2 billion in trade-related transactions with Mexican entities. The inflow of new money during 1983 would be used partly to finance the expected current account deficit; partly to reconstitute the reserves of the Bank of Mexico; partly to pay for the bridge financing previously obtained from the US Federal Reserve and the BIS; and partly, if feasible, for the payment arrears that had built up with the private sector. The limitation was that 'net' new foreign indebtedness by the Mexican public sector should not rise by more that US \$5 billion in 1983.

The international banking community accepted before the end of December 1982 the granting of the US \$5 billion facility during 1983; the credit agreement was signed on 3 March, 1983.

In much the same fashion, new money requirements with banks were repeated in 1984, when Mexico obtained a new credit for the amount of US \$3.8 billion. This time, given Mexico's excellent performance under the 1983 Program, terms and conditions were much better: ten years' tenor with 5½ years' grace, at LIBOR plus 1½ per cent or PRIME plus 1⅛ per cent.

THE RESTRUCTURING OF PRIVATE DEBT

In the past, the Mexican authorities had never regulated, controlled or required the registration in any form of Mexican private sector debt contracted with foreign entities. Private sector activities were considered as quite independent from public sector ones; in any case, they were traditionally small in proportion to the latter. It was then not sufficiently appreciated that such private sector activities could similarly affect, through their debt servicing, the country's overall foreign currency needs for which satisfaction the country's authorities can be deemed to be ultimately responsible. The Mexican Government's efforts initially concentrated upon the country's overall external finances and the foreign debt of its public sector entities; it was increasingly necessary to bring order to private sector foreign debt, which had grown substantially since 1981, and had been in a state of virtual payments moratorium (principal and interest on bank and suppliers debt) from the beginning of August 1982, given that scarce foreign exchange had been wholly absorbed by the needs of the public sector.

The first step naturally consisted in its registration. The registration of private sector debt was useful not only in obtaining the required information, but also in subsequently ensuring that the scarce foreign currency resources eventually transferred to the private sector through the domestic banking system would be used for the required purposes—like payment of interest—and not for less important or even harmful purposes, like speculation and capital flight. The exchange control system, established first in September and subsequently adapted in December 1982, was a vital mechanism for ensuring that foreign currency flows would be directed towards the desired purposes, while capturing the appropriate information.

Upon registration, we learnt that private sector debt to foreign supplies and lenders, excluding the recently nationalised banking system, amounted to approximately US $22 billion and that its amortization schedule was particularly concentrated in the short term: approximately two-thirds of private debt matured within a period of two years. Of the outstanding amount US $18 billion was owed to banks and US $4 billion to suppliers.

It was necessary to find appropriate mechanisms, as in the case of public debt, to restructure the debt profile of private debt to ease foreign currency needs of the country as a whole. Second, it was necessary to regulate the interest arrears to banks accumulated by private sector entities from the beginning of August 1982 to the end of January 1983, when that sector had been crowded out of foreign currency availability. Whilst the reserves of the Bank of Mexico improved from a drastically low level, we needed to regulate the interest arrears to banks, without disbursing the foreign currency to the international banks. A mechanism was designed whereby the Mexican debtor could constitute a dollar deposit with a Mexican bank, through the delivery of documentation and the required local currency at the prevailing exchange rate; the dollar deposit thus created in the Mexican bank, on behalf of the Bank of Mexico, would be in favour of the stipulated foreign bank lender and would earn a market rate of interest payable in cash abroad on a monthly basis. The outstanding amount of the dollar deposits would be gradually reduced until September 1983, subject to the improvement of Mexico's reserves; any amount outstanding at the end of such month would be refinanced with the banks on a medium-term basis. Approximately US $860 million of such deposits were created; the improvement of Mexico's reserves during 1983 allowed the gradual reduction of outstandings to US $280 million by September and the announcement that such remaining amount would be paid in mid–December of that year without the need for any refinancing. By the end of 1983 bank interest arrears had been eliminated.

Another area that required immediate regularisation were payment arrears on debt to foreign suppliers. Such arrears were paralysing the flow of raw materials, spare parts and other equipment needed from abroad; again, with particularly low reserves at the beginning of 1983, it was necessary to find a way of regulating such arrears without temporarily disbursing the available foreign currency. A similar domestic dollar deposit mechanism was instituted for debtors to registered foreign suppliers relating to payments on debts due since 20 December, 1982 up to 30 June, 1983; as amortization payments arose, debtors would be able to constitute domestic dollar deposits with Mexican banks for the required amount against the delivery of domestic currency of the prevailing rate of exchange. The dollar deposits would earn a market rate of interest, payable monthly abroad, and the certificates of such deposits could be transferred to the registered foreign suppliers; payment of the outstanding amount of deposits would be announced subsequently by the Bank of Mexico on the basis of its reserve position.

Approximately US $520 million of such deposits were created covering the above-mentioned period, and the Bank of Mexico announced in August 1983 that 50 per cent of the outstanding amount would be paid in September of that year, and the other 50 per cent would be paid in early March 1984. For payments on maturing debt to foreign suppliers during the second half of 1983, a similar dollar deposit mechanism was created; recovery of reserves again permitted announcement of early amortization of the deposit outstandings.

There also existed in the private sector, through bank or suppliers, debt arising from official export credit agencies in respect to the export of goods and/or services to Mexico. Official agencies are particularly reticent to restructure or postpone amortizations, given that they generally operate with preferential rates of interest. In June 1983, Mexico signed a general agreement with fifteen countries in Paris, that laid down the basis for refinancing over a period of six years with three years' grace—on commercial terms to be agreed with each country agency concerned—the private sector amortizations due during 1983. This would be in the form of a line of credit assigned to two prominent official financial institutions in Mexico specialised in foreign trade activities (BANCOMEXT and NAFINSA), but the underlying commercial risk would not thereby be automatically absorbed by the public sector; if the private debtor were able to deliver on due date sufficient local currency at the prevailing rate of exchange, either of the Mexican financial institutions could draw upon the line of credit from the respective country in order to refinance the payment over the medium term; if the private debtor were not able to deliver on due date the local currency, the credit risk would remain with the original lender without adversely affecting either of the Mexican financial institutions involved. The public sector would be taking over the exchange risk, without the absorption of the underlying private sector commercial credit risk, which remained with the original creditors.

The last part of the restructuring of private sector debt lay in the bank capital amortizations and it is here, as in the case of the public sector, that the large majority of the debt was to be found. First, a substantial improvement in its maturity profile was needed; second, it was necessary to find a mechanism to reduce or even hedge the foreign currency risk for debtors, as the latter had been financially shaken by the Mexican peso's 500 per cent devaluation since early 1982; third, the difficult state of public finances required that subsidies should not arise on this front; and fourth, it was necessary to find a mechanism whereby the Mexican public sector would not assume or absorb the foreign debt of the private sector, as the latter had acted independently with foreign lenders, who should continue to bear the underlying credit risk.

The solution to this multiple problem arose with the establishment of a special mechanism for the restructuring of private sector debt and the hedging of foreign exchange risks, created by the Government as a trust fund in the Bank of Mexico. In Spanish it is known as 'FICORCA'; Fideicomiso para la Corbertura de Riesgos Cambiarios (Trust Fund for Covering Exchange Risks). FICORCA is a complex mechanism with extensive documentation involved, but its conceptual philosophy should be as readily accessible as that of international forward exchange markets: interest rate differentials between two currencies will affect their exchange rate applicable for markets, both currencies are delivered in the future in forward exchange operations; in the case of Mexico, FICORCA is not a market but an established mechanism and the domestic currency is to be delivered at the outset of the operation, but the principle is similar. A given amount of domestic currency delivered today by the borrower to the Bank of Mexico, taking into account domestic interest rates minus the expected rate of depreciation of the currency, should—if treated as a deposit—accumulate sufficiently for the purchase of the desired foreign currency at the future established date at the then prevailing exchange rate, and the Bank of Mexico would take up the responsibility of delivering the foreign currency at such date. One of the main features of the scheme is that it provided the peso credits at cost rates to private debtors who wanted to join the scheme and that the high prevailing interest rate in pesos was partially capitalised depending on each client's cash flow, thereby providing financial feasibility to companies which otherwise would have had to declare bankruptcy.

The FICORCA mechanism was established in respect to foreign currency debts incurred prior to 20 December, 1982 with financial institutions registered with the Ministry of Finance.

The FICORCA schemes had significant benefits for the domestic borrowers, but could only be entered into with the agreement of the foreign lender to restructure the debt over the *medium term*. FICORCA is an ingenious mechanism— without proposing to directly control the restructuring of the foreign debt for the benefit of both parties and the country in general.

The FICORCA scheme gave good results and the overwhelming majority of outstanding bank debt, approximately US $12 billion, was registered prior to 20 December, 1982, a similar FICORCA mechanism was instituted in 1984 for foreign currency debts contracted subsequent to such date. It reflected the continued concern of the Mexican financial authorities to ensure, as far as possible, that new indebtedness contracted by the private sector should, through the benefits of exchange cover, have a medium-term profile. In today's economic and financial conditions, the trend points towards the increasing harmonisation of foreign private sector activities with the macro-economic needs and currency limitations of the country.

THE SECOND RESTRUCTURING OF PUBLIC DEBT

The first restructuring had provided a breathing space on foreign capital repayments until the end of 1984, but starting in 1985 there was an enormous hump of repayments falling due in the next six years, with no possibility of finding sources or voluntary refinance for such magnitudes. Consequently, from the beginning of 1984, the Mexican authorities began to work on a comprehensive restructuring proposal that was subsequently presented to the international banking community.

The proposal entailed the restructuring of US $48.0 billion of public sector debt maturing between 1985 and 1990, the years where the heaviest repayments were concentrated. The restructured repayments would be over a fourteen-year period, with an incremental repayment pattern to provide a smooth upward curve of debt repayment. It was, thus, a complete overhaul of the public sector debt repayment profile. The change can be appreciated from the following graph (Figure 3.2).

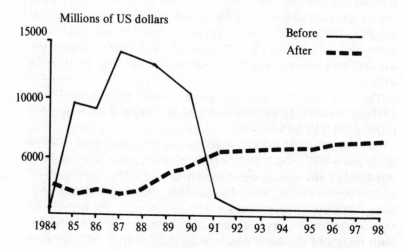

Figure 3.2: *Profile of capital amortization payments before and after the second restructuring (1985–90 maturities)*

The second restructuring would provide for a low starting base of repayments, providing time for Mexico to gradually step up its re-entry into the voluntary credit markets. The package also provided for the total elimination of the expensive prime as a base rate, leaving only LIBOR plus a reduced margin that averaged 1⅛ per cent over the life of the fourteen-year loan, with no restructuring fees to be applied; all of this added up to substantial interest savings over the time period involved of approximately US $5 billion.

A novel feature of this package, for Mexico as well as for other developing countries, was the formulation of a longer-term macro-economic framework, together with extensive and detailed analysis and projections of the external sector of the economy.

The blueprint proposed, on the internal front, a continued reduction in the public sector deficit, and support of private sector activity as the leading force of economic growth in the future; on the external front, it projected continued growth of non-oil exports of around 13 per cent a year in dollars, with appropriate exchange rate and other macro-economic policies; a small current account deficit relative to GDP (around 1 per cent); the growth of total public sector debt at an average of 4.5 per cent a year in nominal terms; within the latter, the growth of debt with multilateral and bilateral institutions at an average annual rate of 10 per cent in nominal terms, with bank debt rising at only 4 per cent a year on average in nominal terms. The overall growth of public sector debt projected to 1990 in nominal terms would result in a negative real growth (after discounting inflation).

All the projections, analyses and figures, amply discussed with the IMF, World Bank and banking institutions, were intended to approach debt management as an *integrated* effort of macro-economic planning together with external indebtedness. Up until then, the approach had been more of a yearly one, concentrating essentially upon current account results (and its required financing), without analysis of the impact of medium-term trends in debt structures and its interlinkages.

Given the longer-term framework of the restructuring, the Mexican authorities agreed to the enhancement of the annual Article IV Consultations with the IMF, so that on a six-monthly basis during the life of the loan an IMF mission would elaborate its internal economic report on Mexico which would subsequently be distributed to all international lenders.

Appraisal of the restructuring package: benefits and limitations.

There is a mistaken tendency to believe that debt restructuring packages, for Mexico or other countries in similar circumstances, are a solution to the external debt problem. This is not the case.

Stripped of all its complexities, the restructuring process

improves the existing debt repayment profile of the country concerned, thereby lessening the need for annual gross refinancing of the external debt outstanding and improving one of the key factors of vulnerability of the country concerned in the foreign exchange and debt arena. By itself, it does nothing to improve the country's current account per-formance, a key indicator of the country's external improvement in future debt servicing capacity.

The debt restructuring process had benefits related to the substantial improvement of the external debt profile (at least in the case of the multi-year restructurings as last obtained by Mexico), thereby relieving the pressure of obtaining the corresponding refinancing amounts which may be limited, inappropriate or otherwise unobtainable, in the absence of suitable market mechanisms. This reduces uncertainty with international lenders and investors (foreign and domestic), reduces latent tension among lenders as to the provision of the refinancing amounts and avoids difficult loan non-renewal possibilities with some lenders, which would have a negative impact on the country's reserves and upon the other remaining lenders. If a lowering of loan margins is achieved, a saving is generated upon the amount of interest that would otherwise have to be paid on the outstanding debt, and, therefore, upon the current account. (It should, nevertheless, be noted that the saving on margins—though significant in itself—is still relative to the actual level of base interest rates, as the major part of the interest payable on outstanding debt remains subject to the interest rate determined by the floating rate basis.)

The limitations of the restructuring process are obvious. With minor adjustments, the interest charges on outstanding external debt continue to accrue, even under the new maturity structure of the restructured debt. It is macro-economic policy itself that will guide economic results towards the desired projections and will thereby influence the future behaviour of the current account by export and import flow adjustments. Current account trends will, in turn, again affect the magnitude of 'new money' packages to finance expected current account needs and reserve growth.

After the suitable restructuring of the external debt profile, the centre-stage lies in the area of *macro-economic policy*, in its ability to effectively generate a sustained—not merely temporary—improvement in the country's current account performance, compatible with recovery of satisfactory economic growth and restored financial stability.

The rest of 1984 and most of 1985 were spent putting the agreements together; the total restructured amount was $48.7 billion.

One of the unwritten understandings that made the multiyear rescheduling (MYRA) possible was that Mexico would not need new money in 1985. In fact, balance of payments projections for the year showed that no foreign loans were required, outside those disbursed by international organisations such as the World Bank and IDB, as well as by bilateral sources. This translated into the lowest request for net foreign financing submitted to Congress by the Mexican Government in thirteen years: $1 billion only, against $15 billion in 1981 and around $3 billion per year from 1977 to 1980.

In fact, $1.2 billion was to be paid during 1985, out of the now restructured $5 billion of 1983 new money. It was the first time since 1982 that repayment of principal of medium-term loans was contemplated.

That year, however, turned out to be more complicated than that.

On the fiscal side economic recovery created pressures on the level of inflation, above those envisaged in the Budget. This forced the authorities to maintain higher than expected interest rates and allow a faster devaluation of the peso, which accelerated further the upward trend of prices. While the first quarter targets were barely achieved, it became clear that the fiscal and monetary targets for June were not going to be met. As mid-1985 rolled by, the increasing fiscal imbalance was coupled with a new wave of speculation against the peso and renewed capital flight.

In July, a 20 per cent devaluation of the peso was followed by a new floating system which sought to stem capital flight. Interest rates were systematically increased to yield positive levels of return, and later in the year, a draconian restriction on the banking system's lending capacity reduced the availability of credit to a trickle.

Of the repayment of $1.2 billion scheduled under the

MYRA, $250 million were paid out in early January and the balance was rolled over to the end of September and early October. There was, in fact, another very large principal repayment that was the object of some controversy. The state-owned oil company, Pemex, had agreed with the Federal Reserve's request in 1984 to gradually reduce the roll-over period of its $4 billion banker's acceptances facility from six months to three months, reportedly to adjust to 'market practice'. This agreement meant that Pemex had to pay down at least US $1 billion of the facility, in order to allow the remaining balance of US $3 billion to satisfy the Fed's requirements. As the now reduced facility was rolled-over for a further two years and the participating 110 banks were paid US $1 billion, some of the Mexican creditors who were not participants in the facility complained loudly about lack of equity. The feeling was further exacerbated as a parallel UK based sterling acceptances facility for Pemex was reduced for the same reasons, at the request of the Bank of England and the British participants.

The Mexican public sector, therefore, repaid around $1.5 billion of principal to banks in 1985, including the US $250 million already mentioned.

In mid–September 1985, two disastrous earthquakes hit Mexico City, causing widespread death and devastation. The next day, while Mexico was rescuing its dead and wounded from under the rubble and debris of thousands of destroyed buildings, a leak from the IMF was printed in *The Washington Post*, stating that Mexico was out of compliance with its IMF agreed targets and had ceased to be eligible for further drawings from the institution.

Although the substance of the mysterious press story was true, its timing became a source of great embarrassment to the IMF, which immediately announced US $300 million emergency loan to Mexico, unprecedented in its size and the speed with which it was processed and disbursed. Other pledges of emergency support by the World Bank and the IDB followed.

By late–September, with telephone communications with Mexico still interrupted, a Mexican mission met the Advisory Group in New York and announced that the repayment of US $950 million agreed as part of the MYRA could not be made.

Reserves were dropping and the earthquake damage was assessed at between US $4 billion and US $5 billion. A message went out to the international financial community. In it, besides the request to roll-over the US $950 million for three months while a more definitive solution was found, the Mexican authorities informed their creditors that they would be requiring net external financing of US $4 billion in 1986, of which US $2.5 billion would be requested from commercial banks. This assumption was later confirmed in the 1986 Budget, sent to and approved by Congress in the following weeks. 1985 ended joylessly. Besides the material and psychological impact of the earthquakes, Mexico ended the year with inflation of 63 per cent, slightly higher than 1984; a public sector deficit of close to 10 per cent of GDP, caused mainly by the interest payments on the domestic debt; reserves US $3 billion as the economy showed clear signs of a slowdown towards the last quarter, notwithstanding a 3 per cent growth rate for the whole year. The price of oil was under severe pressure, having suffered a loss of US $3 to US $5 per barrel in the last days of the year.

The 1986 budget was an exercise in political courage. After a three year period of little or negative growth, and after the brutal effect of the earthquakes, the Government yet again decided to give priority to the fight against inflation. The Budget called for a year of zero growth, where inflation would be reduced to 45 per cent and the public sector deficit halved to 5 per cent of GDP. The US $4 billion net foreign borrowing requirement was mostly to replenish reserves. The underlying assumption for the average price of a Mexican barrel of oil during 1986 was US $22.50, which included a 10 per cent drop from then prevailing prices.

On these bases, an IMF Agreement was hammered out by the Mexican negotiators and was about to be formalised in early February 1986, when the oil price suddenly plunged to single digits and Mexico's original Budget assumption became untenable. The Agreement with the IMF was not signed, as the parties waited for oil prices to stabilise. Rumours about tens of billions of dollars being requested by Mexico were widespread, together with the fear of unilateral default by the world's second largest debtor.

The mood in Mexico was ominous. While the Government had successfully resisted the pressure from some sectors to use the earthquakes as an excuse to stop payments and demand better terms from its creditors, the even more costly drop in oil prices generated a wave of demand for immediately halting payments which included all sectors of society. Even within the Government, where such decisions were usually left to the Minister of Finance, a veritable chorus in favour of a moratorium arose.

From February to June, as oil prices continued to fall, several Mexican missions visited Washington to confer with the IMF, the World Bank and the US financial and political authorities. Most of these efforts, however, proved to be rather fruitless. The public sector deficit was climbing with each month that passed, under the combined pressures of higher than expected devaluation, inflation and interest rates, which made it impossible to forecast the expenditure side of fiscal policy, while the income side was clobbered by falling oil prices.

The IMF would not move without a clearer picture and the US Administration insisted on a 'Programme' which included trade liberalisation, opening to foreign investment, privatisation of public sector companies *and* a reduction of the public sector deficit. Although these principles had already been heralded as part of Mexico's economic policy package for 1986 by the Mexican Government, as they were believed to be mostly for external consumption, rather than clear policy intentions. Hence, the insistence on forcing a quantified, detailed account of such goals, even in the context of a continuously shifting economic scenario, while Mexico continued to offer policy inputs but refused to guarantee or quantify the policy outputs.

This 'dialogue of the deaf' caused increasing frustration within Mexico, and made even the most reasonable and sophisticated observers advocate a harder line of negotiation. The Mexican negotiating team, headed by the Minister of Finance, Jesus Silva Herzog, clearly started drifting towards a stronger response to the international financial community's apparent lack of understanding and support.

After all, Mexico had paid all its interest and even some

principal in 1985, and was continuing to do so in 1986, even under the most critical circumstances faced by the country in recent economic history.

Notwithstanding Silva Herzog's repeated warnings, a deeply ingrained sense of responsibility and a genuine desire to avoid a confrontation was apparently confused with weakness and lack of resolve. Complacency crept in in international financial circles and the initial alarm gave way to the belief that Mexico would not 'rock the boat'.

Silva Herzog's abrupt resignation in mid–June, soon after pronouncing a series of widely publicised and increasingly bellicose statements on the debt problem, seems to have focussed the world's attention on Mexico's plight yet again.

The new Minister, Gustavo Petricioli, unearthed a scheme which had been advocated by the technical team at the outset of the oil price collapse, which would effectively stop all debt-service payments and substitute them for deposits at Mexico's Central Bank, while a satisfactory settlement was achieved.

The scheme was presented to, and discussed with, the IMF, the World Bank, the US Treasury, the Federal Reserve and the Co-Chairmen of the Bank Advisory Group, who collectively decided to avoid a collision course by presenting Mexico with a reasonable alternative which was prepared in great haste. This included the full participation of the new Mexican team, which now included a high-level member of the powerful Ministry of Planning and Budget, in a deliberate display of economic policy-making cooperation, an element which had been sorely missing in prior attempts.

On 22 July, 1986, a 'Letter of Intent' was delivered to the Managing Director of the IMF by the Mexican Minister of Finance. It described an eighteen-month programme (to the end of 1987) which included a number of novel features, as well as a gargantuan infusion of foreign financing by Mexico's creditors of over US $12 billion, plus US $2.4 billion of contingent loans. The programme addressed most of Mexico's concerns:

(a) It acknowledged the full impact of the drop in oil prices in both the balance of payments (estimated at US $8 billion) and fiscal revenues (estimated at 20 per cent of total revenues or 6 per cent of GDP); therefore, it accepted a high fiscal deficit of 16 per cent of GDP in 1986, as well as the resulting three-digit (115 per cent) inflation for the year. Of course, it included a reduction of the fiscal deficit of 3 per cent over the period, as a result of both expenditure cuts and income measures;

(b) It protected Mexico's economy against further sudden external shocks by providing for automatic additional financing were oil to drop below US $9 per barrel for an extended period during the programme;

(c) It provided for additional public investment *and* its financing, in case the recovery of the economy proved to be slower than expected, with automatic adjustments of the relevant quantitative target;

(d) It acknowledged for the first time that Mexico's deficit was the result of the very large nominal interest payments on domestic debt, rather than the result of excessive spending. In fact, it highlighted that Mexico had produced a primary fiscal *surplus* (before interest payments) continuously since 1983;

(e) It emphasised the return to growth, after three years of stressing adjustment. Indeed, it was baptised as Mexico's 'Program for Growth and Structural Adjustment';

(f) It defined the sources of financing to support the growth-oriented angle, roughly along the lines of the debt strategy laid out by Secretary Baker in Seoul, in 1985;

(g) It did not contain any explicit commitment about privatisation, foreign investment or trade liberalisation other than the already shown plans of Mexico on these subjects.

The crisis had been avoided. The banks were relieved. The system was safe. Mexico could look forward to recovery. Now, the effort to raise the financing had to start.

This was easier said than done. The size of the package, the diversity of sources and the complexity of the issues confronting the negotiations with each of them required a whole new approach. It was a delicate balancing act, with each source of financing needing careful attention while at the same time requiring fast progress to create the necessary momentum in the other areas:

1. *The IMF* committed 1.4 billion SDR's (about US $1.7 billion) in quarterly disbursements linked with Mexico's compliance with quantitative targets. The first disbursement was conditioned upon the commitment of the so-called 'critical mass', or 90 per cent of the amount to be contributed by commercial banks; the initial negotiation included the 'Letter of Intent', the 'Technical Memorandum' with the detailed absorption of the mechanics, and the quarterly targets for September and December of 1986.

2. *The World Bank* committed US $2.3 billion of net loans to Mexico over the 1986–7 period. This means that gross disbursements should reach more than US $3.5 billion in the two years, a yearly average of more than double the amounts achieved up to 1985; this seemingly unattainable goal would be made possible by granting Mexico fast disbursing, policy-based loans in key areas of the Mexican economy, rather than through the more traditional project-financing approach.

   Obviously, the implication was that there had to be a higher content of policy conditionality. It was perceived, however, that Mexico's sectorial policy programmes were fully consistent with the World Bank's new conception of their role in financing growth in highly indebted, middle-income countries. How consistent these views really were remained to be seen as the different loans and the specific conditionality in each loan awaited negotiation. The World Bank was placed in the middle of the package. Besides its own project and policy conditionality, the approval by the World Bank's Board of Directors and the effectiveness of certain World Bank loans to Mexico at certain dates were introduced as conditions for the disbursement of the commercial banks' loans, in an unprecedented exercise in cross-conditionality.

   Again, Mexico accepted this feature because it felt

strongly that it wanted to act on the areas where the World Bank offered to cooperate, and if it was going to introduce structural adjustments anyway, it might as well do so and obtain financing at the same time. After all, trade liberalisation and industrial reconversion *do need* generous amounts of financing.

3. *The official bilateral creditors*, organised in the so-called 'Paris Club', also had to join the effort. Their contribution was two-fold: first, they had to accept the longstanding demand by commercial banks to restructure the maturities and, if possible, the interest on their existing loans to Mexico and second, notwithstanding the first, to continue to provide financing to facilitate Mexico's increased imports, a vital feature if the growth element of the programme was to take hold. Under great pressure from the IMF, the World Bank, the commercial banks and ultimately, the US Administration, the Paris Club granted Mexico a period of ten years, including five years of grace, to repay all maturities of principal and 60 per cent of the interest payments falling due between 30 September, 1986, and 1 April, 1988. The package amounted to around US $1.8 billion, and it included an unwritten pledge by the member countries not to withdraw export credits from Mexico. Individual agreements had to be negotiated with each country regarding currencies and interest rates. France, which presides over the Paris Club, also played a key role in the speedy and satisfactory conclusion of negotiations.

The condition of effectiveness of the Paris Club agreement was the effectiveness of the IMF stand-by which, as mentioned before, was conditional upon the commitments by commercial banks which, in turn, will only disburse their contribution if Mexico meets the IMF targets, negotiates certain loans with the World Bank and disburses a minimum of US $1.7 billion from the World Bank *and* a minimum sum from bilateral sources.

Altogether a mind-boggling accumulation of cross-conditionality which has the potential to create almost irresistible momentum or to cause virtually total paralysis, were one of its elements to go wrong.

4. *Japan.* The Mexican Government had been negotiating with the Export-Import Bank of Japan for almost one year for a scheme based on Eximbank's Article VIII, which allows for untied financing to be supplied to developing countries for the development of certain key projects. Since this modality was incorporated in Eximbank's charter only recently, there was virtually no precedent.

After long discussions, three projects were approved by Japan:

(i) The conclusion of the second stage of a steel mill in the Pacific port of Lázaro Cárdenas, which was suspended in 1984 due to budgetary restrictions: US $250 million of Japan's contribution will be channelled to this project.

(ii) The Pacific Petroleum Project, which includes a gas pipeline across Mexico's Isthmus of Tehuantepec, a parallel crude oil pipeline, a petrochemical plant for the production of ammonia, a refinery, and port and storage facilities at both ends; around US $500 million of Japanese financing will go towards supporting this project;

(iii) A further US $250 million to support the Export Development Programme, a World Bank-supported project whose aim is to promote the export of non-oil manufactured products by financing imported inputs as well as machinery required for the production of exportable goods.

The Government-to-Government protocol was signed in November 1986 and the billion dollars were to be disbursed over the next eighteen months.

The projects have a fairly low import content, and an even lower Japanese content, which makes the loan doubly useful: it makes it feasible to develop three priority areas and it has a positive balance of payments effect.

The applicable rate will be 6.1 per cent fixed in yen, and the final maturity for all three projects is fifteen years, with grace periods depending on each project.

5. *A bridge loan* worth US $1.6 billion was negotiated in August 1986, to shore up Mexican foreign reserves. Of the total US $1.1 billion was supplied by eleven OECD countries, plus token contributions from Argentina, Brazil, Colombia and Uruguay, to provide the Latin American 'flavour'. The Bank for International Settlements, representing the European, Canadian and Japanese contributions, insisted in being paid LIBOR plus 1.5 per cent for its loans, a shining example of lack of sensitivity which almost scuttled the deal, had it not been for the US decision to reduce the interest on its share to allow for a reasonable average cost.

The officially funded part of the bridge loan was disbursed at the end of August, 1986 and had been fully repaid by early February 1987, out of the IMF and World Bank disbursements. Mexico's fifty-four largest commercial bank creditors, at the insistence of OECD governments, provided a US $500 million bridge loan which was initially supposed to be disbursed together with the 1.1 billion mentioned above. The banks, however, stipulated as a disbursement condition that the 'critical mass' (or 90 per cent) of the large bank syndicated loan for US $7.7 billion be committed. This happened only on 19 November, 1986. The US $500 million matured on 30 January and were subsequently rolled-over for a further period of ninety days, to be paid out of the syndication proceeds.

6. *The commerical bank 'package'*, for US $7.7 billion, was the backbone of the financial arrangements for Mexico and an important watershed in that it contained contingent facilities for US $1.7 billion which were not present in previous negotiations either with Mexico or with other countries.

After delivering the Letter of Intent to the IMF on 22 July, 1986, the Mexican team started developing a conceptual approach to the new round of negotiations.

Following several weeks of internal discussions, the Mexican proposal was discussed with the US Secretary of the Treasury and his Assistant Secretary in charge of international matters. Neither fell off his chair; both suggested it would be hard to sell; neither attempted to persuade Mexico to abandon it.

The Mexican proposal consisted of:

(a) Debt service of old (existing) loans would be dealt with on the basis of a Constant Present Value Stream of payments which would include both interest and principal, and would be extended over a period which might be as long as twenty-five years. This mechanism of repayment was already being used domestically, to deal with the peso payments of private sector firms to FICORCA.

The proposed mechanism implied that, in the initial years, there would be automatic capitalisation of interest which would be added to the existing stock of debt and paid in the later years. (See Annex I for details of the proposed scheme.)

(b) The truly innovative feature of the proposal was that the resulting stream of payments under the constant present value procedure would itself be modified (accelerated or extended further), depending on the evolution of the ratio between the price of oil and interest rates. The 'normal' ratio was defined as 2.5 times the interest rates (i.e, US $15 per barrel of Mexican oil and 6 per cent for LIBOR would be 'normal' and would, therefore, correspond to the 'unit'). Should the oil price/interest rate ratio move above 2.5, the proposed stream of payments under 'a' above would accelerate, given a higher availability of foreign exchange; were the ratio to move below 2.5 the stream of payments would become smaller, and therefore, the total repayment period lengthened.

(c) The spread over the base rates would be eliminated or, at least, substantially reduced.

(d) To deal with the new money requirements, the original

Mexican proposal suggested that banks accept a World Bank or US Treasury zero coupon bond as collateral, which would be worth the same amount of the new money borrowed at its maturity (twenty years was suggested).

Given that the market value today of such a bond is only a fraction of its value at maturity, the amount required by the Mexicans to buy it could easily be obtained by borrowing a slightly higher amount from the banks, by using Mexico's reserves, or both. Thus, the banks would have no principal risk (only the risk of interest payments), and could, therefore, deal with the regulatory constraints more freely. Given that the principal would have been fully guaranteed, the interest rate could have been fixed at a level determined by negotiation and, conceivably, an element of *real* relief (as opposed to capitalisation, which only postpones payments) could have been achieved.

The Mexican proposal was presented towards the end of August 1986. Once fully understood by the Advisory Committee, it caused shock, rejection, anger, and particularly among the US banks, a rush to complain to the Federal Reserve authorities in Washington about its 'disruptive' nature and the dangerous precedent it established. Canadian banks also found it unacceptable and Japanese banks declared themselves 'astonished' at the suggestion. Even Europeans found it difficult to manage; German banks thought it was 'intellectually stimulating' and the Swiss were the only group to openly support the concept.

In the words of one American banker, the proposal was 'innovative, ingenious, creative, even brilliant, but it won't fly'. Another said they never thought that someone could successfully put together a coherent proposal by taking 'every one of the dozens of different ideas proposed over the last three years regarding debt crisis and mixing them together in a single concept'.

The Federal Reserve authorities reacted with equal strength. Not only did they send word to the highest Mexican authorities that their proposal was unacceptable, they even suggested that it was the result of the evil minds of the

Mexican negotiating team, which should perhaps be removed and substituted by more docile individuals.

The age-old temptation to kill the messenger who is the bearer of bad news surfaced clearly, and the authority and fate of the Mexican negotiating team was the subject of some uncertainty, although fortunately only for a few days.

On 1 September, 1986, in his State of the Union Address, President Miguel de la Madrid strongly defended Mexico's negotiating stance and openly praised the 'skills of Mexico's negotiators'. This was a clear signal that both regulators and banks had to make important concessions, even under a more orthodox approach. It also consolidated the position of the negotiating team.

The Mexican proposal had been thoroughly researched, even in its accounting, legal and regulatory implications. It linked the behaviour of the fundamental elements of the Mexican external sector (i.e. the price of oil, interest rates and debt service) and was intended to substantially reduce the reticence of commercial banks to contribute new money by providing the World Bank or US Treasury guarantee in the form of the zero coupon bond.

Admittedly, it was a complex proposal and the capitalisation feature as well as the linkage of the debt service to oil prices was a new and 'dangerous' precedent. Its analysis and negotiation would have required intelligence, statesmanship and regulatory flexibility. It also would have required time. But, time was in short supply. By September, Mexico had gone without bank credit for more than twenty months, and its reserves had dropped by about US $3 billion. Also, the annual meeting of the IMF and the World Bank was imminent.

James Baker, Secretary of the Treasury of the United States had launched his famous debt strategy in Seoul a year earlier, but without concrete results thus far. A high-profile success was needed to give substance and credibility to the US initiative. Mexico was seen as the only country which could provide it.

To add to the sense of urgency, Jacques de Larosière, Managing Director of the IMF, had recently announced his departure at year-end, and logically wanted to add the Mexican deal to his considerable collection of achievements before he gave his valedictory speech at the end of the September meetings.

The World Bank, now a key player in the debt strategy, had a new President. Barber Conable, after twenty years as a US Congressman, also needed a success to get his presidency off to an auspicious start. Being politically sensitive, he clearly also understood the value of a quick breakthrough in the Mexican negotiations.

As the 'powers that be' consulted and agreed, the Mexican negotiators and the Advisory Committee were still debating what to do with the original Mexican proposal. Then, as they reconvened for a new round of negotiations, notice was served to them that they had to have a 'deal' by the IMF meetings. Deadline: 29 September, 1986.

Although taken by surprise and initially overwhelmed, both the banks and the Mexican negotiators reacted with pragmatism and agreed that in order to meet the deadline, a more traditional package was the only realistic approach.

There was a clear trade-off. The Mexicans dropped their original proposal and the banks started looking at terms and conditions which were obviously more favourable to Mexico than their initial ideas. The banks also dropped their insistence on on-lending and conversion of new money into equity (at par), which would have held up negotiations for much longer.

Negotiations moved to Washington and were taken over by the Chairmen of the thirteen banks in the Committe, the Managing Director of the IMF and his Deputy, the Chairman of the Federal Reserve Board, officials of the US Treasury, the President of the World Bank and his Deputy, and the Minister of Finance of Mexico.

All knew of Mexico's decision to stop normal debt servicing and introduce the old idea of peso deposits if an agreement was not reached by 1 October.

When the agreement was struck, after several all-night sessions, Mexico and its commercial bank creditors had avoided a disruptive confrontation and were facing an awesome task: the implementation of the largest restructuring/new money package ever attempted in the context of a sceptical, even cynical commercial banking community.

It took another three weeks to write what the 'Olympians'

had agreed upon and to negotiate all the details they had overlooked. Finally, on 18 October, the 'Term Sheet' was sent out to the almost 500 banks which were creditors to Mexico.

The Commercial bank package consisted of mainly:

		US $ billions
1.	'Old Debt' previously restructured	43.7
2.	'New Money' of 1983 and 1984	8.6
3.	Private Sector Debts to banks	10.0
4.	'Multifacility Agreement 1986–7'	7.7
	Total	70.0

The 'Old Debt' for US $43.7 billion, which had been restructured in 1984–5 under the MYRA was stretched out to twenty years including seven years of grace. The spread over cost of funds was reduced from $1\frac{1}{8}$ per cent on average $^{13}/_{16}$ of 1 per cent, that is, 0.81 per cent.

The 'New Money' operations of 1983 and 1984 were not touched as regards their term to maturity. Their interest rate, however, was lowered to a cost of funds concept, and the spread was also reduced to $^{13}/_{16}$ per cent. The previous Prime Rate component was eliminated and transformed into LIBOR or CDs, which also yielded important savings given that 75 per cent of such loans were on Prime Rate.

The private sector debt, organised and restructured under FICORCA, could now be paid over the same twenty years with seven years of grace as the old debt, compared to eight years with four years of grace as originally negotiated.

Finally, the US $7.7 billion of new money were negotiated as follows:

		US $ billions
1.	New Money 86–7	5.0
2.	World Bank Cofinancing 86–7	1.0
3.	Oil Contingency Facility	1.2
4.	Growth Contingency Facility	0.5
	Total	7.7

The Oil Contingency Facility consisted of a band from US $9 to US $14 per barrel of Mexican oil. If the price of oil fell below US $9 for an extended period, banks would contribute additional resources to cover the shortfall up to US 81.2 billion. If conversely, oil prices rose above US $14 and stayed there, there would be a dollar-for-dollar reduction in the New Money element. This facility will very probably be used, given the evolution of oil prices.

The Growth Contingency Facility consists of an additional contribution of US $500 million by commercial banks to finance public sector investments with high spillover effects into the private sector, which are labour intensive and with low import component. These investments would be considered above and beyond agreed IMF expenditure targets, in case the economy were to remain sluggish, as measured by the 'Index of Manufactured Production' of the first quarter of 1987 compared to the first quarter of 1986. This facility will probably be used, given the initial indications of first-quarter performance to this date.

All the commercial bank debt of the public sector, both old and new, ended up costing $^{13}/_{16}$ per cent. This rate homogeneity was the result of a Solomonic decision by the Olympians in Washington, in an effort to reconcile the different points of view of the Advisory Group and the demands of the Mexican negotiators. Although not very market oriented, it was clear, clean and easily understood.

Getting the banks to put up the new money was always considered a difficult task. Everybody was aware of it, but the old-timers in the Group and among the Mexicans were particularly cautious and concerned. This concern was reflected in the request for new money that went out to all banks.

The so-called 'base', (as the total exposure by commercial banks to Mexico was called) was calculated at around US $65 billion. The base date chosen was 23 August, 1982. The logic of using a 1982 base was that after that time, almost all new borrowing was involuntary and banks which had lent voluntarily should not be penalised.

Therefore, in order to secure US $7.7 billion (including the contingencies) all creditor banks would have to be asked for around 12 per cent of their 1982 base. This did not leave much room for shortfalls and outright refusals. It was therefore, agreed that all banks should be asked for 12.9 per cent of their 1982 exposure, in order to provide a 'cushion'. In retrospect, this decision was an enlightened one. Without the cushion, the Mexican deal would have taken several months more to complete. Other measures were taken to facilitate the decision by banks. Ten currencies were authorised and banks had the choice of domestic, LIBOR or fixed rate in their home country currency, if they chose not to fund in dollars. Also, conversion to home country currencies was allowed within one year for non-dollar based banks which had earlier participated in US dollars, both in the old debt and in the New Money of 1983 and 1984. Furthermore, the principles which would rule the restructuring and re-lending of the private sector foreign debt under FICORCA became an integral part of the Loan Agreement.

Immediately following the mailing of the term-sheet, high-level representatives of the Mexican Government and the banks, supported by local financial and monetary authorities, engaged in a worldwide 'roadshow' which took them to all major and secondary money centres around the world, explaining the package, informing about the Mexican economy, and identifying potential national and individual problems.

By 19 November, 1986, the 'critical mass' had been achieved; that is, telex commitments for US $6.9 billion or 90 per cent of the target amount of US $7.7 billion had been received. This made it possible to release the bridge loan by commercial banks for US $500 million, as well as the first *tranche* from the IMF Stand-by Agreement, for around US $300 million more. It also released US $500 million from a loan from the World Bank to support trade liberalisation.

The remaining 10 per cent of the commercial bank money, even with the built-in cushion, proved much more difficult to secure. Indeed, it would take five more months, until 16 April, to declare the loan effective and give drawdown notice for the first *tranche* of the package amounting to US $3.5 billion.

In this last stage of the effort, three problems became apparent which seriously threatened the success of the operation:

(a) The poor performance of the United States banking community relative to other countries, given the serious shortfalls of many small and medium-sized regional banks and the outright refusal to participate by around forty to fifty American banks. The main problems were in Detroit, Ohio, Florida and the mid-Atlantic area, including Washington, DC, where local banks all demanded the Mexican Embassy account as a condition to join.

(b) The strong emergence of the 'national quota' concept, mostly aimed at the United States, where banks in many countries would limit their contribution as a group to the same percentage of the target amount which they had contributed in the 1983 and 1984 New Money packages. This prevented non-American banks from bailing out non-participating US banks; as the US situation became bleaker, non-US banks in Europe and Canada actually 'parked' themselves at 11.6 per cent of their 1982 exposure, (instead of 12.9 per cent, as requested by Mexico), while waiting for the US banks to improve their performance.

(c) Many non-US banks, mostly but not exclusively in the Middle East and in some Southern European countries, suddenly discovered that, while they enjoyed getting their regular interest payments from Mexico, they were no longer interested in increasing their exposure. All sorts of excuses were used, mostly blaming it on Board decisions, to avoid the instrumental pressure. Another forty to fifty banks outside the United States were lost, while others decided to contribute token amounts.

The effort to get the last 10 per cent, besides taking five months, was fraught with frustration, disenchantment and tension.

The IMF, the World Bank, the financial and monetary authorities of the OECD countries, the Advisory Group banks and the Mexican team all worked relentlessly and literally around the clock during this period, both at the political and at the individual bank level, to improve the numbers and obtain a politically acceptable participation from all countries, with particular emphasis on the US regional banks.

The result in the end was the bare minimum required to close the deal. The total amount committed was 7.787 million US dollars, that is, an over-subscription of only 1 per cent which was contributed by six of the seven US banks in the Committee to meet the British and Canadian demands for a greater US contribution. The lack of capacity of large US money centre banks to persuade the regionals to participate became increasingly obvious, and the rather aloof and arms-length position which the US financial authorities chose to take, contributed to the lacklustre performance of the United States as a whole.

Non-US banks, and regulators, as well as the Mexican officials were deeply intrigued and frustrated at the apparent lack of consistency in the attitude of US regulators, which had acted so forcefully to arrange the original deal and were now allowing so many important regional banks to enjoy a free-ride while jeopardising the stability of the international financial system and Mexico's economic programme.

At least twice during the process of signing up banks, given the slow progress and the offensive cynicism of some banks, the Mexican authorities seriously considered the suspension of payments. However, the cost-benefit of such a move was no longer very clear. By the end of 1986 and the first quarter of 1987, Mexico's reserve position had improved dramatically as a result of capital repatriation, an explosive increase in non-oil exports and a recovery in oil prices. In addition, more than 90 per cent of the money was already committed, and a suspension of payments could jeopardise existing commitments while it did not assure the participation of the, then, missing banks.

Political pressure, however, was starting to mount. Many economic policy measures and the indispensable confidence of the private sector in the Government's policies depended on the successful completion of the package. The media, both Mexican and international, started to follow the process blow-by-blow, adding to the pressure.

By mid–February 1987, following the unilateral suspension of payments by Brazil, the Mexican authorities and the Advisory Group decided to set a deadline of 20 March to sign the new money agreement and the amendments to the eighty-seven old debt contracts. The decision proved to be wise. A final, all-out effort was mounted by Mexicans and bankers, and even the US regulators decided to join, albeit tepidly.

In the end, 365 banks contributed the new money, an alarmingly low number when compared to the original expectations of at least 400 banks. But, Mexico got its restructuring and its new money, which should be enough to support its economic programme at least through 1988, and can now look at the future with more optimism and certainty. Indeed, the terms and conditions it obtained have become the goal of other countries which are engaged in similar negotiations. After five years of arduous negotiations, Mexico can point to three rounds of restructuring which have transformed its debt profile into a long-term, more manageable stream of payments. It has also obtained the necessary grace period to continue to practice economic policies which will reduce the cost of debt servicing by export-led growth. Moreover, it has succeeded in reducing the cost of the family debt significantly, by reducing spreads, adopting cost-of-funds base rates and eliminating fees.

This should allow Mexico to consolidate its recovery and face the political events of 1987 and 1988 with the assurance which stems from having completely normal financial and economic relations with the rest of the world and the largest even foreign exchange reserves. This, in turn, will hopefully foster domestic confidence and promote investment and savings by both foreigners and nationals, which are crucial to economic growth and the creation of much needed jobs.

The cost, however, has been considerable. A practically flat growth in the last five years, a reduction of around 15 per cent in GDP per capita and a drop of 40 per cent in real wages in the same period speak of the social and political consequences of the debt crisis. A solid, sustained recovery and a lasting solution to the debt crisis—Mexico's and others'—will not be achieved by debt management alone. Mexico has to grow if it wants to overcome its debt crisis and avoid social and political tensions.

Adjustment with growth, the premises on which Mexico's 1986–7 economic programme are based, cannot be successfully maintained by debtor countries without a decisive contribution from developed economies in order to create a more propitious external environment. The threats are very obvious: protectionism is becoming widespread, as a result of severe trade, fiscal and monetary misalignments among OECD countries; interest rates in the United States are creeping upwards, in what constitutes a potentially explosive development in the debt crisis, and one which could seriously set back the 'muddling through' process practised so far; technological change and the absence of effective stabilising mechanisms continue to erode the relative price of raw materials.

Debtor countries will not—cannot—stand idly by as they watch their trade and their payment capacity diminished by an increasing interest burden for reasons completely beyond their control and responsibility. Most debtor governments have used up the political room for manoeuvre they enjoyed five years ago. Standards of living have dropped and their deterioration threatens the democratic process in these countries. Many of the highly indebted, middle income countries in Latin America, Asia and Africa are enjoying democratically elected governments for the first time in many years. But, democracy cannot thrive in the presence of hunger and deprivation. In order to be meaningful, treasured and popularly supported, democracy has to deliver higher levels of welfare after the necessary period of adjustment.

Democratic leaders in Latin America and elsewhere are fully aware of this mounting pressure, and suspension of debt service is a readily available escape valve which they will resort to if forced to choose between their creditors and their constituencies. It is already happening.

Leaders of debtor countries cannot control interest rates, non-tariff trade barriers or the price of their exportable raw materials; but they can and will hit back at an international economic system which they perceive as unfair by not paying interest on foreign debts if only to dramatise their frustration. It is the only weapon which can effectively focus the attention of the international economic agents on the plight of these countries.

In Mexico, these scenarios are not likely to materialise, at least for the foreseeable future. Strong political leadership, old and well established political institutions and the very real possibility of sustained, moderate growth have created, together with the recent financial arrangements, an atmosphere of confidence and stability which is a far cry from the tumultuous days of year-end 1982, when uncertainty was the rule. But, even in Mexico, and even assuming appropriate domestic economic policies, the burden of the debt going forward may prove too onerous in the context of a hostile external environment.

Debtor countries have been responsible; they have been patient; they have played mostly by the rules of the system. Exceptions have been rare and can be explained in their own context (e.g. Peru and Brazil).

But, let's assume now that all sovereign debtors attain a reasonably satisfactory agreement with their creditors, along the lines of Mexico's package. It is still by no means assured that they will then be able to regularly service their debts and eventually refinance the principal through voluntary operations while enjoying economic growth. The permanence—or exacerbation—of negative factors in the international economic environment will frustrate any such target. The choice is clear: if sustained growth by debtor countries is to be achieved, either the international environment improves, or the nominal size of the debt will have to be reduced.

While OECD countries have continuously and repeatedly failed at creating such an improved economic environment (which speaks in favour of attempting other solutions), they have never seriously tackled the question of a coordinated, deliberate effort to alleviate the debt burden of developing countries by creating the adequate regulatory, accounting, legal and political conditions to write down part of such debt.

Already the market is pricing LDC debt at anywhere from 5 cents to 70 cents on the dollar, depending on the countries involved. But, debtor countries are expected to continue to pay full debt service on the total nominal amount of debt. For many commercial banks, this in effect represents a windfall profit. Indeed, in many countries in Europe, banks have already passed on to their taxpayers, in a gradual, painless, almost undiscernible fashion—in the form of loan-loss provisions which are very generously treated by tax authorities—the discount of their portfolios. Winds of change are blowing in the right direction. An increasingly aware US Congress can accelerate regulatory changes if regulators continue to be reticent. US and UK banks have made important write-downs. Whether they will move fast enough remains to be seen.

The progress achieved so far in dealing with the debt problem was extracted by shock treatment from a sceptical and reticent international financial system. The fact that the system has proved resilient and is now stronger than five years ago should not produce complacency. If this new found strength translates into more enlightened, more generous solutions to the debt crisis which allow debtors to grow, then the efforts and sacrifices of so many millions will not have been lost. If, on the other hand, the system uses its resilience and greater strength to avoid change and continue to allocate the brunt of the burden to debtor countries, the ghost of massive, even concerted default may reappear, and uncertainty and confrontation will lay all our efforts to waste.

ANNEX A

28 August, 1986

United Mexican States conceptual framework for a foreign financing strategy: servicing of outstanding loans from commercial banks and new commercial banks financing
Basic objectives The underlying premise of the working proposal is that a successful external strategy must satisfy both the external financing requirements of the Mexican economy and the concerns of Mexico's bank creditors in light of the constraints to which they are subject. The basic objectives of the strategy are:

1. To meet Mexico's anticipated financial requirements for 1986 and 1987 within the framework of its IMF-supported economic programme.
2. To achieve a more realistic matching of debt service requirements and Mexico's capacity to pay and, at the

ANNEX B

Mexico: Public, private and bank external debt
(US $ Billions)

	Registered Public Debt			Bank Debt[2] Funds Channelled To:			Private sector debt	Total external debt
	Long term	Short term	Total	Public sector	Private sector	Total		
	(1)	(2)	(3= 1+2)	(4)	(5)	(6= 4+5)	(7)	(8= 3+6+7)
1976	15.9	3.7	19.6	–	–	1.6	4.9	26.1
1977	20.2	2.7	22.9	–	–	1.8	5.0	29.7
1978	25.5	1.2	26.7	0.8	1.2	2.0	5.2	33.9
1979	28.3	1.4	29.7	1.1	1.5	2.6	7.9	40.2
1980	32.3	1.5	33.8	2.7	2.4	5.1	11.8	50.7
1981	42.2	10.8	53.0	4.6	2.4	7.0	14.9	74.9
1982	49.5	9.3	58.8	4.5	3.5	8.0	18.0	81.8
1985	71.6	0.5	72.1	4.5	3.5	8.0	16.7	96.8
1986	73.5	1.4	74.9	4.5	3.5	8.0	16.5	99.4

Source: Secretaria De Hacienda Y Credito Publico, DGCP.
Notes: 1. Refers to the external debt of Mexican Banks not registered in the public debt.
            2. Preliminary.

12 May, 1987

same time, to minimise the amounts of additional new money to be procured through separate negotiation over the medium-term.

3. To protect the Mexican economy from oil price and interest rate shocks.

4. To achieve a longer-term solution to Mexico's debt problem that will foster the re-establishment of normal access to the financial markets.

Working proposal   The framework for the working proposal consists of three parts that address, respectively, the cost of Mexico's previously re-scheduled commercial bank debt and its 1983 and 1984 new money loans, the repayment profile of this debt and the means of financing Mexico's 1986 and 1987 new money requirements.

1. The eliminations of spreads on previously re-scheduled commercial bank debt and on the 1983 and 1984 new money loans, together with the substitution of cost-of-funds rates for the prime rate, would provide savings of more than US $600 million per annum. These savings would in turn reduce future external financing requirements.

2. To meet the basic objectives outlined above, repayment of the principal of, and interest on, this existing debt would be based on constant present value payments adjusted to reflect changes in the relationship between oil prices and international interest rates.

3. As regards new money for 1986 and 1987, the quality of the banks' asset would be enhanced if a portion of this new money were used to purchase a zero coupon bond issued by the World Bank and pledged to secure repayment of the principal of the new money. The zero coupon bond would have a value at maturity equal to the total amount of new money borrowed. From the banks' point of view, the risk of principal repayment would not be a Mexican portfolio risk, but a World Bank risk. From the Mexican point of view, defeasibility of the additional debt from the outset would improve expectations as to Mexico's economic future.

NOTES

1. For a quantification of external shocks on various Latin American countries, see 'Latin America, The Crisis of Debt and Growth', by T.O. Enders and R.P. Mattione, *Studies in International Economics*, The Brookings Institution, 1984, for Mexico, the external factors are quantified for 1979–82
2. The Bank Advisory Group was composed of the following: Bank of America NT and SA; Bank of Montreal; Bank of Tokyo Ltd; Bankers Trust Co.; Chase Manhattan Bank NA; Chemical Bank; Citibank NA; Deutsche Bank AG; Lloyds Bank International Ltd ; Manufacturers Hanover Trust Co. of New York; Morgan Guaranty Trust Co. of NY; Société Genérale and Swiss Bank Corporation (in alphabetical order).
3. At the time, Mexico was pressing for a longer period of coverage for the amortizations to be restructured, but banks were then totally opposed. In fact, they initially wanted to restructure only one year's maturities (1983) so that Mexico's progress could be assessed annually. This became known colloquially as the 'short-least approach'.

4 The Foreign Debt Crisis and Adjustment in Chile: 1976–86

Ricardo Ffrench-Davis

The debt of Chile with banks rose twice as fast as that of Latin America and of LDCs as a whole in 1977–81 and the 1982 crisis found Chile with a large debt relative to its economic size. Since then, the country has suffered a sizeable negative transfer with bank creditors, only partially compensated by an enlarged access to official funding.

Together with an orthodox adjustment and continued terms of trade worsening, the heavy debt burden explains why Chile is one of the nations with poorer economic performance in 1982–6. With respect to 1981, GDP per capita in Chile fell at a rate almost twice that in the remainder of Latin America.

Section 1 of this chapter examines the size and composition of the external debt of Chile in 1976–81, the macro-economic effects of rising capital inflows into the domestic economy and the use made of them. Section 2 discusses the renegotiation processes in 1983–6, the agreements with the IMF, the nature of adjustment taking place in the Chilean economy, the role played by multilateral funding and debt-equity conversion. Section 3 presents a brief discussion of an alternative approach.

1. GROWING INDEBTEDNESS AND POSITIVE NET TRANSFERS

The effects of the external shock on debtor nations show great diversity in spite of their generalised nature. This diversity is the result of the different size and growth rate of the debt of

113

each country, and of the development and debt strategy they adopted, before and after the crisis.

In Chile the failure of the monetarist experiment in 1974–81 was closely linked with an across-the-board liberalisation of imports and of the financial system. The trade and financial policies adopted made it possible for the foreign debt with banks to grow annually almost 60 per cent between 1977 and 1981 compared with 28 per cent for Latin America. The excessive increase of debt discouraged capital formation instead of supporting it. There were five main reasons for this outcome: the rapid and indiscriminate import liberalisation, particularly of consumer goods; a large exchange rate appreciation; a persistent high real domestic interest rate; an absolute freedom for the market to decide about the use of both foreign and domestic financing (Arellano, 1983), and the difficulty of identifying market comparative advantages or opportunities for productive investment, within market conditions determined by the implementation of an extremely ideological economic policy.

1. Volume and composition of debt

As from 1977 the Chilean external sector witnessed a growing deficit in the trade and current accounts, however, until 1981 the even larger net capital inflows made it possible to accumulate significant international reserves. The flow took place within a framework of expansion of the external sector, particularly of imports of non-essential consumer goods. Non-traditional exports expanded rapidly, but the growth of imports was stronger. As a consequence, the deficit in the non-financial current account exhibited a worsening trend (see Table 4.1).

The capital flow was concentrated overwhelmingly in bank loans to the private sector, with no public guarantee. The flow of capital increased notably as a share of gross domestic investment and GDP. This was partly due to the poor performance of the two latter variables during the seventies. By 1981 the per capita GDP was barely similar to the level achieved in the early seventies. (See Meller, Livacich and Arrau, 1984 and Table 4.2.) The rate of investment in 1974–86 in each year was lower than the average achieved in the sixties

Table 4.1:   *Balance of payments (millions of US$ and index 1980=100)*

	Exports	Imports	Trade balance	Current account	Balance of payments	Non-financial current account	Terms of trade index
	(1)	(2)	(3)	(4)	(5)	(6)	(7)
1974	2,151	1,794	357	-211	-55	-27	185
1975	1,590	1,520	70	-491	-344	-207	111
1976	2,116	1,473	643	148	414	474	120
1977	2,185	2,151	34	-551	118	-186	107
1978	2,160	2,886	-426	-1,088	712	-599	104
1979	3,835	4,190	-355	-1,189	1,047	-514	111
1980	4,705	5,169	-764	-1,971	1,244	-1,041	100
1981	3,836	6,513	-2,677	4,733	67	-3270	81
1982	3,706	3,643	62	-2,304	-1.165	-383	73
1983	3,831	2,845	986	-1,117	-541	631	77
1984	3,650	3,357	293	-2,060	17	-105	72
1985	3,804	2,955	849	-1,329	-99	572	66
1986	4,205	3,126	1,079	-1,203	228	609	72

Source: Central Bank of Chile.
   Columns (1) to (3) are FDB.
   Column (5) only includes Central Bank.
   Column (6) is (4) minus net interest payments and profits.
   Column (7) is from ECLAC.

(Table 4.3). But, the current account deficit and the debt service (amortization plus interest payments) also grew in relation to exports, in spite of the dynamic behaviour of these during the early years of the monetarist experiment (Ffrench-Davis, 1983b, Table 4.2).

As far as creditors were concerned, in 1981 more than 80 per cent of foreign debt was with commercial banks; these shared barely 19 per cent in 1974. In 1982 the Chilean bank debt per capita was over US $1000, compared with US $600 for the Latin American average and US $500 for Brazil (CIEPLAN, 1983). Furthermore, the Chilean bank debt rose by 57 per cent per year between 1977 and 1981, compared with average of 28 per cent for all developing countries. Naturally, neither one of these sizeable rates could be kept up for a long time. For this, both debtors and creditors should be held co-responsible for the resulting crisis, since the latter frequently put pressure on

Table 4.2:   *Official and revised GDP: Total and per capita (1970=100)*

	GDP		GDP p/c	
	Official (1)	*Revised* (2)	*Official* (3)	*Revised* (4)
1970	100.0	100.0	100.0	100.0
1971	109.0	108.0	107.1	106.1
1972	107.6	107.9	104.0	104.2
1973	101.6	103.3	96.6	98.1
1974	102.6	108.9	95.9	101.7
1975	89.4	90.8	82.1	83.4
1976	92.5	94.6	83.6	85.4
1977	101.7	102.6	90.3	91.1
1978	110.0	109.0	96.0	95.2
1979	119.1	117.5	102.2	100.8
1980	128.4	124.3	108.3	104.9
1981	135.5	130.7	112.4	108.4
1982	116.4	112.3	94.9	91.6
1983	115.6	111.5	92.7	89.4
1984	122.9	118.5	96.9	93.5
1985	125.9	121.4	97.7	94.2
1986	133.1	128.4	101.6	98.0

Sources: (1) and (3) from official National Accounts published by the Central Bank. (2) and (4), for 1970–74 are rates of change in Marcel and Meller (1986); for 1974–81 are rates of change in Meller, Livacich and Arrau (1984); remainder years based on rates of change estimated by Central Bank. Figures for 1982–6 are based on provisional official rates of change.

the former to accept further credit and liberalise capital movements.

As far as debtors were concerned, in Chile the growing net inflow of capital was received mainly by the private sector, without a public guarantee. This was the result of a deliberate government policy, which was helped by the change taking

Table 4.3:   *Gross domestic investment, 1960–86 (annual averages in % of GDP)*

1960–70	20.2
1971–73	15.9
1974–81	15.8
1982–86	14.2

Source: Central Bank, gross fixed investment from official national accounts in 1977 pesos.

place in international markets. Thus, nearly two-thirds of Chile's total debt had that characteristic in 1981 (see Table 4.4). The existence of a debt of over US $10.5 billion with no public guarantee by mid–1982, when the crisis emerged, undoubtedly constituted a potentially decisive factor in a process of debt renegotiation.

Table 4.4: *Foreign debt of Chile, 1975–86 (millions of US$ and per cent of total)*

	Total	Private with guarantee	Public and publicly-guaranteed		Private without guarantee	
			Amount	(%)	Amount	(%)
	(1)	(2)	(3)	(4)	(5)	(6)
1975	5,153	21	4,667	85.6	786	14.4
1976	5,392	30	4,434	82.2	958	17.8
1977	5,763	46	4,479	77.7	1,284	22.3
1978	7,153	48	5,198	72.7	1,955	27.3
1979	8,790	76	5,369	61.1	3,421	38.9
1980	11,331	72	5,310	46.9	6,021	53.1
1981	15,700	69	5,623	35.8	10,077	64.2
1982	17,263	62	6,770	39.2	10,493	60.8
1983	18,133	413	9,096	50.2	9,037	49.8
1984	19,746	2,130	13,203	66.9	6,543	33.1
1985	20,190	1,994	14,897	72.7	5,593	27.3
1986	20,757	2,012	15,748	75.9	5,009	24.1

Sources: Central Bank
Chilean External Debt up to 1985, and Boletin Mensual, January 1987, for an estimate for 1986.
All figures refer to disbursed outstanding debt.
(1) Total including IMF and debt payable in domestic currency, and excluding short-term trade credit to non-bank debtors; the latter amounted to US$ 800 million in 1986.
(2) Private debt with public sector guarantee.

2. Macro-economic adjustment and debt dynamics

A massive process of indebtedness such as occurred between 1977 and 1981 had significant effects on several areas of the national economy. Particularly relevant were the general liberalisation of imports and of the financial system. It had deep effects on aggregate demand and its composition, it contributed to a spectacular concentration of wealth, it altered the functioning of the process of saving and investment, and the management of monetary and foreign exchange policies.

Until late 1981 the net capital flow into Chile exceeded the absorption capacity of the national economy, pressing for a faster import liberalisation and exchange rate appreciation. As a consequence, the deficit in the current account experienced a persistent and substantial increase. In spite of this, capital inflows through private debtors grew even faster. The corresponding surplus (positive net transfer or excess of net loans over interest payments) brought about the increase of international reserves witnessed until 1980.

The sizeable capital flows—those applied to financing larger imports as well as those that went to enlarge the international

Table 4.5:   Imports and GDP per capita, exchange rate, and tariffs (Indexes 1970=100)

| | Imports per capita | | | | | |
| | Total | Non-oil | Non-oil current goods | GDP per capita | Exchange rate | Average tariff |
	(1)	(2)	(3)	(4)	(5)	(6)
1974	116.4	97.8	111.1	101.7	130.6	75.6%
1975	87.1	78.5	84.0	83.4	179.0	48.7%
1976	82.0	68.3	67.7	85.4	144.7	35.6%
1977	108.9	95.2	97.2	91.1	120.8	21.7%
1978	126.7	115.9	117.9	95.2	134.1	14.8%
1979	159.5	133.5	137.3	100.8	131.0	12.0%
1980	181.6	162.0	168.4	104.9	114.4	10.0%
1981	209.1	192.2	204.7	108.4	97.2	10.0%
1982	117.6	105.2	115.8	91.6	112.9	10.1%
1983	90.7	78.0	91.2	89.4	135.5	21.0%
1984	106.6	94.8	105.9	93.5	139.5	24.4%
1985	91.6	80.1	83.9	94.2	174.9	27.3%
p1986	84.8	77.4	77.2	98.0	197.7	n.a.

Sources: Central Bank. Cols (1), (2), (3) are CIF, includes zona franca and others. Deflated by index of external inflation (EPI) estimated in Ffrench-Davis (1984). Col (3) excludes Capital Goods. Col (4) 1974–81 are rates of change in Meller, Livacich and Arrau (1984), and Marcel and Meller (1986); 1982–6 are official figures. Col (5) exchange rate deflated by revised CPI and inflated by the EPI. Col (6) is the annual simple average of import tariffs.

reserves—meant that by the early eighties about 40 per cent of all the credit available in the Chilean economy had its origin in foreign funds. In spite of this, substantial differences persisted between domestic and external interest rates, reflecting considerable segmentation in the financial market. In 1981, for example, the real interest rate (converted to its peso equivalent) of foreign debt in dollars was twenty-six percentage points less than the real cost of domestic credit in pesos. This situation was characteristic throughout the period 1975–81 (Arellano, 1983; Ffrench-Davis, 1983b, Table 4.1; Mizala, 1985).

The growing capital inflow made constant appreciation of the exchange rate possible (see Table 4.5). This in turn made it more attractive to resort to external loans; because of the appreciation, their real cost expressed in Chilean pesos was negative during most of the post financial liberalisation period. Thus, the process had a feedback, fostering the inflow of capital which allowed a long process of exchange rate appreciation. Consequently, the nation economy became increasingly accommodated to the massive inflow of financial capital. This was backed up by the belief in the country's official circles that since the debt was mainly private it would be efficiently used (Robichek, 1981, p. 171–2).

Meanwhile, saving and investment ratios were noticeably lower than the levels reached in the sixties; the rate of gross capital formation barely reached an average of 15.8 per cent of GDP in 1974–81, well below the 20.2 per cent average recorded in the sixties (Table 4.3). A growing proportion of the resources were channelled into imported consumer goods, crowding out demand for domestic output and switching savings to consumption. Investment, particularly in the production of tradeable goods decreased. The clearest comparative market advantages in the second half of the seventies were to be found in the purchase of assets at depreciated prices from businessmen heavily indebted in the domestic market. With the exception of a few sectors intensive in natural resources and of luxury building, investment was faced with the difficulty of identifying comparative advantage: the appreciation and instability in the exchange rate, the high real domestic interest rates, the dismantling of public activities that had supported production, the reduction of public investment, the indiscriminate liberalisation of imports, all converged to provide a discouraging framework for productive investment.

Paradoxically, then, in spite of the atmosphere of success that prevailed until 1982 and the close intercommunication between the government and economic groups, the process of investment was weakened during the monetarist experiment

Table 4.6: *Chile: Real wages, other earnings, and unemployment (annual averages; index 1970=100, and % of labour force)*

	Real wages	Family allowance[a]	Average pensions[b]	Public social expenditures per capita[c]	Rate of unemployment[d] %
	(1)	(2)	(3)	(4)	(5)
1970	100.0	100.0	100.0	100.0	5.9
1974	65.0	104.8	51.3	91.7	9.1
1975	62.9	100.8	50.2	75.0	17.6
1976	64.7	93.6	52.3	71.2	21.9
1977	71.4	87.2	57.0	78.7	18.9
1978	76.0	84.8	62.1	79.0	18.0
1979	82.2	82.0	72.1	82.8	17.3
1980	89.3	82.2	74.3	83.5	17.0
1981	97.3	81.6	78.0	84.4	15.1
1982	97.6	80.0	83.5	86.9	26.1
1983	86.9	64.1	83.2	77.6	31.3
1984	87.1	75.8	89.7	76.4	24.7
1985	83.2	55.1	NA	74.0	21.7
1986	84.9	46.1	NA	NA	19.1

Notes: a. The reference in 1970 is the blue collar (obrero) allowance.
      b. Excludes social assistance pensions; includes all other civilian pensions. Taken from Arellano (1987), "La situacion social en Chile", CIEPLAN, February.
      c. The series for the period 1970–82 was taken from Marcel (1984). Figures from 1983 on were estimated using rates of change from Informe Gemines, October 1986.
      d. Includes labour force in government employment programmes PEM = FOJH; excludes disguised unemployment.
         Up to 1985 taken from Jadresic (1986); 1986 is based on the average of the figures for March and September, U. de Chile, Economics Department.
      NA: Not Available

Source: See CIEPLAN (1977) for sources and definition of each item.

(see articles by Foxley, Munoz and Ffrench-Davis in CIEPLAN, 1983).

Beyond the poor functioning of the productive system, it was obvious that the trends exhibited by the external sector could not be kept up for long, even if the international situation had not changed. However, the official opinion was that the process would be self-regulating. It was asserted that since: a) there was a fiscal budget, b) high-powered money was larger than the value of the international reserves, and c) the monetary policy was 'neutral', a foreign exchange crisis could not possibly arise. Despite this, when international financial problems emerged in 1981, the trade deficit represented 11 per cent of GDP, and the current account deficit was 21 per cent. The corresponding excess of domestic expenditure over output was located in the private sector. In fact, foreign loans to the private sector allowed a large and growing excess spending of this sector.

On the other hand, during this period the distributive situation deteriorated (see Table 4.6). Real wages, family allowances, pensions, the rate of employment and social public expenditure per capita were lower than in 1970 in each year of the period 1974–86. Excessive foreign indebtedness was inefficient as well as inequitably distributed, allowing greater growth in the consumption of higher income groups, who were those who benefited the most from this process. The high level of consumption was concentrated mainly in imported goods, as shown below.

The restricted access to foreign credit and high real interest rates in 1982 coincided with a sizeable fall in the price of copper (a product that accounts for half of Chilean exports); furthermore, the Chilean economy was particularly vulnerable as the government had done away with economic regulation mechanisms, and the productive system was weakened and over-indebted. Thus, the external shock was multiplied in the domestic economy and GDP (discounted by the worsening of the terms of trade) fell by 14 per cent in 1982; manufacturing output fell by 22 per cent.

3. The use of debt
The increase of the Chilean debt was used to a large degree to

finance an excess of imports. In fact, an analysis of the period shows that about three-quarters of the rise in the debt was used to increase the import coefficient of the Chilean economy, with the remainder compensating the fall in the terms of trade (see Ffrench-Davis and De Gregorio, 1986). In net macro terms no part was used to finance the creation of productive capacity since the rate of investment was lower during the monetarist experiment than in the sixties.[1]

Table 4.5 shows the evolution of imports, the real exchange rate and the average tariff, for the 1974–86 period. It is noteworthy that the cumulative nominal growth rate of imports between 1977 and 1981 amounted to 32 per cent per annum and its real expansion was 22 per cent which represents a growth three times higher than that of GDP for the same period.

An analysis of the performance of imports shows that 'excessive' imports of non-capital goods amounted to around US \$5.8 billion during the 1977–82 period, that is, throughout the 'boom' period, when the illusion of an economic miracle prevailed. The estimate of excess imports is made in Ffrench-Davis and De Gregorio (1985). If we consider the interest payments accrued to that debt, the total excess expenditure in imports increases to US \$7.7 billion. This figure represents approximately three-quarters of the net foreign borrowing of the Chilean economy during the 1977–82 period, which amounted to US \$9.9 billion (see Table 4.4).

Lastly, these excessive imports occurred as a consequence of the policies adopted in external sphere. The extreme liberalisation of trade, as expressed in uniform tariffs set at 10 per cent, together with an exchange rate that also contributed towards making imports cheaper (see Table 4.5), allowed these to increase beyond what was consistent with the effective growth of the Chilean economy.

2. ADJUSTMENT AND NEGATIVE TRANSFERS: 1982–86

1. Debt renegotiations in 1983–6

There have been four renegotiations with bank creditors, two programmes with the IMF and two SAL agreements with the World Bank in the period 1983–7.

The 1983 and 1984 maturities of the debt of public agencies and banking institutions were renegotiated in 1983, as well as the reinstatement of short-term facilities and a 'new money' agreement for 1983. A further 'new money' agreement was negotiated in 1984. In June 1985, the Chilean Government reached another agreement with the creditor banks to restructure its foreign debt maturing between 1985 and 1987 and obtained new loans for the two-year period 1985–6, in the framework of a three-year IMF extended fund facility arrangement (see French-Davis and De Gregorio, 1985).

In all three cases the new credits have covered a fraction of the interest paid to the same creditor banks (see Table 4.7). In fact, from 1982 onwards, Chile has undergone a substantial net

Table 4.7: Imports and GDP per capita, exchange-rate, and tariffs (Indexes 1970=100)

| | Imports per capita | | | GDP per capita | Exchange rate | Average tariff |
| | Total | Non-Oil | Non-Oil current goods | | | |
	(1)	(2)	(3)	(4)	(5)	(6)
1974	116.4	97.8	111.1	101.7	130.6	75.6%
1975	87.1	78.5	84.0	83.4	179.0	48.7%
1976	82.0	68.3	67.7	85.4	144.7	35.6%
1977	108.9	95.2	97.2	91.1	120.8	21.7%
1978	126.7	115.9	117.9	95.2	134.1	14.8%
1979	159.5	133.5	137.3	100.8	131.0	12.0%
1980	181.6	162.0	168.4	104.9	114.4	10.0%
1981	209.1	192.2	204.7	108.4	97.2	10.0%
1982	117.6	105.2	115.8	91.6	112.9	10.1%
1983	90.7	78.0	91.2	89.4	135.5	21.0%
1984	106.6	94.8	105.9	93.5	139.5	24.4%
1985	91.6	80.1	83.9	94.2	174.9	27.3%
p1986	84.8	77.4	77.2	98.0	197.7	n.a.

Sources: Central Banks. Cols (1), (2), (3) are CIF, includes zona franca and others. Deflated by index of external inflation (EPI) estimated in Ffrench-Davis (1984). Col (3) excludes Capital Goods. Col (4) 1974–81 are rates of change in Meller, Livacich and Arrau (1984), and Marcel and Meller (1986); 1982–86 are official figures. Col (5) exchange rate deflated by revised CPI and inflated by the EPI. Col (6) is the annual simple average of import tariffs.

Table 4.8: *Debt burdens and output performance: Chile and Latin America*

	Total GDP (1986 wrt 1981)		Debt burdens (averages 1985–6)					
	Total (1)	Per capita (2)	Debt/ GDP (3)	Debt/ exports (4)	Inte- rest/ GDP (5)	Inte- rest/ exports (6)	Financial services/ GDP (7)	exports (8)
Chile	-1.8%	-9.6%	125.5%	448.0%	11.6%	41.3%	11.3%	40.4%
Latin America	5.4%	-5.8%	55.1%	371.5%	5.2%	35.2%	4.8%	32.3%

Sources: Estimates based on Central Bank of Chile and ECLAC. Debt includes IMF; exports are of goods and non-financial services; interests are gross payments; financial services are the sum of net interests and profits; GDP was converted into a dollar equivalent with actual 1985 and 1986 exchange rates for Chile; for Latin America 1983 rates were used to estimate GDP in constant dollars, and then adjusted by the WPI of the US.

outflow of funds to creditor banks. That is one reason determining the restricted economic activity, unemployment and low investment prevailing in the past six years.

The effects of the critical external shocks were reinforced within the domestic economy by the nature of the monetarist adjustment policy imposed in Chile. A distinctive feature has been the 'indiscriminate' opening to foreign trade (at present a uniform tariff of 20 per cent since 1985). Official economic policies have resulted in predominant 'overkilling' expenditure-reducing as opposed to expenditure-switching policies, with large output-reducing effects.

The decline in output and the indicators of the debt burden and service in Chile are worse than the average for Latin America (see Table 4.8). There was a recovery in 1984 and in 1986, but it was relative to a depressed previous level. However, terms of trade worsened more for Chile than for the overall region.

Since economic growth was very poor during the monetarist experiment (see Meller, Livacich and Arrau, 1984 and Table 4.2), it turns out that output per capita in Chile in 1986 was on a par with that of two decades ago. In Latin America the decline was also great; however, it declined only to the level of 1977.

Negotiations with the IMF The agreements with the IMF and the creditor banks contain a number of interesting points. Here, we shall focus on the main ones.

Debt renegotiations were conducted by the Chilean Government, despite the fact that initially most of the debt was in the private sector and lacked public guarantee. This is not surprising, of course. It is contradictory, however, to the contentions of the economic authorities until 1982, regarding the 'efficiency' of private indebtedness. Even more contradictory was the public guarantee and subsidies granted after the crisis to a major portion of private debt. These renegotiations, like most such operations of LDCs in the past five years, were preceded by agreements with the IMF, and the corresponding conditionality as regards national economic policies. The standard quantitative performance criteria related to targets on changes in domestic credit, international reserve, short and long-term foreign debt of the public sector, and current account and non-financial public sector deficits. The targets were fixed once a year usually with limits per quarter.

The programmes contain several other controls by the Fund, for instance, restrictions on payments and on transfers for current international transactions. Two of the subjects of control were a 120-days' deferment period on import payments and foreign exchange quotas for tourism. Some other targets such as inflation rates are not formally performance criteria.

The 1983 stand-by agreement with the IMF, which covered a span of two years ending in January 1985, was particularly restrictive. Its provisions on the fiscal deficit had the most serious implications. The fiscal deficit was fixed at 1.7 per cent of GDP for 1983.[2] The actual deficit turned out to be 3 per cent, still a low figure. Accordingly, notwithstanding the fall in GDP by 14 per cent the previous year, output was depressed further in 1983. The low level of economic activity allowed a surplus in the 1983 trade balance of nearly 5 per cent of GDP, as targeted. But both actual exports and imports were roughly 16 per cent below the programme figures. Gross domestic investment was also substantially lower than projected: 10.3 per cent *vis-à-vis* 17.4 per cent. The bulk of the fall, according to the Fund figures, was concentrated in the private sector.

Informal reports indicate that the comparatively low public sector deficit was not imposed by the Fund on this occasion, but sought by the Chilean economic officials. However, an excess over the target was incurred in the last quarter of 1983 in response to a substantial slack of the economy and a large under-utilisation of the other performance limits.

After rising to 5 per cent for 1984, the fiscal deficit target again shrank to 3 per cent in 1985 and to 2.2 per cent in 1986. The two latter targets are part of the three-year extended arrangements made in August 1985 for 1985–8.

The size of the fiscal deficit should be evaluated in the context of the prevailing recession. Deficit composition, too, requires consideration. In the case of Chile, a social security reform made in 1981 meant that the public sector was left to pay existing pensions, and most of the pensions of workers retiring in the five subsequent years, while a large part of the contributions of workers was turned over to private financial companies (Pension Fund Administrators, which lately have partly passed into foreign ownership in debt-equity swaps). To finance such payments, the Treasury must borrow from these companies. As a result, what used to be public sector revenue is now budgetary deficit. The transfer involved is of such magnitude that more than the whole fiscal deficit for 1984–6 was due to the cost for the public sector of the social security reform. Accordingly, discounting the budgetary cost originated by the social security reform, fiscal deficits have been non-existent or very small, in spite of a severe depression in the national economy. Consequently, the fiscal deficit failed to play the reactivating role it had to perform. The counterpart has been considerable under-utilisation of production capacity and a depressed rate of investment.

The other point about the IMF agreement we wish to discuss here is that of imports. Chile's regime is still the closest in the continent to free trade and Chile has agreed with the IMF and in the SAL agreements with the World Bank to keep it so. In a context of great scarcity of foreign currency, this is a serious restriction to economic activity.[3] It is estimated that under the conditions prevailing in 1982–5, if just US $100 million were leaked to non-essential imports, the resulting under-utilisation of domestic production capacity could amount to as much as US $400 million. The result is a consequence of the fact that adjustment was achieved mainly via expenditure-reducing policies, in order to restrict aggregate demand to a level consistent with the availability of foreign currency. Of course, more effective switching policies, affecting the composition of aggregate demand and supply could have been consistent with a larger economic activity.

In general, bargaining on policy conditionally has been negligible and the Government has complied with the targets agreed in both arrangements, with some deviations that have been waived by the Fund.

Negotiations with bank creditors The agreements have been associated with negotiations with bank creditors. In the discussions between the IMF and the Government the amount of total funding required in the period is determined. The Fund conditions the approval of this arrangement on the agreement of other creditors, mainly banks, to provide their quota of funding. Formal discussions are carried out by the Chilean Government with a committee of twelve banks.

In 1983, the amortizations falling due in 1983–4 were rescheduled, non-trade related short-term loans were converted into medium-term debt, a line of short-term trade credits were approved at the level outstanding as of 1 January 1983 for a period of eighteen months. The Government extended (without any charge to creditors) a guarantee on the rescheduled maturities of the private financial sector, took over the debt of private banks that went into bankruptcy, guaranteed the short-term trade credit, and provided large subsidies to private debtors, including a preferential exchange rate for debt service.

The so-called 'new funds' were granted by banks in proportion to their exposure in Chile. The amounts were negotiated separately in 1983 and in 1984.

In 1985, there was a new rescheduling, covering principal

falling due in 1985–7, and the short-term trade credit was renewed. New funds were agreed for 1985–6, part of which were guaranteed by the World Bank.

As regards the terms and conditions agreed with the bank advisory committee, its salient features are (see Ffrench-Davis and De Gregorio, 1985):

a) The terms and interest conditions obtained by Chile are very similar to those of other Latin American countries in each of the renegotiation rounds. This similarity is obtained regardless of the economic situation, the debt composition and burden of each country. For instance, the predominance of non-guaranteed private debt in the case of Chile was not matched by better renegotiation terms.

b) There is a clear trend among creditor banks to reduce their exposure. In the case of Chile, the amount of new money obtained declined steadily from US $1,300 million in 1983 to US $370 million in 1986, and to zero in 1987.[4] The limited amount of new loans shows up more clearly when we consider the non-negotiable maturities that were serviced.

Table 4.7 shows the net outflow of funds in favour of each class of creditor. In 1985–6 the net medium-term flow of funds from Chile to the bank creditors averaged about US $940 million yearly, equivalent to approximately 6 per cent of GDP. In 1987, because bank credits succeeded in lending no 'new money', net transfers climbed to US $1.3 billion.

c) The gap left by negative transfers in favour of private creditor banks is partly offset by lending from multilateral institutions. The level of debt with the World Bank, IDB and IMF rises at an annual average volume on the order of US $700 million. This means a rate of increase of 63 per cent per year between 1982 and 1986 (44 per cent if the IMF is excluded). The rate of increase is extremely high, partly because the level at the beginning of the crisis was low, in response to the previous privatisation of the foreign debt. Space for borrowing from multilateral sources was, in 1982, potentially available, as there had been relatively little borrowing from those sources previously. Space tends to be exhausted as the level used rises, however. After exhaustion, net loans would tend to follow the overall rate of increase of outstanding credit.

In summary, the funding from multilateral sources is important on two grounds in the sphere of financing. Their large net volume contributed to compensate partly for the sizeable net transfers to banks, and simultaneously made feasible their maintenance at such a high level. In total, Chilean net resource transfers as a share of GDP are near the average of Latin America. However, if only net transfers to banks are considered, the results worsens notoriously for Chile, as shown in Table 4.7. The other relevant point is that the available space for net positive transfers from multilateral sources, given present prospects, would tend to diminish.

There have been several threats by some industrialised countries to oppose loans by multilateral banks to the Chilean Government, because of its poor standing on human rights. The more complicated situation for the Government emerged in the discussion of the SAL II loan from the World Bank in 1986, which was approved with only 51 per cent of the votes of the board, with the abstention of the US. The US also abstained in the discussion of loans from IDB. However, the actual results prove that in balance the treatment has been preferential. This can be explained by the orthodoxy of economic policies in Chile, and the fact that at times the Government moves much further in that direction than the IMF or the World Bank would demand. Consequently, there tends to be no bargaining on conditionality, but a willing acceptance of the orthodox approach by the Government. The position of the Chilean Government has been then much in line with the economic ideology of the US government.

The data suggests that the balance up to 1986 has been one of strong support from the US Government for the creditor banks and the Chilean Government, not only by approving credit from multilateral organisations with the World Bank's guarantee on part of the new money, but also by rescheduling maturities and granting loans from the Commodity Credit Corporation, amongst others.[5]

d) Since 1983, refinancing of the debt of domestic banking institutions to bank creditors has been guaranteed by the Chilean Government. In 1983–4 there was no charge for this. Under the terms of the 1985 negotiation a small commission is payable in 1987 (0.5 per cent), 1990 (0.75 per cent) and 1993 (0.81 per cent) for outstanding loans, in case banks demand a public guarantee for them. In addition, the State has contributed to a major portion of debt service by: a) supporting the private banks, most of which, from early 1983 to mid-1986 were under public intervention; b) renegotiating the domestic debt with preferential interest rates; and c) granting a preferential exchange rate, and other subsidies to private debtors.

The debtors of the non-financial private sector have also benefited from various forms of public subsidy to support their debt service. This support, however, does not include a public guarantee. If the private debtor fails to make the corresponding peso deposit at the Central Bank to cover payments abroad, the State does not become responsible for servicing the creditor. Conversely, if the debtor makes the required deposit in pesos[6], the Central Bank assumes direct responsibility for servicing the foreign debt in the same rescheduled timetable of guaranteed debt.[7]

The similarity among the terms and conditions obtained in different cases contrasts sharply with the fact that—contrary to the rest of Latin America, except Argentina—the debt of Chile was predominantly private, without a public guarantee. This feature should have weighed heavily in a renegotiations process; all the more so when the indebted private sector, because of the serious financial stress it was undergoing, was in no position to repay, on its own, its liabilities in the period covered by the renegotiation.

By the end of 1981 the private sector was responsible for 65 per cent of the total debt versus 35 per cent by the public sector. However, as from 1983 this trend was significantly reversed. In fact, at the end of 1986 public and publicly-guaranteed debt accounted for 76 per cent of the total (see Table 4.4).

This phenomenon is due to two reasons. The first and more important one is that the public sector has taken over most of the debt due to the fact that even if the private sector had had the necessary pesos to meet its commitments abroad, the country did not have available the foreign currency to enable them to do so. Therefore, as the public sector was the only one with access to external financial markets, it contracted loans from the same creditors in order to provide itself and the private sector with enough foreign currency to service the debt.

In other words, between 1981 and 1986, the total debt increased by US $5.1 billion. The borrower had to be the public sector, because the private sector had no access, and the funds were used to cover interest payments, of which two-thirds were originally the responsibility of the private sector. Consequently, it implied a further 'nationalisation' of the burdensome Chilean debt. For this reason, the public debt share rose thirty percentage points between 1981 and 1986.

The second reason for the increased participation of public debt was the guarantee granted ex-post to the debt of the private financial sector. In 1981 private debt with public guarantee amounted scarcely to US $69 million, increasing to US $2,012 million at the end of 1986, which explains the ten percentage point increase of public sector participation in the total debt.

This process of 'public nationalisation' of debt has had serious consequences on the bargaining power of Chile, because prior to the emergence of the crisis most of the debt was the exclusive responsiblity of the private sector, which was unable to service its debt on its own. In this sense, Chile was one of the few countries in Latin America whose debt was mainly private, thus, placing it potentially in a better bargaining position than the rest. However, it sterilised this advantage without receiving any significant compensation from creditor banks for the reduction in the commercial risk of their exposure in Chile.

It can be argued that, apart from the effect of decreasing bargaining power, the public guarantee has not represented any cost to the country because creditors have not made it effective. However, the relevant question is whether in fact the private sector has been meetings its commitments with its own funds.

The answer is obviously negative, since private sector payments have been made with substantial State support. Furthermore the State has had to borrow in order to obtain the foreign currency the country does not possess. As discussed above, sizeable subsidies by the public sector were granted through several devices, including a preferential exchange rate.

In the case of the preferential exchange rate, which was in force from August 1982 to December 1986, this has involved the massive transfer of funds towards a segment of the private sector. This subsidy which initially equalled 11 per cent of the official dollar value, reached 40 per cent in June 1985, at which date its gradual elimination was decided.[8] The magnitude of this transfer is estimated at US $2.9 billion. Additionally, in September 1984, the option was granted of converting debt in dollars into pesos, with a cost of US $230 million for the Central Bank. These two subsidies alone amounted to roughly one-fifth of GDP (at 1985 prices).[9]

It can, therefore, be said that, by means of the preferential exchange rate and other mechanisms, the State assumed responsibility for an important part of a debt it did not originally contract.

2. Amortization commitments, new renegotiations and debt-equity conversion.

Without a change in the present debt scenario, the prospects for Chile look dark in the next ten years. Debt was 1.2 times the annual GDP and close to 4.3 times the value of exports of foods and services in 1986. Gross interest payments amounted to 12 per cent of GDP, and net transfers to banks were 6 per cent (see Table 4.8 and 4.7). In brief, the debt burden looks extremely heavy.

The need for continued rescheduling of amortization is

another outstanding feature. Amortizations maturing in 1987 (not rescheduled in 1985) were US $240 million, and in 1988 would have climbed to over US $3 billion if they had not been rescheduled again in 1987.

The overly optimistic estimates made in prior years led to the need to reschedule again the maturities with private creditor banks.

With respect to multilateral creditors a complicated situation also emerges. The large *net* loans received from these official sources will tend to recede if the present framework is projected into the future, because of the exhaustion of the unused margin for borrowing that Chile had (see Section 2.1 above) and because amortization commitments start to rise in these years, following the steep increase in the debt stock with multilateral institutions since 1983. Payment of principal rises from US $24 million in 1983 to US $260 million in 1990. Furthermore, amortizations already committed after the rescheduling agreed in 1987, imply that 60 per cent of all the medium- and long-term debt would be due within the period 1989–95 (see Table 4.10).

Chile's debt burden is so large that there is a clear need for a combination of long-term overall rescheduling, reduction of interest rates and write-down, especially of private debt originally non-guaranteed.

Since mid–1985 there have been transactions leading to a reduction of the debt stock and also some write-downs have taken place (Banco Central, 1986). In May 1985 the Government started a two-tier system allowing the pre-payment of debt with bank creditors. The system is based on the use of debt promissory notes (*pagares de la deuda externa*) sold by creditors with a discount, and on the capitalisation of external loans (debt-equity conversion). The notes of guaranteed debt are being sold, in the international secondary market, with a discount of the order of 30 per cent of their face value.

One of the tiers (chapter XVIII of the Foreign Exchange regulations of Chile) is directed to repatriating capital that has fled or to capture foreign currency from the 'parallel' domestic market. The other tier (chapter XIX) is officially directed to attracting foreign investors. The Central Bank accepts the notes of its direct liability at 100 per cent of their face value.[10] In the case of other debtors, the parties negotiate the terms of the transaction.

In the first eighteen months, about US $670 million or about 3 per cent of the debt stock have been converted: two-thirds of them in the first tier. A sizeable share of funds used to purchase promissory notes abroad are estimated to proceed from the domestic 'parallel' foreign currency market. An incentive to transactors is a sort of capital laundering. The second tier—for an amount of US $190 million—has been encouraged by the discount in international markets and by access to low-priced domestic equity. In this second tier there is a change in the form of the liabilities of Chile, from debt to risk capital, subject to remittances of principal and profits after a certain period.

Additionally, there has been straightforward direct debt-equity conversion of loans originally associated with direct foreign investment under Decree 600 (US $150 million) and write-downs of some private non-guaranteed debt (US $330 million as recorded by the Central Bank).

Criticism of the above mentioned system relate mainly to five points. One is acceptance in Chile at face value of notes that are priced in the market at 70 per cent or less, a price that is actually supported by the Government guarantee and subsidies to domestic debtors, as well as by the large net transfers to creditor banks. The second is their use in buying Chilean firms at underpriced equity. The third is that several of the firms are located in extremely politically sensitive areas and may have a 'strategic' role in national development. Fourth, the repatriated capital or foreign currency taken from the parallel market is used to prepay debt, which otherwise would presumably be rescheduled over and over into the future. Fifth, that FDI in cash is replaced by foreign investment in promissory notes.

3. BASES FOR A NEW NATIONAL APPROACH

The sharp decline in the Chilean economy originated partly in the international crisis that afflicts most developing countries. Its effects, however, have been most intensively felt in Chile. It can be pointed out that in 1986, gross domestic product per inhabitant in Chile was 10 per cent below that of 1981; for Latin America as a whole the figure was only 6 per cent. Chile's poorer performance stems from three major factors. One is the greater indebtedness experienced during the most extreme monetarist period, that is 1976–81. In 1985–6 Chile's foreign debt accounted for more than 120 per cent of total annual output; for Latin America as a whole, this percentage was about 55 per cent. Second, the terms of trade worsened drastically, 21 per cent between 1980 and 1986.[11] The third factor is the orthodox policy approach used in Chile to face the crisis. The external shock was multiplied in the domestic economy, with an abrupt and large fall in economic activity and investment.

The fact is that the debt problem is not being solved. Present prospects are that external financial restrictions and negative financial flows from Chile will be a burden for many years yet. A serious effort towards tackling this burden effectively entails action on three fronts.

On the external front any manoeuvring capability *vis-à-vis* the creditor banks should be utilised firmly. The non-guaranteed debt and the fact that there are negative transfers (more is being paid out than is being received) are potentially significant elements to improve Chile's position. Even under present conditions in the negotiating framework there is room for improvement. Beyond that, the external framework requires modification. This will probably not be possible without cooperation among indebted countries. It is not a question of forming a cartel to discuss collectively the details of each country's debt. What is needed, instead, is joining forces with a view to altering the arbitrary conditions that the cartel of banks and the IMF have imposed on debtors whose weakness is increased by their acting in isolation.

The second front has to do with commercial cooperation to broaden export markets. Reinsertion into economic integration schemes may contribute to expand non-traditional exports. It should be recalled that the Andean Agreement was the main market for Chilean exports high value added during the export boom in 1974–6, which was checked by Chile's withdrawal in 1976. The emergence of democratic regimes in the region and the persistence of the international crisis are potentially encouraging factors for reactivating economic integration with ALADI and ANCOM.

The third is the domestic front. Those responsible for the Chilean economy have proved unwilling to recognise the seriousness and persistence of the present crisis. The clearest signs of such inability is the prevalence of an 'indiscriminate external opening', whereby Chile would continue to suffer negative financial transfers well into the nineties. Another negative element is the extreme 'subsidiarity' approach predominant in Chile, whereby the private sector is expected to be the one to give national development a fresh start. 'Subsidiarity' has led to a renewed privatisation of public enterprises, frequently at undervalued prices. What the private sector could not do under more favourable circumstances during the period 1974–81, it would doubtfully do in the more demanding situation of crisis. Against an originally ideo-logised approach, based on extreme 'subsidiarity' and extreme 'free enterprise' there is the alternative of a public policy leading the design and implementation of a national development programme, directed to reconstructuring the economy and achieving a better balance of power within the domestic economy and *vis-à-vis* foreign counterparties. The private sector, be they large or small companies, cooperative or worker-owned firms, would hardly recover without a dynamic sector acting selectively in their support.

Regarding trade specifically, the domestic market must be reactivated with intensive use of domestic components. To this end, public expenditure should steer clear of non-essential imports and—in conjunction—a selective import regime (plus keeping a 'realistic' exchange rate policy) should be adopted. A differentiated and selective tariff schedule is a key instrument. The main features of an alternative programme have been discussed elsewhere (see CIEPLAN, 1983).

It is a question of saving the foreign currency that is currently spent on non-essential imports; the main point, however, is to prevent the reactivation of domestic demand from leaking abroad to any great extent. Lastly, growth is not possible without enlarged capital formation. Investment should be encouraged.

In brief, there is no doubt that external determinants are responsible for much of the general decline in Latin America and Chile. The response to this should be a decided attempt to improve the external environment, which requires more bargaining power and joint action with other countries. The Chilean economy was more vulnerable than others to external shocks. Chile was unprotected in the face of external events: accelerated indebtedness and indiscriminate import liberalisation created a country increasingly dependent on foreign decisions. Today, the need to reconstruct a road to national development is evident. This entails *selective* economic relations with the foreign sector and a State endowed with strong bargaining and leadership ability.

NOTES

1. This outcome is explained by the incentives provided to consume imported foods and the role played by the financial system in redirecting savings from some sectors of the Chilean economy toward excess consumption of other sections within the domestic economy. See Arellano (1983) on the latter issue.
2. The target was fixed in a given amount of peso. Since actual GDP in pesos resulted in being lower than programmed, that given amount represented 2 per cent of GDP figures. It includes, as current expenditure, the full inflation correction of domestic public debt.
3. For a discussion of an alternative import policy see the author's article in CIEPLAN (1983) and the panel in Ffrench-Davis and Feinberg (1986).
4. The 1987 agreement states no new loans for 1987, and for 1988–90 a 'retiming' of interest payments which would be made on an annual basis, returning to a semester basis in 1991. The agreement implies a postponement from 1988 to 1991–3 of interest payments estimated at US $447 million.
5. For instance, in 1985–6, the CCC rescheduled US $130 million due during the biennium and offered US $180 million in new loans.
6. The government granted creditor banks the right to relend in Chile part of the pesos deposits, while they wait to be remitted abroad in foreign currency.
7. The timetable may be modified in bilateral agreements involving some write-down of private debt.
8. Figure for 1982–5. Since February 1984, exporters and public enterprises were excluded from the subsidy. The subsidy was partly delivered in promissory notes of the Central Bank, which were traded below their face value in the secondary market.

9. See De Gregorio (1985). The estimate does not include the takeover by the Government of a) US $300 million of debt of two banks that went into bankruptcy, nor b) the notably larger cost of subsidies to private banks and economic groups. See Arellano and Marfan (1986) for an analysis of the several subsidy schemes.
10. In chapter XVIII, the Central Bank auctions monthly quotas. It has been capturing an economic rent that has fluctuated around 14 per cent of the notes. In chapter XIX the Central Bank exchanges its foreign debt notes for promissory notes in pesos, which are being sold in the secondary market at roughly 92 per cent of their face value.
11. The figures for Latin American oil exporters and non-oil exporters were 37 per cent and 6 per cent respectively.

REFERENCES

Arellano, J. P. 1983, 'De la liberalización a la intervención: el mercado de capitales en Chile, 1974–83', *Colección Estudios CIEPLAN*, 11, December, Santiago.
Arellano, J. P. and Marfan, M., 1986, 'Ahorro inversión y relaciones financieras en la actual crisis económica chilena', *Colección Estudios CIEPLAN*, 20, December, Santiago.
Banco Central, 1986, *External debt of Chile*, annual issues.
———'Quarterly economic and financial report of Chile', Santiago.
Bank for International Settlements, *Annual Reports*, BIS, Basle.
CIEPLAN, 1983, *Reconstrucción económica para la democracia* CIEPLAN-Editorial Aconcagua, Santiago.
———1987, 'Sintesis Estadistica', CIEPLAN, March.
De Gregorio, J., 1985, 'Deuda externa, escenario económico internacional y cuenta corriente en Chile: perspectives para 1985–90', *Notas Técnicas* No. 68, CIEPLAN, Santiago, March.
De La Cuadra, S. and Desormeaux, J., 1985, 'La renegociación de la deuda externa y el programa económico de mediano plazo', mimeo, Universidad Católica de Chile and Santiago.
Ffrench-Davis, 1982, 'El experimento monetarista en Chile: una sintesis critica', *Colección Estudios CIEPLAN* 9, Santiago, December; and 'The monetarist experiment in Chile: a critical survey', *World Development*, November 1983.
———, 1983a, ed., *Relaciones financieras externas y desarrollo nacional en América Latina*. Fondo de Cultura Económica, México.
———, 1983b, ed., 'El problema de la deuda externa y la apertura financiera en Chile', *Colección Estudios CIEPLAN* 11, Santiago, December; and 'The external debt, financial liberalization and

crisis in Chile', in M. Wionzcek, ed., 1985, *Politics and economics of external debt crisis,* Westview Press, Boulder.

———, 1984a, 'Indice de precios externos: un indicador para Chile de la inflación internacional, 1982–83', *Colección Estudios CIEPLAN* 13, June.

———, 1984b 'Deuda externa y alternativas de desarrollo en América Latina', *Colección Estudios CIEPLAN* 15, December.

Ffrench-Davis, R. and De Gregorio, J., 1985, 'La renegociación de la deuda externa de Chile en 1985: antecedentes y comentarios', *Colección Estudios CIEPLAN* 17, Santiago, September.

——— 1986, 'Origenes y efectos del endeudamiento externo en Chile: antes y después de la crisis', *El Trimestre Económico* No. 213, Mexico, forthcoming.

Ffrench-Davis, R. and Feinberg, R. E., 1986, eds, *Más allá de la crisis de la deuda: bases para un nuevo enfoque,* CIEPLAN, Santiago and Grupo Editor Latinoamericano (GEL), Buenos Aires. Forthcoming in the University of Notre Dame Press, Indiana, USA.

Foxley, A., 1982, 'Experimentos neoliberales en América Latina', *Colección Estudios CIEPLAN* 7, March, special issue, and *Latin American experiments in neo-conservative economics',* University of California Press, 1983.

Griffith-Jones, S., 1986, 'Management of the debt crisis: an analytical framework', *Notes Técnicas* No. 87, September.

McKinnon, R., 1977, 'La intermediación financiera y el control monetario en Chile', *Cuadernos de Economica* No. 43, December.

——— 1981, 'Foreign Exchange Policy and Economic Liberalization in LDCs', in Alternatives de politicas financieras en economias pequeñas y abiertas al exterior, *Estudios Monetarios VII,* Banco Central de Chile, Santiago.

Heller, P. 1986, 'Un enfoque analitico empirico de las causas del actual endeudamiento externo chileno', *Colección Estudios CIEPLAN* 20, December.

Meller, P., Livacich, E. and Arrau, P., 1984, 'Una revisión del milagro económico (1976–1981), *Colección Estudios CIEPLAN* No. 15, December.

Mizala, A. 1985, 'Segmentación del mercado de capitales y liberalización financiera', *Notas Técnicas* No. 69, CIEPLAN, March.

Robichek, W. 1981, 'Some Reflections about External Public Debt Management', in Alternatives de politicas financieras en economias pequeñas y abiertas al exterior, *Estudios Mohnetarios VII,* Banco Central de Chile, Santiago.

Sjaastad, L. and Cortes, H., 1978, 'El enfoque monetario de la balanza de pagos y las tasas de interés en Chile', *Estudios de Economia* No. 11, Universidad de Chile, first semester.

Tapia, D., 1979, 'Apertura al mercado financiero internacional', in *Institucionalidad económica e integración financiera con el exterior*, Instituto de Estudios Bancarios, Santiago.

Zahler, R. 1980, 'Repercusiones monetarias y reales de la apertura financiera al exterior: el caso chileno, 1975–78', *Revista de la CEPAL* No. 10, April.

5 Brazil and the IMF: Logic and Story of a Stalemate

Dionisio Dias Carneiro

INTRODUCTION

Since the Mexican moratorium in August 1982, the Brazilian economy has been facing a long period of abnormal international financial relations. In the first two years of the developing countries' debt crisis, when the rules of the game were at the peak of uncertainty, the Brazilian Government resisted internal pressures to suspend payments of interest on its external debt. At that time there was a good chance that a unilateral moratorium by the Brazilian Government would significantly deepen the disruption of international financial markets. The size of the Brazilian foreign debt and the gloomy forecasts then available pointed to disastrous consequences of such an action.

Simple cost-benefit analyses were not uncommon then, aiming at demonstrating that since the debt crisis would probably last for a long period, chances were that the best course of action for the Brazilian Government would be a unilateral moratorium. In fact, this position was favoured by most of the opposition during the 1982 election campaign. The course of action chosen by the Brazilian Government, until early 1987 however, was to play the game according to what was expected of a country that intended to remain eligible for voluntary loans, even if the foreseeable future did not look particularly pleasant. The implicit expected pay-off was that creditors would take that into consideration when normality returned to international financial markets.

The most important variables for this decision at the time

141

were: the level of international lending rates, the prospects for export growth and the likelihood of return of voluntary finance. After the September 1982 meeting of the IMF Board of Governors in Toronto, it also became clear that the multilateral institutions would mainly be confined to playing a particularly important and delicate role of preventing debtors from defaulting and private creditors from counting losses and quitting.

The aim of this paper is to describe the evolution of the relationship between Brazil and the IMF from detonation of the debt crisis in 1982 up to the end of 1986.

Following this introduction, section 1 summarises the state of the Brazilian economy at the time of the debt crisis, section 2 reviews the peculiar situation of the country at the time it submitted a programme to the Fund at the end of 1982, section 3 describes the steps followed from the signature of the first letter of intent to late 1986. In section 4 an attempt is made at drawing lessons from the Brazilian experience, and finally section 5, written after the moratorium of February 1987, concludes the paper with a brief evaluation of the prospects for the present debt crisis.

1. ADJUSTMENT BEFORE THE IMF

The origins of the recent balance of payments problems of the Brazilian economy go back to the first oil shock in the mid–seventies.[1] At that time, the Brazilian economy imported around 80 per cent of the oil it consumed and the quadrupling of oil prices and the rising cost of machinery and other intermediate goods added US $6.5 billion to its imports in 1974. The current account deficit rose to 6 per cent of GDP and the policy response from the Brazilian Government was essentially to adopt an investment programme whose aim was to enhance the growth of export capacity and substitute domestic production for imports. The shortage of foreign exchange in 1975 led to the adoption of an import controls scheme designed to grant import facilities for those projects aimed either at import substitution or export development. The availability of international finance from private banks encouraged a growth-cum-debt strategy. The level of international interest rates and the prospects for export growth, based on the experience of previous years, led to favourable estimates of the ability to service the external debt in the foreseeable future.

Major developments following the first oil shock may be seen from data on Table 5.1. From 1974 to 1977 the trade deficit had been reduced from US $4.7 billion to US $100

Table 5.1: Brazil: Some macro-economic data

Years	GDP (1)	Indus-trial Output (1)	Infla-tion (2)	Real Wages (3)	Mon-etary base	Exports (4)	Im-ports (4)	Terms of Trade Total (77=100)	n-oil	PSBR /GDP (5)
1971	12.0	–	19.8	63.6	5.6	2.9	3.2	82	65	1.5
1972	11.1	14.0	15.5	68.1	10.3	3.9	4.2	87	72	5.7
1973	13.6	16.6	15.7	73.3	16.7	6.2	6.2	95	82	3.0
1974	9.7	7.8	34.5	74.3	9.4	7.9	12.6	78	78	0.8
1975	5.4	2.1	29.2	82.1	-3.9	8.7	12.2	76	76	1.6
1976	9.7	11.9	46.4	84.7	2.6	10.1	12.4	85	85	2.0
1977	5.7	2.2	38.7	89.3	13.0	12.1	12.0	100	100	4.0
1978	5.0	6.1	40.9	96.7	5.2	12.7	13.7	86	84	2.9
1979	6.4	6.9	77.2	100.0	2.9	15.2	18.1	79	81	2.9
1980	7.2	9.2	110.2	96.0	-15.0	20.1	22.9	65	78	1.8
1981	-1.6	-10.2	95.2	100.1	-22.9	23.3	22.1	55	71	3.1
1982	0.9	-0.2	99.7	109.9	-5.4	20.4	19.6	54	69	2.9
1983	-3.2	-5.5	211.0	94.5	-23.0	21.9	15.4	53	64	0.1
1984	4.5	7.0	223.8	87.3	-20.4	27.0	13.9	58	71	2.2
1985	8.3	8.5	235.1	85.3	2.1	25.6	13.2	55	69	–
1986	8.2[6]	11.7	65.1	–	239.4	22.4	12.9	–	–	–

Notes: 1. Real rates of growth
2. December to December
3. Industry only, deflated by the general prices index (IGP) 1979–100
4. US$ billions
5. Adjusted for inflation, author's estimates, for details see Carneiro (1986 B)
6. Preliminary

Sources: Boletim Do Banco Central (several issues)
National Account Tables (FGV)
International Financial Statistics (several issues)
Conjuntura Economica (several issues)
Fibge-Indicadores Da Industria

million surplus. Imports remained constant in nominal terms at their 1974 level while exports had grown at 13.9 per cent per annum. Crop failures in 1978 brought this trend to a halt. The second oil shock in 1979 contributed to renewed worries about the prospects for the trade balance. Simultaneously, the combined effects of the increase in international interest rates and the piling of debt signalled further trouble on the current account. Even before the interest rate shock, the efforts at controlling the trade deficit had not been sufficient to be reflected in the current account. Interest payments on the accumulated foreign debt had increased from US $700 million in 1974 to US $4.2 billion in 1979, absorbing 27.5 per cent, of export revenues. Debt indicators deteriorated as the net debt-to-export ratio went from 1.5 in 1974 to 2.6 in 1979. On top of that, signs of world recession following the adoption of contractionist macro-economic policies in the industrialised economies undermined the debt-cum-growth strategy as the prospects of world trade growth turned gloomy.

Long-run structural adjustment financed by external indebtedness had proved to be a feasible way to promote economic growth, but the positive response of the domestic economy to the stimuli of priority projects was accompanied by severe tensions in the economic structure. First of all, the increase in the rate of inflation after 1974 from an average of 20 per cent to about 10 per cent per year in the following three years brought the defence mechanism of indexation under stress: savings could still be attracted to domestic financial markets to provide funds for the new investment projects, but governmental guarantee was the only way to try and harness them towards priority sectors. On the other hand, the perception of an unstable rate of inflation, reinforced by repeated and short-lived attempts at demand control, made it difficult for private investors to borrow funds for new projects without some guarantee that inflation (as reflected in prospects of nominal debt service) would stay under control. The result was that the Government increased its role both as investor and as agent responsible for financial intermediation. Limiting the monetary correction on Development Bank loans while guaranteeing full monetary correction on most popular financial assets meant granting special subsidies whenever the rate of inflation went above target levels. Financial instability became a major problem for the monetary authorities with rescue operations commonplace whenever an attempt at monetary control reduced the liquidity of the financial system. In practical terms, the inflationary process became autonomous, with current rates being essentially determined by past rates that fed into current prices via the various indexing schemes in the economy. So the monetary aggregates became essentially endogenous. Minor supply shocks could be neutralised by some contractionary measures, but attempts at severe demand restraint had visible effects on output while the threat of interrupting the structural adjustment investment projects ended up being seen as worse than a tolerable inflation. Thus, an accommodating demand policy became the rule during most of the period, although spasmodic rounds of monetary and fiscal austerity were observed throughout.[2]

The second oil shock contributed to shake the confidence of policy-makers in the possibilities of continuing on the same track. Attempts at real devaluation via an accelerated crawling peg, increases in agriculture support prices and a proposal to increase the degree of wage indexation to control strikes provoked a turnaround of macro-economic policy. Mario Simonsen left the Government and was replaced by Delfim Netto as Minister of Planning. Simonsen had favoured the adoption of a more restrictive macro policy fearing that an increase in the rate of inflation would undermine foreign creditors' confidence and willingness to keep rolling over the external debt, but he was unable to find support from either the President or his supporting party in Congress. Delfim Netto sought less restrictive policies, reduced interest rates and supported the change in the wage law in an attempt to revive the miracle years of the early seventies. The rate of inflation more than doubled from 1978 to 1980.

In the first quarter of 1980, as foreign bankers were increasingly unhappy with the Brazilian Government's odd experiments, and in the face of less than rosy prospects for the balance of payments, Delfim Netto had to announce another major turnaround in macro-economic policies. Interest rates were raised, ceilings on the provision of credit for non-priority projects were established, cuts in non-priority investment

outlays of state companies were promoted. The banks
responded to the change in policies by refinancing existing
debt and providing new money at higher spreads, putting an
end to the financial squeeze.

One may ask at this point why Brazil did not go to the IMF
in support of its stabilisation policies after October 1980.
Bacha (1983) estimates that the decision not to seek IMF support
for an apparently orthodox stabilisation programme may have
cost Brazil around US $400 million of extra interest payments.
The Government seemed to fear that the IMF might require
drastic changes in its long-run strategy of structural
adjustment and restrict its freedom in economic policy. Later
developments suggest that besides being regarded as an
exhibition of Government weakness it could undermine the
already feeble political support for the Government. The loss
of US $3.5 billion in international reserves during 1980
demonstrated the difficulties found by Delfim Netto in
convincing private bankers to remain in the game. But, the fact
that new loans were still available at rising interest costs are a
good evidence that having a market doing business as usual
did make a difference.

The restrictive demand policies initiated in the fourth
quarter of 1980 had two main objectives: to display control
over the trade balance in order to signal to bankers that the
situation was manageable in the short run; and to retain some
control over public sector borrowing so that at least high
priority investment projects could mature. This would buy
time until the growth of export capacity and import
substitution opened enough room for debt service. In fact, US
$3.3 billion dollars were added to exports in 1981 and the trade
deficit of US $2.8 billion of the previous two years was
converted into a US $1.2 billion surplus, although the real
growth of world imports was only 1 per cent.

The Brazilian Government's growth-cum-debt strategy was
being challenged on two fronts. Nationally, high inflation and
the difficulty of controlling the public deficit were the main
signs of macro-economic inconsistencies which had to be dealt
with sooner or later. Externally, growing interest payments,
slower than anticipated growth of export demand and
unfavourable behaviour of the terms of trade led to a continual

postponement of the turning point in the external debt path which would signal the success of the strategy. Internal political opposition to the strategy gained strength both from the conservatives' side, which favoured an immediate attack on inflation, and from the left which pointed to the increasing dependence on foreign money as the main cause of Brazil's economic problems and favoured a unilateral moratorium as part of a programme of economic reforms.

2. THE MEXICAN CRISIS AND THE BRAZILIAN SMOKESCREEN

In 1982, Brazil exported US $3 billion less than in the previous year. This fall in export revenues signalled that the Brazilian economy would not be able to proceed with the long-run adjustment initiated in the mid–seventies, as long as shrinking world markets frustrated efforts to produce a significant trade surplus. For the second year in a row, restrictive domestic policies directed towards reducing domestic absorption were being adopted. The fall in the import coefficient from 9.2 to 6.8 per cent of GDP from 1980 to 1982 (Table 5.2) was insufficient as exports fell by more than US $400 million more than imports and interest payments increased by over US $2.2 billion in 1982 (see Table 5.3), absorbing more than half of export revenues. World recession and the resilience of

Table 5.2:   Brazil: Some external indicators (1979–86) (%)

Items	1979	1980	1981	1982	1983	1984	1985	1986²
Exports/GDP	6.4	8.0	8.5	7.1	10.4	12.3	10.7	8.6
Imports/GDP	7.6	9.2	8.0	6.8	7.3	6.3	5.5	5.0
Net debt/exports	264.0	233.0	231.0	325.0	351.0	292.9	328.6	3.9
Debt service/exports¹	77.0	61.9	71.0	96.6	78.2	66.4	72.1	–
Interest payments/ exports	27.5	31.3	39.3	56.3	43.6	37.3	40.6	41.2
Reserves/imports	53.6	30.1	34.0	20.6	29.6	86.1	88.2	–

Notes: 1. (Amortizations and interest payments/exports)
            2. Preliminary
Source: Boletim Do Banco Central (several issues)

Table 5.3:   *Brazil: Current account deficits and their main components*
              (millions US$)

Years	Trade balance	Net exports (goods and services)[1]	Net interest payments	Deficit in current account
1979	-2827.3	5205	4185.0	10741.6
1980	-2810.4	5931	6111.1	12807.0
1981	1232.1	1631	9161.0	11734.3
1982	780.4	2808	11353.3	16310.5
1983	6470.4	-4063	9555.4	6837.4
1984	13089.5	-11345	10202.7	-44.8
1985	12470.6	-10768	9588.7	267.8
1986[2]	9529.0	–	9225.2	2826.3

Notes: 1. Resource balance (excess of absorption over GDP)
          2. Preliminary
Source: Boletim Do Banco Central (several issues)

domestic inflation to demand controls were the two main reasons behind a general sense of frustration.

On the domestic scene, the political outlook was no less complex. Amidst a heated debate concerning the legislation for the November 1982 general elections, the Government tried to convince the public that going to the IMF would be pointless. The basic argument was that it would be impossible to obtain enough finance from the Fund to match the country's needs. The current account deficit of 1982 was over US $16.3 billion and there would be no chance of obtaining that kind of money from the IMF. Since control over the new Congress and the electoral college that would choose the first civilian President after twenty years of military rule, was at stake, the regime was determined to prevent the prospect of having the country under the scrutiny of the Fund from becoming a hot campaign issue.

From August to November 1982, a smokescreen operation was conducted at the highest levels of power. In August, following the Mexican moratorium, it became clear there would be no way to convince private bankers to keep doubling their bets on Brazil's long-run strategy for adjustment.[3] In September, when the basic strategy of keeping the banks in the game was being articulated by the governments of the industrialised countries and Mr. de Larosière, the Brazilian economic staff started negotiating with Fund officials. They still hoped that the Toronto meeting of the governors of the Fund and the Bank would increase the Fund's financial resources and, thus, at least save the face of the Brazilian authorities: the augmented resources of the IMF would help to show Brazilian public opinion that new conditions prevailed in the international financial markets and that multilateral finance could replace private financing that had become scarce and more expensive. Had the new conditions materialised, an upper credit agreement with the Fund would have been more defensible and politically less of a burden.

The frustration after the Toronto meeting contributed to further erode the domestic credibility of the Brazilian economic team, which had no other choice than to maintain the internal discourse about not going to the Fund.[4] At the same time, it prepared the first mission for immediately after the elections.

Negotiations with private banks started in Toronto, where the role of the Fund was made clear to the Brazilian authorities. Instead of enhanced financial resources, the main asset of the Fund became the political ability of its Executive Director. The financing of Brazil's balance of payments for the second half of 1982 and the following year was part of an emergency operation which had started with the Mexican rescue, and would involve the private banks, multilateral agencies and the Government of the United States. The operation involved emergency funds to prevent unilateral suspension of payments for lack of foreign exchange, an agreement with the IMF based on a programme to limit the need for foreign exchange, and the harnessing of private creditors around packages of financial support which underlined the common interests of preventing a complete disruption of the international financial system.

Emergency funding for the remainder of 1982 was provided by a loan of US $1.5 billion from the US Government and US $500 million from the BIS, together with around US $2.3 billion in short-term money from large private creditors, with the understanding that for the following year the maximum flow of funds available to Brazil would be US $10.6 billion from private banks, inclusive of refinancing, and US $2 billion from multilateral institutions.

As a token of seriousness of purpose, a special meeting of the National Monetary Council voted a formal pledge of austerity for the next year in the form of a document called 'Programme for the External Sector for 1983'.[5] The basic assumptions of the document were that exports would grow by 9.5 per cent and imports would be cut by 17 per cent so as to generate a trade surplus of US $6 billion for 1983. Notwithstanding Government denials it became obvious that the Programme would be the basis for an agreement with the Fund and that furthermore no deal could be reached with the private banks without the formal approval of the Fund.

Three days after the November elections the Planning Minister admitted that Brazil had already been 'adopting an economic policy within the lines recommended by the IMF'.[6] On 20 November the official announcement was made that a programme would be submitted for IMF consideration and that a formal agreement had been reached with the private banks around four points or 'projects' as they came to be called:

(1) The creditor banks would provide new funding of US $4.4 billion to borrowers nominated by the Central Bank.
(2) Repayments due in 1983 amounting to US $4 billion (later the figure was changed to US $4.4 billion) would be refinanced for eight years.
(3) Interbank credit lines related to trade credit, then estimated at around US $10 billion, would be renewed.
(4) Interbank credit lines for Brazilian banks operating abroad would be restored at their levels of 30 June 1982 (the amount then estimated was US $10 billion, later revised to US $7.5 billion).

The formal announcement of a programme with the IMF defines a new pattern of debt-related negotiations for Brazil. Until the 1982 crisis, as long as there was a voluntary market, the problem of finding finance for balance of payments disequilibria depended essentially on the ability to keep good prospects for the future. Adjustment was seen as a long-run process. Any deviations from sensible macro policies, such as happened in the first half of 1980, could mean more difficulties in raising finance and possibly higher spreads. When voluntary lending stopped, the problem was converted from a display of austerity in order to appease the private bankers to one of committing overall macro policies and trade policies with the IMF. Negotiations now were with Fund officials under the general agreement that the banks would follow through.

At first, both Brazilian authorities and creditor banks representatives in the negotiating committees acted as if they believed the emergency situation would not last long; otherwise it is difficult to accept that experienced bankers and monetary authorities could rely indefinitely on commitments with short-term interbank financing as a basis for external debt renegotiation. Whether any of the parties actually believed that, is totally immaterial. The second element of the strategy was to bind the agreements together so as to prevent less exposed banks from disrupting the scheme. This was done first of all by requiring approval of all four projects by all banks involved, before the agreement was valid; second, by the condition imposed that the decision concerning the IMF stand-by credit to Brazil would only be taken after the banks had approved the agreement.

This scheme turned out into a bluff. Difficulties concerning the approval of projects three and four led to the signing of the multi-partite agreement on 25 February 1983 based on projects one and two. The projects related to interbank credit lines in fact had to be negotiated during the whole year of 1983. An estimated US $5 billion of credit to Brazilian banks in August 1982 was no longer available by the end of January 1983.

3. FROM AGREEMENT TO STALEMATE[7]

On 6 January 1983 the Brazilian Government submitted the first of a series of seven letters of intent to the IMF, asking for credit under the 'extended facility' and pledging to adopt what was then called a stabilisation policy directed towards the structural adjustment of its economy in order to reduce its internal and external disequilibria in the period 1983–5. As is the norm, the letter of intent contained essentially a set of measures to control domestic absorption (that is to reduce consumption and investment), so as to adapt the economy to the external constraint defined in the programme approved in October 1982 by the National Monetary Council.

There were several problems with the first letter that may help to explain the painful negotiations of the following period:

(1) The three-year programme was directed towards a 'structural adjustment' which seemed very narrow when compared with the previous adjustment that had already changed the composition of investment, pattern of input utilisation (especially in terms of energy use), allocation of domestic credit, etc., since the first oil shock. The idea of the programme agreed with the IMF was to promote an adjustment based on the reduction of public investment, acceleration of mini-devaluations and correction of some domestic prices in order to increase exports. No consideration was given to the single fact that exports in the previous year had been reduced not because of excessive absorption, but because of the international recession.[8]

(2) Despite the lack of responsiveness of the rate of

Table 5.4:   *World imports quantum (1969–85) %*

Years	Growth rate	Years	Growth rate	Years	Growth rate
1969	11.2	1974	3.1	1980	1.5
1970	9.5	1975	-4.7	1981	0.4
1971	6.4	1976	12.4	1982	-0.8
1972	8.9	1977	5.9	1983	1.8
1973	12.1	1978	3.3	1984	8.9
		1979	6.0	1985	4.2
AVERAGE (69/73)	9.4	AVERAGE (74/79)	4.3	AVERAGE (80/85)	2.7

Source: IMF—International financial statistics

inflation to demand restrictions in the previous two years, no attention was drawn to the role played by indexation: internal disequilibria would be dealt with by the usual prescriptions of setting limits to nominal growth of net domestic credit of the Monetary Authorities and to public sector borrowing. A target of 70 per cent was set for the 1983 rate of inflation, aiming, thus, at a thirty percentage point reduction in spite of the fact that an acceleration of mini devaluations and a cut in subsidies for consumption goods would certainly add to price increases.

(3) The targets for public sector borrowing and net domestic credit were not only completely arbitrary, as noted by Bacha (1983) but also inadequate. Marques (1985) shows that error in the estimated figure for the net domestic credit in December 1982, of around 46 per cent, meant that the target for nominal growth for 1983 would be 13.3 per cent for an inflation target of 70 per cent.[9] The error was corrected in the following letters, but unrealistic figures were the rule for each one of them except for the second.

The targets for fiscal policy turned out to be the most problematic. Successive negotiations were needed throughout the year in order to adapt the concept of borrowing requirements used by the IMF to the complexities of the Brazilian public financial sector. Hardly ever did the targets mean some feasible restriction for public expenditures. During most of 1983 efforts were made to correct the figures that remained out of date due to the inability of the IMF staff to take into consideration the implications of the existence of a large indexed public debt to the setting of realistic deficit targets.[10] Furthermore, the fact that the rate of inflation was by and large insensitive to demand control due to general indexation increased the gap between targets and actual performance throughout the year.

On 18 February, shortly before the date the Brazilian letter of intent was to be approved by the IMF Executive Board, the Brazilian Government devalued the cruzeiro by 30 per cent and had to present a second letter of intent (dated 24

February) in order to adapt the targets to the new situation. A long period of instability was to follow the maxi-devaluation as the Government tried to convince asset holders that a second devaluation would not come and promoted a partial de-indexation of wages to avoid the neutralisation of the devaluation which occurred in 1980.

Heavy speculation against the cruzeiro during most of the year did not result in massive capital flight as in other countries, due to the existence of dollar-indexed government bonds and to the tradition of capital controls.[11] The effects on the rate of interest were, however, inevitable, and added strength to the recessive impact of the contractionary fiscal policy. In an attempt to reduce wage indexation, the Government proposed not less than four changes in the wage law, three of them turned down by Congress. Due to a special constitutional precept that allowed the Executive to legislate in economic and financial matters pending approval by Congress, the successive wage laws managed to reduce wage indexation during the year. The compound effect of accelerating inflation and partial de-indexation was that average real wages in the industrial sector were reduced by 14 per cent from 1982 to 1983.

The importance of de-indexation of wages in the negotiation between Brazilian authorities and the IMF cannot be inferred from any of the official documents exchanged, but may be deduced from the timing of concessions of waivers and the suspension of disbursements.[12] We may learn from this that implicit conditionalities may be more important than explicit ones. Throughout 1983, Brazil had met all the external targets, but this does not seem to have softened pressures to reduce wage indexation. On the other hand, insistence on reducing wage indexation, even against strong opposition in Congress, was part of an effort to curtail the wage bill of state companies as a way to control public spending.

By the end of 1983, following the rebound in world trade and stimulated by the real devaluation of the cruzeiro, Brazilian exports started to grow again. The gain in that year was a mere US $1.7 billion (8 per cent over the previous year) but sufficient to help meet the target for the trade balance, as imports fell by US $4.2 billion. Arrears of around US $2.3

billion arose due to difficulties in the capital account, since only half of the net capital inflow that had been estimated as part of the programme was observed.

In the fourth letter of intent submitted in the year (14 November) the domestic targets were somewhat softened by the removal of the monetary correction of the public debt from the nominal targets for PSBR. Real GDP fell by 3.2 per cent and industrial output by 5.5 per cent, the twelve-month rate of inflation went from 99.7 per cent in 1982 to 211 per cent in 1983 and the inflation-adjusted PSBR was reduced from 2.9 per cent to 0.1 per cent of GDP. Except for the doubling of the rate of inflation, which signalled the difficulties ahead in defining the strategy for 'domestic' adjustment, the programme had attained its main objectives and the rules of phase II could be designed.

Phase II of debt renegotiation looked easier to manage than phase I since the basic rules had become clear to most participants. The experience of the two previous year had proved 'successful' in the sense that no deepening of the crisis had been brought about by debtors' unilateral action, whereas leakages from the creditors' side had been kept down to a manageable size. For Brazil, a new round of the same game meant negotiations between a committee representing the eight hundred creditor banks and the Brazilian Government under the supervision of the IMF backed by the US Government. For 1984, negotiations would proceed on three fronts: the committee representing private creditors, the industrial governments that had backed the first round with special bridge loans and supported the maintenance of trade credit lines in official institutions, under the general heading of the 'Paris Club' and the multilateral agencies (especially the World Bank, the Interamerican Development Bank, and the IMF). The complexity of the negotiations may be evidenced by the basic content of the four 'projects' in their phase II edition:

(i) the so-called 'New Money Facility Agreement', by which a total of 792 private banks pledged to increase their exposure by a total of US $6.5 billion;

(ii) the 'Deposit Facility Agreement' according to which US $5.4 billion of repayments would be rolled over by 554

banks under the coordination of Citibank;
(iii) the 'Trade Facility Agreement' by which 231 banks pledged not to reduce trade credit lines totalling US $10.3 billion under coordination of Chase Manhattan Bank;
(iv) the 'Interbank Facility Agreement' in which Brazilian banks operating abroad would be guaranteed to have access to not less than US $6 billion in the interbank market, from 275 private banks under the coordination of Bankers Trust.

In the absence of an international lender of last resort to prevent private banks from withdrawing their credit when it was needed most, the private banking system backed by the chairmen of the Central Banks of most creditor countries had to perform a coordination task they were not prepared for amongst parties that were only abiding to the rules as long as they feared that a further deepening of the crisis would leave everyone worse off. Incentives to break the rules hinged, thus, on what happened in the environment, that is, on debtors' exports and on creditors' evaluation of the debtors' minimum financial requirement to stay afloat.

In 1984, for the first time since 1979, the external constraint on the Brazilian economy showed sings of softening. On 27 February 1984 a waiver was granted by the IMF board, motivated by the failure of banks to meet their targets in the previous year. Space was open for the definition of less restrictive domestic targets for the fifth letter of intent which was signed on 15 March. This letter was negotiated without any major disagreements between the Brazilian Government and the IMF.[13] On the other hand, improved trade surplus for the first quarter helped dampen speculation around a new devaluation. Manufactured exports responded to the upsurge of world trade, led by the US recovery; at the same time it stimulated demand in the industrial sector and, via inter-industry multiplier effects, in the remainder of the economy.

The recovery initiated in 1984 led to radical change of prospects as to the constraints under which the Brazilian economy would be operating in the following years. The Brazilian economy was seen as being able to grow its way out of the debt crisis. By the end of 1984, when Mexico was pointed to by many as a show case of adjustment and good behaviour, Brazil managed to exhibit a 4.5 per cent growth in its GDP with a record surplus in the trade balance of US $13.1 billion. It was able not only to pay its gigantic interest bill that absorbed almost 40 per cent of export revenues, but balance its current account. Most important of all, the recovery of world imports had been sufficient to show that the efforts made for structural adjustment since 1974 were paying dividends: in spite of a 7 per cent growth in industrial output, imports had declined by US $1.5 billion and the economy had reduced its import coefficient by almost 3 per cent of GDP since 1980. Finally, it should be noted that the improvement of the trade balance from a deficit of US $2.8 billion to a surplus of US $13.1 billion from 1980 to 1984 was obtained in spite of a loss of more than 10 per cent in terms of trade in the same period.

From the end of 1984 onwards the pattern of negotiations between Brazil and the IMF experienced a radical change. The last efforts to play the game by the same rules that had prevailed at the height of the debt crisis were made in January 1985, when the departing Government tried to have the seventh letter of intent approved by the IMF board as part of an effort to obtain a rescheduling of repayments similar to that agreed with Mexico. Failure to have the basic framework for stabilisation approved by the IMF, due to the realisation that domestic targets for the fourth quarter of 1984 had not been fulfilled, postponed the negotiations until after the new Government took over in March. Negotiations with the banks were suspended pending that the (new) Brazilian Government reached an agreement with the IMF.

Both the format and the conditions which presided over negotiations until December 1984 were taken as given by the Brazilian authorities, which limited themselves to trying to get as much finance from whatever source was available. In an emergency situation, the amounts negotiated were based on a strategy which were strictly necessary to keep the country afloat, based on the available estimates of the future behaviour of trade balance. This process was interrupted by the refusal by the IMF board of the seventh letter of intent presented by the Brazilian Government. From January 1985 onwards formal short-lived postponements of the phase II conditions took place every three months.

As the new economic team resumed contact with the creditors in the second quarter of 1985 the role of the IMF in the definition of the stabilisation efforts of the Brazilian economy was under general questioning, and there was no way the new Government could find internal political support for another letter of intent as the country's needs of foreign exchange had clearly declined as shown on Table 5.5.

Table 5.5:   Brazil: Structure of Imports (1979-85), US $ millions and %

Years	Consumption goods	Intermediate goods[1]	Oil	Capital goods	Total
1979	1786	12311	6264	3975	18072
(%)	(9.9)	(68.1)	(34.7)	(22.0)	(100.0)
1980	1387	16957	9372	4619	22943
(%)	(6.1)	(73.8)	(40.9)	(20.1)	(100.0)
1981	1106	16698	10604	4257	22061
(%)	(4.9)	(75.8)	(48.1)	(19.3)	(100.0)
1982	1014	14862	9566	3519	19295
(%)	(5.3)	(76.6)	(49.3)	(18.1)	(100.0)
1983	793	12130	7822	2505	15428
(%)	(5.2)	(78.6)	(50.1)	(16.2)	(100.0)
1984	695	11063	6736	2169	13927
(%)	(5.0)	(79.4)	(48.4)	(15.6)	(100.0)
1985	795	9878	5418	2494	13167
(%)	(6.1)	(75.0)	(41.2)	(18.9)	(100.0)

Notes: 1. Including oil
Sources: Relatorio da cacex
         Fundacao centro de estudids do comercio exterior

During most of 1985 the difficulties of reaching an agreement with the IMF were, thus, quite evident. On the one hand, the fact that Brazil would not be requiring new funds to balance its current account (although it had been transferring abroad more than 4 per cent of its GDP for the last two years) was used as the main agreement for not having to submit the new Government to a narrowing of its space for manoeuvre. On the other hand, bankers as well as governments of the creditor countries stuck to the view that IMF surveillance was an indispensable condition for a multi-year rescheduling. Finally, the IMF staff insisted that the apparent success of Brazilian external stabilisation would be short-lived if the Government did not decide to control public expenditure in order to reduce inflation.

The basic ingredients for a stalemate were, thus, defined. Since Brazil was not expected by the new Government to need new money either from private bankers or the IMF, it put itself in a more comfortable position of being able to make its own choice of domestic policies without stopping paying interest on the external debt. The major weakness of its position was of course due to the high rate of inflation: a 200 per cent annual rate which showed no signs of responding to demand controls. This high inflation had resulted from a long period of adjustment when the efforts at short-run stabilisation had conflicted with the need to carry on the investment projects. Structural and demand forces that fed the continuous spiral of wages and prices were periodically aggravated by the need to correct relative prices during the process of adjustment; the ability of potential losers to transfer at least part of their losses to the Government led the Brazilian public finances to a state of disarray. Most analysts of the Brazilian economy agreed that some kind of domestic adjustment was needed, especially as the country could no longer count on a net inflow of external resources and had to transfer abroad part of its savings.

Fiscal reform is certainly part of the effort which has to be made in order to adjust the domestic economy, and had it not been for the unfortunate experience of the country with the IMF agreement in 1983, IMF support could be seen as important not only to speed up internal reforms, but as a means to have access to additional finance in order to diminish the burden of debt service. After the 1983 experience, however, it turned out to be politically difficult to gather support for another round of restrictive measures under the surveillance of the IMF without need of more finance.[14]

In the first months of the Sarney Government the economic team was clearly divided between two courses of action: to proceed with economic growth as allowed by the availability of foreign exchange or to try yet another round of restrictive macro policies and abide by the Fund's rules. In September 1985 Dilson Funaro was nominated Minister of Finance, and most of the team at the Central Bank who were committed to the idea of applying a monetary shock to control inflation and submitting another stabilisation plan to the Fund were replaced by a team that favoured monetary reform and a de-indexation plan in order to stop inflation. Funaro is an entrepreneur with no formal background in economics and had been a harsh critic of Delfim Netto's policies. As soon as he moved from the presidency of the National Development Bank to the Ministry of Finance it became evident that he would have full support from President Sarney as well as from an important segment of the Sao Paulo industrialists, becoming responsible for the definition of economic policy. His views concerning the main issues that had been dividing the Government thus far were well known as he stated loud and clear his position that Brazil should follow 'its own way' towards domestic adjustment, that economic growth was an essential element for the credibility of any durable strategy for adjustment and that the Government would try to bring the banks back to negotiation without the intermediation of the IMF. The fact that Brazil was finishing its third year of recovery without any sign of deterioration in the current account helped to keep the banks in the game. After all, with so many big problems sprouting everywhere among the indebted nations Brazil was still one of the best available bets, was not claiming for further exposure and was paying the largest spread among the large debtors.[15]

Funaro's stance was kept virtually intact until late 1986. His idea that Brazil should follow its own way towards domestic adjustment led him to place all his bets on the Cruzado Plan of monetary reform based on a sudden de-indexation of the economy, followed by a price freeze at a time when inflation was heading towards a 300 per cent annual rate at the beginning of 1986. He drew on all his stock of credibility not only in gathering internal support for the stabilisation effort but also in trying to convince the banks, the governments of the creditor countries and the multilateral agencies that the chosen course of action was the only way by which sensible domestic adjustment may proceed. On the external front, he has managed to gain some support from the private banks which granted short-lived reschedulings of repayments.

Finding support from the US Government was particularly difficult. At the end of 1986 continuous negotiations were being conducted with the US on several issues, ranging from trade restrictions seen as detrimental to the efforts of the US to reduce its trade deficit to the fact that Brazil had not agreed to seek IMF support for its stabilisation programme. In January 1987, the Paris Club officially agreed to renegotiate the Brazilian debt based upon a mildly favourable IMF report prepared one month before the collapse of the Cruzado experiment. Whereas the relationship with the banks and with the IMF former Managing Director de Larosière has evolved towards a more pragmatic view that a mere favourable appreciation of the IMF in terms of article IV routine reports should be sufficient for a major agreement with creditor governments, it is clear that the many unsettled bilateral issues in the US/Brazil agenda were used to forestall negotiations with the banks.[16]

4. LESSONS AND CONCLUSIONS

Brazil cannot be considered as a typical case in the debt crisis for several reasons that range from the size of its economy and external debt to the pattern of structural adjustment followed since the second half of the seventies. However, the experience of the past years seems rich in interesting aspects that illustrate the difficulties involved in finding solutions to the Third World debt crisis. This section tries to summarise the lessons we may draw from the experience of 1982–5.

First, since no voluntary lending would be forthcoming in all likelihood in the following years, incentives to non-cooperative behaviour dominated the pay-offs both for debtors and for marginal lenders. Heavily committed lenders were the players whose highest immediate interest depended on cooperative behaviour since their most likely pay-off in case of non-cooperation would be bankruptcy. Therefore, finding ways to induce cooperative behaviour was the first task the larger banks and the governments of the industrialised nations set to themselves at the outstart. Formal, as well as informal, support of the chairman of the Federal Reserve System, Paul Volcker, and of the Managing Director of the IMF, de Lariosière, was, thus, of fundamental importance for the pattern of solutions that arose from the Mexican case as described by Gurria in this volume and Kraft (1984). Furthermore, the fact that a non-traumatic solution was found for Mexico was a sign to prevent potentially disruptive actions from other debtors. The system was thus successful in preventing debtors from forming a cartel and creditors to follow their instincts and act separately; this characteristic of the solution was important for the immediate outcome as well as to freeze the case-by-case approach as the norm.

The developments after 1983 also made clear, and this is underscored by the Brazilian experience, that growth is a *sine qua non* condition for the success of any strategy to enhance cooperation. Basically, one has to ensure that the sum of the game may be increased following cooperative behaviour, so that penalties for 'bad behaviour' are effective. One might say, that growth of the world economy 'protects the environment' in which cooperative behaviour can flourish.

The continuation of world economic growth after 1984 and the progress obtained from the reduction of nominal international interest rates, besides being crucial to prevent aggravation of the debt crisis at the international level, allowed for the increase of the relative independence of those countries, like Brazil, which may be able to grow while balancing their current accounts. World trade growth, however, has not been sufficient to promote a sound recovery of the trade balance of large debtors although it has been sufficient to reduce the need for foreign finance. The behaviour of export prices, however, both for primary goods exporters and for the new industrial exporters seems to be one crucial element behind the inability of the post–1983 recovery to significantly reduce debtors' financial needs.

The usefulness of IMF-sponsored programmes to stabilise the domestic economy has been challenged by the Brazilian Government on the basis of its 1982–5 experience.

Failure to recognise the extent and importance of the structural adjustment needed was a major deficiency in most reports that tried to derive prospects for the Brazilian balance of payments at the peak of the debt crisis; and the IMF was no exception to that. It is unlikely that IMF surveillance will actually help diminish the risk for private creditors in the next negotiation for debt rescheduling. However, on the basis of the recent Brazilian experience, local stabilisation experiments will probably have to be supported by a more convincing fiscal restraint before they are taken seriously by creditors.

We might as well say something about the lessons not drawn from the debt crisis. First, one tends to forget that the crisis was derived from the fact that private financial markets have not proven to be good providers of liquidity to solve balance of payments disequilibria, especially if there is no lender of last resort to prevent the system from shrinking when credit is most needed. Second, that IMF 'external' conditionality may be a good way to strengthen the political support for sensible policies to adjust one country when the remainder of the system is operating under normal conditions, but is certainly inadequate to solve global crisis. Third, that the linkages between domestic and external equilibrium conditions tend to be more complex than admitted by the IMF model of adjustment. Fourth, that the system of negotiations that emerged from the debt crisis failed to provide the appropriate incentives for cooperative behaviour from all parties involved in the game, as the present instability of world financial markets indicates. The solutions were perhaps too dependent on personal characteristics of the people involved in the crucial matters due to the lack of an appropriate set of rules for generating an acceptable solution.

The case-by-case approach may be said to have been useful at the start of the crisis, since no single institution was granted the power or the means to provide liquidity either for the illiquid banks or for the debt-ridden countries. Systemic balance requires, however, more than willingness to solve emergencies, especially when the definition of what constitutes an emergency seems to depend on whose banks are illiquid. Continuity of the same strategy after the emergency fades away seems inadequate if a stable environment for trade and finance is the minimum requirement for economic growth in the world economy.

5. CONFRONTATION: THE SOLUTION FOR THE STALEMATE

From early 1985 to the beginning of 1987, when the Brazilian Government suspended payment of interest to private bankers, Brazil evolved from the situation of an independent adjuster to what seems to be the most difficult problem in international finance. The size and composition of the Brazilian medium- and long-term external debt are shown on Table 5.6. The frustrations of the Cruzado programme in the wake of the sweeping victory of the Government party in the November elections prompted a radical change in the way that Brazilian officials dealt with the debt issue. The Brazilian moratorium, however, was not a strategic decision which stemmed from the independence granted by a comfortable and stable reserve position, but a move to prevent rapidly falling reserves from provoking import rationing.

Table 5.6:   *Brazil: Foreign debt and its composition, 1980–5 (US $ millions and %)*

	1980	1981	1982	1983	1984	1985
Loans from official agencies	6,968	7,477	8,007	9,178	12,316	14,639
%	(12.9)	(12.2)	(11.4)	(11.3)	(13.6)	(15.7)
Private sources	46,707	53,774	61,509	69,372	74,696	74,121
%	(86.7)	(87.6)	(87.6)	(85.3)	(82.0)	(79.4)
Consol. old pub. debt	4	3	2	2	1	1
Compensatory loans	–	–	544	2,648	3,968	4,452
%			(0.8)	(3.3)	(4.4)	(4.8)
Other	168	157	136	119	110	100
Total registered debt	53,847	61,411	70,198	81,319	91,091	93,313
%	(100)	(100)	(100)	(100)	(100)	(100)
Unregistered	NA	NA	13,067	10,313	8,674	7,704
Total debt			83,265	91,932	99,765	101,017

Source: Banco Central do Brasil, Relatorio, several issues.

At first sight, one could summarise the story as follows: Brazil has undergone structural adjustment reflected both by the level and the structure of its import requirements, as illustrated on Table 5.6. This adjustment was performed at a substantial internal cost (in terms of higher inflation, growing public sector disequilibria, and postponements of distributive policies for more than a decade). After structural adjustment on both the supply and demand sides was essentially finished, in the first years of the decade, the international financial crisis and the world recession were the main obstacles which prevented Brazil from growing. Although the country had no further need of net transfers of real resources from abroad, the absence of voluntary lending after August 1982 imposed the restriction that in order to finance the current account deficit, domestic policies had to be subjected to IMF approval.

Can we really say that there was anything like a consistent strategy for debt bargaining on the part of the Brazilian authorities up until 1987? A strategy requires a clear view of the most probable scenarios for the international economy. Which scenarios can we imagine were in the minds of the Brazilian policy-makers? During 1980–2 high interest rates were seen as a menace to long-run solvency, but on the other hand, the problem was not peculiar to the Brazilian economy. During this period, negotiation was only with private banks and the episode of 1980 suggested that a mere show of austerity was sufficient to keep bankers in the game.

After the interest shock in 1979–82 the costs of adjustment-cum-debt were raised by the fact that the interest burden was higher, and, therefore, limits for indebtedness without insolvency were narrower. With higher interest rates, liquidity problem could be turned into a solvency problem. As long as the domestic economy was adjusted to possibly lower rates of growth in order to reduce its real resource gap, a return of international interest rates to lower levels would restore solvency.

In the present circumstances, the multilateral institutions were not able to replace the role of private markets both for lack of financial capability and the pattern of conditionalities. This state of affairs is clearly inefficient and does not contribute to the restoration of a minimally acceptable international economic order. Furthermore, less than optimistic trade prospects and deteriorating terms of trade signal an aggravation of tensions between debtors and creditors.

The Brazilian moratorium may have been the first concrete sign of this aggravation, and the quick response of creditors in settling the issues which were pending in the negotiations of other Latin American countries in early 1987 may be read as meaning that the diplomacy of debt bargaining, tested during the Mexican episode may be once again returning to the main scene, with basically the same principles: isolate the 'problem case', be tolerant with the other cases so as to prevent collective action, and flag future rewards to good behaviour.

If the recent post–1982 experience repeats itself we may expect that the governments of the central nations will try to promote more growth to prevent a deterioration of the environment may lead to general disruptive behaviour. This time, however, the task of macro-economic coordination may prove to be more complex than in the recent past. In 1983, US-led recovery was sufficient to reverse the gloomy prospects for the largest debtors. In 1987, the common interests among the industrialised countries may be countermanded by the conflicts pertaining to the effects of a general rebound of the world economy on the US trade deficit. The risks of promoting the obvious solutions require a consensus on sharing responsibilities. Unfortunately, the pattern of the last recovery with respect to trade opportunities, relative prices and the recent US–Japan confrontation on the trade issues does not encourage optimism.

NOTES

1. For a description of the main issues of economic policy following the first oil crisis, see Carneiro (1986a).
2. In Table 5.1 basic macro-economic data are provided for the period.
3. In fact, at the time of the Mexican crisis there were clear signs of deterioration of the quality of Brazilian reserves, due to the fact that Brazilian banks operating abroad found increasing difficulties in refinancing their operations.
4. After the Toronto meeting the position of the Brazilian banks operating abroad deteriorated very rapidly. The liquidity position of the Brazilian monetary authorities had become dangerously dependent on the

possibility of such banks refinancing their operations in the local markets where they operated. According to the testimony of a former manager of the New York branch of BANESPA, to a Brazilian magazine (Veja, December 12, 1982), quoted by Fritsch (1985a): 'the next day, the market just wasn't there any more.'

5. The purpose of the targets and policies defined for the following year was to adjust the economy to a foreign exchange availability of US $14.1 billion. This total would be used to finance a projected debt repayment of US $7.3 billion.

6. Fritsch (1985a p.122). The same author calls attention to the difficulties in reaching an agreement with the banks even after the main policies to be followed by the Brazilian Government in the next year had been settled with the banks' committee and the IMF staff.

7. Portions of this section of the paper are based on Carneiro (1986a), with detailed tables containing data on the evolution of targets and actual performance of critical variables.

8. See Table 5.4 for the growth rate of world import volume.

9. The responsibility for the error is hard to establish, since those targets are usually established in the course of negotiations between local government and Fund officials. The consequences were that the Fund was in practical terms, requiring an estimated contraction of domestic credit by around one-third in the year.

10. Although pointed out by many analysts of the Brazilian scene at the time (for example Carneiro and Modiano 1983), the fact the impact of inflation on nominal value of interest payments on outstanding public debt was finally recognised by the IMF board during the discussion of the 1984 Israel article IV consultation, when some members of the board asked the staff to produce a study in order to change the Fund procedures.

11. Other reasons may help to explain the absence of significant capital flight in the Brazilian case when compared with other Latin American countries: among these the existence of a meaningful growth project which had bound a significant part of private capital to the immediate future of the country. The fantastic private gains during this period in the form of high risk premia and high interest on public debt, however, stand high among the reasons why a higher portion of this financial wealth did not go abroad after the crisis of 1982.

12. Only after the publication of Decree-law 2045, which was the third attempt to reduce wage indexation, was it possible to obtain a waiver concerning the non-fulfilment of clauses of the second letter, and thus have the third letter of intent (15 September) approved by the Board.

13. The reasons for this change in outlook came from two fronts. First, the repeated negotiations of the previous year evidenced the ex-post flexibility which could be expected from the Fund in case some of the targets proved to be unrealistic. Secondly, the criteria for the definition of public deficit targets which was adopted after the fourth letter in fact opened room for the growth of public spending, since for example a conversion of debt of a state company held by the Brazilian

Development Bank into equity held by the same agent allowed an increase in the total Federal borrowing requirement.

14. Since 1984, simulation exercises for the Brazilian current account for the following years projects feasible GDP growth paths of around 5 to 6 per cent per year, under not over-optimistic external conditions, without the need of new money from private creditors. Such exercises gave support for the Brazilian official position.

15. Since negotiations leading to the multi-year rescheduling aborted in the beginning of 1985, Brazil did not benefit from the reductions in spreads which was to come with rescheduling, and, thus, ended up paying $2\frac{1}{8}$ per cent over the prime on the non-rescheduled portion of the debt while on the rescheduled portion the spread was 1 and $\frac{1}{8}$ over the LIBOR.

16. The complexities of the present agenda for negotiations between Brazil and the US with special reference to trade are analysed by Abreu and Fritsch (1985).

REFERENCES

Abreu, M. de P. and Fritsch, W., 1985, 'Latin American and Caribbean countries in the world trade system: past problems and future prospects', Texto para discussao, Dept. of Economics, PUC–RJ, mimeo, Rio de Janeiro, September.

Axelrod, R., 1984, *The evolution of Cooperation*, New York: Basic Books.

Bacha, E., 1983, 'Vicissitudes of Recent Stabilisation Attempts in Brazil and the IMF Alternative', in J. Williamson (ed.), *IMF Conditionality*, Washington D.C. Institute for International Economics.

Carneiro, D. D., 1986a, 'Long run adjustment, debt crisis and the changing role of stabilisation policies in the Brazilian recent experience', Spanish translation published as chapter 3 in *Discussao no. 125*, Departmento de Economica da PUC–RJ, mimeo, Rio de Janeiro, February.

Carneiro, D. D. and Modiano, E., 1983, 'Inflacao e Controle do deficit publico: analise teorica e algumas simulacoes para a economia brasileira', Revista Brasileira de Economia, 4, Oct.-Dec.

――― 1986c, 'Perspectivas del Endeudamiento Externo Brasileno', in R. Ffrench-Davis and R. Feinberg, *Mas Alla de la Crisis de la Deuda*, CIEPLAN-Dialogo Interamericano, Santiago.

――― 1986d, 'Stabilisation policies and long-run adjustment: the Brazilian experience in the eighties', prepared for the UNU/ WIDER Project on Stabilisation and Adjustment Programmes and Policies, mimeo, Helsinki, August.

—— 1987, 'The Cruzado Experience: an untimely evaluation after ten months', presented in the Seminar on Recent Stabilisation Experiments in Latin America, FEDESARROLLO, Bogota, January.

Kraft, J., 1984, *The Mexican Rescue*, New York: The Group of Thirty.

Lago, L. C. do., 1982, 'A programacao de setor externo em 1983: uma breve analise critica', in P. Arida (ed.), Divida Externa, Recessao e Ajuste Estructural', Rio de Janeiro: Paz e Terra.

Marques, M. S. B., 1985, 'FMI a experiencia brasileira', first version, mimeo, FGV, Rio de Janeiro, 1985.

Fritsch, 1985, 'A crise cambial de 1982–83 no Brasil: origens e respostas', in C. A. Plastino e R. Bouzas (eds), A America Latina e a Crise Internacional, Rio de Janeiro: Instituto de Relacoes Internacionais, PUC–RJ, 1985.

6 Peru: The Foreign Debt and Heterodox Adjustment Policy under Alan Garcia

Oscar Ugarteche

INTRODUCTION

Peru's heterodox adjustment programme is the first to begin with a unilateral reduction of payments to international creditors. It is also the only country where heterodox policies have survived the vicissitudes of the international crisis as well as its own structural tensions which brought down the Cruzado and Austral Plans.

This article attempts to identify the structural problems of the Peruvian economy which contributed to its growing indebtedness and to introduce the political variables which explain the handling of loans during the seventies and first half of the eighties. The article will then go on to consider the adjustment policies carried out since July 1985 and their effects. The article will suggest why it was necessary for the Peruvian Government to take unilateral action regarding foreign loan decisions. Finally, the article will analyse the results of the model to date along with its vulnerable points.

BACKGROUND

Peru is no stranger to the problems surrounding the suspension of debt payments. Since Independence, Peru has had four periods when payments were suspended, following periods of fifteen to twenty years of debt contracting. Once payments have been suspended, there follows a similar length period with no foreign credit. The cycle begins again once the economies of the central countries begin to stagnate (Ugarteche, 1986). Why does Peru run into debt and how does its use of these funds lead to a recurring credit cycle ending in a suspension of payments? Circumstances and eras change, but in general it is because foreign savings are obtained as credit only in periods when there is an excess of funds contrasting with the surpluses in industrial economies (Ugarteche, 1986). These periods run from 1822–5, 1853–73, 1908–30, with a hiatus during World War One, and finally 1964–81.

The debt process is like this: the Peruvian Government realises that foreign finance is available for loans; it then evaluates the country's needs for infrastructure or military equipment in order to ensure stability within the armed forces. Neither of these generate or save foreign exchange in the short term, leading instead to a greater need for larger loans in order to finance the balance of payments. At this stage, any fluctuation in the international price of raw materials or limitation of access to international credit may bring about a balance of payments crisis. As paying back the loans becomes increasingly difficult, debt hiring for loan repayment increases, leading eventually in the context already described, to a suspension of payments after three years.

This *credit cycle* begins with an excess of credit supply and ends when the prices of raw materials drop, international interest rates rise and the net transfer of funds becomes negative for the country, as an effect of the international crisis.

THE DEBT PROCESS DURING THE 1964–84 PERIOD

Peru re-entered the private capital world market in 1964 after thirty-three years without access to it. It came back onto the market because it needed to cover a slight external sector deficit, which had been covered since the fifties by limited US Government loans. Faced with the threat of the nationalisation of IPC, Standard Oil's Peruvian subsidiary, the US Government retaliated by cutting off loans from AID and later from multilateral organisations. So, Peru initially borrowed in order to cover the balance of payments deficit of US $40 million in 1964 and later fell into further debt in order to fund infrastructure projects which were part of import-substituting industrialisation policy. The saving/investment gap was around 0.3 per cent of GDP on average, between 1965 and 1968. (See Table 6.1.) Peru had difficulty paying creditor banks in 1967—this was aggravated in the same year when the Air Force decided to renew its equipment. As the US Government objected to making loans for aeroplanes, the Air Force brought Mirage aircraft with a French Government loan from the Finance Ministry and Manuel Moreyra at the Central Bank decided to implement a programme of orthodox adjustment. From the end of 1976, foreign banks restricted their loans; disbursements dropped from US $260 million to US $32 million in 1977. International organisations granted US $38 million in 1976 and US $79 million in 1977. Most of Peru's loans were from the socialist bloc countries and from Western Europe and were tied to weapons.

The orthodox adjustment programme was an attempt to balance the economy and regain access to loans. Renegotiations in 1978 covered US $1,327 million falling due between 1978 and 1981, of which US $780 million was with foreign banks, US $211 million with official Western creditors and US $336 million with socialist countries (Banco Central de Reserva, 1985, graph 32).

There was a slight upswing in credit in 1979 and 1980 but substantial growth took place in 1981 once General Morales Bermudez had left office and a civilian Government had taken over. The NRT with banks was negative between 1977 and 1981. The multilateral organisations did not react either to the adjustment programme, and a substantial positive NRT only appeared from 1980 onwards. The agencies and governments and socialist countries had positive flows and from 1980 the socialist countries began to experience negative NRTs.

The orthodox adjustment in 1978 coincided with an increase in the price of silver and oil in 1979. This meant that income from goods and services exports rose, and the foreign exchange and goods markets were opened up. This resulted in bankruptcies of local manufacturing industry and an increase in unemployment.

The social effects of the 1978 adjustment were felt immediately; the proportion of workers with adequate employment fell from 46 per cent of the workforce to 41.5 per cent between 1977 and 1978 and the rate of underemployment increased from 48.2 per cent of the workforce to 52 per cent over the same period. Unemployment began to increase from 5 per cent in 1978 to 6.5 per cent in 1979 and to 7.1 per cent in 1980. Salaries fell from 46.3 per cent of GDP in 1977 to 42.5 per cent in 1978 and 35.8 per cent in 1979.

A further stand-by agreement was signed in August 1979 so that adjustment policies could be maintained under the pretext of the IMF and in order to continue trying to regain access to credit. The social consequences were catastrophic, as we shall see below (see Figueroa, 1987). It is at this time that Sendero Luminoso took shape and began guerilla activity in the area around Ayacucho (see De Gregori, 1986).

ADJUSTMENT POLICIES AND DEBT IN THE '80s

Four agreements were signed with the IMF between 1978 and 1984. These agreements were: the September 1978 stand-by agreement; the August 1979 stand-by agreement; the extended fund facility agreement, signed in June 1982; and a further stand-by signed in April 1984. (For further details see Thomas Scheetz, 1986.)

The 1978 and 1979 agreements gave the new Government space to open up the economy. Although social conditions in the country had reached a critical pitch, external sector indicators were positive and the major imbalances almost closed, domestic savings increased, and net foreign reserves grew. The fiscal deficit fell from 10 per cent to 5 per cent of GDP during those two years.

The new Government, however, decided to continue opening up the economy, pursuing neo-liberal policies, although not as aggressively as those in Chile or Argentina. Public investment totalled 9 per cent during the 1981–4 period, the highest level for twenty-five years. Loans were obtained totalling current US $3,025 million between 1981 and 1984, more than in any other period studied (Ugarteche, 1986). Of these 23 per cent were for defence, another 23 per cent for hydroelectric projects and road construction, and 18 per cent for debt refinancing. While direct investment in the manufacturing sector absorbed one-quarter of the debt increase from 1970–5, during the 1981–4 period this had fallen to barely 12 per cent. The Peruvian state, therefore, invested massive sums, not in projects which offered direct results, but rather in infrastructure.

The foolhardiness of applying free market economic policies in an adverse international context was one of the factors that led to a crisis shortly after Belaunde came to power. The net resource transfer during the first three years of his Government was negative as a whole, and the cost of the 1978 refinancing together with short-term loans choked the balance of payments. Exports of goods dropped from US $3,916 million in 1980 to US $3,147 million in 1984. Imports of goods totalled US $3,090 million in 1980, rising as an effect of the opening-up of the economy to US $3,802 million in 1981.

The opening up of the economy was explosive in the short-term, given the critical international context. The Belaunde Government's economic policy was, therefore, catastrophic and had to fall back on the IMF in 1982. The adjustment measures were as follows:

— An austerity plan for public sector expenditure.
— Eliminate subsidies for mass consumer products.
— To allow for wage increases below inflation and with lags.
— To restructure the State's entrepreneurial role by privatising companies.
— To maintain a flexible exchange rate policy implying a constant process of mini-devaluations. Set limits for net losses of foreign reserves.
— To open up foreign trade significantly by lowering tariffs, lifting existing import restrictions on some articles and making it impossible to impose exchange controls or trade restrictions.
— To limit the increase in net domestic assets of the Central Bank mainly in order to put a break on expansion and domestic credit to the Treasury.
— To control the money supply and establish tendentially real interest rates.

— To cut back on new public sector foreign borrowing (Figueroa, 1987).

The impact of this set of measures in 1982 led to a 12 per cent drop in GDP in 1983; imports of goods fell by US $1,000 million between 1982 and 1983 to US $2,722 million; private sector investment fell from 9.7 per cent of GDP in 1982 to 6.8 per cent in 1983 and 6.1 per cent in 1984. The impact on employment was seen in the increase in underemployment from 49.9 per cent of the workforce to 53.3 per cent between 1982 and 1983.

Given the nature of the international crisis, the balance of payments continued to deteriorate in spite of these adjustment measures and the management of public expenditure became centred on foreign debt payments. Inflation, fuelled by the pegging of public sector services and utility rates to the dollar, became more acute.

This provoked a new bout of adjustment by means of a new agreement with the IMF in 1984. This agreement, however, had already been broken when it was signed in April because of the size of the fiscal deficit, generated to a great extent by the servicing of the foreign debt. Social pressures prevented the application of further salary reductions while, at the same time, inflation was increasing dramatically. At this time, Belaunde's Government decided to suspend all payments to the banks and began the transfer to Alan Garcia's Government.

SOCIAL EFFECTS

The most visible result of adjustment policies and quasi neo-liberal handling of the economy between 1980 and 1982 was the shift of the share of income accruing to labour (wages) to income accruing to capital. In 1975, 73.7 per cent of national income consisted of wages and the earnings of the self-employed while 26.3 per cent was profits, income from real estate and interest. In 1978, following the first adjustment, 67.3 per cent was payment for work and 32.7 per cent income accruing to capital. In 1984, wage income totalled 58.7 per cent of national income while 41.3 per cent was for capital. This shows how there was a concentration of income in the capitalist sectors.

The role of the State took a new turn as it began to reduce the level of social expenditure in the budget. In 1976, 23.5 per cent of public sector expenditure was used in the health, education, housing and work sectors. In 1984, social expenditure was 16.4 per cent of total fiscal outgoings. Public expenditure on education in constant intis, taking 1977 as the base year (100), dropped to seventy-six in 1979 and sixty-one in 1984. It went from an average 17 per cent of the central government budget between 1970–7 to 11.5 per cent on average between 1978 and 1984. This implied an alarming drop in educational services.

Basic food subsidies, another key factor in economic policy during the seventies were drastically cut back from 1977 onwards. These would have mitigated the effects of the crisis as far as income and employment were concerned. Economic policy, therefore, not only prevented better income distribution but also restricted the role of the State as a redistribution agent. The result was a further deterioration in the nation's nutritional levels. In 1985 food consumption per inhabitant was 26 per cent lower than the already low levels ten years earlier (Figueroa, 1987, p. 45):

One study on food and nutrition carried out in the southern Sierra by AID evaluates the changes in nutritional levels between 1980 and 1983 for children from birth to six years.

Nutritional levels	% of children 1980	% of children 1983
Normal	58.4	32.0
Undernourished	41.6	68.0

(Source: Figueroa, 1987, p 32.)

The effect on the population's health was visible in that deaths from tuberculosis, for example, increased from 17.6 per 100,000 inhabitants in 1977 to 25.8 per 100,000 in 1980, the last year for which information is available. The effects of the crisis and of the adjustment policies were visible as soon as the policies were applied. The effect of the adjustment policies on income distribution has been varied. The greatest contraction was felt in more modern, basically urban sectors, while the handling of the state budget has had a less prejudicial effect relatively on rural areas. This implies that the quality of life of the urban population is nearing that of rural inhabitants, and descending towards levels at which social tensions become more acute.

Social services supplied by the State not only were reduced in scope but also substantially in quality during the years of crisis and adjustment. It was against this background that Sendero Luminoso made its first appearance and began to operate in the most depressed areas of the countryside, where the indicators were even more severe than average and where despair had become a way of life from which death alone offered the only escape.

It is appropriate to point out here that as the quality of life deteriorated and Sendero Luminoso acted almost freely in the poorer areas of the countryside, violence became widespread and the drug trade increased. The drug trade became central to the running of the country's economy with the Banco Central registering purchases from 1984 onwards of US $800 million of foreign exchange placed in circulation annually by drug traffickers. In other words, Peru's income from drug traffickers in 1986 was equivalent to 30 per cent of goods exported as registered in the balance of payments, and it, therefore, played a financial role in the running of the economy.

In 1985, Peru's infant mortality rate stood at 92.7 per 1,000; 44 per cent of children under six suffered some degree of malnutrition: unemployment stood at 11 per cent, while 55 per cent of the economically active population was under-employed.

As far as the economy was concerned, inflation for the year was projected to reach 250 per cent and exports of goods dropped to US $2,978 million, 24 per cent less than in 1980. Debt arrears amounted to US $2,000 million.

THE PERUVIAN SCHEME

Peru's new Government came to power on 28 July 1985 and faced with the economic conditions described above, set out to reform economic policy by first attempting to restrain inflation with all its negative redistributive effects and second by reactivating the economy. The Government's main efforts during the first year were to bring inflation under control and take measures to redistribute income in order to improve the situation of the poorest. In order to do this it started from the premise that too high a percentage of GDP was leaving the economy in order to service the foreign debt. This was why it was decided that, before taking any other steps, medium- and long-term public debt servicing should be limited to 10 per cent of exported goods.This would have two advantages: it would release budgetary funds with which to set up public projects and secondly, it would release more foreign exchange for imports.

Inflation was deemed to have been caused by three main factors: devaluing more than the rate of inflation, thereby refuelling it in a spiralling process; the way interest rates were handled in such a way that they led to increased production costs; and restrictions on wages which hit the domestic market. The prices of public services and goods produced by state companies were pegged to the price of the dollar, devaluation costs were reflected in their prices. This was most evident in the price of gasoline which has repercussions on the prices of all other goods.

The following measures were enacted in August 1985:

a)   Interest rates were reduced from 240 per cent to 45 per cent and later to 40 per cent.

b)   The price of the dollar was devalued by 40 per cent and frozen, creating two markets: the *Mercado Unico de Cambrios* (MUC) rate was 13.90 intis per dollar while the *Mercado Financiero* rate (financial market) was pegged at I/. 17.30. The MUC rate was used for importing basic goods while the financial market rate applies to all other imports.

c)   Energy costs—electricity and oil were de-dollarised.

d)   The minimum legal wage was increased by 50 per cent and later in January 1986 by another 50 per cent in an attempt to re-establish the purchasing power of the poorest sectors of society.

e) Consumer tax was reduced.
f) The policy on prices during the first stage was a selective 'freezing' of a basket of basic consumer goods.

Alongside these measures during the first year there were others to encourage agricultural production and income redistribution for marginal urban sectors:

a) PAIT (*Programa de Apoyo al Ingreso Temporal*— Temporary Employment Programme) was set up in order to create 150,000 three-month jobs in marginal urban areas.
b) Credit mechanisms were set up to support the informal sector with loans to small craftsmen with semi-official guarantees.
c) Interest-free agricultural credit for the Andean Trapezium (a trapezium-shaped group of poverty-stricken provinces in the southern central Sierra), one of the most depressed areas in Peru.
d) Special funds for boosting agriculture, livestock, fishing and small businesses.
e) Protection for Peruvian industry through tariff policy and the use of prior import licences plus bans on the entry of certain luxury and capital goods.

The effect of these measures on the economy was almost instantaneous and there was a substantial drop in the rate of inflation. The Central Bank's calculation for inflation over the first six months of 1985 was for an annual figure of 250 per cent. However, at the end of the year the rate stood at 150 per cent (INP, 1987a). The monthly inflation rate according to the Consumer Price Index dropped from an average monthly rate of 11.4 per cent from January to July to a monthly average of 4.4 per cent. This level was maintained throughout 1986, ending the year with an accumulated inflation rate of 63 per cent (INP, 1987a).

THE 10 PER CENT POLICY AND ITS PROBLEMS

At first the President's speech envisaged suspending debt servicing payments which exceeded 10 per cent of exports. In order to be able to carry out these policies, like the rest of the economic policy, it was necessary that there be a distancing from the IMF. The President's speech in this sense was extremely radical and questioned the institution as such.

However, once it was decided that no help would be sought from the Fund and that a maximum 10 per cent of exports would be paid, the question remained: to whom? How to go about selecting the creditors who would be paid? The answer which emerged was that payments would be made based on the criterion that net transfers of resources should be positive. (Author's interviews with different members of the economic team, Lima, 1987.) This, obviously, would mean limits on strategic creditors such as the socialist block countries. Peru's relationship with these countries is strategic because a large part of the fleet of aircraft and tanks belonging to the Air Force and the Army are supplied by these countries, and the maintenance of this equipment to a large extent depends on the regularity of payments. For this reason it was decided that payments to these countries should be over and above the 10 per cent. According to the agreement signed in 1984 by the previous Government these payments were to be made in kind up to a total of US $343.7 million. Of this, US $45.5 million was paid in 1984, US $162.3 million in 1985 and US $110.9 million in 1986. US $25 million is still to be paid in order to complete the terms of this agreement.

Initially, the agreement involved the socialist block countries purchasing one dollar's worth of goods for every dollar paid back in debt servicing. During negotiations held in March 1987, the Peruvian Government is attempting to reach an agreement of two for one. That is, for each dollar paid out, the countries agree to buy two dollars' worth of Peruvian goods. At the time of writing this article, the negotiations had come to a standstill.

Nor is the debt to the IMF included in the 10 per cent. However, faced with payments totalling US $180 million falling due in 1986, the Peruvian Government had problems meeting obligations without substantially affecting the level of net reserves. For this reason it indicated to the Fund its willingness to negotiate a payment schedule for the US $645 million still due between 1986 and 1988. The Fund was unwilling to negotiate and so Peru made two payments, each of US $35 million as a demonstration of good faith, one in March and the other in August 1986, and then suspended further payments. The IMF then declared Peru ineligible for further loans and the relationship between Peru and the IMF broke down (Interviews, Central Bank, Lima, 1987).

Relations with foreign banks deteriorated similarly from 1984 onwards when the previous Government restricted debt payments. Debt in arrears to banks amounted to US $1,330 million up to December 1984. Unilateral roll-overs during 1985 caused further antagonism. At the end of 1986 there was an attempt to renegotiate the foreign debt over twenty years with ten years grace and 3 per cent interest, including in the total all the interest and payments which had fallen due and not been paid since 1984. This did not satisfy the banks and payments were suspended. However, this unilateral action on the part of the Peruvian Government was based on its absolute conviction that in order to be able to pay, in the medium-term, even a small portion of the service payments due as part of a very long-term renegotiation scheme, the domestic economy would have to be reactivated first.

The fiscal and foreign exchange saving achieved by reducing debt servicing made it possible to implement a scheme for economic reactivation as from mid-1986.

There has been a call lately for a scheme to swap foreign debt paper for new investment. This would be a scheme similar to those in Chile or Mexico, but would not involve swapping debt for already existing equity. The idea is rather to encourage the foreign or national investor to expand existing investments or create new ones by allowing him to use debt paper bought at a discount in the secondary market. Presented for payment in Peru, this document is then reconverted into national currency at a premium depending on the origin of the debt and the purpose of the investment. The Debt Council is still discussing this scheme.

There is also to be an attempt to open Debt Council offices

in Paris and Washington in order to keep track of creditors and to keep them informed of the progress of the Peruvian economy with a view to reaching some agreement in due course. The Paris office would deal with the West European and socialist block creditors while the Washington office would deal with those in the United States and the Pacific.

Total debt payments in 1985 amounted, all told, to US $1,080 million or 36 per cent of exports of goods, falling in 1986 to US $769 million or 30.6 per cent of exports of goods (Central Bank information).

US $142.5 million were paid out during the first quarter of 1987, comprising payments included in the 10 per cent and those which were not. Those that are included in the 10 per cent are defined as: those to international organisations such as IDB, IBRD, IFAD and now the IMF; food loans under the US government's PL 480 programme; payments to OECD governments and private foreign banks, as well as government-guaranteed suppliers. Those not included in—that is, over and above—the 10 per cent are: the Andean Development Corporation (CAF) and the Andean Reserve Fund; ALADI's compensatory loans; payments in kind to socialist countries, and some non-guaranteed suppliers. A total of US $142.5 million was paid out in the first three months, US $61.5 million of which was included in the 10 per cent and US $65 million which was not. This sum represents 22 per cent of quarterly exports which totalled US $643 million (BCR, 1987a).

The problems caused to the balance of payments by debt repayments were not limited to the public sector debt. Once it was clear in July 1986 that an adequate level of foreign reserves could not be sustained if private sector debt payments continued, the 10 per cent was expanded to include it also. Moreover, in July 1986, the remission of profits abroad was prohibited, since these were running at a rate of US $450 million a year. The transnational companies are getting round this. The balance of payments tables show profit remittances of mining and oil companies falling substantially in 1986 from a monthly average of US $31 million in 1985 to an average of US $6.5 million after the measures were announced. However, the 'other private services' item increased from US $3 million per month in 1985 to an average US $30 million per month in

1986. In other words, what previously left the country as the transnationals' profits now goes out in the guise of service payments abroad (BCR, 1987a).

THE PERUVIAN PLAN—MARK 2

The measures taken in August 1985 were aimed at restraining inflation and bringing about an improvement in the standard of living of the poorest sectors of the population. Once inflation had been reduced and income redistribution begun, the model continues on the strength of the reactivation of the productive apparatus. The most delicate parts of the anti-inflationary struggle are the supply bottlenecks occurring as demand is reactivated. The economic recovery which began at the end of 1985 was considered precarious unless investment picked up in 1986. There was 60 per cent installed industrial capacity which could be reactivated without needing large investments. Once full capacity is reached, growth with low inflation can only be maintained by expanding that installed capacity. Only recently, in mid-1986, were measures taken to tackle this problem.

Prices were unfrozen, and talks began with industrialists about prices compatible with the anti-inflationary programme. However, some basic prices remained frozen. Interest rates were kept negative and fixed in order to promote investment. The National Investment Council was set up to supervise investments and channel activity towards the area where it was most needed.

The most important factor preventing an increase in the rate of investment is foreign exchange. In a situation where the trade balance is in the red and the service account also, with zero net transfer of resources, any reactivation of investment with imported technology creates an acute imbalance in the balance of payments.

Conversely, if there is no increase in the rate of investment the pressures of demand are up against a rigid supply structure that will fuel inflation. As we can see, foreign exchange constraints on the one hand, and inflation on the other, leave little room for manoeuvre.

Towards the end of 1986 the recovery of real salary levels reached its peak and a series of additional economic measures became necessary to enable the reactivation of the economy to continue without inflation or the balance of payments veering out of control.

The latest series of measures was announced at the beginning of April 1987. According to the officials who designed them, the main aims are as follows:

Economic policy during the present year should be aimed at sustaining economic growth by maintaining reasonable inflation levels in order to continue a redistribution of income. Complementary measures should be aimed at promoting investments which make it possible for the economy to continue to grow and to transform the productive structure. It should also be aimed at limiting inflationary pressure and the loss of international reserves as well as at restraining any regressive tendency in the redistribution of income ... (INP, 1987b)

In order to do this, a wage increase was granted which for the first time since the new economic policy had been applied failed to match the loss in purchasing power:

Various incentives have been designed to stimulate investment. The National Investment and Employment Fund was set up to encourage the repatriation of capital and its investment in priority activities. A compulsory element has also been incorporated in order to stimulate investment by means of Public Treasury Investment Bonds. Companies which do not invest excess funds in the National Investment and Employment Fund are therefore obliged to buy Treasury Bonds.

Two important measures have been taken in the external sector. These have been designed to speed up tax rebate payments to exporters of non-traditional goods. The foreign exchange licence system was set up to deal with service payments abroad. A foreign exchange budget has been drawn up for importing goods from abroad to ensure that companies only import what they need for production and to prevent the accumulation of stocks. It also makes it possible for imports to be rationalised.

Finally, it was also decided that shares should be sold in public companies in order to reduce the pressure of the State in some economic activities, but without removing its presence altogether.

AN EVALUATION OF ECONOMIC DEVELOPMENTS

There have unquestionably been great achievements following the application of the new economic policy, raising the question of whether it is possible to keep them up for long. One achievement has been the recuperation in GDP which expanded by 9.1 per cent in 1986. So far, in 1987 there was a contraction of the economy in January and a slight slowing down in February (MEF, 1987a). A hopeful sign has been the 18.2 per cent increase in investment during 1986. This could be a sign that reactivation can be sustained if these investments mature during 1987.

Another major success was the fall in the rate of inflation which ended 1986 at 62.9 per cent, less than half of the rate during 1985. However, there was an increase in the monthly rate of inflation from the average 4.4 per cent per month in 1986 to 6.6 per cent in January and 5.6 per cent in February 1987.

It is interesting to note that as from January 1986 there was a reversal of rural–urban terms of trade which have traditionally been biased against the countryside. There has been a substantial redistribution of income from the city to the countryside which has been reinforced by increased prices for agricultural products while the prices of industrial products have remained either regulated or frozen. Employment in the industrial sector increased rapidly.

The economic policy's essential achievement—the improvement in demand as a whole by means of a redistribution of income—has been reflected in wages. Taking July 1985 as the base (100), workers in the private sector had experienced an improvement to 118 by December 1985, 140 by November 1986 and then a drop to 133 by February 1987. Of these, workers in unionised firms had greater increases and smaller drops than non-unionised firms.

The minimum legal wage went through the same process, increasing until October 1986 and dropping subsequently. It may have been this deterioration in wage levels which lay behind the general strike on 19 May. In 1985, the top 10 per cent of income earners earned 59 per cent of national income, but in 1986 this had dropped to 55 per cent. This income was redistributed to peasant farmers, the informal sector and wage-earners (INP, 1987a). According to the National Planning Institute, rural sector wages picked up by 30 per cent during 1986 and this is reflected in greater food consumption by those social strata.

The external sector is the model's most obvious Achilles heel. Traditional FOB exports fell in 1986, particularly because of the drop in oil prices, from US $2,247 million in 1985 to US $1,861 million in 1986. Non-traditional exports also dropped, especially agricultural and fishery products, because of the improvement in the population's feeding levels.

Imports, however, increased from US $1,869 million in 1985 to US $2,523 million in 1986, basically because of increased imports of consumer goods and inputs. Foods imports increased by US $162 million from one year to the other. Industrial recovery had an even greater impact on imports of raw materials and intermediate goods which leapt by more than US $400 million in 1986.

International reserves fell as a result of the trade deficit and of service payments abroad, thereby putting pressure on the unregulated free market exchange rate. A system of mini-devaluations of 2.2 per cent per month was begun in January 1987 in both the MUC and Financial markets.

Peru's foreign reserves should be understood not as net foreign reserves but including liabilities to the IMF once it was decided that these would not be paid for the time being. Thus, Peru's international reserves dropped US $469 million in 1986, but so-called net disposable reserves fell US $394 million. Disposable reserves amounted to US $1,535 million at 15 March 1987 *decreasing by US $100 million per month*. This level of reserves would cover six months of imports at present levels and a further year of falling reserves without the model collapsing.

The gap between saving-investment as a percentage of GDP was 4.2 per cent during 1986, mainly due to a sudden drop in savings from 14.3 per cent of GDP in 1985 to 10 per cent in 1986. This doubtless reflects increased consumption levels but also presents a problem regarding the funds that would be necessary to make the necessary investments. Given that there are practically no foreign loans being contracted, this might suggest that sufficient funds may not be available to invest.

On the fiscal side, in 1986 central Government income was 12.9 per cent of GDP, while total outgoings are 18.8 per cent of GDP, leaving a fiscal deficit of 5.9 per cent of GDP uncovered. (MEF, 1987a pp. 60 and 62). These figures, however, do not include public company deficits, which amounted to another two points of GDP during 1986. In other words, the total deficit was around 8.0 per cent of GDP.

The complications of the Peruvian Plan were made clear in April 1987, when the rate of exchange in the free market went from twenty to twenty-five intis per dollar. The uncertainty created by the heterodox policies and Presidential speeches has led investors into quick profit-taking rather than into investing. The schemes introduced to foster investment centre on increasing the profit rate through subsidies to decentralisation to exports and to the production of basic goods (exchange and interest rates). Given the lack of fresh investment an Employment and Investment Fund was designed that should have increased the profit margins by 50 per cent as the Government would put up one inti for each inti invested and income would be tax free for the investor.

This scheme was toppled when, two weeks after its introduction in April, a forced savings mechanism was introduced through Treasury Bonds at 8 per cent. It was made clear that economic policy was not in the hands of one group but of conflicting groups in the Government.

The Prime Minister, and also Finance Minister, resigned after this and other events occurred, such as a Police Strike and a General Strike organised by the CGTP, the largest confederation of trade unions, in mid–May 1987. The President did not accept the resignation of the Prime Minister making the level of uncertainty even worse in face of which investors started moving funds from the Stock Exchange and Inti savings accounts into dollars.

During July, as a response to the Ministerial crisis and as a way of relieving uncertainty, the President announced a new economic package centred on the same heterodox elements, including wage rises of between 25 per cent and 45 per cent creating an instant improvement in demand levels. Simultaneously, deposit rates were reduced from 40 per cent to 20 per cent and lending rates were reduced from 45 per cent to 32 per cent. The result was that the free market dollar rate shot up again, there being a 100 per cent devaluation between April and July 1987.

Table 6.1:   *Peru: The public foreign debt in the accumulation of capital process (as % of GDP)*

	1965/68	1970/73	1974/77	1978/81	1982/84
Public sector investment	4.6	5.1	7.9	6.7	9.0
+ Private sector investment	10.7	7.8	8.3	8.4	7.5
= Total investment	15.3	12.9	16.2	15.1	16.5
– Domestic saving	15.0	14.7	9.7	16.2	13.4
= gap	-0.3	+1.6	-6.5	+0.9	-3.1

Notes: *Defined as net transfer of funds. Payments less repayments plus interest. Includes only public medium and long term debt.
– Means negative.
Source: Central Bank

Table 6.2:   *Peru: Distribution of national income (%)*

	1970	1975	1978	1981	1984
Wages and salaries	46.7	48.3	42.5	39.7	33.9
Independents	27.4	25.4	24.8	25.9	24.8
Income from property	4.5	3.7	2.8	2.2	2.4
Profits	19.8	21.5	28.6	29.7	35.9
Net Interest	1.6	1.1	1.3	2.5	3.0
TOTAL	100	100	100	100	100

Table 6.3:   *Employment structure (%)*

	1970	1975	1978	1981	1984
Employed	49.4	52.7	41.5	45.3	34.8
Underemployed	45.9	42.4	52.0	47.9	54.2
Unemployed	4.7	4.9	6.5	6.0	10.9
TOTAL WORKFORCE	100	100	100	100	100

Table 6.4:   Foreign public debt by creditor (in millions of US dollars)

	1970	1975	1981	1985*	1986*
Agencies & governments	244	825	1,346	1,795	1,930
International banks	135	1,320	1,524	3,110	3,262
International organisations	172	259	784	1,426	1,529
Socialist countries	0	263	930	1,026	986
Suppliers	394	399	1,543	3,107	3,333
TOTAL	945	3,066	6,127	10,462	11,048

Note: *preliminary
Source: Central Bank

Table 6.5:   Balance of payments (in millions of dollars)

	1978	1981	1984*	1985*	1986*
Exports	1,972	3,249	3,147	2,978	2,509
Imports	1,668	3,802	2,140	1,806	2,525
Trade balance	304	-553	1,007	1,172	-16
Financial services	-646	-1,019	-1,165	-1,011	-831
Non-financial services	48	-318	-221	-170	-304
Current account balance	-164	-1,729	-221	125	-1,055
Long-term capital	444	565	1,089	691	603
Short-term capital and errors and ommissions	-204	660	-721	-536	7
Balance of payments	76	-504	247	280	-459

Note: *preliminary
Source: Central Bank

Table 6.6:   *Public foreign debt payments—short, medium and long term (in million of dollars)*

	1984	1985	1986	1987*
Paying falling due	2,275	2,067	2,059	n.d.
Principal	1,441	1,329	1,453	n.d.
Interest	834	738	606	n.d.
Payments made	590	390	259	142.6
Principal	307	273	154	87.9
Interest	283	117	105	54.7
Payments against earlier maturities	73	227	236	n.d.
Principal	26	74	120	n.d.
Interest	47	153	116	n.d.
Central Bank and Private debt payments	602	463	274	n.d.
Principal	332	282	189	n.d.
Interest	260	181	85	n.d.
TOTAL	1,269	1,080	769	142.6
Arrears	1,308	1,249	1,564	n.d.

Note: *1st quarter 1987.
Source: Central Bank

Table 6.7:   *Saving/investment*

	Domestic Saving /GDP	Investment/GDP	Difference/GDP
1984	14.6	16.1	-1.5
1985	14.3	13.8	0.7
1986	10.0	14.2	-4.2

Source: Central Bank

Table 6.8: Real wages index (July 1985 = 100)

	Private sector	Govern- ment	Minimum income	Total
1985				
July	100	100	100	100
December	118	97	120	97
1986				
July	126	122	116	122
October	140	141	133	141
December	139	130	123	130
1987				
January	135	123	115	123
February	133	117	109	117

Source: MRF, 1987a, p. 52

REFERENCES

Alvarez, Elena, 1980, *Politica Agraria y Estancamiento en la Agricultura, 1969/1977*, IEP, Lima.

Aprodeh, 1986, Datos Estadisticos, diciembre, 1986.

Banco Central de Reserva del Perú, 1985, *Compendio Estadistico del Sector Externo, Lima.*

———, 1987a, *Nota Semanal No. 15*, Gerencia de Investigación Económica, impreso, BCR, Lima, 16 de abril, 1987.

———, 1987b, 'Información Estadistica de la Memoria 1986' especially prepared by messres Jorge Cortés y Elizabeth Merino.

Degregori, Carlos Ivan, 1986, *Sendero Luminoso*, Documento de Trabajo, IEP, Lima, 4ta. edición.

Figueroa, Leonel, 1987, 'Ajuste, Ecónomico y Desarrollo en el Perú: Hacia una Politica Alternativa', mimeo, Lima, BCR, sin fecha.

Instituto Nacional de Planificación, 1987a, 'Evaluación del Plan de Corto Plazo, 1986', mimeo, Lima, marzo, 1987.

———, 1987b, 'Analisis de las Ultimas Medidas de Politica Económica', Informe No. 006/87/INP/DCPE, Lima, 23 de abril de 1987.

———, 1987c, *Plan Nacional de Desarrollo 1987*, Lima, marzo, 1987.

Ministerio de Economía y Finanzas, 1987a, 'Alerta Económica No.

2, febrero, 1987', Dirección General de Asuntos Económicos, MEF, 22 de marzo, 1987.

——, 1987b, 'Informe de Coyuntura', xerox, Grupo Económico, Lima, 30 de marzo de 1987.

Scheetz, Thomas, 1986, *Peru and the International Monetary Fund*, Pittsburgh University Press.

Thorp, Rosemary, 1987, 'The Apra Alternative in Peru: A Preliminary Evaluation of Garcia's economic policies', UNDP report in *The Peru Report*, Vol. 1, No. 6, Lima, June, 1987.

Thorp, Rosemary and Bertram, Geoff, 1978, *Peru 1890/1977. Growth and Policy in an Open Economy*, London: The Macmillan Press Ltd.

Ugarteche, Oscar, 1980, *Teoría y Práctica de la Deuda Externa en el Perú*, IEP, Lima.

—— 1986, *El Estado Deudor. La Economía Politica de al Deuda: Peru y Bolivia 1968/1984*, IEP, Lima.

——Interviews, various dates.

7   Costa Rica: A Quest for Survival

Ennio Rodriguez

INTRODUCTION

Costa Rica emerges as one of the most indebted nations both in per capita terms ($1.631 per capita public debt in 1985) and in the proportion debt service represents of exports (47.9 per cent after rescheduling). The experience of Costa Rica is very important for analysing debt issues on at least three accounts. First, a unilateral moratorium was declared as early as July 1981 when the international debt crisis had still not been recognised by the financial community. In this respect, the evolution of the lawsuit between the Allied Syndicate and three Costa Rican state banks is particularly relevant as it raises a wide number of issues regarding sovereign lending. Second, Costa Rica returned to the 'acceptable rules of behaviour' to deal with the debt problem; in doing so the consequences of conditionality have emerged very clearly, in particular Costa Rica has undergone cross-conditionality earlier and more profoundly than other debtors. This was the consequence of the attempt by the Costa Rican authorities to maintain positive external capital flows. Third, Costa Rica has suffered the small debtor syndrome. Debt reschedulings show a general pattern, but small highly indebted nations with a weak international bargaining position have ended up worse off *vis-à-vis* the banks than larger debtors. For a small debtor access to official and multilateral sources can be, however, more significant, but the cost is increased conditionality.

1. AN EXPERIENCE WITH DEFAULT

Costa Rica arrived at the debt crisis after an unprecedented period of growth. Growth rates had been the highest in Latin America for two consecutive decades and during the seventies growth rates were among the top four (ECLA, 1982). However, after 1979, Costa Rica has undergone the worst crisis since official statistics were collected.

Table 7.1:   Annual rates of variation of Gross Domestic Product—Costa Rica (1970 US$)

1970–5	1975–80	1980	1981	1982	1983	1984	1985	1986
6.0	5.3	0.8	-2.3	-7.3	2.3	6.0	1.6	4.2

Source: Central Bank.

This crisis was the combined result of structural causes and pro-cyclical economic policies. The motors of growth during the previous decades had been a successful effort to diversify primary exports, a dynamic process of import substituting industrialisation within the Central American Common Market (CACM) and an impressive growth of the internal market. This period was also characterised by a structural deficit on current account and a large share of external savings financing capital formation. Capital inflows were, thus, an important condition for rapid development.

The oil shocks of the seventies were absorbed via greater indebtedness and so were the major disequilibria that accumulated towards the end of the decade. There was a major decline of the terms of trade, which coincided for the first time with a reduction of trade among CACM partners. There was an exhaustion of the easy phase of import substitution, but the decline was mainly the result of the political and military upheaval of the region.

Disequilibria in the current account and public finances mounted, but adjustment was postponed thanks to abundant private external finance. Economic policy continued to be based on an expansive public expenditure programme, a reduction of protection, high interest rates, high public borrowing and a fixed exchange rate. The structural difficulties for growth were compounded by an inconsistent attempt to liberalise the economy and continued reliance on external finance to paper-off the engulfing disequilibria it was provoking (Rodriguez, 1983).

In a further attempt to deal with disequilibria, following orthodox prescriptions, foreign exchange markets were liberalised. Credibility in the economic policies had been lost, capital flight was increasing and the floating of the currency only added to the problem of uncertainty. There was a 500 per cent devaluation in eighteen months and attempts to intervene in the exchange markets with further external debts ('dirty float') were unsuccessful. External credibility also disappeared and sources of finance dried up suddenly. The Government opted for a unilateral moratorium.

Table 7.2: Balance of payments (US$ million)

	1970	1975	1979	1980	1981	1982	1983	1984	1985
Trade balance	-64.2	-161.4	-421.3	-459.2	-127.1	72.8	-13.9	-73.0	-180.5
Services	-12.4	-56.4	-133.1	-198.6	-280.6	-377.6	-344.6	-298.0	-165.5
Current account	-76.6	-217.8	-554.4	-657.8	-407.7	-304.8	-358.3	-371.0	-139.5
Capital account	61.2	203.4	435.1	751.2	357.7	431.5	411.5	414.0	
Reserves	11.6	16.7	112.6	-33.4	64.7	-124.8	27.7	-58.0	-92.4

Source: ECLA (1986).

It was August of 1981. The international financial community had no recent precedents as to how to deal with a sovereign debtor's default. From a geo-political standpoint, support for the Sandinista Revolution further restricted Costa Rica's room for maneouvre. External finance dwindled to practically nothing and lawsuits began to be filed in the courts of United States.

Of these cases, the one with the deepest consequences was the Allied Bank International versus Banco Crédito Agricola de Cartago, Banco Anglo Costarricense and Banco Nacional de Costa Rica. The three Costa Rican banks are owned by the Republic of Costa Rica and the Allied Bank International represented a syndicate of thirty-nine banks. This case was brought by the Syndicate after the Costa Rican banks failed to make payments on loan obligations to the syndicate. This default was the consequence of the banks following the decrees of 1981, prohibiting the use of foreign exchange for debt servicing.

In September 1983 Costa Rica successfully completed the first rescheduling of its external debt. All but one bank of the Allied Syndicate, Fidelity Union Bank, joined the rescheduling.

In July 1983 the District Court dismissed the case based on the 'act of state doctrine':

A judgement in favour of Allied in this case would constitute a judicial determination that defendants must make payments contrary to the directives of their government. This puts the judicial branch of the United States at odds with policies laid down by a foreign government on an issue deemed by that government to be of central importance. Such an act by this court risks embarrassment to the relations between the executive branch of the United States and the Government of Costa Rica. (Allied Bank, 566, p. 29a)

In April 1984 the Court of Appeals affirmed the dismissal 'because the actions of the Costa Rican government are consistent with the law and policy of the United States' (Allied Bank, 651, p 16a). The principle of comity (the principle whereby one nation respects the act of another nation) required, therefore, that the actions of Costa Rica be given effects in the courts of the United States.

It was argued that Costa Rica's actions were consistent with United States law based on Chapter 11 of the Bankruptcy Code:

Costa Rica's prohibition of payment of its external debts is analogous to the reorganisation of a business pursuant to Chapter 11 of our Bankruptcy Code ... Costa Rica's prohibition of payment of debt was not a repudiation of the debt but rather was merely a deferral of payments while it attempted in good faith to renegotiate its obligations. (Allied Bank, 733, p 21a)

The consistency of Costa Rica's actions with United States foreign policy was demonstrated by continued foreign aid to the country. Further aid to a defaulting country is barred unless the President advises that it is in the national interest to proceed with assistance to such country. In particular, a letter of the President to Congress was quoted. Several other letters and Congressional resolutions supporting Costa Rica and the Agreed Paris Club Minute rescheduling intergovernmental debt are also cited.

The consequences of this court decision remain unclear. A rather strict interpretation would be that the large banks and syndicate leaders would benefit most as the small banks would be unable to disrupt rescheduling programmes agreed by the majority of banks. However, the train of events seems to suggest that importance was given to another interpretation.

It may have been feared that the court's decision set precedents for a form of judicially-administered international bankruptcy. Following the rationale of the Bankruptcy Code, in which creditors cannot collect payments pending an overall solution, the courts may honour the deferral of payments by a sovereign debtor in severe economic difficulties until a rescheduling agreement is reached.

Allied (Fidelity Union Bank) requested the Second Circuit to review its decision *en bank*. This is a rehearing reserved for exceptionally important cases and seldom granted. The motion was granted as also was the petition of the executive branch to file a brief as *amicus curiae* in support of Fidelity.

The court reserved its decision based on the executive's claim that Costa Rica's actions were contrary to United States law and policy and that the act of state doctrine was inapplicable as it purported to confiscate property in the United States (Allied Bank, 225). Shortly after, Fidelity requested to join the refinancing agreements.

The case is amazing to say the least. For example, the evidence quoted above 'Costa Rica's prohibition of payment of debt was not a repudiation ...' although supposedly based on the same facts is replaced by:

The Costa Rican government's unilateral attempt to repudiate private, commercial obligations is inconsistent with the orderly resolution of international debt problems. It is similarly contrary to the interests of the United States, a major source of private international credit. (Allied Bank, 757, p 25a)

It seems that in the rehearing the panel of judges paid little attention to their prior decision and reasoning (White and Case, Petition for a Writ of Certiorari to the United States Court of Appeals for the Second Circuit, p 5). The argument that Costa Rica's actions were covered under the state of doctrine act and comity quoted above 'A judgement in favour of Allied . . .' remains uncontested. Moreover, the Costa Rican actions did not confiscate any property, the effects were only to affect payments temporarily, so as to enable the Government to restructure its external debt.

It is also debatable if an opinion of the executive branch is sufficient to demonstrate that an action is or is not consistent with applicable United States law and public policy.

The initial court decision recognised that the Costa Rican actions were consistent with principles of insolvency and bankruptcy law, a matter that is not considered in the rehearing.

This rehearing decision raises a wide number of issues. First, the court rejected the actions of the Costa Rican Government taken as a sovereign in its public capacity to remedy severe economic difficulties. It substitutes its judgement for that of the Costa Rican Government. Second, the court deferred to recommendations of the executive, abdicating, thus, its responsiblity and violated the separation of powers constitutionally defined. Third, the court ruled that regarding sovereign debt a single creditor holding less than one per cent of the debt can nullify the attempts of the state to restructure its debt (White and Case, pp. 6–7).

The direct implication of this case is that no legal precedent has been established analogous to the Bankruptcy Code. It rather seems that existing legal precedents and doctrine were set aside in the rehearing once it was feared that to establish an orderly legal procedure for sovereign borrowers undergoing severe payments difficulties could undermine the bargaining capacity of creditors. Another implication is that the legal option for securing payment from sovereign debtors in default has been shown to be costly and useless. It is, thus, not surprising that no recent cases have been filed in spite of an increasing list of defaulters.

2. DEBT RESCHEDULING AND ADJUSTMENT: AN EXPERIENCE WITH CONDITIONALITY

In May 1982 there was a change of Government. The new authorities came into office with massive electoral support and with a clear mandate to deal with internal and external aspects of the crisis. The strategy of confrontation with the international financial community followed towards the end by the 1979–82 Administration was changed. It was perceived that the costs of pursuing the strategy of unilateral default were higher than those incurred by attempting to regain access to fresh funds, particularly given the geo-political significance of Central America.

Relations with Nicaragua were rapidly deteriorating. Diplomatic and border incidents, the constant flow of refugees and heavy emphasis by the press on the 'authoritarian' characteristics of the Sandinista regime caused previously widespread support in Costa Rica for the Nicaraguan regime to practically vanish. Pressure was now mounting for supporting the 'contras'. The Government moved to a policy of neutrality aiming at pacific coexistence with Nicaragua and to open the doors in Washington. This policy has not been warmly welcomed either in Managua or Washington. But, complete defiance of US policy towards Central America stopped and relations improved greatly. US military policy has, however, been criticised by the Costa Rican President. In addition, Costa Rica has proposed recently a peace initiative after Contadora seemed to have run out of steam.

Negotiations with the banking community started with the beginning of the new administration, but progress was slow. The absence of precedents and concern about creating them slowed down progress. It was not until agreement was reached with Mexico that the bankers returned to discuss with the Costa Rican authorities with a clear pattern as to how to deal with debt reschedulings. However, the banks became tougher as precedents were feared once the pattern was established (Castillo, 1986, p.196).

Financial conditions of the first round of negotiations were not untypical for a small debtor: for arrears the amortization period was eight and a half years with a grace period of four years and the interest rate was $2\frac{1}{4}$ per cent over LIBOR or $2\frac{1}{8}$ over Prime Rate for principal payments accruing in 1984, the amortization period was seven and a half years with a grace period of four years and identical interest rates. There was a one per cent commission for rescheduling. A second rescheduling agreement was reached on 29 May 1985 with, as was also typical, better conditions than those obtained in the first round of negotiations. There was no commission for rescheduling, spreads were lower, $1\frac{5}{8}$ over LIBOR or over internal interest rates of reference, and up to 50 per cent of the principal could be converted into the currencies of the countries of each bank.

The strategy of following the rules of good behaviour in order to have access to fresh funds has been successful. Moreover, in 1983 and 1985, positive net transfers have been received. In general, arrears have been allowed to build up when inflows have been delayed and in certain years a deficit in current account has been financed and a moderate reactivation of economic activity has been possible.

Table 7.3: Net financial transfers, 1982–5 (million of dollars).

	1982	1983	1984	1985
Net financial transfers	-14	33	-52	130 [a,b]
Per cent of exports of goods	-1.6	3.8	-5.6	14.6 [a]

Notes: a. Based on ECLA estimates subject to revision; figures rounded to the nearest decimal.

b. Calculated using net capital flows which include long- and short-term capital flows, unilateral official transfers and errors and omission.

Source: ECLA, 1986.

This financial strategy has been a condition for the stabilisation programme. This programme managed to reduce inflation, employment levels returned in 1985 to pre-crisis levels, real income of workers has recovered significantly and real minimum wages are at their highest ever level.

In spite of conditionality, the Costa Rican authorities found some room for manoeuvre and some unorthodox policies figured centrally in the stabilisation programme. The

Table 7.4: Evolution of some indicators (1979–85)

	1978	1979	1980	1981	1982	1983	1984	1985
Consumer price index (per cent annual increase)	8.1	13.2	17.8	65.1	81.7	10.7	17.3	14.6
Real minimum wages (1970)	147.7	151.1	153.5	138.9	131.9	152.7	156.5	na
Open unemployment (per cent)	4.6	5.3	6.0	9.1	9.9	8.5	6.6	6.6

Source: ECLA, 1986; PREALC, 1985.

implementation of such policies are clearly linked with the success of the programme. Moreover, the basic stabiliser measures were implemented before signing the first Standby Agreement with the IMF. Major macro-economic disequilibria were not tackled according to the IMF approach.

The central element of the programme was clearly unorthodox, a monopoly of foreign exchange transactions was established by the Central Bank. Foreign exchange transactions except with the Bank were declared illegal and there was police persecution and prosecution of black marketeers. The most important effect of these measures was over expectations. Capital flight decreased and stability of the foreign exchange market was achieved. The Central Bank attempted a revaluation of the colón based on its demand for hard currency projections of assuming no demand for speculative purposes. The projections and more importantly, expectations were handled adequately, as is reflected by the fact that the rate of exchange in the black market has not been 5 per cent higher than the official rate. This was crucial in the control over inflation. An inflationary spiral never really got started. The price increase of 1982 was a once and for all result caused by the devaluation. The moderate revaluation managed to stop further price increases. The importance of devaluations when analysing inflation in small open economies cannot be overstated. In contrast to orthodox analysis, Costa Rican inflation was not primarily caused by excess demand, but was the result of a cost push due to devaluation. Hence, the importance of intervening in this crucial market. The shock treatment was vital to avoid the psychology of hyperinflation.

Monetary policy included an austere credit programme but interest rates were not raised to the recommended real three-digit levels. Orthodox prescriptions by the IMF were not followed in this respect either. It was rather argued that control over the exchange market would bring inflation down in a short period and that there was, therefore, no need to increase interest rates beyond an estimated 22 per cent. In a few months, as inflation came down, interest rates became positive in real terms. This result avoided a major recession and the cost-push impact it would have had. The agreement with the IMF was reached when price increases were already under control.

The decline in real wages was stopped and during 1984-5 real wages increased. This policy allowed for a reactivation of the internal market, especially during 1985. Orthodox critics constantly refer to this element of the programme as its weak link and overlook the fact that it made the whole programme politically viable. It did have, however, a negative impact on the balance of payments.

The fiscal deficit was around 20 per cent of GDP in 1981 and was reduced to 1.5 per cent in 1985, excluding external debt service; which would have raised it to around 7.5 per cent of GDP. Fiscal expenditure has remained roughly constant in real terms. Adjustment has taken place on the revenue side. There was a tax reform and large increases of the prices and tariffs of public goods and services. Central Government's current revenues increased from 13.6 per cent of GDP in 1981 to 16.6 per cent in 1983. Taxes were 13.2 per cent of GDP in 1981 and increased to 16.1 per cent in 1983. This form of tackling the fiscal deficit contributed to reduce inflationary pressures.

This significant tax reform can only be explained by the political climate of acceptance of the need for adjustment and that its costs should be shared. The social groups that only months before were sending their capital abroad, regardless of the consequences for society as a whole, were now prepared to reduce capital flight and accept increased taxation. The return of credibility on the Government's capacity to handle the crisis and to arbitrate class conflict remains the greatest feat of statesmanship since 1949. In the background other factors had an influence. Decades of rapid growth allowed for a society in which social mobility was the norm rather than the exception. A mature democratic regime was made possible for social discontent to be expressed and meant that there is a tradition of negotiations between pressure groups, classes and the state. The middle classes were also acutely aware of the consequences of social polarisation and conflict, as many of their friends from other countries in the region lived in either forced or self-imposed, exile.

This set of policy measures are not necessarily a recipe for success in other societies. The specifics of past growth, the absence of a psychology of hyperinflation, democracy, fairly even income distribution and political leadership were necessary conditions for achieving the results obtained.

Furthermore, a social compensation programme was created geared to target groups that could be affected by the crisis in 1982. It was financed by extraordinary surcharges on imports. Increased revenues accounted for 1 per cent of GDP. Although an evaluation of this programme is pending, it had significant political and social effects. It reinforced the normal activities of the institutions of the public sector geared to target groups. It included an emergency employment programme, food aid, especially in rural schools, and support for housing and land reform.

This social compensation programme, as has been mentioned, added to an already large social government expenditure. A detailed study conducted for 1982 shows that public sector expenditure which improves income distribution accounts for 15.8 per cent of GDP. (The Gini coefficient improves from 0.3871, before considering the redistributive impact of social expenditure, to 0.3086 after its effects are included (Trejos, 1985).)

Employment and capital shock were also protected by an emergency plan. Enterprises, not necessarily owners, were helped during the adjustment period. The programme lasted eighteen months and ninety enterprises benefited representing

9 per cent of the industrial labour force. Specific measures included financial support (reschedulings and fresh funds) from the state banks to fifty-one enterprises, direct negotiations with creditors to stop lawsuits, fresh capital from new investors, help in securing payments from Central American importers and selling of firms to new investors. Firms that benefited had to fulfil the following requisites: their problems were caused by the recent economic crisis; they were important exporters or significant employers; they belonged to the manufacturing sector or to the production or rendering of basic products or services; and, finally, it had to be shown that with short-term help the enterprises were viable. Given the stringent monetary policy this programme was made possible by the fact that the state banks control over 90 per cent of credit (Presidencia de la República, 1986).

These policies and their impact on some of the indicators mentioned above represent a rather successful stabilisation programme. The crisis is, however, structural. Capital formation has remained at lower levels than before the onset of

Table 7.5: *Gross fixed capital formation as a proportion of GDP and sources of finance of gross capital formation, 1976–85.*

Year	GFKF/GDP	Consumption of fixed capital (per cent of GFKF)	Net national savings (per cent of GFKF)	External savings (per cent of GFKF)
1976	24.2	23.0	41.7	35.3
1977	25.0	21.2	48.6	30.2
1978	28.6	22.4	33.7	43.9
1979	28.0	21.1	24.9	54.0
1980	25.1	19.8	24.4	55.8
1981	19.3	16.4	31.4	52.2
1982	15.0	16.1	34.0	49.9
1983	15.8	13.5	42.2	44.0
1984	18.5	12.2	50.5	37.3
1985[a]	19.3	na	na	na

Note: a. Preliminary.
Source: Central Bank.

the recession. External savings are not financing capital formation in the proportion they historically did, and the uncertainty of the region is also affecting local investors.

Access to external sources of finance has been possible in a context of increasing conditionality. The last years it has been transformed into one of cross-conditionality. Successful implementation of the programme agreed with one funding agency has recently become a condition for execution of the other agencies. This has made international negotiations very complex. Failure to meet one of the conditions may trigger off defaults or impede disbursements in other programmes, consequently, everything may need to be renegotiated. This is costly and time-consuming and generates uncertainty.

Within the frame of cross-conditionality there seems to be a division of labour among conditioning agencies: the IMF in three stand-by programmes has emphasised the current account of the balance of payments, exchange rate policy, fiscal deficit and monetary policy; the World Bank's emphasis has been on reducing public sector employment, a reduction of effective protection and export promotion: USAID has focussed on the privatisation of public enterprises; and the commercial banks have tied disbursements to performance of IMF and World Bank programmes (Lizano and Charpentier, 1987).

Cross-conditionality means that a country can be held hostage by one of the conditioning agencies. The cash flow programme for a given year depends on reaching agreement with each individual agency and meeting all the performance criteria.

An example of the costs of the rigidity of cross-conditionality is illustrated by Costa Rica failing to meet one of the second quarter performance criteria of the 1985 stand-by. The point was, according to IMF officials, just a technicality. Formally, however, a waiver from the IMF Board of Directors was needed. This difficulty coincided with a date of disbursement and rescheduling agreed with the banks. A precondition for these were letters of good behaviour both from the IMF and the World Bank. The IMF could not produce such a letter, until there was a Board meeting, more than a month later. Having failed to meet the pre-conditions,

Costa Rica was unable to disburse and incurred a technical default with the banks. To straighten things out, an IMF Board meeting was required. At this stage arrears had started piling up. A meeting with the Steering Committee was convened, but support during the meeting from the IMF, World Bank and USAID was required. This meant that all grievances with these agencies had to be rapidly sorted out. During the meeting, the cash flow and the whole strategy were again open to questioning by banks reluctant to put in fresh funds. After the Committee's approval, the agreed amendments to the contracts had to be ratified by all the banks. Again this meant that each small bank could air its grievances. At the end, the funds were disbursed and the rescheduling took place. All because of a technicality, top Costa Rican negotiators had to spend a large amount of time in endless meetings and, of course, all costs fell on the debtor, from legal fees to the last wire.

Cross-conditionality clearly raises a number of issues. First, whether the eliminaion of 'market distortions' and privatisation is sufficient for achieving the structural transformation of the Costa Rican economy. Second, there is the political economy question of the costs of implementing these policies which other cases in Latin America and the Caribbean suggest are very large indeed. Third, these funding agencies are conditioning access to fresh funds on the implementation of the same set of policies to a wide number of countries and, consequently, make it more difficult for individual countries to succeed following the same development strategy.

The narrow road of cross-conditionality gives little choice as to destination. The transference abroad of decision centres is such that the descriptions of dependency theorists of the sixties seem rosy.

There is the philosophical problem regarding the direction of conditionality. Its underlying principles are that the market allocates resources better than any form of intervention and that productive activities are always more efficiently organised by private capital. Shock liberalisation of the external and the internal markets is strongly recommended.

Costa Rica has initiated a process of structural adjustment within the frame of conditionality. The direction has not been, however, strictly orthodox. As mentioned above, there have been programmes of social compensation and of protecting enterprises. Wages policy and the reactivation of the internal market have confronted the shock liberalising arguments. Tariffs have been reduced, but gradually and in the frame of the Central American Common Market. Non-traditional exports have been promoted through fiscal incentives and subsidies, but there has been no use of the exchange rate as an active policy instrument. Growth of the public sector has stopped, but pressures to reduce public employment have been resisted. There is a process of privatisation of public enterprise under way.

After difficult negotiations Costa Rica seems to have managed to compensate for some of the costs of the adjustment process and has avoided a shock liberalisation treatment. However, there is little room for manoeuvre to introduce further measures guiding the modernisation of the productive sectors and strengthening political democracy by greater economic democracy. The assumption underlying the philosophy of conditionality is that the state should not intervene, regardless of well-accepted arguments such as infant industry, 'pecuniary' externalities, imperfect markets, in particular in technology, building of dynamic comparative advantage among others. The consequence of conditionality is the inability of the state to deal with cases of market failure which demand intervention for optimum solutions, especially when dealing with the modernisation of the productive sectors.

Another immediate consequence of continued access to

Table 7.6: Stock of public debt, 1982–5 (millions of dollars)

	1982	1983	1984	1985
Commercial banks	1,111.3	1,393.5	1,408.6	1,457.8
Multilaterals	857.9	967.9	976.1	1,034.4
Bilaterals	511.0	690.0	736.0	948.1
Bonds	131.0	113.6	113.2	75.0
Deposit certificates	301.8	193.5	187.0	183.6
Suppliers	48.8	48.0	34.2	48.7
Total	2,961.8	3,406.5	3,455.1	3,747.6

Source: Central Bank.

external funds is the increasing level of indebtedness. Although in the short term this seems the less costly option, the fact remains that until a different solution to the debt problem is found, Costa Rica's situation is becoming increasingly difficult.

3. IS SMALL BEAUTIFUL?

As has been mentioned, a pattern for debt reschedulings has emerged. Two rounds of negotiations have taken place and the third one is under way. This pattern and the definition of rounds have been defined primarily by the Mexican reschedulings. But, there is also another sense in which bankers understand Mexican negotiations. They have become the yardstick with which to judge the financial conditions other debtors can obtain. Small debtors unable to pose a risk to the large banks have had to confront tougher financial conditions in their reschedulings. Interest rates and commissions have been higher, grace and amortization periods have been shorter and access to fresh funds more difficult (Bogdanowicz-Bindert, 1987; Monge, 1987; Rodriguez, 1987). Mexico has become a yardstick for measuring political clout and creditworthiness, it is, thus, not surprising that small debtors face tougher conditions.

Moreover, there is evidence to suggest that the IMF is tougher on conditionality required from small nations' stabilisation programmes (Williamson, 1987). This suggests that political considerations do emerge in the supposedly technical policy packages of the IMF. The weakness of political clout of small nations is, thus, further complicated as they also get harsher treatment from the stabilisation programmes of the IMF.

Smallness has meant that relatively small amounts of official or multilateral funds can mean positive net transfers of external savings. This compensatory funding is unthinkable for large debtors as the amounts involved are unmanageable in the current situation of international capital flows. Small is, however, not necessarily beautiful, as such funds are available only under very tough cross-conditionality.

Smallness and good behaviour following the rules of conditionality may not be sufficient for attracting fresh funds. Figures of net transfers in Latin America seem to suggest that geo-political importance is another necessary condition.

Small nations with a less diverse productive structure, a narrow export base, a small internal market and low savings potential have suffered very severely under the debt crisis. It is, thus, not surprising that announced or non-announced complete or partial defaults (Costa Rica recently added to the list) have been rather common in this group of nations. The system seems to have an inbuilt incentive for small nations to drop out as the negative consequences are less feared nowadays. It does mean, however, a loss of access to short-term credit which in countries like Costa Rica is very substantial. A widespread wave of defaults might spread to large debtors as well.

Unfortunately, the short-term perspective of the banks and a rigid pattern have so dominated the approach to the debt problem that no special solutions to the special cases have been seriously considered beyond academic circles.

There should be a case-by-case approach in which the differences between creditors and debtors are considered. The financial community can very well experiment with creative solutions with small debtors. If a case-by-case approach was really adopted the fear of precedents would disappear, as by definition there would be no precedents.

REFERENCES

Allied Bank, 566 F.Supp. at 1444, Appendix C.
Allied Bank, 733 F.2d at 26, Appendix B.
Allied Bank, 757 F.2d at 522, Appendix A.
Bogdanowicz-Bindert, C. 1987, 'El caso de los países pequeños latinoamericanos'. CABEI. *Deuda externa: el caso de los países pequeños latinoamericanos.* EDUCA, San José.
Castillo, C. M., 1986, 'La crisis internacional de la deuda: la experiencia de Costa Rica'. Ffrench-Davis, R. and Feinberg, R. E. (eds), *Más allá de la crisis de la deuda,* CIEPLAN, Diálogo Internamericano, Grupo Editor Latinamericano, Buenos Aires.

—— 1982, 'Estudio Económico de América Latina', 1981. Costa Rica', Santiago.

—— 1984, 'Anuario estadistico de América Latina', Santiago.

—— 1986, 'Anuario estadistico de América Latina', Santiago.

Lizano, E. and Charpentier, S., 1987, 'La condicionalidad cruzada y la deuda externa', CABEI, *Op. cit.*

Monge, L. A., 1987, 'La deuda externa de los países latinoamericanos pequeños'. CABEI, *Op.cit.*

PREALC, 1985, 'Modernización del mercado de trabajo y crisis en el istmo centroamericano', Santiago.

Presidencia de la República, 1986, 'Programa de ayuda a las empresas', mimeo, San José.

Rodriguez, E, 1983, 'Del crecimiento sostenido a la recesión: en busca de alternativas', *Pensamiento Iberoamericano*. No. 4, Julio-Diciembre.

Trejos, J.D. 1985, 'Costa Rica: los programas estatales de carácter social y su impacto en la distribución del ingreso familiar', mimeno, Universidad de Costa Rica, IICE.

White and Case, 'Petition for a write of certiorari to the United Sates Court of Appeals for the Second Circuit'.

Williamson, J., 1987, 'La condicionalidad del FMI en los países pequeños', CABEI, *Op.cit.*

8 Economic Crisis and Foreign Debt Management in Venezuela*

Ana Maria Alvarez De Stella

INTRODUCTION

External vulnerability has characterised Venezuela from the 1920s coinciding with the transformation of the country from agriculture-based to petroleum-based, from a rural country into an urban country seventy years later. The external vulnerability is linked to the enormous dependency on petroleum; petroleum represents around 28 per cent of the real GNP, 72 per cent of the income of the treasury, 13 per cent of gross investment, 95 per cent of the exports and only 1 per cent of total employment.

Owing to the country being a mono exporter, Venezuela has experienced the tragic consequences of this vulnerability and this situation has been accentuated, in that it has not known how to take advantage of the substantial petroleum income— there has been no clear definition of a coherent model of development.

The importance of petroleum for the economy has distinguished us from other Latin American countries.

This paper is in three parts: the first, in which the main aspects of the origin of the present economic crisis and the measures of adjustment, taken from that date to the present,

* This chapter forms part of the project *The Debt Crisis in the 1980s and its Impact*, directed by Dr Stephany Griffith-Jones of the University of Sussex, England to whom I am grateful for her constant support and useful comments, likewise to Dr Miguel Rodriquez (IESA, Venezuela) and to Dr Felipe Pazos (BCV, Venezuela).

are outlined; the second part is dedicated to an analysis of the process of renegotiation of the foreign debt; and, the third part includes comments about the impact of the negotiation on an international level, and the form in which the Accord was obtained.

1. FUNDAMENTAL ASPECTS OF THE RECENT ECONOMIC CRISIS IN VENEZUELA

The origins of the economic crisis that Venezuela is experiencing go back to 1979. From this year until 1984, restrictive policies were applied which have only resulted in a greater stagnation of the economy: in spite of the extraordinary external resources obtained, Venezuela experienced persistent 'stagflation' in these years. In this resides the great paradox which explains the recent economic history of the country.

In explaining the crisis in the foreign sector, which has become more acute since 1982, we will outline as fundamental factors the adoption of incorrect economic policies implemented since 1979, and the lack of national confidence which initiated the enormous capital flight especially from 1980 onwards, becoming more pronounced at the end of 1982 and the start of 1983.

Added to this was the deterioration of the petroleum market and the maintenance of an unfavourable differential between the external and internal exchange rates in 1980–1.

In the evolution of the external sector of the economy we distinguish two periods, the first from 1974 to 1978, characterised by the explosion of petroleum prices and the subsequent unprecedented increase in petroleum revenues, and the post-1979 period in which the economy entered into recession, in spite of the rise in petroleum prices experienced in 1979 and 1980.

Prior to the first period, the external sector benefited from the stability of the balance of payments since the Second World War until the start of the 1970s. A favourable foreign reserves position was thus reached.

The economic decisions were designed taking into account

the particular conditions of a mono exporting country and with the clear objective of increasing the accumulation of capital. With this aim, the petroleum sector was given the central role in the process of development, and the public spending was given the role of transmitting the petroleum revenues to the rest of the economy. Additionally, it was clearly established that industrial and agricultural development would be oriented towards the substitution of imports, which in practice implied the adoption of consumption habits of industrialised economies, destined to produce principally for the middle and high income brackets.

(1) The meaning of the oil boom in Venezuela

1974 brought with it an epoch of splendour to the external sector of the Venezuelan economy—petroleum revenues tripled, bringing an increase of exports from US $11,290 million in 1974 (see Table 8.1). The Government launched an ambitious public investment plan in basic industries (steel, aluminium, electricity, etc.).

Consequently, between the years 1974 and 1977, public spending stimulated aggregate demand and the economy experienced a phase of expansion: consumption and private investment responded vigorously. The excess of public spending had a negative impact on the balance of payments, after a surplus of the current account in 1974 of US $5,735 million.

The macro-economic results of the period 1974–78 were rather favourable, non-petroleum GNP grew substantially (around 9 per cent between 1974 and 1977), and inflation stayed under control owing both to the policy of price subsidies and availability of foreign exchange, which allowed imports to rise.

(2) The external debt in the years after the oil boom

The debt contracted between 1974 and 1983 served to finance the flight of private capital abroad, which led to the acquisition of financial and non-financial assets. The economic policies adopted in these years, which were based on the stimulus of aggregate demand as a way of furthering the real internal supply of goods and services, and on an increase in public

Table 8.1: Venezuela: some indicators of the external sector (Millions of US $)

Years	Exports (FOB)	Oil exports	Imports (FOB)	Trade balance	Current account balance	Net international reserves
1974	11,290	10,762	-3,876	7,414	5,760	n/a
1975	8,982	8,493	-5,462	3,520	2,171	n/a
1976	9,324	8,802	-7,337	2,005	254	n/a
1977	9,661	9,225	-10,194	-533	-3,179	n/a
1978	9,174	8,705	-11,234	-2,060	-5,735	11,513
1979	14,370	13,673	-10,004	4,356	350	15,976
1980	19,275	18,301	-10,877	8,398	4,728	18,890
1981	20,181	19,094	-12,123	8,058	4,000	19,069
1982	16,516	15,659	-13,584	2,932	-4,246	14,164
1983	14,759	13,778	-6,409	8,350	4,427	14,433
1984	15,967	14,794	7,262	8,705	5,418	16,764
1985	14,178	12,862	-7,388	6,790	3,086	17,168
1986	8,686	7,218	-7,700	986	-1,628	n/a
1987ᴾ	10,338	8,700	-7,432	2,906	-279	n/a

Notes: ᴾ = Projections

Source: Central Bank of Venezuela, *Statistical Annual Report, Economic Annual Report.*

spending to finance the ambitious requirements of the Fifth National Plan, stimulated imports. This led to the adoption of consumption habits which were distant from reality.

Two stages can be distinguished in the development of the external debt during the period after the oil boom. During the first stage, from 1974 to 1978, the external debt rose around US $13,000 million, US $10,500 million of which was owed by the public sector. However, the consolidated balance of the current account registered a surplus of US $200 million, which indicates that *the country was generating internal savings sufficient to finance the whole of its investment* and, therefore, the total increase of the public foreign debt was used to finance the accumulation of public sector assets abroad, which rose to around US $10,000 million, whilst the private sector increased external assets by almost US $4,000 million.

The result of this was that sectors in deficit (state companies, private firms, banks, etc.) had to resort to external finance as a way of obtaining foreign resources. This was the case of the decentralised public enterprises, which built up foreign debt to cover their operational deficits.

One should also mention Venezuela's ease of access to the markets, by being classified as Triple 'A' by the main Rating Agencies Standard and Poor's, and Moody's. All the above shows the high level of responsibility of the International Banks in the debt question, a fact which has important implications for present negotiations. Effectively, even when several of these firms were encountering administrative and liquidity problems, they had access to credits since the Republic acted as guarantor of last resort (this can be proved in practice—in the restructuring of the public foreign debts, the Republic of Venezuela has assumed the external obligations of nearly forty state companies).

The second stage of the external debt coincides with the second oil boom, from 1979 onwards, and is characterised by external resources serving to finance the massive private sector capital flights abroad, which were stimulated, fundamentally by the over-valuation of the Bolivar until February 1983 and the financial policy adopted in 1980-1 to control internal rates of interest in the face of the spectacular rise in external interest rates. This, given free convertibility and a fixed exchange rate

Table 8.2:   *Impact of the Venezuelan external debt (billions of US $)*

Years	Consolidated current account balance (1)	Total debt (2)	External in total debt (3)	Increase (4)	Increase in external public debt (5)	Increase in total external assets (6)	Increase in public assets (reserves+FIV+ PDVSA) (7)	Increase in private assets (8)
1973	nd	2.0	1.5	na	na	na	na	na
1974–8	0.2	15.2	12.0	13.2	10.5	13.4	9.6	3.8
1979–83	9.3	35.0	27.0	19.8	15.0	29.1	−0.1	29.2
1974–83 (total)	9.5	35.0	27.0	33.0	25.0	42.5	9.5	33.0
1984	5.2	33.5	25.5	−1.5	−1.5	3.7	2.4	1.3(P)
1960–85(E)	22.10	na	na	na	na	na	na	na

Notes: P   = Preliminary
n.a. = Not available
E   = Estimated

Source: Rodriguez, M. *op. cit.* (1986ii) based on Central Bank of Venezuela: *National Accounts Annual Report* and Cline, W., *Venezuela's External Debt*, Institute for International Economics. Washington, DC.

for the national currency, stimulated even more capital flight, making the National Banking System borrow to invest abroad and take advantage of the differential in interest rates.

(3) 1979–83: Internal and external crisis

What followed the economic boom of the period 1974–8 were various years of dramatic changes in the economy which were characterised by persistent stagflation—especially between 1979 and 1983, in spite of the abundant external resources which the State was still receiving.

In the period 1979–83, three successive recessive stabilisation plans were implemented. This explains the collapse of private investment in the period 1974–8 (from 21 per cent to 12 per cent as percentages of GNP).

The country had between 1974 and 1983 resources to finance its own investment; it was not justifiable to have a level of indebtedness that rose by around US $35,000 million, and which contributed principally to finance private sector assets abroad, which totalled around US $33,000 million (see Table 8.2).

(a) Consequences of the First Adjustment, 1979–82 When the Christian Democrat President Luis Herrera Campins came to power, a programme based on fiscal austerity and economic liberalism was put into practice. The following priority was established: control of the fiscal and external deficit through a real contraction of public spending and through price and tariff liberalisation. In addition, internal interest rates were frozen which initially served as an attempt to stimulate private investment. In practice, this contributed to the flight of capital. One of the most controversial arguments for this flight of capital, which has been criticised for its tragic consequences[1] is the following: it would allow the control of liquidity, reducing international reserves and, thus, alleviating inflationary pressure.

Interest rate control was maintained until August 1981, when the rates started to compete with international rates; and this partially detained the capital flight abroad. However, when the petroleum market weakened in 1982, the flight of capital became greater, being pushed by the over-valuation of the Bolivar. The enormous flight of national savings meant that economic agents with deficits, like state companies, private firms and commerical banks to incurred foreign debts, thus producing a substitution of national financial intermediaries for international ones.

During the years 1979 to 1981, the hoped-for growth in the economy did not occur, leading to additional foreign loans and further flight of capital. However, international reserves did not reflect these problems—by now they had risen from US $11,513 million on 31 December 1978 to US $19,069 million on 31 December 1981 (see Table 8.2).

In 1982, international reserves decreased by US $4,905 million (including those of PDVSA) with respect to 1981. This occurred as a reaction to the fear of a devaluation of the Bolivar, the influence of the Mexican foreign debt crisis, and the slowness of the Government in taking corrective measures and not taking its opportunity to renegotiate the foreign debt—all aspects which provoked further large-scale flight of capital. However, the centralisation of reserves in the BCV (as from September 1982) and the revenues from new borrowing by the public sector prevented the reduction in reserves being more acute.

(b) The 1983 foreign exchange crisis The speculative movements against the exchange rate in face of possible devaluation and/or exchange control, the high concentration of maturity dates of short-term foreign debt and the uncertainty of the petroleum market were factors which stimulated even more the flight of capital, and this situation led the Government to suspend foreign currency sales in February 1983—after nearly twenty years of free exchange rate convertibility and a fixed exchange rate. The measure and its possible consequences created uneasiness in international financial circles and gave rise to a polemic between the Government (Finance Ministry) and the president of BCV centred on whether differential exchange rates or a straight devaluation should be the methods to put a brake on capital flight.

The argument was won by the Finance Ministry whose thesis was based on the idea that disequilibrium should be corrected in a segmented manner; for this RECADI was created (the Differential Exchange Rates Regime). The new system of exchange had three exchange rates. First, the Bs 4.30/$ was maintained (this had been in force since the 1960s) and the Bs 6.00/$ was adopted. Then, in March 1984 the system was modified and the dollar at Bs 7.50 was incorporated—this implied an average devaluation of 41 per cent but continued to be segmented. Exchange control was not considered.

One of the most controversial themes which arose from the BCV Finance Ministry polemic was the recognition of the private foreign debt at the preferential dollar rate. The Government justified this recognition as necessary for the re-establishment of international creditworthiness (around US $5,400 million corresponded to private sector debts), and that this would ease negotiations on the public foreign debt. In addition, it was argued that not to recognise dollars at Bs 4.30/$ for legitimately-contracted private foreign debt would endanger the solvency of numerous private firms, thus, negatively affecting national production and employment.

In various telexes referring to deferral of the payments of foreign debt which preceded the Renegotiation Accord, the creditor banks demanded that the private companies should obtain preferential foreign exchange. Even though the creditor banks demanded neither guarantee nor state assumption of private debt, in practice they did impose their criterion that *it was not possible to separate one problem from the other*.

In addition to the exchange measures adopted in the face of the crisis in 1983, the Government implemented controls on imports by means of quotas, a fiscal policy was implemented, which succeeded in reducing public spending by nearly 27 per cent and a monetary policy with high rates of interest.

On the basis of this programme of adjustment it is worth posing the following question: were these adjustments which allowed an improvement in the current account at the expense of a reduction in GNP really justified? A contraction in the economy had been produced when really an adjustment to correct over-valuation and some quantitative restrictions on the import of goods and services would have been able to alleviate the disequilibrium of the current account when it had been registered in 1982 (See Rodriguez, 1986). With respect to this, the figures speak for themselves. In 1983, GNP dropped by 4.7 per cent and the non-petroleum GNP by something more than 5 per cent, whereas the current account went from a deficit of US $4,246 million in 1982 to a surplus of US $4,427 million in 1983.

In effect, it would have been possible to maintain, or increase, public spending—with positive implications. But, in reality the contraction of public spending again caused a reduction in public and private investment and an increase in private sector saving both at home and abroad. In conclusion, transfers of these savings on an internal and external level led to this sector in 1983 becoming a net creditor abroad to the volume of US $30,000 million.

(4) Sharpening of the recession: adjustments in 1984, 1985 and 1986

The adjustments implemented from 1984 by the Government of President Lusinchi can be summarised as follows: the maintenance of a conservative public spending policy, combined with a moderate devaluation, resulted in the sharpening of the recession, bringing with it the deepening of social problems, for example, that of unemployment (13.4 per cent in 1984, 12.1 per cent in 1985 and 10.5 per cent in 1986).

The intention to correct over-valuation brought about in 1984 a new official rate of Bs 7.50/$, maintaining the Bs 6.00/$ rate to favour and strengthen the petroleum industry. The adjustment of relative prices resulting from this devaluation showed itself in higher inflation—11.9 per cent in 1984 compared to 7.0 per cent in 1983. It should be emphasised that the combination of devaluation with a restrictive fiscal policy brought as a result what we could call contractive devaluation, according to which '... the clause in relative prices originating from the devaluation produces a strong redistribution of income to a sector with a higher marginal propensity to save' (Rodriguez, 1986).

With respect to the balance of payments, the current account registered a surplus of more than US $5,000 million. Already for this year negotiations were under way with the creditor banks to sign an agreement for the foreign public

Table 8.3: Growth in GNP (1968 prices) per cent

Year	GNP Total[1]	GNP Petroleum	GNP Non-petroleum
1974	6.1	−11.1	9.8
1975	6.1	−22.2	11.1
1976	8.8	−0.8	9.8
1977	6.7	− 2.5	7.8
1978	2.1	− 1.7	2.5
1979	1.3	− 7.1	0.8
1980	−1.9	− 7.0	−1.5
1981	−0.3	− 3.4	0.0
1982	0.7	− 7.2	1.4
1983	−5.6	− 4.7	−5.7
1984	−1.3	0.3	−1.5
1985	0.3	− 3.3	0.6
1985*	3.0	0.3	3.2
1987[2]	0.8	3.6	0.6

Notes: 1. Includes import duties
        * Estimated figure
        2. Projection

Source: BCV

debt. In the interim, disagreements arose between the Government and the IMF regarding the requirements suggested by that institution as a previous stage to the conclusion of an agreement with the banks.

The principal requirements of the IMF consisted in a pronounced rise in gasoline prices, proposals for a unified exchange rate in the short-term, even though multiple exchange rates would be acceptable as a transitory measure, the need to eliminate subsidies on mass consumption goods, a policy of commercial liberalisation and free capital movement, the controlling of public sector nominal salaries, and an attempt to implement a restrictive policy on private sector salaries. Finally, the IMF opposed the preferential treatment of the foreign private debt, indicating with respect to this that the Government should assign specific resources to this in the national budget.

In view that there was no need to resort to IMF financing, the country put into practice its own adjustment programme which in reality turned out be very similar and in some aspects more demanding than the programme of the IMF would have been. To respond to the demands of the creditor banks, the Government prepared each quarter its *Economic Memorandum*, which contained recent information and projections for the economy, based on details contributed by various national organisations. Once it had been made clear that Venezuela was not disposed to the signing of accords with the IMF, this text came to be the banks' way of following the Venezuelan economy; the IMF has continued in its traditional role through the consultations provided for in article IV of its Constitutions. On Venezuela's initiative these consultations are carried out twice a year. Additionally a Commission set up in August 1984 by the Government and being made up by the Finance Ministry, the Ministry of Energy and Mines, the Central Planning Office (CORDIPLAN) and the President of the BCV, publishes quarterly the *Quantified Economic Programme* (PEC) which sets out the annually fixed targets for fiscal, monetary and exchange policy.

Even though 1985 was expected to be the year of economic recovery, it turn out to be another year of stagnation, again attributable to the contractive economic policy pursued by the Government. Once more, the Government had a high level of resources which might have suggested future economic expansion. However, the Government opted for using a good part of its surplus to amortize the public debt (external and internal), in spite of persisting economic stagnation. Regarding the private foreign debt, there were several modifications.

One of these was the Exchange Agreement No. 5 of January 1985 which contemplated giving a new facility to the private sector, which would allow firms producing public services and financial societies to cancel their foreign debt servicing at the preferential rate of Bs 4.30/$ by acquiring zero coupon bonds[2] which would be sold at a discount. The mechanism was not successful.

The beginning of 1986 was dominated by the deterioration of the petroleum market and a reduction in petroleum revenues. This led the Government to implement a policy of expansion, especially through the three-year Public Investment Plan (*El Plan Trienal de Inversiones Publicas*) for the period

1986 to 1988. This allowed, for the second year running, the economy to show a real rate of growth after the recessive 1980 to 1984 period (see Table 8.1).

One of the most important events of the year was the signing of the Public Foreign Debt Renegotiation Agreement on 26 February.

In July 1986, the President of the Republic promulgated twenty-one economic measures to confront the crisis. Among the most relevant aspects were the elimination of the dollar at Bs 4.30 and the substitution of a Bs 7.50 rate for the payment of the public foreign debt and the rate of interest on the private external debt. As would be expected, the sharpest criticisms of the new exchange system came from the private sector which did not stop emphasising the negative impact of the measure.

Some days after the outline of these economic measures, the Government decreed that the private foreign debt was to be converted into bonds issued by FOCOCAM (previously mentioned). The international creditor banks would be obliged to accept these bonds as a method of debt payment. This mechanism implied that the Republic would assume the total weight of the private foreign debt—approximately US $6,000 to 7,000 million—and that the creditors would receive payment for this debt through fifteen-year bonds issued in dollars with a coupon of 5 per cent. This measure lasted a month owing to objections from the creditor banks (the bonds were not attractive), and from that date there was no clearly-defined scheme for the settlement of this debt until December of the same year when the new exchange agreement was introduced.

In 1986, crude oil prices reached an average of US $ 12.89 a barrel, which meant a corresponding fall in petroleum revenues of US $5,644 million—a determining factor in the deficit on current account. In addition, the enormous capital movements abroad for the amortization of the public and private foreign debt and the additional capital flight, still continuing in spite of the exchange measures taken, generated a deficit on capital account of around US $2,000 million. This was reflected in a reduction of US $3,892 million in international reserves which fell to US $9,858 million.

In December of that year the Government introduced new

economic measures, based on the adoption of a new exchange rate of Bs 14.50/$—a devaluation of nearly 100 per cent with respect to Bs 7.50/$. This rate would be applicable to the majority of external transactions, with the exception of some essential imports and other special transactions for which the Bs 7.50/$ would be maintained. The parallel market continued functioning for the remaining transactions. Here the US currency averaged around Bs 24.72/$ during the year.

Also, in order to control speculation in the free market, the BCV limited the operations of the foreign currency exchange houses, limiting their role to act as intermediaries in this market. Also, from the middle of the previous year, the Central Bank had been requiring a special deposit of 100 per cent from the banks which kept assets in foreign currency. In general, the central issuing institution directly controlled exchange activity according to the Exchange Agreement No. 1, but until the date that this work was finished there has been no talk of exchange control in the strict sense of the phrase.

Another important aspect of the December 1986 economic measures, was the adoption of a new mechanism for the settlement of the private foreign debt—at the preferential rate of Bs 7.50/$ over eight years. For this, the new Exchange Agreement No. 2 establishes that those firms which wish to opt for a guarantee at this rate should set up a trust fund in the BCV by surrendering a set premium. State firms were permitted to service their own external debt, by adopting this mechanism, rather than settling the debt at Bs 14.50/$.

The deterioration of the petroleum market from the beginning of 1986, impelled the Government to re-open talks with the banks, in accordance with the 'Clausula de Contingencia' (contingency clause). Talks concluded with a new agreement on 27 February 1987. This agreement contemplated the improvement of financial conditions and of the amortization period laid out in the original agreement.

However, debt servicing payments in 1987 (including the US $1,500 million to be settled for capital amortization of the private foreign debt) represent more than 30 per cent of the BCV's foreign currency revenues, and more than 64 per cent of petroleum exports. Nevertheless, higher petroleum revenues are foreseen in 1987 owing to the increase in price. However,

Table 8.4: *Maturities of the public foreign debt by type of debtor (million US dollars, estimates made at the end of 1986)*

	31-12-82	31-12-83	31-12-84	31-12-85	31-12-86
Financial entities	6,876.5	6,767.3	6,314.66	6,211.11	6,164.6
Development corporations	2,833.6	2,788.6	2,591.47	2,548.15	2,539.6
State companies	8,818.6	8,678.4	8,077.85	7,989.50	7,831.5
Mixed companies					
(public and private)	14.2	14.0	15.72	15.34	7.9
Credit funds	569.1	560.0	511.87	530.86	494.8
Central Government	8,809.1	8,669.1	8,239.13	7,724.07	7,910.9
Autonomous institutes	1,719.1	1,691.8	1,585.50	1,524.11	1,508.1
Total	29,640.1	29,169.2	27,336.2	26,543.2	26,457.7

Source: Finance Ministry

the high level of debt service pending with the banks makes it imminent to again obtain money to cover debt service. In this way talks with the banks continue, in order to achieve placement of international bonds or some form of bank finance. In addition to covering debt servicing requirements there is an urgent need for resources destined for internal activity.

In spite of the expansive policies which the Government has planned, the recent exchange rate measures could generate a growth in inflation such that the increase in internal aggregate demand would be limited.

2. THE RENEGOTIATION OF THE VENEZUELAN PUBLIC FOREIGN DEBT

The situation of the public foreign debt reached intolerable levels from the end of 1982. Amortizations due had reached a level of almost US $30,000 million, as a result of inadequate planning which led to payments concentrating on the short-term. This was attributable to the smaller amount of financial support by the Government to state companies, including them to become indebted abroad under onerous financial conditions —specifically at variable rate of interest with very short-term maturities, taking advantage of the fact that domestic legislation was totally flexible in this respect (until 1976) that the international banks were disposed to concede new finance.

As one can deduce from these figures, the foreign debt affected principally Central Government, State companies and financial entities. For 1983 the situation was such that it would have been necessary to make use of more than 77 per cent of estimated income from export to settle all the maturities of that year.

(1) Evolution of the Venezuelan foreign debt
On examining the evolution of the Venezuelan foreign debt, one can appreciate that from mid-1970 debt servicing constituted a growing percentage of exports, remaining above 30 per cent between 1982 and 1984 and continuing at a high level with a pronounced rise in subsequent years.

Table 8.5: *Projections for international reserves and the public foreign debt (million US dollars and percentages)*

	1984	1985	1986	1987	1988	1989	1990
BCV international reserves	12,500	13,750	9,858	9,100	8,800	8,800	8,800
Public foreign debt	27,300	26,500	25,300	24,900	23,600	21,900	20,000
Debt servicing to exports[1] (percent)	39.2	35.2	58.3	47.7	34.4	35.0	32.4

Note: 1. Includes amortizations corresponding to new credits from multilateral, bilateral, suppliers and other sources.

Source: Memorandum Economico (real figures to January 1987)

The Venezuelan foreign debt for the end of 1983 was concentrated (86 per cent) in foreign banks. The results are not very different on analysing the distribution for the end of 1986. The high percentage of the public and private debt contracted with commercial banks makes the country more vulnerable and dependent on private financial sources.

The Government asked the international banks for the first deferral of payments in (March 1983) as no Agreement of Renegotiation had been reached. These deferrals were originally ninety days each, but in 1986 were shortened to a thirty-day period.

The renegotiation started off with the creation of a banks' Advisory Committee, which consisted of thirteen banks, and which was chaired by Chase Manhattan Bank, Bank of America and Lloyds Bank which continue to be co-presidents. Discussions began in February 1984, and on this date the country designated an advisory commission for the refinancing of the public foreign debt constituting high level functionaries of the Finance Ministry and CORDIPLAN in addition to important private sector leaders, one of whom was acting as president of the Commission. People with good knowledge of banking and sympathetic to the party of Government were chosen. After overcoming various rounds of proposals and counter-proposals the Renegotiation Agreement was signed on 26 February 1985, being revised in February 1986.

(2) Renegotiation strategy

From the start of the talks the Venezuelan Government had the following objectives and parameters for the renegotiation of the public foreign debts:

1. To eliminate delays in the servicing of the financial debt and the payments of commercial debts of the public sector.
2. To look for a permanent solution so there would be no need to renegotiate the agreement—in practice this had proved impossible.
3. To formulate an adjustment programme acceptable to the IMF, without this implying the implementation of a programme backed financially by the IMF. One of the

arguments for Venezuela of not going to the IMF was that the country did not want to ask for new banks credits to honour the servicing of the restructured debts, but rather to look for bilateral and multilateral. credits in case of need.

4. To solve the administrative problems which were hindering the registration of the private external debt.

5. Re-financeable debt was defined as the pending maturities (up to 22 March 1983 to date) with a level of up to US $21,976.9 million. Non-refinanceable debt was considered to be the US $5,477 million originating from issues of bonds by the Republic or other public bodies, private holding of obligations to the bearer issued by the said bodies through one or more banks. Debt with multilateral or bilateral organisations was excluded given that this would have implied negotiating with the Club of Paris, subject to an agreement with the IMF. Also, non-refinanceable debt was considered to be credit lines and very short-term holding—money market lines, terms and call obligations—contracted by some agencies of Venezuelan public financial institutions, and finally, public sector commercial debts originating from imports required by state company and the debts with contractors and suppliers. The non-refinanceable debt should be paid on maturity. Additionally, it was decided to cancel immediately 1982 maturities for a figure of US $219,5 million even though this implied discriminatory treatment of certain creditors.

6. With reference to the plan for the amortization of capital and interest, the Advisory Commission established a ceiling of US $4,000 to 5,000 million a year, assuming that payments would have a tendency to decrease.

3) Principal aspects of the renegotiation of the foreign debt: to convert the crisis into something manageable

This phrase was used by the Finance Minister, Dr Manuel Azupurua Arreaza, when he presented the details of the renegotiation of the public foreign debt to the National Congress in February 1986.

Renegotiation had been proposed to the international banks in June 1983, but in spite of many efforts it was not until nearly two and a half years later that the first version of the Agreement materialised. By this time, the world climate regarding the debt was becoming more demanding. During negotiations various propositions from Venezuela and the creditor banks came up.

The fact that the negotiations to conclude the Renegotiation Agreement took so much time had both advantages and disadvantages for the country; advantages because one could negotiate better financial conditions and would not start to pay the capital until the Agreement had been signed—this became an unexpected period of grace; disadvantages, because with the exception of this year penalties for late payment had to be made.

One of the most controversial themes in this process was the recognition of the private sector debt. A Committee was set up to continue negotiations of this debt and the Government committed itself to granting the foreign exchange required for the servicing. Each time a new deferral was agreed to, the creditor banks brought up the problem of the private foreign debt; a clarification was asked for on the accumulated amount of gross obligations maturing in December 1984—these amounted to US $6,000 million to 7,000 million—and an implementation of administrative proceedings with RECADI was required which had the effect of lightening the private foreign debt servicing.

In spite of all the controversy about preferential dollars for the private sector debt and the subsequent risk of fraud, preferential treatment was granted for private debt which had been legitimately contracted abroad—at Bs 4.30/$ for capital payments and Bs 7.50/$ for interest payments. This system was maintained until the recent economic measures of 1986 in which the Bs 4.30/$ were eliminated. In December 1986, it was decided that the debt should be paid at 7.50/$ on payment of a premium, or at the new controlled rate of Bs 14.50/$.

The treatment of the private foreign debt was an enormous concession to the creditor banks which should have strengthened our negotiating power.

Why did Venezuela not renegotiate with the help of the

IMF? One of the main decisions made in negotiation strategy was that the Government firmly believed that the debt renegotiation should not imply a stand-by agreement. This rejection of the IMF's financial-logistic support had much to do with the economic demands of this organisation, even though it should be recognised that in practice 1984's adjustment programme included measures as orthodox as those of the IMF.

May 1983 saw the start of talks with the IMF. The organisation proposed a series of macro-economic recommendations as a previous condition to setting up a stand-by agreement. In addition, exchange rate unification was insisted upon, a situation which the Government did not contemplate for the short-term. However, in June 1983, the IMF evaluated the Government's economic programme giving the green light. In the renegotiation process it was agreed to keep the IMF informed about the economic progress achieved and to this date there have been regular IMF consultations.

4) Financial conditions of the public foreign debt agreement

There were three parts to the restructuring of the public foreign debt—the Republic's direct debt, the debt assumed by the Republic and the direct debt of the decentralised bodies.

Financial conditions of the restructuring of the public foreign debt—February 1987 (Amendment)

Financed amount: US $21,088 million (including US $750 million initial payment and the remainder being restructured balances which were revised from US $20,538 millions to US $20,442.40 million). Maturities for the years 1983 to 1988 were renegotiated.

Guarantee:	The Republic of Venezeuela
Period:	Fourteen years (final date: second quarter 1999)
Commission:	None
Amortization:	Initial payment of US $750 million

(completed). Quarterly payments rising from fourth quarter 1987 (see Table 8.6).

Interest rate:	LIBOR: Adjustable domestic rate of creditor

country or fixed rate (to be determined on signature of the Agreements). The preferential rate was eliminated. Interest to be paid quarterly.

Financial Margin: 7/8 per cent over LIBOR. This rate to be revised from those banks opting for fixed rates in order to reflect a margin comparable to 7/8 per cent.

Legislation and jurisdiction: New York state laws with exclusive jurisdiction for tribunals in Venezuela, New York, England and other member countries of EEC, Canada, Japan, Switzerland, Spain and Hong Kong.

Table 8.6A: *Amortization schedule of restructured debt as proposed in 1987 Amendment*

Years	US $ millions
1985	0.00
1986	666.00[a]
1987	334.00[a]
1988	400.00
1989	700.00
1990	1,050.00
1991	1,250.00
1992	1,450.00
1993	1,650.00
1994	1,850.00
1995	2,050.00
1996	2,250.00
1997	2,450.00
1998	2,650.00
1999	2,338.00
Total	21,088.00

Note: a In 1986, 88 per cent of the down payment was cancelled (US $750 millions), and the outstanding 12 per cent will be paid in 1987.
Source: Amendment of the Debt Restructuring Agreement.

Additionally, the following conditions were agreed on: *Economic Continuity System*: A programme of adjustment was agreed to go through the Quantified Economic Programme (PEC), already mentioned, which is discussed at Governmental level and whose information is contained in the Economic Memorandum presented to the banks each quarter.

Relationship with the IMF: On Venezuela's request the IMF is to carry out the consultations outlined in Article IV of the Articles Agreement each month.

Special clauses in the Agreement: The agreement contained three special clauses:

i)   *Currency option clause:* This was included at the request of some creditor banks not domiciled in the USA who preferred settlement of their debts in their own currency taking into account the problems which could be brought about by keeping the credits in dollars. Such creditors could exercise the conversion option in the following currencies: Belgian Franc, Canadian Dollar, German Mark, Dutch Florin, European Currency Unit (ECU), French Franc, Italian Lira, Japanese Yen, Pound Sterling, Spanish Peseta and Swiss Franc.

In the February 1987 Amendment new opportunities of money conversion were included. The total amount for conversion into other currencies would be US $3,000 million.

ii) *Re-lending facility:* Intended for public debtors who wished to settle part or whole of their debts in advance for liquidity reasons. In this case they would deposit such payments in the re-lending fund and, thus, see their financial charges reduced. The mechanism consisted of reassigning the debt of an official body to another one or to a private firm and had two parts to it: a) Repayment, advance payment of whole or part of the debt of the public organisations that wished to do so. Each creditor, however, has the opportunity of not accepting the option which corresponds to that payment; b) Re-lending, consisting in the power of each creditor bank to re-lend either partially or totally what he holds in the Re-lending Fund in which are deposited the amounts destined for prepayments to potential borrowers once the Republic informed the banks of the entities and/or sector which can receive such re-loans. At the moment it is expected that five state firms are to make prepayments for US $1,300 million.

iii)   *Contingency Clause:* Contemplated as a result of the 1986 Mexico earthquake and in face of a weakening petroleum market. The February 1987 Amendment invoked this clause.

iv)   *Non-Completion Clauses:* The Agreement stipulated the following: a) cross default, in case of any public organisations not paying their foreign debts to the minimum amount established in the Agreement the creditor banks with 66 per cent of the restructured debts could declare due the obligations deriving from the restructuring treaties; b) the violation of any of the Agreements; c) if Venezuela lost eligibility for IMF credit; d) if operating reserves fell below US $2,000 million; e) if the legislation serving as base for the restructuring was suspended in some important aspects.

However, the most important reasons for non-completion would be the presumption of the majority of the creditor banks that the Republic, or any borrower in the public sector, was not paying the debt or did not have the capacity to pay the restructured debt, or proof that the adjustment programmes were incompatible with the continued servicing of the debt— this is to say that the country did not expect a solid external position which would allow the payment of that servicing.

Additionally, the 1987 Amendment mentioned that the obligations of some public sector entities could be converted into investments in accordance with a debt capitalisation programme.

3. THE RENEGOTIATION AGREEMENT FOR THE VENEZUELAN PUBLIC FOREIGN DEBT— COMMENTARIES AND PERSPECTIVES

In spite of the satisfaction at Government level and in some private circles derived from concluding the Renegotiation Agreement for the Venezuelan public foreign debt, discontent has been expressed and criticism has been formulated in no small measure. From the ethical point of view, some have argued that the debt has been contracted by a few and enjoyed by more, and will now have to be paid sacrificing the whole country (Echevarria, 1986).

Venezuela arranged a multi-annual renegotiation agreement with the banks and keeps the IMF informed twice a year about economic results through the ordinary consultations which the IMF holds with Government representatives in accordance with the stipulations of article IV of the organisation's Articles of Agreement.

The financial conditions in the restructuring agreement of the Venezuelan public debt can be compared with that of present conditions in other countries. However, even when the financial margin was reduced from $1\frac{1}{8}$ per cent to $\frac{7}{8}$ per cent in the 1987 Amendment, one should stress that Argentina and Mexico obtained a margin of less than $\frac{3}{16}$ per cent—Venezuela could have succeeded in getting the same. In relation to the period of the renegotiation, Mexico got twenty years and Argentina nineteen years for part of US \$25,300 million and both included grace periods, whereas in the Venezuelan case the period remained at fourteen years and without grace periods.

Once the renegotiation of the foreign debt had been achieved, expectations abounded about the possibilities that Venezuela could re-enter the private capital markets. Up until now, only multilateral credits, principally from the IDB, some guaranteed export credits conceded to state firms have been agreed. At the moment talks are under way with the banks aimed at securing new finance to cover the requirements of the internal economy. Recently, negotiations were held about a placement of US \$100 million's worth of bonds on the Euromarket.

The implementation of the Agreement was delayed owing to problems which had occurred in the interim such as the necessity to invoke the contingency clause in face of recent events in the petroleum market and the uncertainty about the system of preferential treatment which would be applicable to foreign debt after the elimination of FOCOCAM.

According to CEPAL figures, the net transfer of resources

Table 8.6B: *Venezuela: Net transfers of resources (millions of US$ and percentages)*

Years	Net capital income[1] (1)	Net payments of profits and interests (2)	Transfers of resources (3)=(1)−(2)	Exports of goods and services[2] (4)	Transfers of resources/ exports of goods (5)=(3)/(4)
VENEZUELA					
1983	−4,116	2,113	−6,229	14,759	−43%
1984	−3,858	1,352	−5,210	15,967	−33%
1985	−2,573	2,338	−4,911	14,178	−35%
1986	−2,660	1,740	−4,400	8,686	−51%
LATIN AMERICA					
1983	3,200	34,300	−31,100	102,400	−31%
1984	9,200	36,200	−27,000	114,100	−24%
1985	2,400	35,300	−32,900	109,000	−31%
1986	8,600	30,700	−22,100	95,200	−24%

Notes: [1]. Includes short- and long-term capital, official unilateral transfers and errors and omissions.
   [2]. In the case of Venezuela, only exports of goods are included.

Source: CEPAL, Economic and Development Bulletin—December 1985.
   BCV, Quarterly Bulletin.

from Latin America has risen from 1981 onwards, putting these countries in the position of being net exporters of financial resources. The case of Venezuela is important given that resource transfer abroad have been higher than the Latin American average (in relation with exports); see Table 8.6. Resource transfer averaged around US $5,000 million between 1983 and 1986 (about 38 per cent of average exports of goods in those years).

Expectations are that these resource transfers will continue to be negative now that Venezuela is almost the only country in the region which in its negotiations with the banks has always insisted on settling amortization payments of debt according to the time schedule established, while other countries have limited themselves to paying interest, and Brazil even declaring a moratorium on interest payments in February 1987. Consequently, Venezuela has also been the only country amongst the leading five of Latin America which succeeded in reducing the total of its public debt between 1982 to 1986, from $33.4 billion to $32.4 billion.

Another negative aspect is the capital flight which has persisted despite the exchange measures applied.

In Chapter 1 of this book Dr Stephany Griffith-Jones correctly argues that when net transfers are negative, the debtor country will potentially have more power in deciding not to pay, in not making the transfers and in resisting the demands of the lender even to the point of imposing its own conditions.

Based on these ideas, one can conclude that if the net negative resource transfers abroad are higher for Venezuela than the figure for the whole of Latin America, this would imply that the country had extra negotiating capacity to impose its criteria on the creditor banks. The high level of international reserves and the concessions granted on the private debt further strengthened the Venezuelan negotiators' position.

The enormous concessions made on private foreign debt can be explained if we take into account that great part of the handling of the renegotiation of the public foreign debt was at first in the hands of high-level representatives of the private sector. In addition, there were pressures on the part of the creditor banks as existing in the case of countries whose private external debt had reached very high levels.

1) Implications of the Renegotiation Agreement of the public foreign debt.

As a result of Venezuela achieving the Renegotiation Agreement on public foreign debt in February 1986, and later modified in February of this year, debt servicing was reduced, both in terms of interest and capital amortization. On extending maturities to 1999, according to the 1987 Amendment, once the whole of the initial quota (US $84 million) is to be settled by the end of this year, between 1987 and 1989, 6 per cent, and during the years 1990 to 1994, 35 per cent will be paid, whilst the highest charges will be transferred to the period 1995–9 where the remaining 58 per cent are to be settled—all based on increasing amortization quotas, as seen in Table 8.5. If to this is added what must be paid for the non-restructured debt and the interest on both debts, the chronogram of payment for public foreign debt will imply annual outgoings of around US $3,000 million in the coming years.

The capacity to face such payments will undoubtedly depend on the levels reached by international reserves—this being subject to the variable of petroleum price and to the possibility of obtaining new bank lending.

2) Possible alternatives

Any alternatives must imply action both on the internal and external levels. Externally, the Renegotiation Agreement for the debt permits the lightening of the load of debt servicing. However, it would be necessary to implement a policy of becoming indebted in accordance with the global strategy of economic growth, within the objective of complementing internal savings.

Some measures have been taken to stimulate the non-traditional export sector. Additionally, it is urgent to implement control on capital flight, which is one of the factors negatively affecting the capital account. Further a debt equity scheme was adopted which it is hoped will marginally reduce the level of foreign debt.

CONCLUSION

The economic crisis experienced by Venezuela since 1979, is to a large extent attributable to the lack of economic policies with a global strategy of growth, capable of facing the reality of a country with a high and fluctuating petroleum income. A large part of the foreign debt of the country served to finance capital flight.

We have attempted to outline the experience of the renegotiation of the Venezuelan foreign debt having shown as central aspects, on the one hand, that even when it was not anticipated institutionally, the fact was that in the negotiations the problems of the renegotiation of the public foreign debt was linked to the pending debt payments on foreign private debt. This, demonstrated the creditor banks' view that the country's debt should be considered as a whole.

It was emphasised that Venezuela would renegotiate the debt, without going to the IMF, a special feature in the recent renegotiations of the debt on an international level. However, it is worth asking to what extent this was advantageous to the country—this question arises when we ask ourselves whether one could really obtain more external credit without counting on the organisation's support, and if the creditor banks' way of following the economy would be a sufficiently acceptable alternative for them through the lifetime of the agreement.

With respect to the handling of foreign debt, Venezuela could have explored to a greater degree our negotiating capacity, taking into account the enormous concessions given to private foreign debt and the size of negative transfers.

Besides obtaining relatively advantageous conditions within this context, we should emphasise that the Agreement was a response to internal pressures both from the private sector and the political parties, both of whom were active participants in defining negotiating strategy, in the negotiation of the Agreement, and in discussions of the treatment of the private foreign debt.

The Renegotiation Agreement was modified in February of this year in some of its terms owing to the deterioration of the petroleum market.

Finally, we would like to indicate that the success or failure

Table 8.7: Restructured and non-restructured debt (as of December 31, 1983) (millions of US $)

Restructured debt		
Certificates of deposits	2,010.10	
Short-term obligations	8,779.50	
Medium-term obligations	10,006.50	
Endorsements	1,180.80	
Restructured debt total		21,976.90 (80%)
Non-restructured debt		
Bonds	1,163.40	
Multilateral institutions	415.60	
Bilateral institutions	267.00	
Bilaterals: with commercial banks	1,692.20	
Suppliers	1,240.50	
Letter of credits	246.10	
Obligations due as of Dec. 31, 1982	221.60	
Money market: B.I.V.*	177.60	
Other obligations	54.00	
Total non-restructured		5,477.90 (20%)
Total external public debt		27,454.80 (100%)[a]

Notes: * Industrial Bank of Venezuela

[a] According to recent estimations Public External Debt for that year was US $27.616 millions.

Source: Ministry of Finance.

Table 8.8.: Venezuela: External public debt service projections (millions of US $) (As of 10-07-87)

	Restructured debt			Non-restructured debt			Total principal	Total interest	Total
	Principal	Interest	Total	Principal	Interest	Total			
1984*	0	2,142	2,142	2,308	807	3,115	2,308	2,949	5,257
1985*	0	2,143	2,143	2,378	630	3,008	2,378	2,773	5,151
1986*	0	2,027	2,027	1,009	1,213	2,222	1,009	3,240	4,249
1987	666	2,024	2,690	714	592	1,306	1,380	2,616	3,996
1988	335	1,517	1,852	617	424	1,041	952	1,941	2,893
1989	400	1,465	1,865	829[a]	363	1,192	1,229	1,828	
1990	700	1,439	2,139	1,084	275	1,359	1,784	1,714	3,498
1991	1,050	1,475	2,525	778	164	942	1,828	1,639	3,467

Notes: Payments of principal according to the Restructured Agreement 1987 includes US $84 millions corresponding to the down payment of 1986.

* Real Figures

[a] In 1988, US $805.5 millions of Bonds hold by BIV, BANAP and Central Bank of Venezuela were not included.

[1] Estimated Libor Rate were: 6.680% (1987); 6.700% (1988); 6.700% (1989) and 7.00% (1990).

[2] Since 1988, interest rate adopted was a fixed rate of 9.00 + 1⅛% annual.

Source: Ministry of Finance.

Table 8.9: External registered public and private debt (US $ millions)

I. EXTERNAL PUBLIC DEBT				78%
Commercial banks		25,291.60	(90%)	
Restructured debt	20,422.40[a]	22,783.00		
Non restructured debt	2,360.60			
Other creditors (Non restructured debt)		2,508.60	(10%)	
Bonds	1,725.40			
Suppliers	518.30			
Multilateral institutions	200.80			
Bilaterals	64.10			
II. EXTERNAL PRIVATE DEBT		7,177.10		22%
Commerical banks	5,163.10			
Other creditors	2,014.00			
TOTAL EXTERNAL DEBT		32,468.70		100%

Note: [a] This Figure has been updated in 1987, after Credit Tables conciliation

Source: Ministry of Finance and Central Bank of Venezuela

of the renegotiations will be evaluated on the one hand by how the economy can support the weight of debt servicing (taking into account the new petroleum background), and on the other hand, the possibilities of access to international credit. With respect to this, an opportunity to finance on a multilateral base has been established, but it is necessary to look at the possibility of obtaining credits from alternative sources, mainly international financial markets.

NOTES

1. Following Rodriguez, the 1980 and 1981 inflation was due to cost inflation, inertia and structural problems. Not being the consequence of excess demand or liquidity, it was not justified to follow a policy of contraction on aggregate demand since this would result in damage to real production and to employment.
2. The scheme would allow the debtor (only when debtor and creditor are in agreement) to acquire zero coupons issued by the Treasury, but not to a level greater than 30 per cent of his pending balance in the foreign debt recognised by RECADI.

REFERENCES

CEPAL, 1985, *Balance Preliminar de la Economía de Latino-americana 1985*.

Conesa, Eduardo, *Fuga de Capitales de América Latina, 1970–85. Argentina, Brasil, Chile, Colombia, México, Perú, Venezuela*, Inter-American Development Bank.

Consejo de Economia Nacional, *El Bono Cero Cupón y el Refinanciamiento de la Deuda Externa*, Caracas, No. 4, April 1985.

Cordova, Armando, 'Un Diagnóstico de la Crisis Económica Venezolana', *Revista Latinoamericana de Planificación*, Vol. XIX, No. 74, México, June 1985.

Diaz Bruzual, L., 1984, *Crisis y Recuperación*, Editorial Oeste, Caracas.

Echevarria, Oscar, 1984, *La Crisis Económica de Venezuela. Mito y Realidades*, UCAB, Caracas, Second Edition.

——— 1986, *Deuda ... Crisis Cambiaria, Causas y Correctivos*, UCAB, Caracas.

Fajardo, Julián Antonio, 1985, *El Endeudamiento Externo en Venezuela*, Promotion Work, Colegio Universitario de Caracas, Caracas.

Gonzales Rubi, Rafael, 1983, *Venezuela. Las Vicisitudes de la Crisis. Sección Latinoamericana*, Comercio Exterior, México.

Hausmann, Ricardo, 'Venezuela: Politicas de Ajuste y Reactivación', Mimeo.

Marquez, Guillermo, 1983, *La Economia Venezolana en la Década de los 70 (1970–83)*, Monte Avila Editores.

Ministerio De Hacienda, *Memoria*, Various years.

Naim, M. y Piñango, R., 1984, *El Caso Venezuela. Una Ilusion de Armonia*, Ediciones IESA, Caracas.

Palma, Pedro, 1986, *Fococam, Un Nuevo Esquema para el Pago de la Deuda Privada Externa*, Caracas.

Palma, Pedro, 1984, *The Debt Problem. A Debtor's Point of View*, IESA y Metroeconómica, Caracas.

Pazos, Felipe, *Politica de Desarrollo Económico*, Collection of Articles, Reports and Bulletins 1949–84, Banco Central de Venezuela.

Petkoff, Teodoro, 1986, 'Nuevos Criterios para Refinanciar la Deuda Externa', IV Congress of Economics of the Andean Countries, Caracas, 22–25 April 1986.

Republica de Venezuela, '*Memorándum Económico*', 17 May 1985.

Rodriguez, Miguel, 1986, *Notas sobre el Ahorro, la Inversión y el Endeudamiento Externo Venezolano*, Seminar on Savings and Investment in Latin America, CEDES, Buenos Aires.

——— *Consequences of Capital Flight for Latin American Debtor Countries*, IESA, Caracas.

Romero, Hugo, 'La Balanza de Pagos y la Reorganización del Sistema Cambiario', *Revista del BCV*, January/March 1987, p 299.

Sistema Economico Latinoamericano (SELA), 1987, *América Latina en la Economía Mundial: Problemas y Perspectivas*, Siglo Veintiuno Editores, México.

Venezuela, Summary of Proposed Terms of the 1987 Amendments to the Restructuring Agreements, Caracas, 1 April 1987.

Zambrano, Luis, 1986, *Politicas Econoîmica, Reactivación y Crecimiento*, Instituto de Investigaciones Económicas y Sociales, Universidad Católica Andrés Bello.

Zambrano, Luis, Riutort, Matías, Vainrub, Charlotte, and Chi-Yi-Chen, 1983, *Notas sobre las medidas sugeridas por el Fondo Monetario Internacional y sus Implications*, Instituto de Investigaciones Económicas y Sociales, UCAB, Joint Themes No. 2, Caracas.

9 Unmanageable—Toward Sub-Saharan African Debt Bargaining?

Reginald Herbold Green

Per capita output in low-income Africa has declined so drastically over the last 15 years that most of the gains of the modern era have been wiped out. Today, low-income Africa is poorer than it was in 1960. (A. W. Clausen, World Bank, 1986)

Africa's debt burden is now intolerable. We cannot pay. You know it and all our other creditors know it. It is not a rhetorical question when I ask, should we really let our people starve so that we can pay our debts? (Julius K. Nyerere, OAU Chairman, 1985)

THE INVISIBILITY OF AN ICEBERG: SSA EXTERNAL DEBT 1960—84

The term 'debt crisis' has, at least in the North and among bankers or academic specialists, tended to mean crises threatening the solvency of major commercial banks and the stability of the international monetary system. In those terms it is reasonable to argue that Sub-Saharan African states (even collectively) do not pose a 'debt crisis' because their gross commercial bank borrowing is of the order of $25 billion, even excluding write-offs or reserves already provided and potentially offsettable deposits.

On the other hand, in SSA, the term 'debt crisis' is taken to mean levels of external debt to all creditors whose servicing imposes unmanageable burdens relative to export earnings if paid, and almost equally unattractive loss, not only of commercial credit, but also of concessional finance if allowed to go into, or remain, in, default. By that definition—which is the one used in this chapter—about three-quarters of SSA's

245

forty-six states have either a fully-fledged external debt crisis or are on the brink of one.

The only SSA economies one could seriously propose as both truly plausible credit risks from a commercial bank lender's point of view and prudent potential borrowers for general purposes from their own are Botswana and Cameroon. A few more may be plausible cases for consolidation and roll-over loans or for commercial borrowing (preferably on a non-recourse project tied basis) for fairly safe, high-yield, export-oriented projects. Zimbabwe and Kenya may be examples on a general basis; non-recourse project tied loans (albeit realistically more likely to be export credit agency than commercial bank financed) may be sound for lenders and borrowers for very strong projects even in very weak economies, for example, the Songo Songo/Kilwa natural gas to ammonia/urea project in Tanzania and gold mining rehabilitation and expansion in Ghana.

This perception of an SSA debt crisis is a recent one—at least outside the chronic *de facto* default cases such as Zaire and the Sudan. Even at continental level within SSA it dates only from 1982–3. At international agency and academic level general recognition began to develop only from 1984–5.

The basic available data on SSA external debt and debt service are set out in the tables annexed to this paper. As noted below they are, even now, not very accurate (in some cases not at all accurate), but they do demonstrate that continentally, and for most countries, SSA has a nearly unmanageable debt burden.

The parameters of the invisible
SSA external debt was small and its service—with a few exceptions—sustainable and sustained until 1974. Most of the countries had become independent in 1960 or later and, in retrospect, in the 1960s SSA faced much less unfavourable international economic contexts than over 1971–5 or from 1979 to date. External debt was rising rapidly but from a low base and, except for a handful of countries with strong export bases, most of it was from governments (including their export credit agencies) or multilateral development finance institutions.

Even as of 1986, total SSA external debt (including all arrears and short-term financial institutional credit, as well as all medium- and long-term obligations) was in the range of $100 to $140 billion or under 15 per cent of total developing countries' external debt. Commerical bank debt stood at about 25 per cent of the total ($25 to $35 million) or perhaps 5 per cent of total commercial banks developing countries' exposure. At country level it was still smaller—looked at from a global perspective—with no debtor over $25 billion, only three over $10 billion and only five over $5 billion.

The 1986 levels of debt, however, were—as show in the tables—high relative to GDP as was the debt service level.

The 1973-86 debt buildup has had four phases:

1. 1974-5 borrowing to ride out 1973-5 drought and terms of trade (including, but not limited to, oil) shocks.
2. 1976-9 borrowing to speed up growth (which did indeed rise to a sustained four year rate of over 5 per cent—SSA's best period) made possible by sharply improved export earnings and commercial banks' willingness to lend less selectively especially to countries with low initial debt service ratios.
3. 1980-2 borrowing to ride out what was at first believed to be a short-term shock like 1974-5.
4. Post-1982 borrowing—substantially from arrears and/or rescheduling—to avert import strangulation or open default.

The SSA debt profile has—relative to other regions—higher proportions of multilateral agency loans, IMF drawings, short-term credits and arrears. This worsens the debt management problem. The first two categories are formally non-reschedulable and the last two are peculiarly hard to reschedule in practice. The latter three are also omitted from, or only partially recorded in, many international debt tabulations.

Other parameters of invisibility include very incomplete national recording with pre-crises estimates in several cases at, or under, 50 per cent of post crises tabulations as well as a case-by-case approach concentrating on one country at a time.

In addition to obscuring the continental nature of the problem, this approach tended to cause attention to be focussed almost totally on what the debtor had done wrong. Arguably this was a plausible focus to the early 1970s when only a handful of countries—for example, Ghana, Sudan, Zaire—had congenitally dismal economic performance records, but it has become palpably unrealistic since 1979.

THE VIEW FROM SSA

As noted above, SSA debt service to export ratios are approaching 50 per cent. By IMF calculations they were about 40 per cent in 1985 (including IMF and short-term debt service). By 1987 low income SSA economies are likely to be paying 20 per cent of export earnings in interest on external debt alone. In extreme cases scheduled interest and repayments—even with most debt concessional—actually exceed export levels, and in many—for example, Ghana—they amount to over 60 per cent of gross grant and loan inflows even in the context of substantial World Bank/IMF backed structural adjustment programmes.

Despite the relatively low pre-1974 debt levels, the external debt service problems of some SSA economies are not new. Prior to 1975 over half of all rescheduling agreements involved SSA economies. In 1986 over twenty SSA states sought Paris Club reschedulings, for some for the eighth or ninth time.

The perception and actual levels of debt sevice burdens in SSA are not uniform. At one extreme, Botswana has less external debt than external reserves and only moderately more interest due on debt than receivable on reserves. At the other extreme are twelve low income economies which the World Bank indicated in 1986 could never in fact repay their external debt. The twelve are Benin, Gambia, Liberia, Madagascar, Mali, Mauretania, Niger, Somalia, Sudan, Tanzania, Togo and Zambia. However, if one takes all poor countries with 1986-7 debt service ratios over 30 per cent on the World Bank's basis (which is probably one-third below the total actually payable), Guinea-Bissau, Senegal, Sierra Leone, Uganda, Zaire and Mozambique enter this category. Côte d'Ivoire, Nigeria and Gabon have similar debt service ratios but are less poor and arguably could eventually repay subject to extended reschedulings.

Some tactical implications

For most SSA economies grants and new loans exceed interest and amortization actually paid (which is substantially less than payable). The net flow has—according to Overseas Development Council estimates—fallen from $10 billion in 1980 to $4.9 billion in 1985. The 1987 estimated recovery to $7.3 billion (partly due to reschedulings) seems unlikely to be sustained unless very substantial extended reschedulings become the norm. World Bank data for IDA eligible countries (excluding Mozambique) show a net inflow before rescheduling of $5.1 billion annual average over 1980–2, $3.0 billion over 1983–4 and $2.7 billion projected over 1986–90. Including rescheduling, the annual net flows become $6.2 billion, $4,8 billion and $5.0 billion respectively. However, both non-concessional and IMF flows had already gone negative by 1985.

The SSA and individual net resources inflow countries cannot afford to institute unilateral rescheduling/servicing action beyond the point at which this would seriously jeopardise new flows. As a result, they have tended to build up commercial (trade) and subsequently government debt service arrears quietly on a semi-ignored, semi-condoned basis rather than take Peru-like initiatives. Nigeria—a net outflow country—did take a tentative Peruvian stance, but with an exports proposed ceiling of 40 per cent, it was, when promulgated, adequate to pay all interest and about half of principal amortization. In the event, it came unstuck because of the 1986 oil price collapse. The 1985 Sudanese statement of a one per cent of export earnings ceiling was really a rephrased 'won't pay because can't pay' cry of pain and the Zairean declaration is seen widely as a bluff or negotiating gambit, not a statement of real intent.

For the least developed and some other low income SSA economies, full write-off of some bilateral concessional debt has proven attainable. Except for the USSR, USA and Japan, major creditor governments have retrospectively converted loans to these states into grants. However, since some—for example, the UK—charged the stream of waived repayments against their aid budget, the degree of additionality is somewhat problematic.

But, non-reschedulable borrowing from multilateral agencies (basically the World Bank/ODA, IMF and African Development Bank) represent a high proportion of SSA borrowing and debt service. For the IDA eligible group they represented 17.5 per cent before (25 per cent after) rescheduling over 1980–2 and 22 per cent before (29 per cent after) rescheduling over 1980–4 with 1986–90 projections of 29 per cent respectively.

While, in principle, humanitarian considerations (in respect to bilateral and IDA concessional finance) and support for Bank/Fund approved stabilisation/structural adjustment programmes can be used to press for substantial reschedulings, in practice coordination is hard. Indeed, the World Bank has been sharply critical of bilateral representatives at Consultative Group meetings adopting rescheduling targets which the same governments then declined to meet at subsequent Paris Club sessions.

1986–95: PROJECTIONS ASND PREMONITIONS

There is little reason to project any substantial improvement in the external economic context confronting SSA and most of its national economies over the period to 1995. External balance improvement since 1981 relate overwhelmingly to import cuts, which are by now eroding not only national product but also attainable export levels.

Real interest rates for SSA are even higher than global totals suggest. External interest and principal are paid in (or literally from the proceeds of) exports. Therefore, the nominal interest rate needs to be adjusted by the nominal export price change to determine real interest, for example, if interest is 10 per cent nominal and export prices fall 10 per cent then the effective real interest rate from the debtors' perspective is 20 per cent even if creditor country inflation of 4 per cent makes the real interest rate from their perspective 6 per cent. Export price changes have a similar effect on amortization. With few exceptions SSA exports have poor nominal, let alone real, price prospects. They may stabilise or fluctuate around 1987 levels, but even in nominal terms there are frequently 40-50 per cent below mid-1970s highs.

To date special facilities and structural adjustment programmes have been seriously under-financed. With the number of SAPs rising and the use of IMF credit to plug shortfalls in other finance less and less adequate, this problem seems more likely to become worse rather than better over 1987-95.

Overall, World Bank projections for SSA show negligible or negative real per capita GDP growth to 1995—from a 1985 per capita base averaging about 25 per cent per capita less than the late 1970s. The debt service/export and debt/GDP ratios also either improve very slowly or worsen in these projections. For the low income countries even after more generous rescheduling than has typified 1980-6, the World Bank projects 1986-90 import capacity per capita as below either that of 1980-2 or of the mid-1970s.

PRELUDES TO NEGOTIATIONS—NATIONAL

It is hard to describe SSA debt negotiations to date as satisfactory to anybody with the possible exception of commercial banks in some of the London Club reschedulings. That several countries are now seeking their eighth or ninth rescheduling is perhaps in itself adquate evidence—the breathing space is not large or long enough for revival of the economies; the creditors remain largely unpaid. The IMF record is rather parallel. With the potential exception of Zimbabwe, no major post-1978 higher credit *tranche* drawer has been able to restore adequate growth levels while repaying IMF drawings on time other than by re-drawing.

SSA Paris and London Club renegotiations have not been innovative even by the standards of these bodies. Until 1986, the central tendency for Paris Club reschedulings was to roll-forward official debt arrears plus eighteen to twenty-four months payments of principal (and sometimes interest) with five years grace and five further years to repay principal (less for interest and arrears). While good faith clauses on subsequent reschedulings of further years of payments on the rescheduled loans are common, their actual utilisation has been much less so.

Several multi-stage (twelve to eighteen months payments rolled forward each time) reschedulings have been concluded, for example, for Zaire and the Sudan. Each has had elaborate conditionality and monitoring. Their defects include: the massive misallocation of debtor personnel time required to monitor, report, confer, renegotiate them; gross under-financing (even on paper) of accompanying new financial packages; total absence of lender performance monitoring; overall macro-economic assumptions which are—taken together—frequently so optimistic as to make the arrangements about as stable as a house of cards in a typhoon.

While Paris Club reschedulings now usually follow a consultative group financing meeting, they are not institutionally linked to it. More seriously, they rarely provide even short-term debt service burden reduction equal to the amounts set down—by the same governments wearing their consultative group hats—in the macro-economic and balance of payments projections agreed by the group and very often authored by the World Bank. The World Bank has explicitly blamed at least one adjustment programme collapse—Zambia 1984—on this non-coordination.

The IMF does not formally reschedule but in practice seems to have become locked in with respect to its larger SSA drawers. The only way most of them—for example Ghana—can repurchase on time is likely to be by immediately redrawing. While this may maximise long-term IMF influence, it is a peculiar way either to provide long-term structural adjustment or short-term bridging finance. In the better funded structural adjustment programmes—for example, Ghana—heavy IMF drawings in early years are used to cover a general lag in initial bilateral pledging and disbursement but from year four on (when the grace period expires) IMF scheduled repurchases tend to be similar to the projected financing gap.

As a result, the IMF seems rather disposed to use its Structural Adjustment Fund (retreaded Trust Fund with concessional interest rates and longer repayment periods) primarily to refinance part of maturing stand-by drawings, which is arguably not the most efficient allocation. It does reduce pressure on both the Fund and the borrower, albeit the Fund is now seeking tougher conditionality on SAF use than on second credit *tranche* drawings.

Commercial arrears have proven to be a very costly form of external borrowing. In extreme cases they have the result of forcing an economy to revert to cash payments on or before arrival or to externally confirmed letters of credit fully offset by counter deposits. Even more generally they result in premiums of up to 30 per cent on goods sent on credit because of non-, or delayed, payment risk with consequential losses of principal or extra interest charges for the un-, or late, paid seller.

They have also proven to be almost impossible to reschedule except in respect to insured arrears taken over by government export credit guarantee agencies which have been covered under the Paris Club umbrella. Nigeria did negotiate rescheduling, but the agreement broke down within two years in a welter of principal and amortization defaults. The initial problem with rescheduling is the number of creditors but the ultimate one is cost. Many SSA economies have outstanding commercial arrears of 50 per cent to over 100 per cent of annual export earnings.

Do-it-yourself reschedulings have been rare and, with one special exception, rather unsatisfactory. Nigeria's attempt to reschedule (especially on short-term bank lines of credit and on commercial arrears) and to set a 30 per cent to 40 per cent of export earnings debt service to exports cap, without a prior Fund (or Bank) agreement rapidly unravelled.

A more common form of do-it-yourself has been semi-selective massive run-up of arrears on medium- and long-term debt service, as a semi-condoned partial default or debt service cap. While one may suspect some of the run-ups represented inability to manage rather than conscious management, others—for example, Tanzania from 1982—were seen as interim debt service burden limitation tactics. This approach has in several cases bought time but it is hard to see how at least the commercial arrears portion of the overhang can be unwound. That problem is even more acute when—as in Sudan, Zambia and Liberia—substantial repurchase arrears with the IMF block a new IMF agreement until cleared and, thereby, as a second step, block any general, formal rescheduling.

Zimbabwe did manage a 'take it or leave it' rescheduling in 1984 which was both inventive and largely successful. It related to blocked balances awaiting remittance at some unspecified future date which prior to that point could be deposited—at up to 15 per cent in 1984—and the interest remitted immediately. These were converted into 4 per cent government stock with eight to twelve years' maturity. The net present value, as well as the current debt service, were evidently very sharply reduced so that the official presentation of the measures as safeguarding convertibility of interest and liquidation of principal would appear to be a none too subtle piece of sarcasm. Amazingly the creditors—and even financial journals—accepted this rescheduling with little adverse comment.

In addition, the blocked balances could be used to finance approved domestic investment—*de facto* a form of equitisation. In that event dividends (as on all post-September 1979 approved foreign equity investment) would be remittable.

The reason for external acceptance would appear to be the history of the specific debts (or arrears) in question. They represented interest, rent, dividend and amortization or asset liquidation payments due under the illegal Rhodesian regime which were blocked by that regime's exchange controls. Because of their origins and the total inconvertibility of principal and interest from the mid-1960s to 1980, it is likely that these arrears were considered to be a special case and that similar treatment of other external debts (by Zimbabwe or any other SSA state) would not be received equally benignly.

Since 1984, Zimbabwe has been seeking to avoid a standard Paris Club rescheduling—at least partly because with a large budgetary deficit which is primarily the counterpart of defence expenditure imposed by South African aggression against Zimbabwe and its neighbours, an IMF agreement on standard terms is seen by Zimbabwe as dangerously inappropriate to its circumstances. The results of this stance—very limited concessional finance flows, a 1980-2 post-independence borrowing spree and a 1984-on strategy of accepting only quite concessional or very long-term loans—has created a debt service crunch. If Zimbabwe could achieve a moderate current account surplus through to 1990, the repayment hump would be over but the price of doing that would be drastic intermediate and capital goods imports cuts, quite possibly reducing output by up to 20 per cent.

Zimbabwe is steadily repaying its IMF drawings and propose to liquidate them. It argues that six-year 8 per cent money is not particularly desirable and, perhaps more convincing, that it needs to restore first line liquidity to have it available when a genuine shock (e.g., drought) impact needs to be bridged. The peculiarity is that the Fund, Bank and several bilaterals oppose this apparently orthodox approach to the use of Fund credit presumably because it would limit macro-economic conditionality leverage especially if Zimbabwe sought neither a SAP nor a Paris Club rescheduling.

Tanzania's alternative strategy approaches have related much more to adjustment than to rescheduling as such. Until 1984 they were somewhat hard to decipher because internal dialogue blunted their thrust. Their chief differences from standard versions appear to turn on avoidance, where practicable, of massive shocks; institutionalisation of small, frequent changes (e.g., in respect to the exchange rate, a sector in which Tanzania has adopted an approach very similar to Zimbabwe's); protection of mass access basic services and lower-income household; priority for rehabilitation over new projects (now conventional wisdom not so in 1979 when Tanzania first emphasised it), a very high priority to avoiding major inflationary pressures and determination to avoid if at all possible rates above 30 per cent while seeing 10 per cent as a short to medium (three year) target.

By 1985, it had adopted two further planks—basing its external finance package on an articulated projection of import requirements for rehabilitation and 4 per cent annual growth beyond those financeable from export earnings and reaching agreement with the Bank and bilaterals on firm financial commitments before seriously seeking to reach final agreement with the Fund.

Tanzania eschewed rescheduling attempts—other than partial, semi-condoned building up of arrears—prior to 1986 for two reasons. In the absence of an IMF agreement a Paris Club one clearly could not be obtained and in any event a twelve-to eighteen-month roll-forward would need constant renegotiation. In 1986 Tanzania shifted its stance because consultative group pledges fell short of meeting minimum import requirements by the order of $300 million (or nearly 30 per cent of the import target) and the consultative group was willing to call for a multi-year rescheduling.

Tanzania's proposals for ten years' roll-forward of interest and principal payments including arrears—that is, all 1985-95 service on Paris Club covered debt—with repayment spread over the next ten years were serious ones but proved non-negotiable. However, it did get arrears and 1986-7 principal and interest payments rolled forward (to the extent of 97.5 per cent of all payments otherwise due including arrears) with five years grace and five to repay (i.e., repayment over 1992-2202). While a new roll-forward of 1987-97 (or 2002) payments on these loans will fairly clearly be needed, one year guaranteed and two more implicitly promised on the same terms if the 1987 and 1988 Consultative Group meetings so recommend, was seen as a long enough initial breathing space to be worth agreeing upon; the 1986-7 reduction of debt service was estimated as of the order of $276 million (almost 70 per cent of probable visible export earnings).

PRELUDES TO NEGOTIATIONS—REGIONAL

OAU efforts to organise an SSA-Creditor regional debt conference to agree guidelines for rescheduling/partial writedown/new funds allocation have not succeeded to date. The 1986 General Assembly Special Session was on African economy in general, not external debt in particular. Proposals to Special Session did call for at least $35-40 billion rescheduling to complement $45 billion new money over 1986-90 but did not make the total of $80-85 billion (of $125 billion proposed total fixed investment) external support clear. In the event—unlike most of the rest of proposals—the debt proposals (as a result of a *de facto* OECD, Latin American, Socialist European 'coalition' of very different objections) were not adopted in General Assembly Resolution. That resolution does recognise the existence of a debt problem but its only creditor commitment is to avoid net financial transfers from an SSA economy to a creditor economy.

There have been some subsequent responses. One has been to seek to set up a monitoring system to cover creditor as well as debtor performance (more generally North as well as SSA performance) since the resolution is in quasi-contractual form. Some confusion has arisen as UNDP—using the World Bank as its contractor—appears to view itself as the logical monitoring agency while the UN Economic Commission for Africa, the African Development Bank and most African states think a World Bank/ECA or World Bank/ADB monitoring team would be more appropriate.

EEC countries have responded with—and gained OECD blessing for—longer grace periods and repayment phasing up to perhaps ten plus ten years subject to some (apparently not necessarily IMF) policy conditionality. There is also broad agreement on the need to lower interest rates which would apply primarily to export credits and other non-ODA loans, made particularly explicit in the British initiative. While the EEC favours retrospective conversion of development loans to grants for poor SSA countries that is still not favoured by the two major OECD members—USA, Japan—who have not done it already.

Attempts—surprisingly by the usually conservative UMOA (the West African CFA franc states)—to create a united front representation to the Bank/Fund have been deferred. However, Zimbabwe Finance Minister Bernard Chidzero has used his Development Committee chairmanship to push the African debt term-lengthening and interest-lowering case, one which appears to be gaining a more favourable hearing since the middle of 1986.

A REVIEW OF NEGOTIATIONS TO DATE

Most SSA external debt renegotiatons have been aimed at

preventing import strangulation. In some cases, for example, the Côte d'Ivoire, this end was sought before massive arrears had been piled up or imports had been cut below the minimum levels necessary to operate the economy. In others—for example, Nigeria—it was taken after a crisis had recently broken out with arrears piling up and imports falling away but before a process of decline had taken firm hold. A third set of cases, for example, Zambia, came well after such a process had taken hold with arrears very high, imports very low and even ninety-day commercial (bank or other) trade credit virtually a thing of the past. A final category, for example, the Sudan, involves repeated reschedulings following the failure of successive previous ones to yield a breathing space.

Intellectually, there has been a shift to defining goals in terms of the amount, period of deferral, grace period and repayment which would provide time and economic space to restore imports, economic growth and (usually less articulatedly spelled out) exports adequate to resuming debt service. In fact, this goal has rarely been acceptable to creditors so that, while partially reflected in the 1986 Tanzania Paris Club agreement, it is more prominent in submissions such as that of the OAU to the 1986 United Nations General Assembly Special Session on SSA than in actual reschedulings.

Quite frankly, the majority of the reschedulings have been viewed as buying time—usually a little time—by debtors and creditors. Neither usually really believed they solved the problem, but they did avert collapse and provide a few quarters for something good to turn up.

The reduction in gross transfers of financial resources payable in debt service as a proportion of exports have usually been in the 15 per cent to 25 per cent range during the effective period which has usually been one and one half to three years. However, five years roll-forward and an initial reduction in gross external debt service of over two-thirds of visible exports has been achieved in the 1986 Tanzania rescheduling.

The present discounted value of the future debt service streams has in general been reduced by 10 to 20 per cent. Because grace periods have tended to be limited (up to five years) as have those for repayment (usually not in excess of five years after the grace period), the time profile of external debt and the repayment hump in it has been rolled forward more than lengthened. No significant gains have been made on the financial terms of commercial borrowings—indeed on balance they have worsened. That result is all the greater in cases in which non-interest-bearing arrears have been consolidated into interest-bearing notes, for example, Nigeria.

Private sector external loans are a relatively small portion of SSA external debt. Apart from a handful protected by external escrow accounts, for example, to Valco (Volta power and aluminium) and Mobil Zaire (offshore oil field), they have probably fared about as well or badly as official or officially guaranteed state enterprise borrowing. In general, SSA states have not taken on obligations to repay if the private borrower is unable to meet the local currency equivalent of debt service due. However, in the case of commercial arrears there have been cases—for example, Nigeria—of substituting a government obligation for a private sector one, but more because the private borrower had discharged his obligation in local currency but remittance to the creditor had not been possible then because the state accepted liability for unpaid, non-guaranteed private (or parastatal) debts.

Almost all Paris Club and the post-1980 commercial bank renegotiations have been tied to an IMF upper credit *tranche* agreement as a pre-condition for opening negotiations. Since 1982 there has generally—but not universally—been a link to a World Bank structural adjustment programme. Indeed in two 1986 cases—Tanzania and Nigeria—the basic agreement was with the Bank and the Fund one was consequential on it.

The amount of adjustment required is hard to measure empirically. Because most agreements since 1970 have been in a context of import strangulation, increased imports, reduced gross debt service and increased gross inflows (largely on concessional terms at least in principle) have been standard goals even on the part of creditors. The amount and period of adjustment upward of possible imports has usually been self-evidently too low and too short to allow restoration of growth and of sustaining it after resumption of debt service. In several cases quite clearly the fact that rolling repayment forward solves nothing because a substantial portion can never again be serviced has been quite deliberately fudged.

The deals to date have—with few exceptions—been good only in terms of objectives defined as putting collapse or at least rapid economic decline a few quarters forward. Even in that sense some have been unsuccessful, for example, Sierra Leone, Liberia, Sudan and earlier Zambia and Zaire reschedulings. The main causes were lack of options—or of a clear negotiating position based on coherent medium-term projects and strategies—on the SSA side and a lack of willingness to set precedents or accept that much of the debt was irrevocably bad on the lenders' side. The World Bank has sought to redress this imbalance by providing scenarios, but the Paris Club has been rather unwilling to accept their implications as to length of rescheduling, grace, repayment let alone increased conditionality and/or open partial or full write-offs.

Whether most of the deals served anybody's interests is a moot point. In general at the end of the day the debtors had heavier debt burdens and lower real imports and the creditors more debt outstanding and in quasi-default and lower real exports to the debtors. Commercial banks in some cases, for example, Côte d'Ivoire, Kenya, Gabon, Mauritius, have been able to claw down their exposure and in others, for example, Sudan, Zaire, Zambia, have had more time to write it down gradually by setting up reserves over a period of years.

A BACKGROUND AND CONTEXTUAL REVIEW OF RESULTS

Most SSA governments—reading World Bank, IMF and OECD forecasts—expected 1979–80 to be followed by a rapid recovery (analagous to that following 1974–5). This did lead to *ex post imprudence in borrowing*—especially borrowing short—and in running up trade credit arrears and IMF drawings to 'ride out' the storm. Whether it really affected most rescheduling approaches is unclear—they were in large measure desperate crisis management (or juggling) sorties rather than reasoned bridges to recovery attempts. The handful of pre-1979 substantial users of commercial bank credit—for example, Côte d'Ivoire, Nigeria, Kenya, Malawi,

Zambia, Gabon—may have hoped for resumption of normal lending by the banks up to, say, 1982 but probably did not put much faith in it, especially as they could hardly afford to use much more of such expensive money.

At one level *net transfers have influenced or even dominated tactics*. Because SSA as a whole has (including grant aid) a positive overall financial resource transfer position, true go-it-alone positions have been very rare. The one true exception was Nigeria over 1983–5 when it was making unilateral proposals from a position of net resource outflows. By 1986 its (oil) exports had fallen so sharply in import capacity terms that it felt forced to turn to rescheduling on an agreed basis plus massive World Bank borrowing to approach an *ex ante* balanced financial transfer position. The Sudan's nominal following of Peru's approach is slightly unreal—the Sudan was not actually paying as much as it promised, has been unable to meet its own ceiling (i.e., to pay that much) and is hopelessly in default to the IMF.

In a different sense falling net inward transfers and limited debt renegotiation prospects (at least through 1985) have led some countries—notably Tanzania—to use quasi-condoned arrears build-up as an alternative to formal rescheduling so long as it did not affect grant bilateral aid. In these cases World Bank—and less uniformly IMF—service has had priority to achieve inflows from the Bank and to keep open the possibility of a subsequent agreement with the Fund.

SSA states until 1984 at the earliest were *not very creative in proposing non-standard debt reschedulings*. Those that saw them as necessary, like Tanzania, also viewed them as unattainable and preferred semi-condoned, quasi-default to even more unsatisfactory Paris Club model reschedulings which would have broken down as soon as grace periods began to expire if not before. The OAU submission to the Special Session and the Tanzania Paris Club proposals in 1986 do represent a more innovative and assertive stance. Both tend to concentrate on long (five to ten year) interest, arrears and principal roll-forwards with at least five years' grace on each rolled amount and ten years' subsequent repayment. Interest rate reductions have not featured equally prominently in these proposals and write-offs have been posed as a challenge to the handful of major Governments (USA, Japan, USSR) who have not acted on the 1979 agreement to convert loans to low income economies retrospectively into grants.

These post-1984 proposals arguably *attempt to make a virtue out of weakness and smallness.* That is they argue that unless SSA is to remain forever dependent on emergency aid, forever in danger of starvation, forever a shrinking export market for creditors and forever prone to extreme insecurity, then, both massively larger concessional resource inflows and very substantial grace periods on over half external debt payments are needed. Without them, rehabilitation, recovery and structural adjustment to higher earned import (export) levels are seen as unattainable.

Pressure for open unilateral action has rarely been high. This is partly because mass public opinion on this type of issue is rarely mobilised in SSA and partly because unilateral action—except debt service capping to spread out a repayment hump as in Nigeria—was usually perceived by those looking at the issue as likely to reduce inflows more than outflows. In other words, the cost/benefit analysis tended to be negative. Pressure for *de facto* unilateral action, that is, 'can't pay, don't pay,' has been more common when governments believed it would be condoned (especially by commercial non-bank trade creditors and export credit agencies).

SOME SALIENT CHARACTERISTICS OF RESCHEDULING

No SSA economy has secured a rescheduling without a prior IMF agreement. The supposed Nigerian exception is unreal— Nigeria did negotiate a stand-by on higher credit *tranche* terms but for a maximum drawing level of zero. Tanzania, in 1986, negotiated an agreement with the World Bank which also convened a consultative group meeting *before* an IMF agreement was reached. While this sequence clearly led to modifications in the Fund's position, it did not affect the Paris Club's insistence that the agreement be in place before a rescheduling meeting could be convened.

Clear alternative adjustment strategies have not been very common in SSA. Ghana's in 1982 caved in as did Tanzania's over 1981–4. Zimbabwe's had precluded a new Fund agreement and imperilled the World Bank's financing new programmes which, taken by themselves, it actually endorses. Nigeria's and Tanzania's alternative strategies—and their apparent ability to persevere in them despite costs—do appear to have resulted in somewhat less conventional IMF agreements; less dependence on short-term high-interest IMF finance; a greater share of World Bank finance (on Bank terms for Nigeria and IDA for Tanzania) and—perhaps—somewhat less limited easing of short- to medium-term debt service burdens than have typified other reschedulings. But, both have been quite tough in their overall adjustment packages even though Tanzania has insisted on and won considerably more flexibility in timing, a near avoidance of an overtly externally imposed initial 'big shock' adjustment and a bias in expenditure toward basic services for poor people.

The cost of winning some independence of structuring adjustment was high for Nigeria and Tanzania and remains high for Zimbabwe. Whether the freedom of manoeuvre won will recover the cost remains to be seen. In the case of both Nigeria and Tanzania the alternative strategy clearly could not be made to work without an additional import capacity from reduced debt service outflows and/or increased financial inflows. But, because both states appeared willing and to some degree able to struggle on without a conventional rescheduling, mounted energetic (if not very successful) real external and fiscal deficit reduction programmes and did adjust prices (including the exchange rate) significantly the Bank and the bilateral sources came to see their efforts as worth backing and the Fund, rather more grudgingly, went along.

This would not have worked however had either wanted large IMF drawings. Nigeria will not in fact draw under its stand-by. It has negotiated toward borrowing comparable amounts at similar interest rates but with longer grace and repayment periods from the World Bank. Tanzania's drawings are also low for the start-up of a structural adjustment programme.

Debt rescheduling as opposed to devaluation has rarely been highly politicised in SSA except in the sense of affirming that debt service does not have a higher priority than averting starvation. Devaluation has been politicised, but possibly more in a mirror image macho response of 'no devaluation, now or ever' in reaction to the IMF's apparent 'devaluation is good for your soul and cures all ills' recipe than as a genuinely internal debate. Certainly that seems to have been the case both in Nigeria and Tanzania in which rather rapid initial and subsequent sliding devaluation proved politically attainable and sustainable once it could be seen as backed by a domestic case and not as a response to IMF demands. *Rescheduling decisions and negotiating parameters have in almost all cases been taken/set up by a limited number of ministers, senior officials and expatriate advisors in Treasuries and Central Banks.* In some cases these may have been teleguided by hired merchant bank advisors, but the degree to which their influence went further than tactics and data organisation is a moot point—the banks and the Treasuries/Central Banks, perhaps predictably, tell quite different stories.

Oddly, the most politicised rescheduling—or at any rate rolling-over—case is Zimbabwe which has not rescheduled. The internal lineup is not stable—the Reserve Bank of Zimbabwe has for some years seen external debt service and external debt reduction as absolute priorities, while enterprises (who face reduced import allocations) back either rescheduling or replacement borrowing with Finance and Planning holding the balance and apparently somewhat variable on how much import—and thus, output—reduction it is willing to pay to 'get over the external debt hump'.

The 'precedent' argument is beginning to fall away in SSA. SSA is now perceived as a continent in structural economic crisis requiring special treatment. Admittedly, this is a government rather than a commercial bank perception and is only now approaching possible implementation so far as debt rescheduling is concerned. However, creditor government and government guaranteed loans are dominant in SSA and commercial banks might follow a Paris Club lead. That is a plausible scenario at least in cases—for example, Sudan, Zambia, Zaire—in which they know that standard approaches will fail to secure even full interest service much less debt repayment.

Arguably the Tanzanian and Nigerian deals are significantly better than average—especially if macro and sectoral adjustment freedom of manoeuvre is taken into account. Because of the cost of holding out until they were achieved it is unclear how many governments will choose to seek to follow them if citing their parameters as precedents does not itself produce some softening of terms. A government needs to perceive itself as having a strong support base (military in Nigeria, mass in Tanzania) to venture down that road. Learning has probably been largely from what went wrong with other countries' reschedulings (too little, too late, too short) but only in Tanzania and Zimbabwe has this evidently influenced strategy and tactics. Both chose to delay formal debt rescheduling proposals until they believed they had the rest of an adequate financial resource transfer package in place, that is, Zimbabwe is still formally resisting the idea of a Paris Club rescheduling.

Until 1985 it is hard to argue that rescheduling terms changed much either continentally or for individual states. From 1985 there are some signs that World Bank and consultative group projections of short- to medium-term debt service reductions necessary to allow structural adjustment are influencing the Paris Club toward longer rollforward, grace and repayment periods and may in the future result in some concessions on interest rates.

SELECTED ISSUES AND TARGETS: NATIONAL

From the balance of payments projections of the eighteen to twenty most seriously indebted SSA economies the following appear to be the minimum conditions for a stable rescheduling which would have a good chance of holding up without a series of subsequent additional reschedulings:

1. all official arrears plus five years (in the worst affected eighteen, ten years) of principal and interest payments to be rolled forward,
2. the grace period on each rescheduled payment to be ten years,
3. repayment to be phased over the ten years following expiry of the grace period,
4. interest on all rescheduled items to be held to 3 per cent or the initial rate, whichever is lower, that is, a reduction of 50 to 67 per cent in guaranteed or government export credit rates,
5. at least for the low-income category (defined either in World Bank terms or more broadly as under $1,000 per capita in 1984) past development loans to be converted into retrospective grants by the USA, Japan, CMEA countries and—for the SSA debtor countries in respect to which conversion have not yet been made—Federal Germany,
6. at least some export and supplier credits (especially those supporting inherently unsatisfactory projects) to be written off (as Sweden has done in the case of Tanzania).

Rather less drastic steps may be adequate for middle-income countries whose bottom line problems are a hump in their debt profiles and, in several cases, a heavy backlog of commercial arrears. Roll-forwards of three to five years annual principal (but possibly not interest) with repayment over the next seven to ten might well be enough for the Côte d'Ivoire and Nigeria, for example.

Formula-related debt service or more accurately formulae with trigger points setting off rescheduling would be useful. However, a tie of gross debt service to export earnings is too blunt an instrument. At least two measures would be needed— gross debt service to exports and net financial resources inflows relative to GDP or GDP *per capita*.

Commercial arrears whether to financial or new financial institutions need to be consolidated and rescheduled. The problem is that in the cases in which they are large no very satisfactory way forward now exists. There may be a case for letting such arrears remain, paying all new import bills on time and waiting for a more prosperous context to launch serious rescheduling talks on this component of external debt.

To operate debt management convincingly enough to encourage creditors, to agree to multi-year or quasi automatic successive eighteen–month reschedulings requires much fuller and more accessible data than most SSA states have. That data needs to be held in a form allowing simple programming of new debt levels in local currencies, SDRs or USA dollars when exchange rates alter—a test many present recording and retrieval systems do not pass.

REGIONAL INITIATIVES: TOWARD AMBIANCES AND GUIDELINES

Individual SSA economies are not large enough nor individual SSA governments audible (nor well staffed enough) to argue the macro- (or mega) economic case for larger reschedulings, interest rate reductions and partial, selective write-offs. To create a climate of opinon open to such proposals is a process which the 1985 OAU economic summit and the 1986 Special Session may have begun albeit more in putting across the general economic malaise and African states' determination to take a lead in restructuring than in respect to external debt and its rescheduling as such.

Guideline formulation—and dialogue with OECD, CMEA, OPEC and large South economy creditors—is an area for regional coordination. The first step would be for SSA states to agree on negotiable guidelines. The ECA, ADB or Centre for African Monetary Studies (or all three) could provide inputs including data and options.

Negotiable guidelines will probably need to be differentiated. GDP and external debt per capita, adequacy of import levels and debt service/exports ratios, degree of import strangulation and gaps between actual and nominally possible production and population and output growth should probably be among the organising characteristics.

Presentationally SSA/Africa needs a clearcut, simple approach backed by respectable data summaries and technical annexes. But, it also needs spokespersons and a team to carry on dialogue in actual working groups which would presumably then report back to a larger, higher-level body empowered to promulgate the guidelines. Whether that body should be UNCTAD's Trade and Development Committee, the Fund/Bank Development Committee or the UN General or ECOSOC Assembly requires further consideration.

Regionally, greater monitoring capacity in respect to creditors is needed—few African countries can monitor creditor action in a timely way and ECA or OAU should be able to gain economies of scale. However, there is still not full acceptance that monitoring should be a two-way process with representatives or organisations of both creditors and debtors participating.

WHERE NOW? A TACTICAL REVIEW

1. SSA needs substantial *de facto* write-offs for up to twenty economies. Whether they are to be higher levels of very concessional or grant aid used to repay harder loans (e.g., IMF Trust Fund credits to repay normal drawings); open write-offs (as with Sweden taking over payment of commercial loans to Tanzania from its enterprise sector or the USA and Japan adopting the consensus on retrospective grant aid to the least developed/other low income); and/or rescheduling with long grace and repayment periods and reduced interest which combine to reduce net present value significantly is secondary.

2. For a much broader group of countries—who may need rescheduling for fairly extended periods plus modest concessions on interest not wholesale write-offs on medium- and long-term obligations—some means to achieve practicable rescheduling management for commercial arrears is needed. What is practicable varies from the generally insolvent to the substantially illiquid and also depends on how willing Consultative Groups and the Paris Club (hopefully merged for SSA reconstruction and rehabilitation work) are to accept

substantial use of forex to clear these arrears, necessarily at the price of further deferring official debt service or of increasing the minimum levels of new money needed. The import cost, trade finance and routeing convenience and even availability costs of operating with substantial levels of such arrears are so high that this topic deserves far more attention—especially by creditor governments—that it has received to date.

3. SSA is so small that to have the weight to negotiate guidelines for external debt reconstruction (indeed to call attention to the fact its concerns really do have an objective counterpart in the interests of creditor economies) it needs to achieve a form of SSA (perhaps under OAU serviced by ADB and ECA auspices)—Creditor (including Bank/Fund) strategic negotiations. These would seek to:

    a. agree on parameters of problem as they confront different actors,

    b. on requirements for resolving it acceptably to all (or most) actors; as well as

    c. instruments for doing so; for

    d. two to four categories of economy (e.g., hopelessly-indebted low and lower middle income, over-indebted lower middle income, temporarily insolvent lower middle income, viable),

    e. define criteria for categorisation and application of instruments.

4. A one-off all-actor conference by itself (as opposed to a series of working groups and consultations leading to a broadly agreed package presented to such a conference for ratification) is not a realistic way forward. Any single meeting would almost certainly be incompletely factually grounded on both sides and would also probably begin from very different—and partly inaccurate—perceptions by all actors both of their own and others' interests and possible areas of overlapping

interest. Therefore, it would hardly be likely to be adequate for reaching an articulated set of operational decisions. However, an initial commitment to go beyond mere consultation and an interim one as to principles to be worked out are probably needed to get the process started.

5. The process needs to be presented, and actually viewed, as a *complement to country level negotiations* setting a set of parameters within which such country negotiations are to take place and as a central monitoring point for negotiations, agreements, implementations and results rather than as a substitute for them. Nobody envisages a single negotiation covering the diverse (and to a substantial extent unknown) external debt of forty odd economies and arriving at directly implementable results for each.

6. *SSA negotiations and agreements on principle for categories of debtors should be defined formally as having no direct linkage to other regions and categories.* (By demanding such linkage at the 1986 General Assembly Special Session the Latin American states in effect ensured that OECD and CMEA creditor country opposition to including any formal forward progress on SSA's external debt in the final resolution would prevail.) The linkage value will, in fact, exist but by analogy and more for the Bolivias probably the Paraguays and perhaps the Perus, not the Mexicos or the Brazils. *Logically the OAU and the Cartagena Group might usefully have an early technical level meeting followed by a joint ministerial one to reach an agreed modus vivendi in this area.*

Table 9.1: Country groupings, Sub-Saharan Africa

Market borrowers[a]	Official borrowers[c] (30)		Diversified borrowers[d] (10)
Congo	Burkina Faso[ae]	Mali[ae]	Benin[ae]
Gabon[b]	Burundi[be]	Mauritania[ae]	Botswana
Ivory Coast	Cape Verde[b]	Rwanda[be]	Cameroon
Nigeria	Central African Republic[e]	São Tomé and Príncipe[b]	Ethiopia[e]
	Chad[e]	Senegal[e]	Kenya[e]
	Comoros	Seychelles[b]	Lesotho[be]
	Djibouti[b]	Sierra Leone[e]	Mauritius[b]
	Equatorial Guinea[b]	Somalia[ce]	Mozambique[ce]
	Gambia[ce]	Sudan[ae]	Niger[e]
	Ghana[ae]	Swaziland[b]	Zimbabwe[b]
	Guinea[ae]	Tanzania[ae]	
	Guinea-Bissau[ae]	Togo[ae]	
	Liberia[ae]	Uganda[ae]	
	Madagascar[ae]	Zaire[ae]	
	Malawi[ae]	Zambia[ae]	

Notes: a. Countries that obtained at least two-thirds of their external borrowings from commerical sources from 1978 to 1982.
b. Countries with no rescheduling and no external arrears during 1980–85.
c. Countries that obtained two-thirds or more of their external borrowings from official creditors from 1978 to 1982.
d. Countries that obtained at least one-third of their external borrowing from both commercial and official creditors in 1978–82.
e. Low-income countries included in World Bank study referred to by Agarwala.

Source: IMF, World Economic Outlook, October 1985.

Table 9.2: Some economic indicators for Sub-Saharan Africa (billion dollars and percentage change)

	1976	1977	1978	1979	1980	1981	1982	1983	1984	1985
Imports										
Value of goods and services	20.6	23.3	28.2	32.5	40.7	39.1	36.4	33.8	33.0	33.1
Unit value price index	57.9	63.4	71.3	83.9	100.0	98.0	93.5	89.5	87.2	86.7
Value of goods and services (including Nigeria)	31.7	37.8	43.3	48.6	63.4	64.0	56.2	48.7	44.8	44.5
Volume, annual change	-4.6	5.7	8.5	-4.9	5.0	-6.0	-4.5	-9.5	-0.1	2.1
Exports										
Value of goods and services	16.9	19.8	20.9	25.2	30.1	27.1	25.2	24.5	25.7	25.3
Unit value price index	58.3	73.3	74.8	88.7	100.0	90.9	81.0	78.5	80.4	78.3
Value of goods and services (including Nigeria)	27.8	32.5	32.5	43.2	57.7	46.5	38.1	35.5	38.1	37.6
Volume, annual change	5.4	-6.1	3.9	1.3	2.8	-0.5	5.1	0.3	8.7	3.2
Real GDP growth	3.8	1.4	1.9	2.1	3.2	1.9	0.5	0.6	1.9	1.3
Change in consumer prices[b]	20.0	28.0	22.2	26.7	26.1	30.9	19.6	30.2	18.3	18.6
Terms of trade										
Index	100.7	115.7	104.9	105.7	100.0	92.7	86.7	87.7	92.2	90.3
Annual change	9.6	14.9	-9.3	0.8	-5.4	-7.3	-6.5	1.2	5.0	-2.0
Nonoil commodity prices										
Annual change	32.1	36.6	-13.1	14.4	1.2	-18.2	-8.3	7.8	4.5	-8.3
Reserves										
Ratio to short-term debt	2.7	2.2	1.9	2.1	1.6	1.2	0.9	1.1	1.1	1.2

Notes: a. Excludes Nigeria, unless otherwise indicated.
b. Weighted averages.

Sources: IMF, *World Economic Outlook*.

Table 9.3: External debt outstanding (billion dollars, unless otherwise noted)

	1975	1976	1977	1978	1979	1980	1981	1982	1983	1984	1985
Sub-Saharan Africa											
Total debt	16.2	20.7	26.3	33.5	41.9	53.7	62.4	77.7	85.6	88.9	n.a.
Medium- and long-term	15.4	18.7	23.7	30.3	38.2	45.1	51.3	56.7	68.4	70.3	72.8
Publicly guaranteed	14.0	17.3	21.9	28.5	35.8	42.2	48.2	54.9	66.6	68.5	70.9
Of which (percentage share)											
Multilateral[a]	18.9	19.3	19.7	20.4	20.0	21.3	21.5	21.8	20.2	22.0	24.3
Bilateral[b]	48.0	48.6	44.7	40.6	42.9	42.8	43.2	40.2	38.6	40.5	41.2
Financial institutions[c]	17.2	19.0	22.0	26.6	28.2	27.6	28.4	32.7	30.8	27.2	24.1
Other[d]	16.0	13.0	13.6	12.4	8.9	8.3	6.9	5.3	10.4	10.3	10.1
Non-publicly guranteed	1.4	1.5	1.8	1.8	2.4	2.9	3.1	1.8	1.8	1.8	2.0
Short-term	0.1	1.0	1.6	1.9	2.0	2.5	2.9	7.2	2.9	3.5	3.5
Outstanding use of Fund credit	0.6	0.9	1.0	1.3	1.7	2.0	3.4	4.0	5.1	5.3	6.0
Arrears	n.a.	n.a.	n.a.	n.a.	n.a.	4.2	4.8	9.8	9.2	9.9	n.a.
(number of countries)	(n.a.)	(n.a.)	(n.a.)	(n.a.)	(n.a.)	(19)	(22)	(23)	(21)	(22)	(n.a.)

Notes: a. Loans and credits from the World Bank, regional development banks and other multilateral and intergovernmental agencies.
b. Loans from governments and their agencies (including central banks) and loans from autonomous public bodies.
c. Loans from private banks and other private financial institutions and publicly issued and privately placed bonds.
d. Suppliers' credits, external liabilities on account of nationalised properties and unclassified debt to private creditors.
n.a. Not available.

Source: IMF, *World Economic Outlook*.

Table 9.4: Sub-Saharan Africa: Ranking according to debt outstanding, end-1985

Country	Total[a] (billion dollars)	Debt outstanding	Distribution of medium- and long-term publicly guaranteed debt (percentage share)			Scheduled interest payments ratio[b]	Debt-export ratio[c]	Debt-GDP ratio[d]
		Use of Fund credit (million dollars)	Multilateral creditors	Bilateral creditors	Financial institutions and other			
Nigeria	16.6	(0.0)	8.3	17.9	73.8	13.0	134.6	21.5
Sudan	8.3	(664.9)	15.5	67.6	16.9	68.8	1,232.4	100.1
Ivory Coast	8.0	(621.7)	26.0	28.2	45.9	16.6	238.1	116.9
Zaire	5.3	(721.0)	15.1	65.2	19.7	17.3	258.3	203.5
Zambia	4.2	(761.6)	21.0	58.0	21.0	39.7	464.0	455.3
Kenya	3.5	(485.7)	54.2	27.1	18.7	8.7	224.8	57.3
Tanzania	3.4	(21.1)	39.7	56.0	4.2	23.3	743.3	62.5
Mozambique	2.6	(0.0)	8.9	55.7	35.4	68.6	1,518.6	129.2
Zimbabwe	2.4	(264.1)	11.1	17.6	71.3	12.5	164.3	20.0
Madagascar	2.3	(161.4)	22.1	59.7	18.1	21.9	634.1	101.8
Senegal	2.3	(241.1)	28.4	54.8	16.8	18.5	285.1	93.4
Ghana	2.2	(656.0)	36.0	43.9	20.1	21.6	324.9	21.2
Ethiopia	1.9	(49.5)	46.8	41.4	11.8	9.0	339.4	36.5
Cameroon	1.8	(0.0)	34.8	41.8	23.4	4.2	74.0	21.7

Somalia	1.5	(142.2)	30.2	65.5	4.4	7.5	909.1	205.1
Mauritania	1.4	(30.3)	26.8	62.6	10.7	15.8	378.5	215.0
Guinea	1.3	(12.6)	20.4	66.0	13.7	3.2	254.7	74.4
Congo	1.3	(0.0)	22.4	36.7	40.9	7.2	105.2	60.9
Mali	1.2	(80.7)	34.2	63.3	2.6	10.4	563.8	138.4
Uganda	1.2	(282.4)	51.0	38.8	10.2	12.4	279.2	33.1
Liberia	1.0	(225.6)	34.3	46.2	19.5	9.9	215.6	103.8
Niger	1.0	(66.7)	36.3	37.8	26.0	21.2	322.3	64.0
Malawi	0.9	(133.9)	36.3	23.2	13.5	18.6	343.0	78.7
Benin	0.8	(0.0)	35.6	12.6	51.8	16.4	326.0	78.9
Togo	0.8	(62.5)	39.5	54.0	6.5	6.8	315.7	114.7
Gabon	0.7	(0.0)	6.6	31.9	61.5	3.3	34.3	21.5
Burkina Faso	0.6	(0.0)	68.3	27.4	4.3	9.2	366.6	73.4
Mauritius	0.6	(159.3)	45.0	29.4	25.6	10.7	103.5	63.1
Sierra Leone	0.4	(78.4)	38.2	41.1	20.7	23.2	314.9	57.2
Burundi	0.4	(0.0)	62.8	29.3	7.8	9.8	312.3	40.2
Botswana	0.3	(0.0)	56.2	28.7	15.1	3.3	38.8	40.8
Rwanda	0.3	(0.0)	78.0	22.0	—	4.8	175.5	19.6
Central African Republic	0.3	(28.4)	49.8	41.4	8.8	6.7	169.1	58.0
Guinea-Bissau	0.3	(3.1)	46.9	41.3	11.7	38.6	1,042.0	129.4
Swaziland	0.2	(9.9)	51.0	33.8	15.2	4.9	75.6	57.8
Gambia	0.2	(27.2)	52.5	30.9	16.6	9.8	271.3	109.6
Chad	0.2	(8.7)	65.4	25.4	9.1	3.3	197.7	256.0
Lesotho	0.1	(0.0)	90.8	7.1	2.1	1.7	45.3	59.1
Comoros	0.1	(0.0)	47.1	52.9	0.1	9.1	625.9	123.1
Equatorial Guinea	0.1	(7.9)	19.6	55.9	24.5	16.7	473.9	125.7
Djibouti	0.1	(0.0)	18.8	24.0	57.3	1.1	53.0	23.8

Table 9.4: continued

Country	Total[a] (billion dollars)	Use of Fund credit (million dollars)	Debt outstanding			Scheduled interest payments ratio[b]	Debt-export ratio[c]	Debt-GDP ratio[d]
			Distribution of medium- and long-term publicly guaranteed debt (percentage share)					
			Multilateral creditors	Bilateral creditors	Financial institutions and other			
Saõ Tomé and Principe	0.1	(0.0)	48.4	45.1	6.6	12.7	579.0	295.1
Cape Verde	0.1	(0.0)	50.6	40.4	–	7.7	212.8	96.7
Seychelles	0.1	(0.0)	16.0	76.5	7.4	–	90.0	51.7

Notes: a. Excludes areas, includes medium-, long-, and short-term, publicly guaranteed and unguaranteed debt, plus outstanding use of Fund credit.

b. Scheduled interest payments and charges for use of Fund credit over exports of goods and services.

c. Total debt outstanding plus outstanding use of Fund credit over exports of goods and services.

d. Total debt outstanding plus outstanding use of Fund credit over nominal GDP.

– Zero or negligible.

Source: IMF, *World Economic Outlook:* IMF, *International Financial Statistics;* and Fund staff estimates.

Table 9.5: External debt service (billion dollars, unless otherwise noted)

	Actual											Schedule	
	1975	1976	1977	1978	1979	1980	1981	1982	1983	1984	1985	1986	1987
Sub-Saharan Africa													
Interest[a]	0.8	0.9	1.1	1.4	1.9	2.7	2.8	3.5	3.7	4.2	5.2	6.6	6.0
Amortization[b]	1.3	1.6	1.5	2.2	2.5	3.5	3.8	3.3	4.4	6.1	7.9	8.6	9.2
Total	2.1	2.4	2.6	3.5	4.4	6.2	6.6	6.8	8.1	10.2	13.0	5.2	15.2
As percentage of exports of goods and services	8.8	8.7	8.1	10.9	10.2	10.8	14.2	17.8	22.9	26.9	34.7	39.4	37.9
Interest payments ratio[c]	3.2	3.1	3.5	4.2	4.5	4.7	6.0	9.1	10.4	11.0	13.7	17.2	15.0
Debt-export ratio[d]	66.7	74.0	80.3	102.3	96.1	85.0	123.0	177.2	214.5	207.7	217.6	n.a.	n.a.
Implicit average interest rate[e]	5.8	4.1	4.4	4.1	4.6	5.5	4.9	5.1	4.8	5.3	6.3	n.a	n.a.

Notes: a. Includes charges on use of Fund credit.
  b. Includes IMF repurchases.
  c. Interest payments over exports of goods and services.
  d. Total debt outstanding over exports of goods and services.
  e. Interest payments ratio over debt ratio.
  n.a. Not available.

Source: IMF, *World Economic Outlook.*

Table 9.6:   Investment, savings, and resource balance, Sub-Saharan Africa (percentage of GDP at current prices)

	1980	1981	1982	1983	1984
Gross domestic investment	22.5	24.8	21.2	18.5	14.5
Gross domestic savings	21.9	17.2	13.3	13.0	13.9
Resource balance	–0.8	–7.9	–8.0	–5.7	–0.6
Memorandum item					
Gross domestic investment (percentage of GDP) in South Asia	23.4	23.0	23.2	22.9	22.9

Source: World Bank data.

Table 9.7:   External debt of Sub-Saharan Africa, revised estimate, 1984 (billion dollars)

	IMF estimate	Revision	Total
Long- and medium-term[a]	68.8	10.3	79.1
Short-term[b]	4.8	21.6	26.4
Arrears[c]	9.4	5.6	15.0
IMF	5.1	–	5.1
Total	88.1	37.5	125.6

Notes: a.   Revision of 15 per cent estimated on recorded government guaranteed debt, due to general omissions, failure to update for currency fluctuations, and private external debt.
b.   Estimated at 25 per cent of long-term debt (excluding normal ninety-day or less commercial bills). That estimate corresponds roughly to data for a handful of countries for which detailed studies have been done, for example, by the World Bank.
c.   Re-estimated on fragmentary data. Includes arrears of interest as well as principal, of commercial payments not financially intermediated and of invisibles (e.g., airline ticket sales.)

Source: Reginal Herbold Green and S. Griffith Jones, 'Sub-Saharan Africa's External Debt Crisis,' in *Third World Affairs—1986* (London: Third World Foundation, 1986), p. 26.

Table 9.8: Sub-Saharan Africa: Net use of IMF credit (SDR million)

	1982	1983	1984	1985	1986
Total purchases[1]	1,285	1,805	1,046	740	573
Repurchases	241	352	505	623	851
Total purchases less repurchases	1,045	1,453	541	117	–278
Net use of fund credit[2]	678	1,237	505	105	–227
Trust Fund repayments	1	13	60	103	153
Net flow of finance	677	1,224	445	2	–380

Notes: 1. Includes reserve *tranche* purchases.
2. Excludes reserve *tranche*.

Source: IMF

Table 9.9: Official multilateral and commercial bank debt restructuring, sub-Saharan African countries, 1980–5. Amount restructured (million dollars)

	1980	1981	1982	1983	1984	1985
Central African Republic						
Paris Club	–	72	–	13	–	8
Commercial banks	–	–	–	–	–	–
Equatorial Guinea						
Paris Club	–	–	–	–	–	36
Commercial banks	–	–	–	–	–	–
Ivory Coast						
Paris Club	–	–	–	–	356	234
Commercial banks	–	–	–	–	–	501
Liberia						
Paris Club	35	30	–	17	17	–
Commercial banks	–	–	30	–	–	35
Madagascar						
Paris Club	–	140	107	–	89	135
Commercial banks	–	147	–	–	195	–
Malawi						
Paris Club	–	–	25	26	–	–
Commercial banks	–	–	–	57	–	–
Mauritania						
Paris Club	–	–	–	–	–	78
Commercial banks	–	–	–	–	–	–
Mozambique						
Paris Club	–	–	–	–	404	–
Commercial banks	–	–	–	–	213	192

Table 9.9:   continued

	1980	1981	1982	1983	1984	1985
Niger						
Paris Club	–	–	–	36	26	40
Commercial banks	–	–	–	–	26	–
Nigeria						
Paris Club	–	–	–	–	–	–
Commercial banks	–	–	–	1,935	–	–
Senegal						
Paris Club	–	75	74	72	–	117
Commercial banks	–	–	–	–	78	20
Sierra Leone						
Paris Club	37	–	–	–	25	–
Commercial banks	–	–	–	–	25	–
Somalia						
Paris Club	–	–	–	–	–	122
Commercial banks	–	–	–	–	–	–
Sudan						
Paris Club	–	–	80	536	269	–
Commercial banks	–	498	55	790	838	–
Togo						
Paris Club	–	232	–	300	75	35
Commercial banks	69	–	–	84	–	–
Uganda						
Paris Club	–	30	19	–	–	–
Commercial banks	–	–	–	–	–	–
Zaire						
Paris Club	–	500	–	1,497	–	400
Commercial banks	402	–	–	58	64	–
Zambia						
Paris Club	–	–	–	375	253	–
Commercial banks	–	–	–	–	73	61

Notes: – Zero or neglible.

Source: Fund staff estimates.

REFERENCES

Africa Economic Digest, 1985–7.

Green, R. H., 1986, *Third World Sovereign Debt Renegotiation 1980–86 and After*, IDS (Sussex) Discussion Paper 223.

Green, R. H. and Griffith-Jones, S., 'External Debt: Sub-Saharan Africa's Emerging Iceberg' in T. Rose, 1985, *Crisis and Recovery In Sub-Saharan Africa,* OECD Development Centre, Paris.

Griffith-Jones, S. and Green, R. H., 1984, *African External Debt and Development: A Review and Analysis*, IDS (Sussex), (xerox) —consultancy report commissioned by UNCTAD for African Centre for Monetary Studies.

Helleiner, G. K., 1985, 'Aid and liquidity: the neglect of Sub-Saharan Africa and others of the poorest in the emerging international monetary system', *Sub-Saharan Africa: Towards oblivion or reconstruction?*, Special Issue, *Journal of Development Planning*, No. 15.

Kadhani, X. and Green, R. H., 1986, 'Zimbabwe: Transition to Economic Crises, 1981–83 Retrospect and Prospect', *World Development,* 14–8, 1986.

Lancaster, C. and Williamson, J., 1986, *African Debt And Financing*, Institute for International Economics, Special Report No. 5, Washington, DC.

Organisation of African Unity, 1986, *Africa's Submission To The Special Session Of The United Nations General Assembly On Africa's Economic And Social Crisis*, Addis Ababa.

United Nations, General Assembly Special Session Resolution on African Priority Programme For Economic Reconstruction, 1986, New York.

World Bank, 1985, *The External Debt of Sub-Saharan Africa: Origins, Magnitude and Implications for Action* (K. I. Krumm), Working Paper 741, Washington, DC.

———, 1984, *Toward Sustained Development in Sub-Saharan Africa: A Joint Program of Action*, Washington, DC.

———, 1986, *Financing Adjustment with Growth in Sub-Saharan Africa, 1986–90*, Washington, DC.

World Council of Churches (Advisory Group on Economic Matters), 1985, *The International Financial System: An Ecumenical Critique*, Geneva.

10 The Coordination of the Latin American Debtors: Is there a Logic Behind the Story

Diana Tussie

INTRODUCTION

The debt crisis has produced the most drastic economic decline for the economies of Latin America since the depression of the 1930s. But, unlike the thirties, regional governments have tried to make efforts to coordinate their actions to ameliorate the consequences of the crisis. Latin America's leaders have called for a redefinition of the debt issue. They have argued that the debt is overtly political and must lead to negotiations among the governments of the United States, Western Europe, Japan and Latin America. It is important to emphasise that the call for political talks about the debt and its consequences have not been accompanied either by threats to organise a debtors' cartel or by major defaults as in the '30s, although there are some in Latin America who think that this is a desirable course of action.

This essay will first give a brief account of the efforts of Latin American governments to coordinate their responses to the debt issue. The chronological account in this first part falls rather neatly into the three phases outlined in Griffith-Jones' introductory essay in this volume. During the first phase (1982–4) the creditors' formula for dealing with debtors was hammered out without any counterproposals from the debtors' side. The second phase covers the 1984–5 period during which negotiations proceeded along the given track with some emphasis by debtors to alter at the margin the broader strategy imposed by others. During the third phase (1985–6) debtors became more active in their search for alternative procedures. The final part of the essay will then attempt to explain the underlying logic of the debtors' collective action and the reasons for its disappointing record in fundamentally modifying the international distribution of the costs of adjustment between debtors and creditors, although it may have produced fruitful results in other more narrow respects.

PHASE 1—DEBTOR INDIVIDUALISM (1982–4).

The origins of the current debt crisis are well known and need not be repeated here. Mexico's announcement in August 1982 that it was unable to service its debt set in motion a rescue operation led by the United States Government and the adoption of an IMF stabilisation programme in September 1982. Brazil soon realised that it could no longer raise sufficient funds in the market to cover its debt payments. The United States in December 1982 provided an emergency bridging loan while the banks, the Government of Brazil, and the Fund worked out an adjustment package and new funding. Argentina was next to signal its inability to pay and Latin America's debt crisis, by early 1983, had become widespread.

From August 1982 until January 1984 each of the debtors responded to the debt crunch as if faced with a problem of short-term illiquidity. Not one of them considered the option of unilateral action—neither individually nor in concert with the other debtors—which might have implied then a serious risk of an international financial collapse. Thus, a series of rescheduling operations were designed to provide emergency finance, the so-called 'rescue packages'. The cost of these packages to the debtors are, in general terms, very onerous. According to ECLA estimates the majority of debtors suffered a deterioration in terms (changes in commission, spreads and amortization periods) of between 100–250 per cent; this is estimated by ECLA to have implied an increase of around 20 per cent in the real financial cost of credit (Devlin, 1985).

The case for a short-term approach was argued on the assumption of an expanding world economy and future recovery of private bank lending. A steering role in this respect was played by international institutions involved in forecasting world economic trends. The over-optimistic assumptions of debt-related forecasts turned out to be a form of rationalisation useful in persuading debtors to adopt the rescue packages. Confronted with such predictions no country was tempted to default. Default would have meant the need to bring about instant adjustment without further external financing and an embargo on future loans.

Given the prospects, it was thought that a way out could be found in seeking short-term breathing space from foreign exchange constraints by reducing the debt service ratio. In the words of Mario Simonsen, 'A growing economy with expanding exports would hardly seek confrontation with its creditors' (Wiesner, 1985). At first, the implications of these assumptions did not appear to have further consequences. On the contrary, from most debtors' point of view (particularly for the major debtors) the short-term perspective offered them the hope of instant fresh money to alleviate adjustment and promptly renewed access to capital markets. Yet, once the mechanism of debt rescheduling was set in motion, over-optimism turned out to have more than a passing implication; it played a crucial role in setting the parameters of the negotiations and in determining the subsequent distribution of the costs of adjustment between debtors and creditors.

In August 1982 Mexico confronted a situation in which coordination with potential allies was rendered impossible. Initially, the crisis caught everyone by surprise and each debtor struggled merely to stay afloat. An opportunity to cooperate was missed for want of the appropriate mechanism. There was then no established communication network that might have permitted countries to coordinate their responses. A joint strategy requires that the actors involved understand each other, are sure of their codes for signalling intentions and responding to each other's signals and, moreover, are aware of each other's patterns of individual behaviour so that reactions became predictable.

The fact that Mexico confronted the debt problem as a short-term liquidity crunch and that the Government decided to go it alone—as had Nicaragua and Costa Rica before—set a precedent for future negotiations. As most bargaining handbooks will agree, 'Precedent seems to exercise an influence that greatly exceeds its logical importance or legal force'. (Schelling, 1963).

But, though the debtors at that point lost their opportunity for joint action, the creditors did not. Paradoxically, the number of banks involved played in their favour. It was inconceivable that banks acting separately could recover their losses, or that a reasonably orderly and successful negotiation could be carried out with as many as the initial 1,300 banks involved in the Mexican rescheduling. Moreover, by August 1982 there were already strong precedents of creditor coordination to be found in the Paris Club for official creditors and in the steering committees that private banks had set up for dealing with the Polish, the Nicaraguan and the Costa Rican debt crises.

As soon as the first series of debt rescheduling was concluded, Ecuador's Christian Democratic President, Osvaldo Hurtado took the initiative to seek a common political response. In February 1983, President Hurtado requested the executive secretaries of the Economic Commission for Latin America (ECLA) and the Sistema Economico Latinoamericano (SELA) to lay out a set of proposals for cooperation on the debt front. As a result, a Conference of heads of government was convened in Quito, Ecuador in January 1984. The Quito meeting took place in the midst of great uncertainty about the capacity or even the willingness of the Latin American governments to continue to service their debts. The beginning of 1984 was marked by a succession of interest rate rises. Furthermore, Venezuela refused to go to the IMF, Brazil's letters of intent with the IMF required frequent revisions as targets were not met (see D. Carneiro's article in this volume) and lastly, President Alfonsin's new Government in Argentina announced that it would be seeking to redress the rescheduling terms agreed by the outgoing military government. Discontent was widespread within the region; the failure seemed to sow the seeds for regional organisations to step up their efforts to create a common front on the debt issue.

As a result of the Quito meeting, a plan of action was agreed upon calling for longer repayment periods, no increase in the cost of the debt as a result of rescheduling, a linkage between debt servicing and export earnings. The Quito meeting served the purpose of at least slightly shifting the focus of discussion from the narrow technical and financial points to the social and the political implications. 'The presidents and foreign ministers assembled in the Ecuadorean capital were communicating a message. The debt was political' (Roett, 1985, p. 232).

There were, however, some misgivings among the governments that the political initiative might be withdrawn from their hands if left to the regional organisations SELA and ECLA. So Quito may indeed have been a landmark in the efforts to seek a common front but it did not have much immediate practical impact. The solidarity of the major Latin American debtors almost immediately went through a crucial test with Argentina's open confrontation with the international banking community in the first half of 1984. Shortly after Alfonsín took office the Government declared a moratorium on capital and interest payments and announced its intention of undertaking an evaluation of the legitimacy of the debt contracted by the military. In March 1984 the stand-by agreement signed by the military was suspended. Although Argentine officials stressed that the Government had no intention of breaking with the international financial community and was only seeking a give-and-take attitude together with more time to put its house in order, bankers became concerned with the possibility of disruption and a change in the rules of the game. Argentina was 'expected to be a tough negotiator' (*Financial Times*, 1 February 1984). Being self-sufficient in food and energy and conducting most of its trade with the USSR, it was seen to be in the strongest position to cope with possible retaliation from creditors. Yet, despite these sources of apparent strength the Government was not prepared to take a go-it-alone approach and initiated contacts to seek backing from regional governments to confront the IMF and the banks. It was then that the force of precedence was seen at play. With Mexico as well as Brazil and Venezuela in the fold with refinancing agreements in progress, rather than line up behind the Argentines, the other debtors sided with the creditors urging Argentina to come to terms. If Mexico had previously lacked time to coordinate its moves with other countries, by the time of Argentina's duel, Mexico believed that the worst was over and that, therefore, an association with a rebellious debtor might hurt it, backfiring as a penalty in subsequent renegotiations. Argentina, however, tried to buy time and stuck to its refusal to pay interest up until the end of March 1984. At the Annual meeting of the Inter-American Development Bank held in Punta del Este in March 1984, Colombia, Venezuela, Brazil and Mexico, fearing that an Argentine default might harm their own creditworthiness, extended a bridging loan to induce Argentina to cancel interest arrears.

Ironically, this coordinated action among central banks—wherein the major Latin American debtors applied friendly but firm persuasion to discipline Argentina—was the foremost example of Latin American solidarity during this entire period. (Feinberg, 1986, p. 13)

Yet, despite the other debtors' interest in bringing Argentina back to the fold, by mid-1984 it became evident to all that the short-term strategy of debtor adjustment was forcing disproportionately high costs on them and that, moreover, some political stance had to be taken against the increased burden being imposed by the steady climb of the US prime lending rate. In May 1984, Presidents Alfonsín of Argentina, Figueiredo of Brazil, Betancur of Colombia and de la Madrid of Mexico called for a ministerial meeting to identify initiatives that might contribute to a longer-term solution. The Cartagena meeting convened in June in a period of relative weakness of debtor solidarity. Bolivia and Ecuador had suspended payments and after widespread riots in Santo Domingo, the Dominican Republic had broken off its negotiations with the IMF. Of the major debtors, Argentina remained without an IMF accord while Mexico, Brazil and Venezuela were going through a period of relatively smooth relations with their creditors.

Although the countries had agreed on the need to take a joint political stance, there were some misgivings and even disagreement as to what the outcome of the meeting ought to be. Only a week before the meeting the Brazilian Finance Minister declared that the idea of convergence with other governments for debt renegotiation was 'a non-fun joke' between those who did not understand the workings of the international financial system. In Argentina, however, before boarding the plane to Cartagena the Minister for the Economy was quoted as saying that the purpose of the meeting was to try to 'modify the international financial framework' governing the relations between creditors and debtors (*La Razón*, 21 June 1984). Argentina was hopeful that she would not be left alone in her rebellion against the dictates of the IMF.

Much of the international press argued that the Cartagena meeting would provide the setting for a debtors' revolt or a debtors' cartel that would lead to a collapse of the international financial system. But, the governments themselves despite their disparate stances were all very cautious. They feared that aggressive tactics might needlessly provoke government and public opinion in creditor countries into retaliating. The final communiqué of the meeting stressed the willingness of debtors to honour their debts and to continue within the case-by-case framework (Art.8). With the possible exceptions of Argentina and Bolivia, at that time, every other country judged that its own case had special features that warranted preferential treatment and that such conditions could not be put at risk through collective negotiations, the outcome of which would be unknown. Venezuela counted on its strong reserve position and judged that it did not need new credits or an IMF stand-by; Mexico counted on its special relationship with the US to extract more favourable treatment; Brazil had its trade surplus and smaller debtors believed that the size of their debt allowed them more room to manoeuvre. This is a dynamic that Cline has called 'credit-rating self-preservation': no country would want to tarnish its own image through association with less meritorious partners. Moreover, the undeserving behaviour of any one debtor elevates debtors which carry on with the adjustment burden to a position of, 'by comparison, preferred credit risks' (Cline, 1983, p. 92). Credit-rating self-preservation, therefore, means that it will be in the interest of the other debtors to isolate the one among them that is unwilling to abide by the established rules of the game. So Argentina's hope of gaining some political backing from the meeting was at least partially disappointed.

The dynamics of 'credit-rating self-preservation' are not just a figment of the debtors' imagination. The creditors had clearly decided to present a common front and to pursue a strategy of 'divide and rule' which would isolate rebellious countries and reward cooperative ones. On the one hand, as soon as Argentina's duel with her creditors began, the *Financial Times* reported that a feature of the talks was the apparently increased unity amongst the creditor banks.

In the past US banks have veered towards making concessions to the borrower when balance sheet deadlines loom. This time there seems to be no gulf between them and their European counterparts. Argentina's brinkmanship has thus brought its creditors closer together. (*Financial Times*, 12 March 1984).

On the other hand, the Reagan Administration was ready to dangle 'carrots' in front of governments to prevent them from straying from the IMF-sactioned austerity path and to soften their radicalism *vis-à-vis* Cartagena. One such carrot, for example, was a USAID 60 million dollar loan rushed to Peru in June 1984, 75 per cent of which was tied to meeting IMF targets (*Latin American Weekly Report*, 29 June 1984). Simultaneously, Peru was granted Latin America's largest PL 480 programme by means of which the US unloaded its excess wheat and rice at concessional terms (*Latin American Weekly Report*, 22 June 1984). President Belaúnde only belatedly and timidly adhered to the principles agreed at the Cartagena summit, although just a few months before, the Government had been through a tug-of-war on whether or not to ahead with the letter of intent presented to the IMF. At that time some officials had thought that Peru could get much better terms if it waited for Argentina's and Bolivia's confrontation with its creditors to exact concessions; but Belaúnde decided to go ahead. Later, when the Cartagena meeting was being planned, the Peruvian Government's first reaction was to recommend that the whole debt issue be aired in the OAS (of which the US is a member) even though the organisation had already undergone such a test the year before. At a Conference convened for that purpose in September 1983, the US Under-Secretary of the Treasury, Beryl Sprinkel had indicated that the debt issue was no matter of concern:

this extreme situation is only temporary. Once significant adjustments are made, the underlying strength and promise of our economies will re-emerge with dynamism and vitality. Most importantly, confidence is being restored. We look forward to working with you to hasten the arrival of that day, and to working with you thereafter in achieving the potential of this beautiful hemisphere (in Roett, 1985).

Tighter coordination was, thus, difficult to achieve. Not only were there political differences among the regional governments. Within the same Government questions of timing and policy reversals occurred which could lead to the Government veering between confrontation and cooperation with its creditors in accordance with a changing assessment of short-term costs and benefits.

PHASE 2—THE ESTABLISHMENT OF A CONSENSUS (1984)

Although Argentina and especially Bolivia (which had formally suspended payments the year before after a dramatic fall in the price of tin) had approached the conference with hopes of organising some liaising mechanism for debt discussions, most other countries opted for more cautious tactics and refused to go beyond an agreement to exchange information on a purely informal or *ad hoc* basis. A Bolivian proposal put forward during the preceding 'technical' meeting to create a debt negotiating commission was rejected (*Carta de Política Exterior Mexicana,* IV, No. 3, 1984, p. 15).

As has been indicated, to dispel any threat of a debtors' cartel the final communiqué underlined the signatories' willingness to honour their debts and to continue their adjustment efforts (Art. 8) as well as to keep within the case-by-case approach (Art. 10). But, in exchange for a commitment to 'good housekeeping', the signatories made some demands.

It had become evident by then that one of the reasons why rescheduling was imposing such onerous costs on debtors was that the key variables affecting the general level of interest rates were beyond the control of the two actors most involved, the commercial banks and the debtor governments. Thus, negotiations with the banks could affect the payments to banks on spreads over the market interest rate, as well as the fees and commissions charged by the banks, but these elements had only a fairly marginal impact on total debt service incurred; however, the banks could do practically nothing to influence the general level of interest rates, as this was determined by government policies in industrial countries. Not only was the level of interest rate far more important than the elements dependent on the banks' discretion, but furthermore it was by far the most important single factor in determining the overall magnitude of debt service obligations. Neither could banks, and particularly those of the US, allow interest payments to be overdue, without having to exclude them from accrued income, unless the regulatory authorities allowed such a procedure; thus any form of interest capping would have implied losses for the banks. (See Griffith-Jones' paper in this volume.)

To overcome the limited nature of the negotiating forum, the Consensus called for a 'political dialogue' involving the creditor governments. Moreover, they asserted that the debt problem owed its origins to a drastic change in the conditions under which the loans had been contracted. 'These changes were originated in the industrialised countries and were beyond the decision power of the region' (Art. 7), therefore the signatories demanded that debtors and creditors share responsibility in the search for an adequate permanent solution Lastly, they demanded equity in the distribution of the costs of adjustment. Adjustment would need to be tackled symmetrically in debtor as well as creditor countries if it was to be achieved effectively. To this effect 'they pointed out the urgent need for measures to stabilise interest rates without impairing anti-inflationary goals (Art. 12).

These were the broad principles on which the signatories agreed, the principles they wanted creditors to accept. But, there was more than pleading and wishful thinking at Cartagena. The inability to agree on collective negotiations did not preclude an agreement on a set of specific proposals. They aimed directly to establish a frame of reference for future negotiations so that the burdens of adjustment might be alleviated. To this effect the signatories sought measures aimed at obtaining an 'immediate and drastic reduction in nominal and real interest rates in international markets' (Art. 18.A), temporary mechanisms to soften the impact of high interest rates, such as concessional loans or IMF compensatory finance (Art. 18.D) and the rescheduling of interest payments to accommodate falls in export earnings (Art. 18.F).

There was also agreement on a set of more narrow proposals seeking to squeeze softer terms from creditors at the time of rescheduling: the application of interest rates reflecting the real market costs of funds (Art. 18.B), the reduction of intermediation margins and other related costs to a minimum and the elimination of fees and commissions (Art. 18.C), the extension of grace periods and repayment periods and lastly, the consideration that rescheduling should not pre-empt export earnings over and above 'a reasonable percentage' compatible with an adequate level of economic activity (Art. 18.G). However, it did not manage to set out operational guidelines that might, for instance, propose maximum acceptable debt service ratios.

Barely two months after the get-together at Cartagena, Mexico obtained its multi-year rescheduling agreement. As put by *Business Week*, 'Favourable terms on Mexican loans will be helpful ammunition against more intransigent debtors' (*Business Week*, 10 September 1984). When the next meeting of the Cartagena Consensus was convened in September in Argentina coinciding with the country's payments deadlines, again the Government found that it was unable to muster support for a confrontational strategy. It may be that because debtors had suffered a severe deterioration in the financial conditions of their loans and because the parameters of the negotiation had been already limited so as to give priority to these issues, most debtors were mainly concerned with achieving improved financial terms for future rounds. There were no new initiatives at Mar del Plata but the invitation to creditor governments to engage in a direct political dialogue was renewed.

The final communiqué of the second meeting made a tacit reference to the Mexican deal as having applied some of the principles that the Consensus had advocated at Cartagena. At the third get-together in Santo Domingo in February 1985 delegates decided to stop pressing for the idea of a summit with western governments in order to await the results of the April meetings of the IMF and World Bank. Some interpreted this moderation as a consequence of the improved treatment from creditors, in particular to Mexico, and the hope that given good behaviour it could be extended to other debtors. (Duran, 1986). From Santo Domingo there was a call for these terms to be granted to other debtors as minimum conditions for future renegotiations. In fact during 1984 and particularly during 1985, a significant improvement was achieved in the negotiated cost of credit; spreads declined, rescheduling commissions were drastically reduced or eliminated and amortization periods increased significantly. Furthermore, the period of consolidation of debts was considerably extended as multi-year reschedulings were extended to several other debtors: the Dominican Republic and Venezuela rescheduled repayments over four and Chile over three years.

PHASE 3—THE SEARCH FOR NEW SOLUTIONS (1985–6)

By the beginning of 1985, the worst of Argentina's protracted confrontation with its creditors was over. The banks had used a skilful strategy sticking to their demand that an IMF programme was a must and then 'waiting until the economy went into such a tail-spin that the recalcitrant debtor must come crawling back to the table' (*Business Week*, 12 August 1985). The Argentine Government had indeed let the economy go out of control; it had counted too much on the benevolent attitude of creditor governments to the newly-born democracy and it lacked a coherent alternative adjustment strategy. As a senior US banker said after a meeting with Argentine negotiators, 'We expected to get facts and figures, a detailed picture of the country's medium- to long-term economic plans. All we got were some platitudes about Argentina's new democracy' (*Financial Times*, 1 February 1984). By early 1985 Argentina was ready to undergo an IMF-sanctioned austerity plan.

Yet, gradually through 1985 there was an increasingly

widespread realisation that the classical adjustment strategy was being proved wanting. On the side of the debtors there seemed to be a somewhat more organised search for alternatives to ensure that debt servicing would not jeopardise growth. On one hand, Fidel Castro convened a large and notorious gathering in Havana and made an appeal to the Latin American governments to repudiate their foreign debts. Although no serious immediate consequences ensued, the event as such added a new element of urgency to the issue. On the other hand, Peru became the first country in Latin America (after the replacement of President Belaúnde by Alan García, in July 1985) to attempt to put into practice the Cartagena Consensus proposal that only 'a reasonable percentage' of export earnings be dedicated to debt servicing. Until mid-1985 practice had established that the continuation of debt servicing be paramount; it should proceed according to an agreed schedule from which other goals should follow. This resulted in debtors then having to 'adjust' so as to be able to make payments according to schedule. The Peruvian decision to impose a 10 per cent ceiling for the servicing of medium- and long-term debt shifted the emphasis so that growth should not be sacrificed. The focus was placed on the attainment of a minimum rate of growth which would determine the maximum possible debt servicing capability. If such an approach were to be generalised, it would imply that it would be the international financial system which would have to 'adjust' to the minimum growth targets fixed by debtor economies.

A few months after Garcia's and Castro's statements a U-turn occurred on the side of the creditors. The new approach was outlined by the US Secretary of the Treasury, James Baker, at the meetings of the IMF and World Bank in Seoul in October 1985. His proposal was to make available about $29bn net new lending over three years to ease the financial problems of the fifteen middle-income most indebted countries. Of this sum, private creditor banks were expected to contribute $20 bn, the rest to be provided in loans from the World Bank and the multilateral development banks (in the case of Latin America, the Inter-American Development Bank), raising lending levels by 50 per cent. This inflow of much needed fresh funds would take place under the continuing supervision of the IMF, although the policies of the debtor countries would be geared to fostering economic growth. With the Baker plan the emphasis was shifted from the financial to the economic implications of debt servicing. Moreover, it was an explicit recognition that the short-term strategy could not be sustained indefinitely. From the point of view of the members of the Cartagena Consensus it could be viewed as a step in the right direction since it reflected some of their demands. It admitted that the debt problem could not be resolved satisfactorily if it impeded growth in the indebted countries, it recognised the need for additional financing and, with the US Treasury coming out into the open in the search for a stable solution, it tacitly gave in to the demand that creditor governments become involved.

When the Consensus subsequently met in December in Montevideo for an evaluation of the Baker initiative, further progress was made along the road of concertation: on the one hand, there was a renewed impetus provided by the novel Brazilian interest in the Consensus and on the other, there was the establishment of a new mechanism, a monitoring committee. The change in the Brazilian political regime in March of 1985 had not initially meant a drastic change on the issue of debt management but by mid-year a new economic team was sworn in. The team headed by Dilson Funaro was from the start committed to doubling per capita income by the year 2000 and consequently keen on arresting negative transfers of resources. The final communiqé of the Montevideo Conference was heavily influenced by Brazilian proposals. It stressed that the restoration of economic growth was a necessary but not a sufficient condition to solve the problem. Equally important was a commitment to retain the benefits of growth at home for which there must be a commitment to reverse negative flows and to reduce real interest rates to 'historic levels'. The document also included a proposal to link transfers abroad to a minimum growth target, a policy that Brazil subsequently announced that it might put into practice by setting a ceiling of 2.5 per cent of its GNP that would be available for debt servicing. The group described the Baker initiative as a 'positive step' but 'inadequate'.

With the catalysing slide in oil prices, a second impetus at the Montevideo gathering was provided by Mexico and Venezuela's expected income shortfall. The feeling that debt servicing was a paramount obligation of debtors without there being sacrifice from any other of the players suffered further erosion. A monitoring committee made up of Argentina, Brazil, Mexico, Uruguay and Venezuela was formed to evaluate the progress of negotiations and to propose alternative options if necessary. The agreement to set up a monitoring committee hinted at the increasing willingness and ability of the big debtors to keep each other informed of their actions and, if necessary, to call upon members to extend the scope of their mutual support.

When Mexico's plight in August 1982 had signalled the onset of the debt crisis Latin America lacked any concentration mechanisms that could be called upon, if only to be used as psychological tactics. With no back-up, cash-strapped governments had to face their creditors one by one as the crisis peaked in countries at different times. By the end of 1985, in just a year and a half of existence, the Cartagena Group might not have fully coordinated the disparate views and differing national needs of the Latin American debtors. But, it had succeeded by the tacit threat of unleashing a domino effect, in establishing itself as a strategic deterrent, a back-up instrument in case of need. This point will be elaborated further in the following section when the logic of the joint strategy is discussed.

Second, it had established some basic negotiating para-meters. Although the formation of a cartel had been dismissed and the case-by-case settlement never seriously questioned, it had managed to coordinate individual initiatives so that mutually reinforcing effects could be expected. By the end of 1985, the Cartagena Group could claim some credit for having forced the international financial community into being more flexible and for having persuaded the US administration that growth would have to be encouraged if a way were to be found out of the debt crisis. The philosophical heart of the Baker Plan had endorsed the idea of growth.

Although most countries believed that they could clinch better deals individually than collectively, they also believed that the back-up provided by the mere existence of the Cartagena Group for their individual negotiations was crucial. When Mexico and Venezuela following the oil price tumble called for an emergency meeting of the monitoring committee in February 1986 in Punta del Este, it was clear that they were exercising 'one of the few options that might have an impact both on their own electorates and in the eyes of the international financial community'. (*Financial Times*, 6 February 1986).

The Punta del Este meeting endorsed the view that individual policy decisions could converge and have mutually reinforcing results. The final communiqué stated that 'the emergency actions (that may be taken by individual countries) will receive the solidarity and support of the rest of the signatory countries to the Cartagena Consensus'. In other words, the signatories hinted that Mexico might not be left alone. Whatever path it took, confrontational or not, would be supported, perhaps even followed, by the rest of the group. The veiled threat was further tightened by a declaration that 'given the high degree of interdependence, any external factor affecting a particular country or a group of countries provokes important effects and reactions in the rest of the nations'. At this point it seemed that the coordinating mechanism that Argentina and Bolivia had desired and lacked in 1984 had been set up and was ready for use, should Mexico require it. One can suppose that all that Mexico subsequently believed it needed was the mere commitment to the threat of joint action. As G. O'Donnell (1985) has pointed out creditors confronted with the possibility of a debtors' alliance will immediately offer 'side payments' or bribes to prevent its consolidation. The existence of the Cartagena Consensus has helped debtors by inducing higher bribes.

During 1986, after a two-year period of accommodation, the logic of the collective strategy of the debtors seems to have surfaced with some clarity. President Alan Garcia remarked during his visit to Uruguay in April: 'we never pretended a consensus on idential steps' (*Clarin*, 14 April 1986). Keeping within the format of case-by-case settlement the Cartagena Consensus created ground so that individual strategies had mutually reinforcing effects. Such a linked-step strategy meant that, for example, after Mexico's inauguration in 1986 of a contingency facility and automatic finance linked to a minimum growth target, Argentina required similar terms. Argentine negotiators also demanded and obtained—although only for 'old debt'—the same interest margin of $\frac{3}{16}$ per cent over LIBOR that had been granted to Mexico.

THE LOGIC OF THE JOINT STRATEGY

In addition to requiring skill and audacity, a negotiation takes place in the context of a balance of power. To begin with, as in most realistic situations, the debt interaction cannot be characterised as one of pure conflict, a zero sum game. The element of conflict is indeed present, yet the situation can best be described as one of mutual dependence, a non-zero sum game, that demands some kind of collaboration among opposite parties even if only in the avoidance of mutual destruction. In effect, from the vantage point of creditors there has been a continuous awareness that to maintain the balance of power ways had to be found to avoid debtors from falling into despair; they had to prevent governments in debt-ridden countries from feeling that it was better to pay the price of sanctions than continue the normal service of debts. At the onset of the debt crisis, as we have discussed in the previous section, over-optimistic forecasting served to persuade debtors to accept the rescue packages. By 1985, when because of persistent high interest rates and falling export prices, over-optimism was seen as such, Baker's proposal was launched creating new incentives for cooperative behaviour. To successful adjustors it promised increased funds and room for growth-oriented policies laying fresh ground for a renewed game of mutual dependence.

Why were debtor governments so prone to accept the confines of this balance of power? From the focal point of the debtor government it is unrealistic to assume that its policies are the outcome of a unified actor pursuing a single goal. A full analysis of its choices and actions in this bargaining process should include an understanding of the basic power configuration on which it rests, in other words, reference should be made to the political determinants which affect a government's set of preferences. (c.f. C. Fortin). The fundamental issue to settle here is, to what extent are policy-makers genuinely prepared to carry out the ultimate threat, collapse of negotiations? By collapse we are referring here to an outcome leading to a protracted and more or less irreversible conflict between the debtor government and the banking community, international financial organisations and creditor governments, implying possibly some degree of de-linking of the debtor economy from the Western world economy.

The degree of acceptability of this outcome on the part of the government policy-makers will be a function of their assessment of: (a) the harm that the collapse of negotiations will bring to the economy, to particular sectors within it—notably those representing the political bases of the state and to the ability of the government to command economic resources; and (b) the political response within the country: how would interest groups, political parties, the mobilised populace respond to the conflict following the collapse and its economic consequences? (Fortin, 1986).

Because of the risk of domestic upheaval, the will to carry out the ultimate threat requires the will to accept likely changes in the domestic balance of power. It is quite reasonable then for policy-makers devoid of revolutionary leanings to conclude that it is less costly to keep renegotiations going than to precipitate a break with creditors. For governments treading a middle-of-the-road path, as Simonsen held: 'a growing economy with expanding exports would hardly seek confrontation with its creditors'. After such cost-benefit calculations it is not surprising that they were inclined to look for some ground for cooperation with creditors so long as these were also willing to reward cooperative behaviour (Axelrod, 1984).

In this sense, the debt bargaining context is more like a prisoner's dilemma than a game of chess. Both sides can potentially do well by mutual cooperation or can do poorly by mutual defection. A fundamental point here is that both sides are aware that the opposite party is not unconditionally willing to make the most feared move since the damage may be worse to the threateners than to the opposite party. 'It is typical of strategic threats that the punitive action—if the threat fails and has to be carried out—is painful and costly to both sides. The purpose is deterrence *ex ante* not revenge *ex post*' (Schelling, 1963, p. 185).

In such a situation the greatest cost of the debtors' ultimate threat, the threat to default collectively was the risk of having to carry it out. Unconditional commitment to this sort of threat, therefore, was self-defeating. The debtors were, thus, caught in a sort of trap in which the credibility of their threat to default was greatly impaired. Moreover, credibility could possibly be enhanced by avoiding an explicit articulation of the threat, that is by mere implication. By letting it hang in the background the probability of a resort to joint action appeared at once more real and less provocative. So the best possible strategy was appearing to be reasonable and merely to insinuate that a sort of domino-theory-contagion was not ruled out. Yet, the debtors then had to solve the following dilemma: how could they show they seriously considered collective default when it was an option that they would in fact prefer not to carry out, and *at the same time* employ that option as a deterrent to extract concessions from creditors? Bargaining theory has held that maximum credibility may be extracted from this sort of threat by leaving as little room as possible for discretion in carrying it out (Schelling, 1963). Faced with such a situation an actor can of course bluff to persuade the opposite party falsely that the costs or damages to the threatener would be minor or negative; he may pretend that it believes the costs to be small or, alternatively, he may threaten that he *may* act rather than he will. The key to this sort of deterrent is that one may or may not carry out the threat; the final decision is not altogether under the threatener's control. The threat does not take the form of 'I may or may not according to rational calculations or choice' but rather, 'I may or may not and even I cannot be completely sure'. The element of uncertainty may come from chance, accident, third party influence, or an ingredient in the situation that neither party can entirely predict or control. In early 1986, the debtors were clearly converging from individual bargaining positions into this kind of strategy when they repeatedly highlighted the element of uncertainty introduced into the debt scenario by the increasing pressure of public opinion. This was the implication to be drawn from the statement made by Mexican Finance Minister, Jesús Silva Herzog, in early February, to the effect that governments are responsible first to their people and then to their creditors. Argentine Minister for the Economy, Juan Sourrouille carried the same message to the April meeting of the IMF/World Bank Development Committee, 'the patience of the people is reaching the point of exhaustion'.

Once the ingredient of uncertainty was introduced at the Punta del Este gathering into the collective strategy of the debtors, together with a purposefully undefined commitment to greater solidarity,[1] the scene was re-set for a new phase of brinkmanship tactics. This time Mexico was at the front yet with the backing of the Consensus. Whereas Argentina's brinkmanship in 1984 had by force of circumstances been solitary—part of its failure having been due to its isolation—Mexico's brinkmanship in 1986 had some backing from the Consensus of Cartagena. This may be one of the elements explaining the favourable deal obtained by Mexico, though clearly not the main one.

The issue of brinkmanship as a bargaining tactic now raises the problem of the different implications of the collective and the individual threat of collapse. The cost to creditors of collective action is quite obviously much greater. Therefore, if faced with the danger that a serious alliance of debtors may arise, they will be inclined to make side payments in order to prevent such a joining of forces. The more probable and imminent the formation of an alliance, the more urgent creditors will feel that they must redouble their efforts to tempt potential deserters (O'Donnell, 1985). Each debtor government, however, moving towards an alliance and faced with the offer of side-payments then will assess the situation as follows: acceptance of such immediate and tangible advantages keeps its domestic balance of power unchallenged while considerably enhancing its bargaining position *vis-à-vis* its creditors. In other words, the plausibility or even the mere insinuation of the debtors' alliance serves as an excellent bargaining chip. It has opened the way towards a better deal by forcing creditors to make concessions that they might not have been ready to consider before the debtor seemed prepared to promote or join the coalition. The threat of contagion turns out to be a question of individual tactics.

The point is, therefore, that so long as debtors are not left to fall into despair—which seemed to be the situation in FBS until Baker's proposal—brinkmanship is an individual initiative of debtors. Individual unilateral action is obviously less costly to creditors than joint action; in a game of mutual dependence it is concurrently more credible. Brinkmanship as a bargaining tactic:

> involves getting into the slope where one may fall in spite of his own best efforts to save himself, dragging his adversary with him . . . Brinkmanship is thus the deliberate creation of a recognisable risk of war, a risk that one does not completely control. It is the tactic of deliberately letting the situation get somewhat out of hand, just because its being out of hand may be intolerable to the other party and force his accommodation. It means harrassing and intimidating an adversary by exposing him to a shared risk, or deterring him by showing that if he makes a contrary move he may disturb us so that we slip over the brink whether we want to or not, carrying him with us. (Schelling, 1963, p 200)

Bargaining strength in this context lies in what is weakness by other standards, or rather, has reversed weakness into strength. The risk of unilateral action, or responsibility for avoiding such a course then is made to depend on what the creditors do. The credibility of the deterrent, and the power of the weak party has stemmed from the fact that the possibility of unilateral action is not limited to the situation in which a cool decision will or can be taken. It is not made to depend on preference or commitment, the final decision is left to chance. It is then up to the creditors to estimate how far they must concede to avoid precipitating collapse. 'To share a risk with the enemy may provide him with an overpowering incentive to lay off' (Schelling, 1963, p. 194)—which here can be translated into inducing creditors to force up their rewards in bilateral negotiations.

The success of brinkmanship is thus measured by the ability to obtain a deal that maximises the availability of foreign exchange to the debtor economy, that is, a 'good deal' in financial terms. The price paid, however, is the persistence of the overall balance of power, one in which negative net transfers have not been reversed or even much reduced (c.f. Griffith-Jones in this volume). This is a gloomy note on which to end a discussion of the prospects of debtor coordination. Yet, successful brinkmanship has an additional dimension. Not having either to implement the threat of contagion or to make it clear that one would refrain from recourse to it, has left its credibility intact for the future—an element of considerable value given the fact that the debtors are faced with an ongoing process of renegotiations as to how and when the debt is to be serviced.

CONCLUSIONS

Since 1982 the debt burden has engulfed Latin American debtors in a severe economic and financial crisis. The debtor countries are far from having regained their capacity for sustained growth, and given the persistent drain of resources abroad, the perception remains that a permanent and equitable solution to the question is not yet at hand. Governments are still confronting the same difficulties and the same alternatives as five years ago. The institutionalisation of the eleven-nation Cartagena Consensus as a permanent regional forum for consultation on debt matters has changed the bargaining context but does not seem to have significantly altered the overall balance of power *vis-à-vis* creditors.

Part of Cartagena's limited impact can be explained by reasons of precedent and timing. The crisis found creditors prepared for coordinated action while sovereign borrowers, being used to negotiate on an individual basis, were ambivalent as to the implications of setting up a supra-national body which would require some transfer of sovereignty. The setting up of such a body would have required a shared perception of problems and considerable degrees of political affinity in addition to a communications network which was then lacking. From this point on creditors took advantage of the natural obstacles of forging a debtors' alliance and pursued a wise strategy of divide and rule. The strategy was assisted by the timing of debt rescheduling: crisis peaked in countries at different times. It was also facilitated by debtors' initial hopes of a normal return to capital markets, and, therefore, by their perceived need to preserve their credit rating by not waging a war with the international financial community. These hopes were cleverly fuelled by the optimistic forecasting of creditor institutions.

By 1984, it became clear to debtors that the crises were not conjunctural phenomena that could be dealt with by short-term adjustment. It also became clear—at least to a number of them—that the persistence of debtor individualism was leading to excessively uncritical acceptance of creditors' interest in maximising payments. But, by then the confines of the balance of power had been firmly set. Moreover, debtor individualism offered the immediate advantage of allowing the extraction of short-term concessions from the divide and rule strategy of creditors. In principle, however, many governments believed in some degree of coordination with other debtors on general issues. The most pressing of these general issues, one for which no alleviation could be sought under the current negotiating framework, was that of high and increasing real interest rates. On this the debtors were united; throughout 1984 and 1985 they made repeated appeals on the need to bring down interest rates and to engage in a direct political dialogue with creditor governments to work out a global solution. The Baker initiative partially yielded to these demands by shifting the emphasis from the financial to the economic dimension of the debt problem; and by giving debtor governments some hope of a respite it ensured that despair did not push debtors to rock the boat.

Because most Latin American governments have tended to view the existence of the Cartagena Group as a bargaining chip to be traded for certain concessions at the negotiating table, collective appeals have remained within the realm of the general declaration of principles. Cartagena has not drawn up an operational plan, for example, agreement on a maximum limit to debt servicing or net transfers, concrete proposals for interest capping which might have narrowed the bargaining context in a manner more favourable to the debtors. Concurrently, failure to agree on operational criteria has implied that the Cartagena Consensus could resort to only one crude threat, a threat that has deterred creditors from optimising their short-term debt collection position but has not compelled them to work out a longer-term global solution.

Will debtors need to forge a tighter alliance in order to obtain a long-term global solution? A tighter alliance would require, in the first place, the willingness to set up a permanent secretariat; it would require that some decision-making power and resources be transferred to it, that governments become bound to it and accept being hostages of each other. Such a step, utopian as it may be, would greatly enhance Cartagena's prospects as a meaningful alliance and would undoubtedly induce creditors to seriously consider a debt relief programme. Yet a debt relief programme need not depend solely on the improbably prospects of a tighter alliance. Leading banks have not only been increasing their capital substantially, they have also been building up substantial loan loss reserves against their debtor country exposure. Reducing the interest payment burden—via capitalisation, for instance—would not cost the banks anything directly; it might even make financial sense. Regulators might require that they take capitalised interest payments out of reported profits and use them to bolster capital or loan loss reserves. But any such reduction in profits might be more than offset by the strengthening of the capital structure and the realistic prospect of steadily reduced exposure to rocky sovereign borrowers (Kaletsky, 1987).

So what role remains for the Consensus of Cartagena? Cartagena's impact has been limited yet not neglible; it has served, as we have seen, to coordinate bargaining tactics for mutually reinforcing effects. As such its credibility is intact. To enhance it and to keep up the momentum the group might in future need to set up more frequent periodical meetings at a technical level to exchange information on the narrow issues of the negotiations, for example, debt-equity swaps, conditionality, etc., an area in which much remains to be done and one in which, with comparatively little investment, rewards can be easily reaped. If such a breakdown of potential areas of cooperation were tackled, a step-by-step strategy might find debtors better equipped for a situation in which a more radical approach was required. It took OPEC over a decade from its initial contacts in the early sixties to turn into a meaningful cartel in the seventies. Likewise, quiet step-by-step diplomacy in a non-urgent environment can set up a mechanism which debtors might want to trigger at the right opportunity. All efforts of cooperation require a process of learning by doing.

NOTES

I would like to thank Mike Faber, Carlos Fortin, Judith Evans and the contributors to this volume for their stimulating comments on a first draft. The paper was also inspired by talks with government officials who might wish to remain anonymous. My special thanks to Stephany Griffith-Jones for persistent questioning. The usual caveats apply.

1. 'Because of the high degree of interdependence in Latin America, any external factor affecting a particular country, or group of countries, provokes important effects and reactions in the rest of the nations'. (See Appendix—Communiqué issued at Punta del Este, 28 February, 1986).

REFERENCES

Axelrod, R., 1984, *The Evolution of Cooperation*, New York, Basic Books.

Cline, W., 1983, *International Debt and the Stability of the World Economy*, Washington DC, Institute for International Economics.

Devlin, R., 'La deuda externa vs. el desarrollo económico: América Latina en la encrucijada', Santiago, *Colección Estudios CIEPLAN* no. 17, octubre 1985.

Durán, E., 'Latin America's external debt: the limits of regional cooperation', *The World Today*, Vol. 45, No. 5, May 1986.

Feinberg, R., 1986, 'Latin American debt: renegotiating the adjustment burden', mimeo.

Fortín, C., 1986, 'Politics and debt crisis management in Latin America: A framework research', mimeo.

Kaletsky, A., 'Don't cry for Brazil', *Financial Times*, 28 February 1987, p. 9.

O'Donnell, G., 'External debt: why don't our governments do the obvious?', *CEPAL Review* No. 27, December 1985.

Roett, R., 'Latin America's response to the debt crisis', *Third World Quarterly*, April 1985, Vol. 7, No. 2.

Schelling, T., 1975, *The Strategy of Conflict*, New York, Oxford University Press.

Wiesner, E., 'Latin American Debt: Lessons and Pending Issues', *Papers and Proceedings of the 97th Annual Meeting of the American Economic Associations*, May 1985.

Periodical publications
Business Week
Carta de Política Exterior Mexicana
Clarín
Financial Times
La Razón
Latin American Weekly Report

11 Power, Bargaining and the Latin American Debt Negotiations: Some Political Perspectives

Carlos Fortin

INTRODUCTION

International debt rescheduling negotiations may appear at first sight as ideally suited for analysis through formal models. Two distinct parties, the debtor government and the creditor banks, confront each other on issues of an apparently quantifiable nature—how much will be paid and when—on which they have clear-cut preferences: the creditors to recover as quickly as possible their capital and interest, the debtors to pay as little as possible over the longest possible time. All the various trade-offs appear also quantifiable. These are precisely the situations in which formal models of bargaining, whether economic—such as bilateral monopoly[1]—or strategic—such as game-theoretic[2]—recommend themselves.

Yet, a little reflection suggests that those types of models are insufficient to understand the kind of external debt bargaining processes that the studies in this volume deal with. To begin with, it is clear that what is being negotiated about is not only the financial features of rescheduling but more general issues of macro-economic policy in the debtor countries, which have large implications for their development prospects and for the welfare of different sectors of their populations. The calculus of utilities involved is, on this count, much more complex than the formulation above suggests, not least because those issues are inextricably linked to divergent theoretical and ideological perspectives.

Second, and perhaps more seriously, these models are not conceived to incorporate systematically an analysis of power.

This is most evident in the case of economic models, where the relative power positions of the parties are only introduced as determinants of their utility functions; the latter are assumed to reflect fully any differences in resources or capabilities, and after they are fixed, the parties are assumed to be symmetrical.[3] This, of course, immediately removes a crucial—perhaps the most crucial—component of the bargaining interaction in debt rescheduling negotiations. In the case of game-theoretical models, there is room for introducing capabilities and power in the decision rules, but this can only be done at a high level of abstraction.[4] The actual power processes that take place within the debtor government cannot be included in the analysis inasmuch as game-theoretical models assume fixed utilities and pay-off matrices[5]; by contrast, the fact that states and governments are subject to continuous and changing political pressures, to which they often respond by modifying their utilities, is outside the scope of the models. This is, however, again of the essence of the bargaining contexts we are talking about; we are not so much interested in finding a determinate 'solution' for the bargaining game as in making sense of a series of interactive encounters, leading to a concretely determined outcome.

Any realistic explanation of the bargaining processes examined in the preceding studies must incorporate the two dimensions suggested above; some elaboration of them is, therefore, in order at this point.

1. THE CONTENT OF RESCHEDULING

Chapter 1 above identified the outcomes to be explained in terms of:

a) *the kind of debt rescheduling deal arrived at,* with indicators such as the resulting change on the net transfer of financial resources from, or to, the country; the change in the net present value of the debt; and financial aspects of the deal.

b) *the degree of adjustment required as a condition of the deal,* measured in terms of key economic variables such

> as GDP, employment, investment, income distribution, the current account of the balance of payments, inflation, etc., and
>
> c)   *other variables*, such as the treatment of loans to the private sector, trade preferences, large contracts, etc.

The systematic introduction of an emphasis on the political aspects calls for some further comments on the last two dimensions.

1. Adjustment

In its broadest sense, it refers to restoring the balance in the external accounts—in particular, reducing the deficit in the current account of the balance of payments—either through short-term change in some macro-economic variables or through long-term restructuring of the economy. These objectives can in principle be achieved through a number of policy packages, including some containing heterodox measures, such as import restrictions or multiple exchange rates.[6] However, the kind of 'adjustment policies' that are part of debt rescheduling negotiations are those espoused by the IMF and the World Bank, and based on a broadly defined—that is, in some respects 'fiscal'[7]—monetary approach to the balance of payments. In practice this approach defines adjustment policies essentially in terms of the reduction of aggregate demand, economic liberalisation, and the opening of the economy to the rest of the world. Since these policies normally have a contractionary impact, thus, affecting the real income of different sectors of the population, the extent to which they are included in debt rescheduling agreements is a crucial component of the analysis of the renegotiations from a political viewpoint.[8]

A point to be noted here is the complex and sometimes contradictory relationship between adjustment and the specific features of the rescheduling deal. *Ceteris paribus* the willingness of a government to introduce strict adjustment policies along the lines advocated by the IMF should increase its chances of obtaining a 'good' rescheduling deal, since creditors would trust the programme adopted to increase the repayment ability of the economy. In principle, therefore, there should be a direct relationship between the two variables: the more orthodox the adjustment package agreed, the better the rescheduling terms. However, the *degree* of adjustment required—in the first sense above—is by definition a function of the state of the economy and its main macro-economic balances, notably its external accounts; the latter in turn are greatly influenced by the rescheduling, which sets the level of outflows in the services account and generally affects the external resources that will be available to the economy. Thus, a favourable deal will make the need for drastic adjustment less pressing.

2. Other variables

Among them the most relevant in terms of political analysis is the treatment of the debt of the private sector. This is obviously the one area of negotiations in which pressures from various economic groups will be especially evident, and the links between the government and indeed the state—which enters the negotiations as representative of the national interest—and sectional and class interests within the national society will manifest themselves. This point will be taken up again below.

2. GOVERNMENTS AS POLITICAL ACTORS

Often analyses of international bargaining assume the state to be a unitary actor with clearly-defined preferences which in some sense correspond to the utility function of the national society as a whole. Taken literally, the three assumptions implicit in this description are unrealistic. The state is not a unitary actor but one composed of various sub-actors (agencies, bureaucracies, individuals) which, in turn, respond to influences and pressures from various non-governmental actors (classes, interest groups, political parties); as a result there is often not a single, univocal and transitive set of preferences (although at a given point in the actual bargaining sequence there might be); and, furthermore, whatever set of preferences ultimately prevails is likely to be representative not of a single national utility function, but rather of the interests of certain sections of society which might be contradictory to those of other sections.

In the case of Third World societies and states this already complex panorama is further complicated by the fact that those societies and economies are inserted in a particular—'dependent'—way in the international context; some of the relevant actors are, therefore, external, notably international capital, and some of the internal actors develop links with the external ones which serve to 'internalise' the influence of the latter.

At the same time, however, it must be recognised that certain outcomes in the negotiations are 'in the national interest' in that they are beneficial to the economy as a whole and, therefore, to all relevant social actors; and that they will weigh heavily in the preferences of decision-makers and negotiators. Important questions here include the extent to which the decision-makers are able to specify clearly the outcomes which are in the national interest and the extent to which they have enough autonomy from political pressure to be able to pursue them in the negotiations even if they may conflict with sectional interests. These points will be taken up again below.

Some conceptual distinctions in relation with the state appear, therefore, appropriate.[9] In contemporary political analysis the term is used to include two closely-related but distinguishable notions. On the one hand, it refers to the power coalition of classes and groups whose interests are being fundamentally pursued by the development model adopted. Terms such as 'the social bases of the state' or 'the class nature of the state' refer to the state in this sense. On the other hand, the state is also a set of institutions and personnel through which state policy and action is decided, organised and implemented.

A full analysis of the political determinants of state action should include in the first place reference to the groups whose fundamental interests are being furthered by the state. These can be conveniently categorised in terms of sectors of capital: industrial, commercial, financial or agrarian, in the understanding that there will be interpenetration and combination; do the interests of the popular sectors—workers, peasants, urban dwellers—have a place in the dominant coalition of interests? What is the importance of foreign capital in its various forms—for example, productive capital through direct foreign investment, banking capital through financial flows—in that coalition? What are its links with domestic private capital and with state enterprises? What is the importance of the latter and their managers?

In this connection the analysis of some of the more industrialised countries of Latin America in the late 1970s put forward the hypothesis of the existence of a 'triple alliance' composed of state capital, foreign capital and private domestic—predominantly industrial—capital.[10] According to this analysis, the dynamic agent of accumulation in the model was the multinational enterprise but the state played a central role in defining the conditions for the presence of the multinationals as well as a growing role in accumulation itself through state companies often in association with foreign capital. Domestic capital was in a subordinate but still dynamic position. The social bases of the state here were, therefore, the managers of state enterprises, the local managers of international companies and the local bourgeoisie, notably industrial. By contrast, other cases involved state power configurations dominated by domestic financial and commercial capital, in alliance with international—predominantly banking—capital. While the popular sectors and their interests were fundamentally absent in both configurations, the exclusion is considerably more drastic in the latter; the former, as an industrialising model, requires some degree of incorporation of the popular sectors both as labour and as consumers.

While it is not being suggested that there is a simple correlation between the analysis of the social bases of the state—which, in effect, operates at the level of the fundamental logic of the state rather than of its behavioural characteristics —and state action, the understanding of the basic power configuration which the state represents is a necessary background variable for examining in more concrete fashion the issues at hand. In principle, the higher the influence of *financial* and *international* capital on the state—given the development model adopted—the more likely that the government will exclude a breakdown of negotiations as an acceptable outcome. Conversely, the higher the importance of industrial capital and state enterprise, the more likely that the goal in the negotiations will include reference to 'growth' with preference to the stability of the international financial system.

Turning to the more observable level of the state as a set of institutions and personnel, a first issue to be noted is precisely that of the relation between the social bases and the state managers and institutions: how autonomous are the latter? It has been suggested that the regimes described as 'bureaucratic-authoritarian' exhibit a larger degree of autonomy with respect to social pressures and influence than more pluralist regimes;[11] therefore, the ideological orientations and the immediate interests of the state political personnel become particularly relevant to understand state behaviour. Other questions to be asked here have to do with the structure of government organisation: the number and the type of agencies involved in various functional areas, and their formal and informal division of labour. In particular, the extent to which the executive branch is responsible before an elected organ, be it a Parliament or some other, is, as will be discussed below, relevant to the bargaining position of the government negotiators.

In terms of the relationship between the state and the body politic, the basic features of the regime to be considered include the degree of *pluralism* (elections, freedom of the press, of association and political activity, multipartidism); and the degree of *mobilisation* of the population by the state or the government parties or movements, with special reference to grass-root forms of political participation. Terms like democratisation sometimes tend to conflate the two; in effect they are not only different but in some cases might be contradictory. Conversely, some authoritarian—that is, not conventionally pluralist regimes may be highly mobilising.

3. TOWARDS REALISTIC MODELS OF INTERNATIONAL DEBT BARGAINING

We, therefore, need models of international debt rescheduling bargaining which can capture the richness and complexity of the concrete reality of those processes, including their political dimensions. Such models, to be sure, will be indeterminate and will not exhibit the elegance and parsimony that are such attractive features of the economic and game-theoretical approaches. Important building blocks for new models have already been provided by a number of contributions on bargaining in general, and international bargaining in particular, notably the manipulative,[12] the process analysis,[13] and the power-dependence[14] approaches. This section will attempt to take advantage of those contributions to explore some concepts which may be useful in understanding international debt rescheduling negotiations as political processes and the behaviour of debtor governments *qua* political actors.

1. Objectives

A political analysis of the outcomes of international debt negotiations must start with a detailed consideration of the objectives and goals that the debtor governments set for themselves in the negotiations, and their political determinants.

A first and fundamental question here is, to what extent are government decision-makers prepared to accept that the negotiations may not reach agreement, and to take unilateral action? Such action need not be a full repudiation of the debt, but a redefinition of its terms and conditions based on criteria other than purely market ones.

Two cases must be distinguished here. The threat, or even the implementation, of unilateral action by the debtor government might be essentially a bargaining tactic, aimed not at ending the negotiations but at extracting concessions from the creditors leading to an acceptable deal later. For this to work, the action must have a sufficiently serious negative effect on the creditors to force them to make concessions. Evidently, if the government is not prepared to go through with a true breakdown of the negotiations, a miscalculation as to the reaction of the creditors, their home governments and international financial organisations will result in a climbdown and possibly in an even worse deal. This type of case has been the subject of particular attention from bargaining theorists of the manipulative approach.[15]

On the other hand, unilateral action might be aimed, in the absence of agreement, at implementing a state of affairs that the debtor government regards as a reasonable solution to its predicament. This will, in all likelihood, not be a complete repudiation but rather the setting of limits to the amounts to be paid, thus creating some incentive for the creditors not to retaliate. The purpose is not to inflict harm on the creditors in order to pressurise them into an agreement acceptable to the debtors—which will, by definition, fall short of the unilateral action threated or undertaken—but to implement an acceptable solution in the absence of agreement. In reality, it is likely that any unilateral action will contain elements of both types.

Even the second type, though, may lead to a protracted conflict with the banking community, international financial organisations and creditor governments, which might in turn require substantial structural adjustment away from integration in the world capitalist economy.

The degree of acceptability of this outcome on the part of the government policy-makers will be a function of their assessment of:

a) the probability that unilateral action will lead to retaliation on the part of creditors, home governments and international financial organisations,

b) the probability, and the extent to which, such retaliation will harm the economy, particular sectors within it—notably those representing the bases of the state—or the ability of the government to command economic resources, and

c) the political response within the country: how would interest groups, political parties, the mobilised populace respond to the conflict and to its economic consequences? In other words, what will be the harm to the ability of the government to command political resources (legitimacy and support?).[16] In this connection it is conceivable that powerful economic groups within the country may regard the stability of the international financial system as an overriding value to be preserved; sectors of the financial bourgeoisie would take that view for obvious reasons of self-interest, particularly if their activities are internationalised. Indeed, in the context of high levels of capital flights in the period preceding the negotiations it is possible that economic groups other than financial would also be concerned with preserving the smooth operation of the international capital markets to protect their financial assets abroad. Evidently, import-export sectors will not wish to jeopardise international trade in general and that of the country in particular. It is equally likely that important elites within the countries may value highly the integration of those economies and societies in the world market, which afford them the opportunity of interaction with their counterparts in the industrialised countries and of access to a comparable lifestyle.

A second issue in connection with the objectives that government negotiators adopt has to do with the distinction between the different types of outcomes identified under 1 above, and particularly between rescheduling and adjustment. It can be assumed that governments will always prefer deals that maximise the availability of foreign exchange for the economy, that is, 'good' deals in financial terms (everything else being equal and given appropriate discount rates for future flows). A different question is the extent to which the government has the capacity to evaluate alternative packages from this viewpoint.

With respect to 'adjustment' the situation is somewhat different. Policies of restriction of public expenditure and of economic liberalisation might be wanted by decision-makers independently of the renegotiations and even though they might entail a purportedly initial sacrifice of growth, investment, standards of living, etc., as a price to be paid for future 'sound' growth. This preference might be a function of ideological positions of government decision-makers or of sectors among them (it has been suggested, for instance, that Ministry of Finance officals tend to take a more monetarist view than those of Industry or Planning Ministries or agencies[17]). It can also be a function of pressures from economic and social groups from which the government draws support. Thus, at some point in their development, both domestic industrial capital and international capital with productive operations located in the country might exert pressure to reduce the importance of state enterprises in the productive sphere, inasmuch as they regard them as unfair competitors. Industrial capital will equally press for the elimination of restrictions on downward wage flexibility. Financial capital, in turn, will urge the elimination of restrictions on capital flows and on interest rate levels, and generally the deregulation of capital markets. Commercial capital oriented towards imports will press for the liberalisation of foreign trade.

Clearly, some of the policy preferences of the various sectors of capital will differ. For example, industrial capital producing for the internal market will probably not welcome the liberalisation of imports, might oppose devaluation on the grounds that it will increase the cost of their imported inputs and will probably resist the freeing of interest rates; *vis-à-vis* the debt renegotiations it will probably emphasise the objective of 'growth' to a greater extent than financial or commercial capital. Such clashes of preferences will be partially reflected within the state apparatus in terms of different institutional sectors, agencies and even individuals. An important question here is the extent to which the state, or sectors of it, have developed clientelistic relations with private interests which could make parts of the state apparatus into spokesmen for the special interests of the private groups concerned; or conversely, the extent to which the state apparatus and personnel have developed relative autonomy from private groups and can, therefore, arbitrate in the clash of preferences and/or pursue their own view of the national interest.

In this perspective, the debt renegotiation exercise may be understood as offering an opportunity to committed government policy-makers and their socio-economic support groups to introduce structural changes by presenting them as externally imposed requirements for renegotiation.

As for the third type of outcome identified under 1 above, the treatment of the private debt, its link with the question of internal pressure group politics is, as already indicated, obvious, involving issues like the identification of the type of debtors that would account for most of the private debt, the characterisation of their behaviour *vis-à-vis* the negotiations and an assessment of their influence in the government's position.

2. Capabilities

The issue here is, what accounts for the relative success of different actors in debt renegotiation bargaining? In general terms, the degree of success of a given actor in a bargaining process can be said to be a function of the clarity and detail with which its objectives are specified; of the actors' capabilities, that is the resources it commands that could be used to put pressure on the other party in order to reach a favourable agreement, or to resist the other party's pressure, both during the negotiations and in the event of a break up; and the strategies and tactics of the actor in the actual bargaining, including the perception it has of the goals, capabilities and strategies and tactics of the other actors.

Zartman's concept of negotiations in terms of the identification of an agreed formula followed by the working out of details through proposals, concessions and specific agreements is useful at this point,[18] provided the formula stage is not regarded as purely—or even primarily—technical problem-solving. Since it involves defining the agenda for negotiation and, therefore, adopting a view as to what the issues are in the conflict, it will often be the case that the outcome hinges directly on the capabilities, that is, the relative power of the actors. Capabilities will also be central in the subsequent process of detailed negotiation. We, thus, need to explore the concept further.

The first question here is, capabilities for what? The answer seems to be threefold:

i)   the ability of the government *to agree*, that is, to reach a decision about the acceptability of a proposed deal and to persuade all relevant political actors within the country to go along,

ii) the ability of the government *to implement* a given

agreement: this is particularly applicable to adjustment deals,

iii)   the ability of the government to apply economic pressure on the creditors and to withstand possible retaliatory action from the creditors. This can be further disaggregated into the *resource* available to the government and the *ability of the government to use* those resources.

The complex nature of the relations among these three dimensions and between them and the objectives and tactics of the government should be emphasised. To begin with, the first two types of capabilities can have positive or negative effects on the outcome depending on the context of the negotiation. Thus, while 'the power of a negotiator often rests on a manifest inability to make concessions and meet demands',[19] that is, on the absence of a capability to agree, the presence of a capability to implement an adjustment programme can be an important bargaining asset to strike a more favourable rescheduling deal.

Turning to the third type of capability, their impact will be closely linked to the objectives of the government in the negotiation and to the tactics used. If unilateral action is threatened as a bargaining tactic, it will be the more effective the more it can harm the creditors. It follows that the larger the debt, the higher the capability of the government in this respect. By the same token, though, the higher will be the cost of concessions for the creditors; thus, small debtors might find it easier to get better terms. It also follows that the larger the net negative resource transfers, the higher the capability of the government (see chapters 1 and 4 above).

If unilateral action is not aimed at forcing concessions by applying pressure on the creditors but rather at implementing a given solution in the absence of agreement, the more important type of capability is the ability to withstand retaliation.

Again, the two dimensions are closely related. It would appear that the size of the economy and its importance as a trading partner to the home countries of the creditors are resources enhancing the capability of the government in both respects. These elements operate in various ways. The debtor government has potential allies within the creditor countries among those economic sectors for which the debtor economy is a market or a source of imports, while at the same time being able to threaten trade retaliation measures in case of breakdown of negotiations. The size of the economy increases the probability of diverting trade of response to a trade boycott from the creditor countries, or of self-provisioning. A substantial amount of direct foreign investment from the creditor countries in the debtor economy also enhances the latter's capabilities again, both by creating potential allies within the creditor country, and by opening the possibility of retaliatory measures affecting the sunk investment. Conversely, a high level of dependency of the debtor economy on trade, investment, technological and aid flows will reduce its capability to withstand retaliation.

The preceding discussion leads to the issue of the impact of internal political structures and process on the capabilities of the negotiating government. Three aspects appear as particularly relevant:

i)   The degree of pluralism and openness of the political regime. This refers not only to the existence of elections but, more generally, to open political debate, freedom of expression, association and political activity and the existence of a multi-party system. The more pluralist and open the political system, the greater the bargaining power of the government, because of the need to reach a deal that can be accepted by the relevant internal political forces— including to varying extents the popular sectors. As already indicated, this dimension is related to, but different from, that of mobilisation and, more generally, of support for the government in power. In principle, a pluralist regime will command the broad assent of a larger proportion of the population than a non-pluralist one. The support for the government in power and its policies will, however, probably be less widespread and less intense than in a mobilised non-pluralist regime (i.e. a revolutionary government).

Therefore, the more pluralist and open the political process, the more difficult it might be to implement an agreement, especially an adjustment programme, and the more difficult and complex might be the task of mobilising resources and support to carry out unilateral strategies or resist retaliation from the creditors. At some point, however, the latent support for the pluralist regime can be turned into support for the confrontational stance of the government. An important issue here is the extent to which the rescheduling and the related adjustment questions are a matter for public debate or conversely, are played down by the government as technical, 'non-political' issues.

ii)   The degree of internal differentiation of the governmental structures and personnel. In principle, the more differentiated the decision-making apparatus of the government and the more the constitutional controls over the executive branch, the more the bargaining power of the government. However, a similar caveat applies in that the existence of various levels of decision-making with, in some cases, conflictive perceptions might prejudice the bargaining position of the government by preventing a clear specification of goals. Important questions in this connection include: which government agencies and organisations are involved in defining the goals and the negotiating strategy, and implementing them? Which ones are involved in the actual negotiations? Are there differences in views and approaches among them? To what extent do those differences—if any—reflect those of interest groups external to the government? To what extent are they perceived and/or used by the creditors to reduce the effectiveness of the government negotiators (e.g. do creditor banks use their close links with local banks to try and influence the position of the financial agencies of government against that of other governmental units, such as the planning office)?

iii)   The degree of stability of the government. The question here is, to what extent is the government perceived as able to enter into commitments that will be honoured through time? A government about to complete its constitutional period is in a disadvantageous position to either agree to substantial concessions or issue threats that will need to be carried out after it has been replaced. As often stability and continuity are perceived as higher in authoritarian than in democratic regimes, this factor might temper the notion that politically open regimes might enjoy a more favourable bargaining position. The issue here is the credibility of the government and its policies in the medium term.

Finally, a discussion of capabilities should not neglect the possibility of a country taking advantage of possible geopolitical considerations *vis-à-vis* the governments of the main creditors in order to secure a better set of deals.

3. Strategies and tactics

Capabilities can only secure objectives in bargaining if deployed adequately. Strategy and tactics in bargaining, thus, play a role in determining the outcome; indeed, one of the characteristic features of the new approaches to bargaining which stemmed from the critique of the economic and game-theoretic models is their emphasis on strategy and tactics as means of manipulating and altering both preferences and the perception of capabilities, an emphasis that sometimes exaggerated the real incidence of these sets of variables.

In the types of negotiations under discussion here a fundamental question of strategy and tactics has to do with the extent to which concerted bargaining or action among the debtors is undertaken or threatened. This, however, is not purely a question of strategy, but has to do also with capabilities: a debtor's cartel—if consistently carried out—results in the creation of power, rather than simply in altering its perception. On the one hand, the deployment of that power, particularly inasmuch as it must be consistent with the persistence of the cartel in the face of centrifugal forces, involves complex issues of strategy and tactics.

Other important elements under this rubric include the

extent to which the debtor government takes the initiative in the structuring and conduct of the negotiations, and the extent to which it is prepared to threaten or undertake unilateral action.

4. LATIN AMERICAN DEBT RENEGOTIATION: THE POLITICAL FACTORS

The preceding discussion and the categories introduced in it should help us interpret the evidence contained in the case studies in this volume in terms of the political factors affecting the behaviour of debtor governments. Rather than rehearse that evidence as a whole or propose a detailed, comprehensive interpretation, this section will highlight the central findings and will place them in the context of the discussion above. It should be understood more as an indication of the potentialities of the approach and a preliminary identification of areas for further research, than as a fully-fledged application.

1. Government Objectives and the Identification of the Formula

It emerges from the studies that, with some qualifications to which we shall come later on, the Latin American debt negotiations that began in 1982 were dominated by the 'formula' agreed by the Mexican Government and its creditors in August of that year. This broadly defined the kinds of negotiating actors involved, the range of issues to be negotiated, the range of outcomes to be considered—and those excluded—and the range of strategies and tactics to be legitimately employed. The overall approach entailed the acceptance by the debtors of the fundamental market parameters of the international creditor-debtor relation, as expanded in the practice of the IMF to include policy conditionality. As the studies also show, this definition was basically favourable to the creditors and to the detriment of the debtors. Why did the governments go along with it?

A first answer is more or less evident from the case studies: the immediate cause was the fact that the governments adopted as their overriding objective the avoidance of an all-out confrontation with the creditors. The 'formula' was the result of a self-imposed limitation: the objective of the negotiations was to maximise financial relief but within the boundaries set by the creditors, their governments and the international financial institutions. This definition of objectives was made known to the creditors. The case of Mexico was the first and clearest. Following the announcement of the suspension of payments on the public debt in August 1982, the Government agreed to the setting up of a Bank Advisory Group composed of the thirteen largest creditor banks. This was, in effect, the other party in the negotiations, acting in representation of all creditor banks, but, at the same time, it was an *advisory* group for the Mexican government for preliminary discussion of ideas and for working through the final proposals and their technical implications. The approach adopted evidently both limited the scope of the objectives to be pursued in the negotiations and excluded the possibility of unilateral action. This non-confrontational approach was adopted also by Brazil in its 1982 restructuring and by Chile and Venezuela in their 1983 negotiations.

The next question, of course, is why did the governments adopt this self-imposed limitation on their objectives and strategies? The answers here are complex and vary from country to country; they do, however, go back to some of the categories discussed above. To begin again with the case of Mexico, in terms of economic and political capabilities relevant to the negotiating process, the country was objectively—and was perceived to be—in a weak position. Economically, it was undergoing a crisis: as Villarreal shows, at the end of the year GDP had fallen by 0.5 per cent, the deficit of the public sector was equivalent to 16.8 per cent of GDP, inflation was 98.8 per cent and the current account deficit was US$6.2 billion, equal to 29 per cent of the value of exports. On the political front, the period of the incumbent in the Presidency had only a few months to run, and, therefore, the Government was perceived as lameduck and probably unable to implement any strong position that it might adopt in the negotiations. Also, the extent to which Mexico was effecting net negative transfer of resources was still limited and in any case probably unknown to the negotiators on both sides; perhaps the strongest capability of the debtor government in this context was, therefore, not available to Mexico.

Thus, both the ability of the Government to carry out any possible threat of unilateral action and the capacity of the economy to withstand its consequences were doubtful, and this, in all likelihood, weighed significantly on the adoption of a non-confrontational stance. This calculus was reinforced by the view among government decision-makers that the difficulties were temporary and that normal lending would be resumed soon, a view that reflected the received wisdom of international analysts and the market at the time. There was, therefore, a reasonable argument based on capability analysis to justify adopting the non-confrontational position. Yet, it would again appear that the crucial factor in that decision was a matter of preferences and goal-setting on the part of the relevant Mexican decision-makers: it was the view that no action should be taken that could endanger the international financial, and indeed, economic system. Preserving the stability of the world financial system was put at the top of the objectives of the Mexican negotiators. This can itself be justified in terms of the interests of the Mexican economy, which is highly dependent on international trade and external finance; in addition, however, this no doubt reflected the preferences of technical personnel in the Finance Ministry, who seemingly took charge of the process until 1986. Indeed, the weaknesses of the Government because of the impending presidential change probably contributed to giving the Finance Ministry a freer hand.

The studies do not go into the pressure group and public opinion politics surrounding the negotiations at this stage, and this is an area in which further research might be enlightening. One would expect to find a substantial view among powerful economic groups that a non-confrontational position should be adopted. The highly internationalised character of the Mexican economy and its business class, their ties with the US economy and the importance of the financial sector as intermediary with the world economy would clearly operate in that direction. So would the fact that in the period immediately preceding the crisis and the negotiations there was a massive capital flight, with the 'Errors and Omissions' item of the balance of payments going from a surplus in 1979 to a deficit equal to 41 per cent of the exports of goods in 1981. There is little doubt that it was not in the interest of the wealthy that a crisis of the international financial system should be provoked by Mexico's action. On the other hand, it would appear that the issue did not enter the public debate at that time, but was rather treated by the government as 'technical'. As will be seen below, this contrasts oddly with the case of Brazil, where, despite the fact that it was still a military dictatorship, a spirited public debate took place in 1982 on whether the debate should be repaid or not, with the opposition parties openly calling for a repudiation. In sum, while there were specific, conjunctural factors that may explain the decision of the Mexican government to accept the terms of reference proposed by the creditors, it would appear that deeper, more lasting political features of the Mexican system were also operating in the same direction.

In a sense, the Brazilian case is the opposite from this viewpoint. The conjunctural reasons for the initial acceptance of the 'formula' were not too different from the Mexican ones. In particular, the military government in power at the end of 1982 valued highly Brazil's integration in the world economy, and was not keen to risk it through unilateral action. Even more than in Mexico, the Government in Brazil saw the difficulties as temporary, and trusted the economy to be able to resume dynamic growth within a reasonable time; for that, keeping good relations with international banking was essential. On the other hand, there were factors that anticipated the possibility of a change in the future. Brazil had already embarked on a gradual process of dismantling the military regime that had ruled the country for nearly twenty years, and this had created a degree of open political debate and political accountability on this particular issue which seems to have gone further than that in democratic Mexico. This, as Carneiro shows, explains the reluctance of the Brazilian Government to enter into a formal agreement with the IMF until 1983, that is, after the elections of November 1982. Second, the Brazilian business sectors, and indeed, the economic decision-makers in the military period, had adopted long before an endogenous growth strategy, and placed great priority on maintaining the dynamism of the economy; this is one of the reasons why there had been no substantial capital flight in Brazil. As the concluding chapter indicates, as long as the growth of the economy was perceived as compatible with the service of the debt, there was no call for unilateral action. However, it would soon be clear that the compatibility was illusory, and, together with the re-emergence of the popular sectors in the political arena as a result of the democratisation, this would have important implications for the management of the debt issue later on.

No such qualifications were present in the case of Chile, as Ffrench-Davis' chapter amply demonstrates. There the goal of maintaining good terms with the international financial community was overriding, reflecting both the class basis of the Chilean military dictatorship and the nature of the economic model that had been implemented since 1973.

In the case of Venezuela, again the high integration of the economy in the world system and the perception that in the long run the oil wealth of the country would see it through the crisis if only its creditworthiness could be restored led to the adoption of the Mexican formula, complete with a Bank Advisory Group. Capital flight was even more massive in Venezuela than in Mexico, and this no doubt added to the pressure to avoid confrontation.

2. Politics and the adjustment issue
The Mexican formula included the principle that the rescheduling of the debt was conditional to the adoption of an adjustment programme along the lines prescribed by the International Monetary Fund and monitored by them. Mexico itself signed a formal agreement with the Fund in December 1982 and a second one in 1986. As indicated, Brazil refused to do so throughout 1982, but was already implementing a policy along the lines demanded by the Fund and in November that year submitted the programme to the IMF. After that it produced seven letters of intent, the last in January 1985. Chile signed two agreements with the IMF and two Structural Adjustment Loans with the World Bank. Costa Rica signed a Stand-By Agreement in 1983 and a SAL later.

Venezuela did not enter into an agreement, but also introduced policies along the required lines and agreed to periodic monitoring by the Fund.

The content of the various programmes was essentially orthodox and contractionary, although in some cases it included heterodox measures, such as quantitative import controls in the Mexican agreement of 1982 and the foreign exchange regime in the Costa Rican agreement of 1983. In all cases, the initial impact was recessive; this was particularly so in the case of Mexico, whose GDP fell by over 5 per cent in 1983. Furthermore, it involved surrendering some control over economic policy, a phenomenon exacerbated by the linkages among the various conditionality regimes (cross-conditionality) again particularly strong in the Mexican 1986 agreement and in the Costa Rican case.

The adjustment packages, however, were not always an imposition of the foreign creditors. In effect, in all the countries concerned the prevailing view among those in charge of economic decision-making was that an adjustment programme was necessary for the economy to recover equilibrium, that the causes of the disequilibrium were essentially those identified by the monetary and fiscal approaches to the balance of payments and that, therefore, the kind of adjustment programme required was of the sort prescribed by the IMF. In most cases, such programmes had begun to be implemented even before the debt negotiations started, and in at least two cases the programmes went beyond what the IMF was requiring (Chile and Venezuela). In effect, therefore, the adjustment issue as such was not part of the negotiating strategy of the governments; they conceded the point to start with, and with it the point about conditionality, although, to be sure, the specifics of each programme were a matter for negotiation. An exception to this was Brazil, whose preference for growth strategies led it repeatedly to exceed the IMF agreed targets. Venezuela appeared as an exception but, in fact, it was not: although outside a formal agreement with the Fund, the programme implemented was more orthodox than the Mexican one.

3. Politics and the self-assertive phase

The studies make it clear that the year 1985 was something of a watershed in the history of the negotiations. Unilateral moves had already taken place in early 1984, notably the Quito meeting of Heads of State and the Argentine moratorium; but they were effectively neutralised by the action of the creditors and their governments, as the Tussie chapter ably demonstrates. By contrast, in 1985, the situation appeared ripe for an increasing show of self-assertiveness on the part of the debtor governments.

It is also clear from the studies that this more self-assertive attitude of the governments in 1985–6 was largely a result of internal political factors. In Peru, the unorthodox economic programme adopted in August 1985 and the restriction of the service of the external debt to 10 per cent of the value of exports reflected the need of the new Garcia Government to respond to an internal context of political radicalisation which was beginning to endanger the bases of support of the populist government party. In addition, it reflected an heterodox analysis of the adjustment problems of the Peruvian economy, which is well presented in Ugarteche's chapter. In this sense, the Peruvian stance was the most radical, not only because it went further in taking unilateral action at the time, but because it did so on the basis of a rejection of the central tenets of the economic wisdom prevailing in the international financial circles.

The Brazilian case is somewhat different. Brazil also rejected the contractionary prescription of the IMF in September 1985, and resumed an approach that privileged growth over the need to balance the current account and end inflation. This was as a result of the transition to democratic rule, when the new Government received, and needed to retain, the support of substantial sections of the Brazilian popular sectors. Furthermore, the new stance—as Carneiro shows—also reflected the views of the industrialist class, notably that of Sao Paulo with whom the new Minister for the Economy, Funaro, had close links. The combination of these political factors led to a more self-assertive position, which laid the ground for the 1987 moratorium. However, it would appear that the foundations for this stance are less radical than in the Peruvian case; the Brazilian moratorium came closer to a tactical move, whose purpose were, in the short run, to ease the external financial constraint, and in the medium term to extract better terms for a reinsertion of Brazil in the international financial circuit.

Mexico is yet, again, a different case. There the fundamental adherence to the parameters of the 'formula' remained unaltered until 1986. Indeed, as Gurria indicates, the 1986 proposed budget, before the oil price collapsed, still embodied a zero-growth approach despite the fact that there had been three years of little, or no, growth in which the country had had to make a major effort to continue servicing the debt, and that the economic conditions had substantially worsened as a result of the earthquakes of September 1985. The fall of oil prices in February 1986 made the targets agreed in principle with the IMF unreachable, but the Fund refused to take a more lenient approach. The debate, which had moved into the public arena at the time of the earthquakes, intensified, with the possibility of unilateral action being raised by growing sectors of public opinion.

It would seem that at this point the control of the process by the Finance Ministry was challenged by other sections of the Government who favoured unilateral action. This possibility was becoming increasingly credible, particularly when in June 1986 one of the first moves of the new Finance Minister was to make public an old proposal effectively involving a moratorium.

All the indications, therefore, were of a major change of attitude within the Mexican Government, and no doubt this perception was the determinant factor in the efforts at accommodation made by the IMF, the World Bank, the US Government and the creditor banks, leading to the July 1986 agreement with the IMF. This involved important concessions by the Fund on the adjustment front (although the commitments entered into were backed by an even stronger conditionality than in previous agreements). At this point, it would appear that some sectors within the Mexican Government felt that the conditions existed for an attempt at a more radical departure from the 'formula' and this was embodied in the rescheduling proposal made in August 1986 and discussed in detail in the Gurria chapter. But this was clearly going beyond what the political decision-makers in the Government were prepared to back. In the face of strong opposition from the banks, the Government instructed the Mexican negotiators to abandon the proposal and settle for a conventional package. The latter, to be sure, turned out to be considerably more innovative and favourable to Mexico than any preceding one, but by essentially returning to the 'formula' Mexico chose to remain within a framework in which as Villarreal indicates, the fundamental problem is not solved: the service of the external debt exceeds the real payment capacity of the Mexican economy and necessarily entails a serious curtailment of investment, growth and employment possibilities as well as a loss of living standards. Evidently, the complex Mexican political context sets limits to the extent to which the Government feels it can push unilateral action. Within those limits, the Mexican negotiators have been able to obtain terms which represent a major improvement on past experience.

4. Politics and the private debt

The issue of the treatment of the private external debt is one in which the impact of internal political force and pressures—interacting with international factors—is most directly and immediately felt. Not surprisingly, this is the area in which the studies show a greater degree of variation on the approaches adopted by the different countries. In the concluding chapter of this volume Griffith-Jones presents a detailed comparison of the cases on this score, and I shall not anticipate it here, except to say that the countries seem to fall within a continuum: at one extreme the Chilean Government effectively accepted responsibility for the bulk of the private debt and in addition granted large subsidies for servicing it; at the other, the Mexican Government refused to do either. In between, Venezuela did not assume the private debt but did provide large subsidies in the form of preferential exchange rates. While the case studies do not go into the domestic politics of these different approaches, some broad indications can be gathered from them. In the Chilean case, the decision appears as the result of the great leverage that domestic financial sectors have on the Government, a situation known to the creditors. In effect, according to Ffrench-Davis, the Chilean Government did not treat the issue of the private debt as a part of the negotiations, and as a result the Government guarantee and massive subsidies involved were granted without any attempt at extracting reciprocal concessions from the creditors.

In the case of Venezuela, it would seem that the main determinant was external pressure from the creditors, although no doubt the domestic sectors involved also exerted pressure. Interestingly, the IMF opposed the subsidies, at least in the form adopted, that is, through differential exchange rates. This whole area is one on which further research could greatly illuminate the overall question of the political determinants of debt renegotiation behaviour.

As indicated at the beginning of this section, this brief review was not intended to provide a comprehensive political analysis of the Latin American debt negotiations. Its more modest purpose was to point to some central issues on which a political bargaining model of analysis can be helpful both for understanding the available evidence and for suggesting issues for further research. The crucial incidence of political factors in what is often portrayed as an essentially technical process should, however, have become apparent. In particular, the discussion highlighted the impact of internal political forces and processes. This aspect is often neglected even in political analyses of the debt issue, which tend to concentrate on the interaction between the debtor government and the other actors, while incorporating the conception of the government as a simple, unified entity.[20] I would argue that abandoning this conception and introducing political and power processes in the analysis of the behaviour of debtor governments is essential not only for making sense of the past, but for approaching the most challenging aspect of the exercise, the design of possible future courses of action that will solve the debt problem, as distinct from simply postponing it. The next chapter will take up this last set of issues in some detail.

NOTES

1. The classic statement of the bilateral monopoly model is Zeuthen, F., 1930, *Problems of Monopoly and Economic Warfare*, London, Routledge and Kegan Paul. For an overall presentation of economic models of bargaining, see Coddington, A., 1968, *Theories of the Bargaining Process*, London, George Allen and Unwin. See also the useful overview and readings in Young, O. R., ed., *Bargaining. Formal Theories of Negotiations*, Urbana, University of Illinois Press, 1975, Part Two, pp. 129–42.
2. Luce, R. D. and Raiffa, H., 1957, *Games and Decisions*, New York, John Wiley; Rapoport, A., *Two-person Game Theory*, Ann Arbor, University of Michigan Press, 1966; Young, *op. cit.*, Part One, pp. 21–129.
3. Young, *op. cit.*, p. 133. See also Bacharach, S. B. and Lawler, E. H., *Bargaining. Power, Tactics and Outcomes*, San Francisco, Josey-Bass Publishers, 1981, pp. 8–9.
4. Young, *op. cit.*, pp. 30–1.
5. Zartman, I. W., 'Negotiations as a Joint Decision-Making Process', in Zartman, I. W., ed., 1978, *The Negotiation Process: Theories and Applications*, Beverly Hills, Sage Publications, p. 73.
6. See for instance, Kaldor, N., 'Devaluation and Adjustment in Developing Countries', *Finance and Development*, vol. 20, no. 2, June 1983, pp. 35–7; specifically on Latin American, Gurrieri, A. and Sainz, P. 'Is there a fair and democratic way out of the crisis?', *CEPAL Review*, no. 20, August 1983, pp. 127–48.
7. Sharpley, J., 'The Potential of Domestic Stabilisation Measures in Developing Countries', in Killick, T., ed., 1984, *The Quest for Economic Stabilisation: The IMF and the Third World*, London, Heinemann Educational Books, pp. 55–85.
8. For discussions of the political aspects of stabilisation programmes, see Nelson, J. M., 'The Political Economy of Stabilisation: Commitment, Capacity and Public Response', *World Development*, vol. 12, no. 10, October 1984, pp. 983–1006, Moore, M., 'On the Political Economy of Stabilisation', *World Development*, vol. 13, no. 9, September 1985, pp. 1087–91; and Haggard, S., 'The Politics of Adjustment: Lessons from the IMF's Extended Fund Facility', *International Organization*, vol. 39, no. 3, Summer 1985, pp. 505–34.
9. For a discussion of the concepts that follow see Fortin, C., 'The relative autonomy of the state in Latin America: some conceptual aspects', in Tussie, D., ed., 1984, *Latin America in the World Economy*, London, Gower. For applications to specific cases see Anglade C. and Fortin, C., eds, 1985, *The State and Capital Accumulation in Latin America*, London, Macmillan.
10. Evans, P., 1979, *Dependent Development*, Princeton, Princeton University Press.
11. On bureaucratic authoritarianism, a useful introduction is Collier, D.,

1978, *The New Authoritarianism in Latin America*, Princeton University Press.

12. Schelling, T.C., 1963, *The Strategy of Conflict*, Oxford University Press.
13. Zartman, *The Negotiations Process. Theories and Applications, op. cit.*
14. Bacharach and Lawler, *op. cit.*
15. See, for instance, the discussion on threats in Schelling, *op. cit.*, pp. 124–31.
16. An intriguing variation related to this point is the case of a government which is genuninely prepared to face a collapse of the negotiations and might even be confident of the internal response to such a stance, but is on the other hand fearful retaliation on the part of international financial organisations and home governments amounting to destabilisation and conceivably leading to an overthrow.
17. Fitzgerald, E. V. K., 'The state and the management of accumulation in the periphery', in Tussie, D., ed., *op. cit.*, pp. 130–1.
18. Zartman, 'Negotiation as a Joint Decision-Making Process', *op. cit.*
19. Schelling, *op. cit.*, p. 19.
20. An important exception is Kaufman, R.R., 'Democratic and authoritarian responses to the debt issue: Argentina, Brazil, Mexico', *International Organization*, vol. 39, no. 3, Summer 1985, pp. 473–503, although concentrating almost exclusively on stabilisation, as distinct from debt rescheduling, issues.

12 Conclusions and Policy Recommendations*

S. Griffith-Jones

INTRODUCTION

In attempting to analyse the management of debt crises in Latin America and Africa, from 1982 to the present, several difficulties present themselves. *In the first place, we are analysing an extremely complex process, whose final outcome is not yet known.* In some ways, it is like analysing a play or a drama in the theatre at a time when only two, or perhaps three, of the acts have actually taken place, and in circumstances when nobody—including the actors—know the full script. In particular, in mid-1987, it is somewhat difficult to visualise the outcome of Brazil's unilateral action, which may be fairly influential in determining the evolution in the rest of the Latin American countries. *Second, analysis is made more difficult due to the differences between rhetoric and reality.* For example, since mid-1985 in the analysis made in industrial and developing countries alike, there seemed on the whole to emerge a consensus that debt crises management, as practised till then, was both unsustainable and undesirable, given the existing future likely trends in the world economy; it was, therefore, concluded that new ways had to be found and rapidly implemented to handle the problem, which would

*This paper attempts to summarise the conclusions of the case studies and draw implications for the future. I am grateful to my project colleagues: Ana Maria Alvarez, Dionisio Carneiro, Ricardo Ffrench-Davis, Angel Gurria, Ennio Rodriguez, Diana Tussie, Oscar Ugarteche, Rene Villarreal, as well as to David Glover, for their valuable comments on a first draft at our workshop in Ciudad de Mejico; I also gratefully acknowledge Clark Reynolds' insightful and detailed comments. I thank Lucy Nichols for her research assistance.

allow for growth in debtor economies. In spite of this consensus, at least at the level of rhetoric (see, for example, bi-annual Interim Committee Declarations, found in *IMF Surveys*) two years later, effective multilateral action has not been taken, except for specific countries (e.g. the Mexican 1986-7 deal) or for limited and insufficient measures (e.g. the Structural Adjustment Facility created for low-income Sub-Saharan African countries).

1. THE KEY QUESTIONS

At the beginning of this book (and project) three questions, seen as key were posed (see Chapter 1).

The first question asked was why were the deals on debt and adjustment, agreed and implemented since 1982, *so much closer to the interests and aims of creditor institutions than of debtor countries?* The question seemed even more relevant after mid-1985, when the above-described broad consensus emerged—in developed and developing countries—that debt crisis management was unsatisfactory, *particularly for debt or nations' growth and development prospects.* However, the new actions taken multilaterally, within the broad umbrella of US Treasury Secretary Baker's initiative—though positive in themselves—did not, at least until 1987, amount to a new way of handling the problem, and therefore, unfortunately did not overcome the basic limitations of the approach developed since 1982.

Given this evaluation, which is increasingly accepted in a vast variety of circles, supplementary questions arise: why have debtor governments been so patient during such a long period of large negative net transfers, and why have most of them (except for the Peruvian Government) not followed unilateral actions earlier and in a more consistent way? Furthermore, given that the debtor governments have been so patient in servicing debts at levels which have in several cases contributed to cause major declines in investment, employment, real wages, and social welfare expenditure, why have the societies in those nations been so patient?

It should, however, be emphasised that since mid-1985, a

number of Latin American and African governments have either taken or seriously threatened to take, unilateral action. Particularly in early 1987, the picture changed significantly, especially as the Brazilian Government suspended interest payment on its bank debt, and as Ecuador, as well as a number of other small Latin American governments took similar action. The future evolution of debt crisis management will, to an important extent, be determined by the outcome of Brazilian negotiations, as well as the impact on bargaining of the large loan-loss provisions made by US and UK banks in mid–1987.

The situation for Sub-Saharan low income African debtors has been somewhat different as Reg Green points out in his chapter. As most low-income African countries still receive positive net transfers (due to official grants and concessional flows), they are in a different bargaining position from most Latin American countries (heavily indebted with private banks and with negative net transfers) as cessation of debt servicing to banks by these African countries could jeopardise the larger positive inflow from official sources. In spite of this, several African countries have built up arrears, mainly on commercial but also on government debt servicing, 'quietly, on a semi-ignored, semi-condoned basis'. Most unilateral declarations of a ceiling for debt service (such as that of Sudan in 1985) were based on a 'won't pay because can't pay' attitude, rather than a long-term strategy. However, the May 1987 Zambian unilateral imposition of a very low ceiling on external debt payments (together with its dramatic abandonment of a programme drawn up with the IMF) seems a more deliberate attempt than that of other African cases, to pursue a more radical stance on debt and adjustment.

The second question posed was to what extent were there differences in the debt/adjustment deals reached by different countries? What reasons could contribute to explain such differences?

The third question posed was how the debt rescheduling/new money adjustment deals varied from year-to-year, after 1982? Have qualitative changes been introduced?

An additional, fourth and perhaps crucial question relates to the future search for an alternative more 'positive sum' framework of debt management. This clearly consists of two elements, when viewed from the point of view of debtor countries and governments: a) what are more appropriate technical solutions than the ones adopted until now, such that debtors' growth and development can be safeguarded without threatening the stability of the international banking system? b) what tactics and strategies should debtor governments pursue to make the adoption of such measures feasible?

2. ATTEMPTING TO EXPLAIN THE NATURE OF THE DEALS REACHED

Looking at the first set of issues, the fact that major debtors governments (except for Peru) have not consistently pursued a line of unilateral action is itself one of the main reasons why debt rescheduling/new money deals continue to be closer to the interests of creditors than that of debtors.

Amongst the reasons why such unilateral actions were not taken by major debtor governments was the *uncertainty* of the impact of such actions on the international banking system, and more importantly, on the funding of world economic activity and trade; more than the fear of retaliation against their own trade flows, which experiences like that of Peru seem to show is not very serious, debtor governments legitimately feared in the past the risk of declining volumes of world trade, that could accompany a possible disruption of the international banking system.

The threat to the private banks' solvency of unilateral action by major debtors has increasingly diminished since 1982, as private banks strengthened their capital base and have increased their loan-loss provisions, as well as expanded their non-LDC business far more than their LDC lending. As a consequence, the risks to the private banks' solvency from LDC default are seen in industrial countries to have diminished quite significantly, though clearly not totally.

Thus, even before the major loan-loss provisions made by Citibank and other US, as well as British banks, a 1987 British All Party Parliamentary Group report[1] concluded that 'American banks are now more vulnerable to domestic energy, farming and housing loans than to LDC debt. For most of the major banks, simultaneous default (collective or coincidental) by a number of large Latin American debtors would shake them; *a single default would be absorbed.* A similar conclusion was reported in January 1987 by Salomon Brothers[2], when it stated that 'the 34 major US banks they track should be able to write off some US $20 billion, or nearly 40% of their total cross-border lending to Argentina, Brazil, Mexico and Venezuela by 1989, without impairing equity ratios.'

As Table 12.1 indicates, levels of loan-loss provisions vary quite significantly among countries. Until late 1986, they were highest in continental European countries, such as Switzerland, Netherlands and West Germany; the lowest provisions rates were, until May 1987, made by banks based in the USA, the UK and Japan. For US banks, provisions were already high in 1986, however, for countries that have ceased or limited payments of interest for over ninety days; thus for Peru's loans, it was reported[3] that an initial provision of 15 per cent was required. Since May 1987, a radical change occurred in the loan-loss provisions made by the twelve major US banks, most of which had by the end of June 1987 made such large loan-loss provisions that those reached almost US $10 billion, and around 25 per cent of those banks' loans to developing countries. The US banks' action was followed in mid-1987 by very large loan-loss provisions by two major US banks, National Westminister, and Midland Bank International, and by several major French banks.

Though a fairly important part of developing countries' debts to private banks have been written-down or written-off banks' balance sheets, this has not led to corresponding debt forgiveness. Furthermore, practically all debts of most LDC debtors, are traded by creditor banks at a discount on secondary markets; this seems further clear evidence that these banks do not think it likely that they will recover the full value of their outstanding loans. However, in debt servicing and even in debt rescheduling operations, *debtor countries are still obliged to service the debt at its full original face value*, which is indeed no longer its market value. Indeed, taking the debt of twelve major borrowers as an example (which underestimates

Table 12.1:   *Problem sovereign debt reserve levels, June 1987*

Belgium	No specified percentages but there is a requirement to provide. Reserve levels vary but probably average around 15 per cent.
Canada	10–15 per cent reserve required by end October, 1986 for thirty-two designated countries. All the major banks will meet the requirement in 1986. Higher levels of reserves are expected to be required after October 1986.
France	No formal rules but most major banks have set up large reserves. BNP and Société Générale are running at over 30 per cent; Crédit Lyonnais has somewhat less.
Germany	No formal rules but tax authorities generally helpful. Most major banks have reserved between 30 per cent and 50 per cent.
Japan	Amount per country varies but Ministry of Finance 'guidance' stipulates an average maximum 5 per cent against exposure to thirty-six problem countries. Virtually all banks have reached this level and, with the fall in the value of the dollar, banks have been required to write back their reserve to the 5 per cent limit. Early 1987 offshore company established to take over part of Japanese banks' loans to countries that may not be able to repay their debts.
Netherlands	From 5 per cent to 100 per cent on countries specified by the central bank. Most banks now have a reserve of around 20 per cent of problem sovereign debt.
Spain	Bank of Spain circular requires from 1.5 per cent to 100 per cent on country groupings defined in circular. Most major banks have around 10 per cent, and some more.
Sweden	From 35 per cent to 80 per cent on countries selected by Bank Inspection Board. Most banks' reserve levels now average around 50 per cent.
Switzerland	General guideline that banks should maintain reserves of at least 20 per cent against problem country exposure. Banks left to decide which of their exposure falls into this category. Most major banks have reserved between 30 per cent and 50 per cent.
UK	No formal rules. Reserves vary from 100 per cent to very little. Large banks running at around 5 per cent–10 per cent, at end 1986. National Westminster made provisions of almost 30 per cent on loans to thirty-five countries in payments difficulties or rescheduling their debt.
USA	Varying percentages on Poland, Nicaragua, Zaire, Bolivia, Sudan and Peru. No rules on others. Most large US banks had 5 per cent or less for all problem sovereign

> debt at end 1986. In May–June 1987, most of the major
> twelve US banks made large provisions, such that
> their total loan loss reserves reached around 25 per cent
> of 'doubtful' LDC loans.

Source: IBCA Banking Analysis Ltd, *Real Banking Profitability*, November 1986, Newspaper clippings *Financial Times*, June 1987.

the problem), US banks holding some US $77 billion in book assets could sell those assets at only $50 billion on the secondary market, that is at *only two-thirds* their face or book value.[4]

Far higher bank loan-loss provisions, as recently made by large US banks—and previously by Swiss and other banks— clearly have advantages in the long-term for debtor developing countries. It reduces uncertainty about the risk to banks' solvency and stability should debtor governments take (or be forced by circumstances to take) unilateral action. *Furthermore, it strengthens the possibility for intermediate solutions*, that have been amply discussed in a variety of circles, which would imply LDC governments would service the debt, but with some element of forgiveness, either attached to the level of the debt and/or of the interest payments.[5]

Paradoxically, however, the strengthening of banks' loan-loss provisions—and even more the requirements by bank regulators to make provisions against new loans to those sovereign debtors for which provisions were made—has *possibly reduced* the willingness of banks to increase their lending to LDC debtors. Differences between levels of provisions and regulations on provisions (and their tax treatment) in different creditor countries also make it increasingly difficult to make collective arrangements, for negotiating and distributing (amongst banks) new money, as the chapter by Gurria on the difficulties for arranging the 1986–7 Mexican deal clearly illustrates. *In the short term* and within the framework of traditional packages of debt rescheduling/new money, the strengthening of the banks' balance sheets by increased loan-loss provisions may have some problematic effects for debtor countries; however, these problematic effects should not be exaggerated, as there was already very little new net bank lending to Latin America and Africa in recent years (see Chapter 1).

In the medium term, and within a context of a new framework or a new phase of handling the debt problem, the existence of large loan-loss provisions in many of the major banks provides important range of manoeuvre for solutions which recognise that the real market value of the debt is no longer its face value, and that reductions should either be made of the level of the debt itself, or of debt servicing of it. It is likely that pressure from debtor governments, as well as from enlightened private actors and/or governments within industrial countries, will necessarily play a major role in the transition to the next step. Thus, in a medium-term perspective, banks' greater ability to absorb LDC losses should strengthen the confidence with which debtor governments can use threats of (or even in extreme cases) take unilateral action, without fearing as much as in the past that such threats or actions would endanger the stability of the international financial (and even trading) system. Furthermore, the availability of significant loan-loss provision in banks' balance sheets makes more feasible the adoption of a framework for managing debt, which implies that banks' acknowledge some losses and that debtor governments reduce their level of debt servicing (without this implying an increase in the total level of debt). Such a package would clearly also further increase the role of industrial governments in the deals either by increased lending, subsidising banks' losses, or take-over of discounted bad debts (the latter measures already being pursued by the Japanese Government).

It is interesting that bankers and bank economists are not only expecting something like this to happen, but are saying so publicly. For example, Holley, *op. cit.*, concludes his study arguing that a debt consolidation on concessional terms 'would certainly be preferable to a seemingly endless series of negotiations, that would inhibit long-term policy-making on both sides and would not excessively affect banks' standing in the market'. There also seems to be a gradual, but consistent, trend in public opinion and in political circles within industrial countries towards a view that new ways of handling the debt problem need to be found, which will imply some element of discounting such debt or its servicing; amongst the reasons for this shift is not only a wish to improve development prospects in debtor nations, but also trade and investment prospects for industrial nations.[6] We will go back to the need for searching for alternative ways to manage the debt problem. Before that we will return to the reasons why major bank debtor governments have not until now taken more consistent unilateral action on the debt issue or have not until now bargained in a tougher way for a better deal.

An important element may have been a more long-term perception of costs and benefits obtained by debtor countries from their links with the international fiancial system, than is obtained by looking only at the massive negative net transfers for the debtor economies since 1982 (for the very high magnitude of those net reverse transfers, as proportion of

Table 12.2: Net resource transfer (NRT) as percentage of GDP and exports, 1982-6[a]

	Average NRT as proportion of average GDP[b]		Average NRT as percentage of average exports of goods[c]
	1982–5	1986	1987
Brazil	–3.2	–4.1	–30.6
Chile	–3.4	–2.6	–16.4
Costa Rica	0.03	–1.6	–1.1
Mexico	–7.7	–1.9	–46.9
Peru	–1.0	–0.9	–4.9
Venezuela	–10.0	–10.2	–39.8
memorandum			
Argentina	-6.1	-3.3	-43.5

Notes a. NRT (net resource transfer) is equal to net capital inflows less payments of profits and interest. Net capital inflows include long- and short-term capital flows, unilateral official transfers and errors and omissions. Figures were in US$ of each year.
b. GDP in 1982 US$, 1982–5; for 1986, GNP in 1986 US$.
c. Exports of goods in US$ of each year; 1986 export figure is an estimate, based on December 1986 CEPAL report.

Sources: CEPAL, *Notas sobre la economia y el desarrollo de America Latina*, several years for net resource transfers, IDB, *Economic and Social Progress in Latin America*, several years for other variables.

Table 12.3: *Real net resource transfer, deflated by the barter terms of trade as a percentage of GDP, expressed in 1984 US$, 1973–85*

	1973–81	1982–85	1973–85	Ranking of case studies best to worse
Brazil	1.5	–2.9	0.2	2
Chile	4.8	–3.0	2.4	1
Costa Rica	4.4	2.3	2.4	1
Mexico	2.8	–5.4	0.2	2
Peru	0.6	–0.7	0.2	2
Venezuela	2.4	– 10.5	–1.6	3
Memorandum				
Argentina	0.2	–6.0	–1.7	
Colombia	0.7	2.4	1.2	

Sources: (a): net resource transfers in nominal values, from Table 4, J. Eclac, 'Latin American Debt: Resource Transfers, Investment and Growth'. Mimeo, Inter-American Development Bank, October 1986. The figures differ somewhat from ECLAC figures given above, because they do not include grants and aid, which is particularly significant in the case of Costa Rica.

(b): terms of trade figures, by country, from UNCTAD *Handbook of International Trade Statistics, 1986 Supplement.*

(c): GDP figures, same source as (a).

GDP and exports, for the different countries analysed in this study, see Table 12.2 and column 2, Table 12.3).

Indeed, debtor governments may have compared the large positive net transfers which they had received, particularly during the seventies, with large negative resource transfers since 1982, and felt especially initially, that the net impact on their economies of the total period was still positive or at least zero. With such a perception, the incentive to take unilateral action would be reduced, particularly if, and while, a reversal of the sign of net resource transfers *was seen as likely to occur in the near future. Around 1986*, that perception began to change; this was reflected for example, in the analysis made by the Inter-American Development Bank, which estimated in its 1986 Annual Report that in nominal terms, the negative net transfers from Latin America as a whole since 1982 had roughly wiped out the entire net inflow of capital generated in the massive petrodollar recycling of the 1970s.

As the evaluation of costs and benefits of the link with the international financial system takes place basically at a national level, it seems useful to calculate the total net resource transfer to and from the countries we are studying over the 1973–85 period.

A technical, but clearly relevant, issue to determine the correct measure is the choice of deflator. Measurement in current US dollars of every year clearly provides only a first, and rather imprecise, approximation. The second option is to use a deflator which reflects inflation in the US, which has a connection with import prices of Latin American countries, given the high proportion of imports from the US. The third option, and in our understanding the most precise one, is to deflate net resource transfers by an index which reflects the different countries' terms of trade.

What we are trying to measure is to compare the real value in domestic resources of the additional foreign exchange obtained by a country when net transfers were positive with the real resources used by the country to make negative net transfer of foreign exchange. Massad and Zahler[7] have suggested that it is most precise in such circumstances, when making an evaluation from the point of view of the debtor country, to use as a deflator the country's terms of trade, as this would reflect most precisely the real social price of net resources obtained by and extracted from the debtor country. Though the use of terms of trade index as a deflator may not incorporate all the effects of world inflation on the real value of total net resource transfers, it does reduce the margin of error involved.

As can be seen in Table 12.3, by the end of 1985, the real net resource transfer, taking the whole of the 1973–85 period, was negative for Venezuela (and Argentina), and around zero for Brazil, Mexico and Peru; indeed if the 1986 figures are added, the net resource transfer for Brazil, Mexico and Peru would also be negative. For all these countries, by late 1986, there had been no net contribution in net resource transfers from the international financial system, since 1973, *even though their stock of debt had grown significantly*. The situation is slighlty better for Chile and Costa Rica (particularly the latter if grants and aid are included), but even in those two cases a continuation of negative net transfers at the levels of recent years would imply that the net contribution from external capital flows since 1973 will become zero or negative, while their external debt has increased very significantly during that period. If this perception is combined with the prospect of continued negative net transfers for future years (as projected by most international institutions and independent observers) the net contribution over the long term of international capital flows will increasingly be seen as negative by the major debtors.

Even if the net resource transfers are deflated by a price index reflecting only domestic US inflation, (as a proxy for the price of imports of those countries), the total net resource transfer for the whole period 1973–86 is *negative* for Argentina and Venezuela and only very marginally positive for Mexico and Brazil; however, the outcome is somewhat more positive, if US inflation and not terms of trade is used as a deflator for Peru and Chile, and particularly for Costa Rica. It is specially noteworthy that for the whole of Latin America, total net resource transfers, deflated by US inflation, for the whole 1973–86 periods are around $50 billion (1984 US dollars), in spite of the fact that the region's external debt during the period grew by over $200 billion. Thus, even if deflating only by US inflation, and thus ignoring the additional effect of terms of trade deterioration, the total net transfers to the region could become zero or negative before 1990, if negative transfers continued at their very high 1982–6 level.

We can, thus, conclude that by the late eighties, practically all Latin American countries will have stopped receiving positive net transfers from the international financial system, even though the whole period since 1973 is taken into consideration and whatever the methodology used to estimate them; as a result, Latin American governments' resistance to continue making such negative net transfers can be expected to be strengthened.

Naturally, our assessment is too aggregate, as it does not examine the use made by the borrowers of the positive net transfer of funds in the initial period. The welfare effect for the debtor economy as a whole will be different if the resources were mainly invested in productive and effective projects, were consumed domestically, or were exported as private assets abroad, a key point to which we will return below. In this aspect, the welfare effects of borrowing on the national economy are more positive, the larger the proportion of those additional resources which were used in expenditure that increased growth capacity of the economy and/or their ability to generate additional future foreign exchange flows.

This leads us to a third element in the exploration of why debtor governments may not have taken more consistent unilateral action or even tougher bargaining positions. Most analysis centres on 'the national interest', that is, the interest of the debtor country as a whole, assumed to be represented by its government. This concept is too aggregate, given the complex social and political realities of debtor countries, which are reflected in the actions of governments.[8]

In terms of the special interest of those wealthy citizens, who benefited from the huge inflows of the seventies by increasing their consumption levels domestically or exported their wealth abroad and who have been more sheltered from the cost of adjustment to negative net transfers and deteriorating terms of trade in the 1980s, the net impact of those external flows may still be seen as positive. For poorer and more vulnerable groups, who may have benefited somewhat from improved living standards as a result of positive net transfers of financial resources, but who have been severely affected by negative net transfers—bearing a disproportionate share of the cost of the adjustment—the net balance may be very negative.

To the extent that wealthier groups had a larger influence on debtor governments than poorer groups, this may have discouraged unilateral action or tougher bargainng. However, to the extent that broader strata of the population are affected by slow growth or recession, to the extent that democratisation in several of the major debtors implies a far greater influence for the interests of the poor and the vulnerable, and to the extent that even wealthier groups perceive as potentially unsustainable the huge 'social and human' cost of adjustment, without a clear perception of improvement in the near future, the balance within debtor governments can be expected to shift (and has broadly been shifting), either to far tougher bargaining positions and/or to unilateral action. As was discussed in Chapter 1, this shift broadly corresponds to that indicated by bargaining theory. Major changes in negotiating posture are likely to occur when—in assessing the concessions made by both sides—it is found that there was 'unfair advantage' to one of the sides, in this case the debtor countries, and particularly to the poorer and more vulnerable groups within them; the change in negotiating position arrived as a result of this evaluation relates not only to how closely the negotiator responds to his own constituents (as bargaining analysts correctly point out) but also to who his main constituents are at the time.

To the shift of power and perceptions within debtor nations, should be added the shift of perception within industrial countries, where concern has been growing, within government, representatives in international financial institutions, and more broadly in the media and in public opinion, of the excessive human cost of adjustment of developing economies to the debt problem and to the deteriorating international environment.[9]

Part of the reason why governments, and peoples, have been so patient in servicing their debt, even at the cost of large domestic sacrifices of adjustment, are country specific and often related at least partly to non-economic variables. For example, several countries faced the initial stages of the debt crisis at a time when their countries were beginning a return to democratic rule, after years of military dictatorship. Such processes, in countries like Argentina, Uruguay and Brazil, imply a number of delicate domestic negotiations for the creation of new institutions, for the establishment of political coalitions, for mutually acceptable relationship between civil society and the armed forces. The difficult and complex nature of the tasks already facing governments may have inclined them, particularly initially, to avoid an additional potential source of tension or conflict with international creditors and financial institutions. Thus, the youth and the potential fragility of the new democratic governments seem to have inclined them towards a more conciliatory and conservative approach in international economic relations. However, when popular pressure has mounted for higher real wages and employment (or a recovery of previous levels), these new democratic governments have hardened their stance towards the international creditors and have increasingly placed minimum economic growth on the agenda of negotiations with them.

On the other hand, the lack of patience of the Garcia Peruvian Government and its unilateral and somewhat defiant actions can also, to an important extent, be explained by political variables. As is discussed in the chapter by Ugarteche, the Garcia Government faced since mid-1985 not only a difficult economic situation, but also a very tense political situation, with an extremely serious challenge to the Government's stability (and that of democracy in Peru) coming from the extremist Sendero Luminoso guerrillas, and with a country that lacked both a sense of future and of national unity. President Garcia's unilateral action on debt, as well as particularly the uncompromising harshness of his language towards foreign creditors and international financial institutions, can thus, to an important extent, be explained by the 'need' to find an 'external enemy' that provides a catalyst for national unity; naturally, the particularly severe trade-off between growth in Peru and servicing the debt fully provided an additional incentive for unilateral action, especially given strong democratic pressures for growth and increasing living standards of the very poor.

The priority given by a country's government and society to economic growth, in relation to other objectives, also has a large impact on the government's attitude towards debt servicing. For example, as is discussed in the chapter by Carneiro, the Brazilian Government and entrepreneurs give very high priority to economic growth; recession is seen as extremely undesirable, both by the Government and the private sector. While full debt servicing was consistent with high economic growth, the Brazilian Government continued to service debt in a timely way; however, when a conflict arose between growth and debt servicing in early 1987 (exacerbated by excessively expansionary macro-economic policies, as discussed below), the Brazilian Government suspended temporarily servicing of the debt to private banks. In Mexico, the priorities of objectives seem somewhat different to those in Brazil. Mexican entrepreneurs and the Mexican government seem to give far higher priority to objectives different from growth, than their Brazilian counterparts. Thus, stable and friendly relations between the Mexican Government with foreign creditors, as part of a harmonious relationship with industrial countries, and particularly with the US, are seen by Mexican entrepreneurs and Government as an important policy objective; it is within such a harmonious context, that the private sector will be more willing to invest domestically. If relations between Mexico and the outstide world are not seen to be clear and harmonious, and/or domestic confidence of private capital diminishes for other reasons (e.g. high inflation, over-valued exchange rate), then an important part of domestic savings leaves the country as capital flight. Thus, in an economy such as that of Mexico, with practically no capital controls, with such an 'internationalised' entre-preneurial class and with such close proximity and growing integration to the US economy, the Government seems objectively to be (and feel) constrained in its bargaining on debt and in the design of its macro-economic and development strategy by the need to avoid massive capital flight and to avoid disrupting friendly relations with its important neighbour.

Similarly, in Venezuela, the Government and the entre-preneurs seem to attach higher priority to objectives other than growth. For example, a major stated policy objective of the Venezuelan Government has been to be able to return to 'voluntary' market borrowing. In such a context, any radical, or even unorthodox option, of limiting debt service payments would be very counter-productive to its major policy objective. Furthermore as discussed below, the Venezuelan Government has even made fairly large amortization payments, partly with a view to increasing the country's 'creditworthiness'. However, at the time of writing, it would seem very unlikely for Venezuela to be able to seize important new sources of finance on the private capital markets.

3. COMPARISONS BETWEEN COUNTRIES

a) Net transfers and policy conditionality

In analysing the deals on debt rescheduling/new money adjustment that different Latin American countries have agreed with their creditors, it becomes clear that there are certain important trade-offs between the quality of the financial package and the conditionality of the adjustment. It should, however, be stressed that the trade-offs are basically within a fairly narrow range, as since 1982 for almost all the Latin American countries analysed here and for almost every year examined, *net resource transfers* have been negative and conditionality on their economic policies has in several cases been fairly heavy. It is absurd that *conditionality* is being applied *ex post*, well after the net resource transfer from abroad has been made and spent, and at a time when the net contribution from foreign creditors is clearly negative; in fact, debtor governments are being told how to allocate their *own resources*, so they can generate a surplus for making a net transfer of resources abroad. Independently of ideology, conditionality clearly makes far less sense in the current context, than in one when financial flows make a positive contribution to countries' resources.

A very relevant variable for the type of financial deals obtained seem to be size, as small countries, particularly if they have geo-political importance to industrial governments or can make a special case on humanitarian grounds, can more easily obtain positive net transfers. A clear illustration of this is Costa Rica, the only Latin American country in our sample to still obtain positive (though very low) net resource transfers since 1982 (see Table 12.2) and also one of the two countries doing best, if the whole 1973–85 period is evaluated (see Table 12.3). The reasons are clear; large (in proportion to the countries' economy) official flows are feasible financially, because these flows are small in relation to the US budget; they are actually made, to an important extent (though not only) because of Costa Rica's geo-political importance to the US and particularly because it borders with Nicaragua. (The magnitude of aid flows to Costa Rica has risen dramatically since 1983[10]; while total aid (ODA) flows from industrial countries to Costa Rica and averaged less than US $30 million between 1979 and 82, they rose to an average of above US $200 million between 1983 and 1985, almost a tenfold growth!) Undoubtedly, other reasons also contribute to explain the relatively favourable deals obtained by the Costa Rican Government, such as the design and implementation (since 1982) of viable macro-economic packages and the good technical level of the negotiating team. However, clearly the relatively small size of the Costa Rican debt and economy, as well as the country's geo-political importance to its main creditor country, are the major reasons for explaining the relatively positive financial outcome.

As Rodriguez clearly points out in his study, the cost of positive net transfers for small countries is very heavy conditionality, often exercised simultaneously by different international financial institutions (the latter is now called cross-conditionality). As Rodriguez illustrates such heavy cross-conditionality not only generates an extreme form of dependency of national economic policy on foreign decision-makers, but is also extremely inefficient, due to its heavy administrative cost, both in terms of time of senior decision-makers and actually in financial terms.

As Green describes, low-income African countries have, particularly since 1984, bargained mainly on a case of smallness and (very genuninely) of weakness. This argument is based on humanitarian concerns (avoidance of starvation or extreme deprivation for large numbers of people) though to a lesser extent, also on the possibility of reversing a decline of important markets for industrial countries and avoidance of political instability. The modifications obtained, particularly in rescheduling (with the Paris Club and with private banks but also in other fora) have only been granted in the African case, once IMF agreements were in place. Cross-conditionality is a very common feature in Sub-Saharan Africa, for example, Structural Adjustment Loans from the World Bank (which include a significant amount of policy conditionality) are far more common in Africa than in Latin America.

The only fairly large Latin American economy that has had World Bank Structural Adjustment Loans (SALs) is Chile. Furthermore, since 1983, Chile has almost continuously had

IMF upper credit *tranche* agreements, and has on the whole complied with its performance criteria better than any other Latin American country. More broadly, the orthodoxy of Chilean economic policies—which as Ffrench-Davis points out often exceeds that of the IMF or World Bank—has made it easier for Chile to obtain slightly better deals in terms of net resource transfers than other Latin American debtors, largely due to a fairly large increase in public flows.

There seems in this case to have been a 'trade-off' between obtaining a slightly better net resource transfer deal than for other countries (see Table 12.2), related to an important extent to the fact that the Chilean Government has been willing to adopt both very drastic and very orthodox adjustment packages, and implement them successfully, particularly since 1985. Indeed, it could be argued that the Chilean Government only bargains genuinely on debt rescheduling and new flows, but *not* really on the type of adjustments, as its views on the subject are as orthodox, if not more, as that of international financial institutions. Two caveats seem useful here; first, Chile has obtained such slightly preferential treatment, in spite of concern amongst several of its creditor governments (as well as other governments) about the country's extremely slow transition to democracy, and poor human rights records, reflecting perhaps the overriding importance attached by international financial institutions till now to Chile's commitment to orthodox adjustment and to financial objectives, such as inflation control, and its punctuality in servicing its debts. Another caveat is that although Chile's NRT outcome is less bad for the 1982–85 period than other Latin American countries, it is still strongly negative; however if the whole 1973–85 period is combined (see Table 12.3 again) Chile together with Costa Rica gets the relatively biggest contribution of positive net transfers from capital flows.

A somewhat different trade-off seemed to emerge in the deal signed in 1986 for Mexico. The Mexican Government was able to negotiate in 1986 both a fairly gradual and unorthodox adjustment package (see chapter by Villarreal), as well as a fairly favourable financial deal, in terms of net resource transfers, changes in maturity of the debt, spreads; furthermore, new ground was broken by the innovative elements in the package, such as the contingency clauses for minimum growth and protection against oil price fluctuations (see chapter by Gurria), as well as the acceptance by the IMF of a new concept for measuring the fiscal deficit (see chapters by Villarreal and Gurria).

This favourable deal cannot merely be attributed to the clear geo-political importance of Mexico to the US and to the size of the Mexican debt to the banks; the importance of these elements was enhanced by the fact that after very tough bargaining—in which the possibility of unilateral action was a clear option—the Mexican Government accepted a multi-laterally agreed deal, which though very favourable, had no purely concessional elements in it.

The Mexican bargaining experience of the 1986–7 package (as described in detail with an insider's insight in the chapter by Gurria) shows that better financial deals (the negative net transfer for the 18 months after the deal is being implemented will either be shaply reduced or possibly even fall to zero!) seem to be struck within the multilateral framework of negotiations, by governments that have clear objectives in their bargaining stance, that are willing to threaten unilateral action (with a clearly studied and broadly supported—within the government—option for such action), but that permanently continue a conciliatory dialogue with creditor governments and international institutions. Because international financial markets are so influenced by perceptions, respect for formalities (such as keeping key actors informed of changing developments, using friendly and conciliatory language, expressing the wish to reach agreement, as well as willingness to service the debt in the long term even when short term unilateral action is being presented an option) is of great importance. In that sense, the radical rhetoric used by the Garcia Peruvian Government in criticising its bank creditors and the IMF (though explained by domestic political reasons and pressures) was in some ways more damaging to Peru's relations with some of its creditors and lenders (such as the Inter-American Development Bank and the World Bank) than the unilateral action itself taken by the Garcia Government; this is particularly because the previous Peruvian Government (under President Belaunde) had, in fact, been during its last year servicing less of its foreign debt than the Garcia Government has!

Even though the 1986–7 financial Mexican package was so favourable, it had not enabled, at least until mid-1987, economic growth. This is particularly surprising, as Mexican foreign exchange reserves reached in mid-1987 their highest historical level, reflecting that, at least temporarily, foreign exchange scarcity was not the main constraint to growth. Slow growth was only partly due to the constraints placed on economic policy by IMF performance criteria. Additional constraints on economic policy making arose partly from the Government's need to pursue policies that avoid flight of private capital (and as far as possible encourage return of capital already fled). This leads to policy objectives such as very high real interest rates, necessary to avoid capital flight, but clearly counter-productive to private productive investment growth.[11] Thus, as pointed out above, in economies very open in their capital flows, with a very internationalised entrepreneurial class, there are additional (domestic) constraints imposed on government policy—to those coming from the policy conditionality attached to IMF or World Bank lending, and to the broader constraints on growth posed by limited availability of foreign exchange and of domestic savings. The problematic effects of this additional restriction on economic policy-making, as well as the broader deeply negative effects of capital flight on national economies, poses the question whether some greater degree of capital controls may not, in fact, be desirable for Latin American economies. Clearly such controls would be difficult to implement, particularly in Mexico, but such difficulties may outweigh the benefits of such measures.

The country in our Latin American sample which gets the worst result in terms of real net resource transfer is Venezuela. This is, to an important extent, due to the fact that, as Alvarez describes, between 1974 and 1983 the external debt did not basically fund trade deficits, as in most other Latin American countries, but its end use was the export of private assets abroad. Indeed, according to the estimates provided by Alvarez (see Table 12.3), the total increase in the foreign debt between 1974 and 1983, of US $33b, corresponded exactly with the estimated increase in private assets; most of this accumulation of private assets occurred in the 1979–83 period, when the bolivar was overvalued and per capita GDP systematically declined. The lack of profitable domestic opportunities, related to economic decline, and particularly fears of devaluation, provided incentives for capital flight, a process which was eased by lack of any capital control. As the level of total foreign debt declined since 1983, the flight of capital has continued, though at lower levels than in the 1979–83 period.

The magnitude of the capital flight from Venezuela during 1982–5 is estimated to have been so large that on fairly conservative estimates, it represented around 75 per cent of the total negative net transfers (of around 10 per cent of GDP) from the country during that period.[12] If such figures are correct, then 'only' 2.5 per cent of Venezuelan GDP was transferred abroad during 1982–5, as a result of larger debt servicing than new inflows of capital. Though this sum is still very high it is more comparable to that of the rest of the large Latin American debtors (see Table 12.2). The key issue, in an effort to stem negative net transfers from Venezuela, thus seems to be the definition of an alternative economic policy and development strategy to that pursued in recent years, such that will stem the very large capital flight from the country. A second important issue is that Venezuela has, during 1982–6, not obtained significant new credits from the private banks, and has not only serviced interest, but also amortized some capital, thus reducing the level of its total foreign debt.

Table 12.4:   Capital flight flows, from selected Latin American countries

	Capital flight from 1982–85, US$ of each year[a]	Capital flight as % of negative net transfers 1982–85[b]
Venezuela	17.0	75%
Mexico	23.3	49%
Argentina	9.9	67%

Source   (a) Conesa, *op. cit.* in[11]

        (b) Net transfers figures based on CEPAL, *Balance Preliminar de la Economia Latinomericana*, December 1986.

There are at least two other Latin American countries where the issue of capital flight was in the early eighties (and potentially may again become) as important as the types of deals reached with foreign creditors, in influencing the level of total financial net transfers. As discussed above, one of them is Mexico; the other is Argentina. As can be seen in Table 12.4, between 1982 and 1985, capital flight is estimated to have represented 49 per cent of negative net transfers for Mexico, 67 per cent for Argentina and 75 per cent for Venezuela. Increased capital flight since 1980 in those three countries both contributed to cause and was accelerated by the debt crisis. A more fundamental solution to the debt crisis than has been found until now could potentially contribute also to limiting capital flight, if it contributed to restore growth and confidence, while reducing uncertainty. However, the issue of controlling capital flight must also be given importance per se; in particular, the possible need—at this stage of their development—for greater government controls on capital flows requires further exploring, given the excessive 'internationalisation' of the process of financial intermediation in some Latin American countries, and the relatively smaller size of capital flight in countries (such as Brazil) where more capital controls have always existed.

Returning to the subject of conditionality, it is noteworthy that the Venezuelan Government has been able to resist signing an agreement with the IMF, which allowed it somewhat greater autonomy in its economic policies; however, as Alvarez points out, the adjustment policies adopted by the Venezuelan Government were in several aspects as (if not more) contractionary and orthodox as those recommended by the IMF. The form of monitoring adopted, via Economic Memoranda prepared by the Government and by bi-annual Article IV consultations, was, however, fairly innovative. The ability to systematically resist an agreement with the IMF as a condition for rescheduling is partly related to the fact that Venezuela has had very large foreign exchange reserves, continued to serve the interest on its public and publicly-guaranteed foreign debt, and merely requested a rescheduling of most amortization payments, *without requesting any new money from the private banks, as part of the package negotiated.* The Venezuelan Government did not request 'involuntary' new lending from the private banks; furthermore, it has even made fairly substantial amortization payments.

The Garcia Government in Peru has tackled the trade-off between financial deal and policy conditionality in a different way from that of other Latin American debtors; since 1985, it has both taken unilateral action on debt and has embarked on its own adjustment programme, openly rejecting IMF conditionality and even suspending repayments on previous IMF loans (see chapter by Ugarteche). At least at the time of writing (mid–1987), the results of these actions have been positive both in terms of the financial deal on net transfer (see Table 12.2 and Table 12.3), in its effect on the country's growth record in 1986 and early 1987, as well as in the extent to which economic policy has favoured or protected more the poor and the vulnerable.[13]

Indeed, partly as a result of Peru's unilateral action of limiting payments on debt which released some foreign exchange, the Peruvian economy in 1986 was the fastest growing in Latin America. However, the fact that debt payments were limited, has by no means eliminated the constraints for economic growth. Thus, in mid–1987, very rapid growth plus weak prices of Peru's exports, and policy mistakes, such as overvaluation of the exchange rate, are leading to accelerating inflation, and—even more pro-blematically—to rapidly-declining foreign exchange reserves. Though unilateral action limiting debt service payments has freed foreign exchange resources allowing for higher growth in the Peruvian economy, it has not by itself laid the base for sustained growth.

Unless growing macro-economic imbalances are revised in time, there is a risk that in Peru, the heterodox or alternative (to the IMF) economic policy package will run into severe problems. The failure of heterodox macro-economic manage-ment in Peru would follow on from the failure of the unorthodox, anti-inflation plan Cruzado in Brazil (described in Carneiro's chapter); it is often the inability of developing country governments to design, negotiate domestically and implement technically coherent and politically viable hete-rodox macro-economic packages, which forces these governments ultimately to go to the IMF. Clearly in the Peruvian case the political pressures on the governments are great; given the sharp declines in previous years of income of the more vulnerable groups and the pressure from the extremist Sendero Luminoso, the Government finds it politically difficult to control real wages and its own special expenditure; on the other hand, unless real wages and social expenditure are controlled, a growing and eventually unsustainable macro-economic disequilibrium will develop, which may threaten much of the progress achieved both in terms of economic growth and income distribution.

From the point of view of international financial flows, the Peruvian experience has shown that after two years of unilateral action no legal response has come from the creditor banks to confiscate assets or other drastic measures; the only 'cost' of the unilateral action, as regards creditor banks, has been their curtailment of short-term credit lines. It could be argued that the Peruvian case is exceptional, as it is not a 'major' debtor (though it is a medium one) and due to the fact that Peru has become a sort of 'basket case', given its more or less widely-recognised inability to pay. However, it should also be stressed, in this context, that the creditor banks' response to the Brazilian unilateral action in 1987 of suspending interest payments, has been equally—if not more—low key. As a consequence, there seems to be growing—though obviously not conclusive—evidence that creditor banks will tend to respond to unilateral action defensively, by curtailing short-term credit lines, but not aggressively, for example, by legal actions. Naturally, the risk of legal action or of curtailment of intra-bank lines is always present, even though existing experience seems to indicate it as unlikely.

On the other hand, the Peruvian Government's suspension of payments to the IMF (and its failed attempts to reschedule payments to that institution) has had negative effects. Suspension of payments to the IMF, as well as Garcia's harsh critique of the Fund, seems to have seriously inhibited new credits from the World Bank and the Inter-American Development Bank, with negative effects on the Peruvian economy.

It seems noteworthy that successful resistance to accept

IMF conditionality has been more widespread (Brazil since 1985, as well as Venezuela and Peru) and began far earlier, than unilateral action on the debt front in Latin America. This is particularly clear in the evolution of the Brazilian Government's position, which since 1985, adopted its own macro-economic programme, without IMF supervision, but continued to service the debt until February 1987, when it adopted unilateral action.

The fact that the Brazilian Government did not reach an agreement with the IMF in 1985 and 1986 implied costs, such as the fact that its financial deals with the banks were less attractive, for example, as relates to level of 'spreads' than, say, those of Mexico, and more importantly implied a lack of new credits from private banks. However, the freedom to define its own macro-economic policy, allowed the Brazilian Government to pursue growth-oriented policies. As can be seen in Table 12.5, during the 1985-6 period, per capita GDP growth in Brazil (at 5.8 per cent) was by far the highest in Latin America, and well exceeded the Latin American average (at only 0.8 per cent during the two years). Two very important caveats should, however, be made here. First, sustained growth in Brazil in the mid-1980s was made more feasible than in other Latin American (or indeed African) countries, due to the structural adjustment investment in tradeables and capital goods so effectively carried out by the Brazilian Government in the 1970s (see chapter by Carneiro, for a clear discussion). Second, even though the Brazilian Government launched an innovative and unorthodox macro-economic stabilisation programme to curtail inflation (the Plan Cruzado), policy mistakes in the Plan's implementation—such as excessive monetary expansion, excessive real wage increases, insufficient corrections to public enterprise prices—implied that severe financial disequilibria emerged, leading both to extremely high levels of inflation and to a drastic reduction in the balance of payments trade surplus.[14] Though impressive, the levels of growth reached in certain sectors were clearly unsustainable; this was particularly so in the industrial sector, where total production grew by 34 per cent between March and October 1986, with non-durable consumer goods production growing by 43 per cent in the same seven months!

Table 12.5:　Latin America: evolution of GDP per capita (% changed)

	1981	1982	1983	1984	1985	1986	Accum ulated varia tion 1981–6
Latin America excluding Cuba	–1.9	–3.7	–4.7	0.9	0.4	1.2	–7.6
Brazil	–4.2	–0.8	–4.8	2.6	5.9	5.7	4.0
Costa Rica	–5.0	–9.7	–0.0	5.1	–1.7	0.4	–11.0
Chile	3.5	–14.5	–2.2	4.3	0.7	3.2	–6.2
Mexico	5.4	–2.6	–7.6	0.9	0.1	–6.3	–10.4
Peru	1.3	–2.5	–14.2	1.2	–1.0	5.9	10.1
Venezuela	–3.9	–4.1	–8.2	–3.7	–3.2	–1.0	–21.9

Source: CEPAL, *Balance preliminar de la economia latinoamericana*, 1986.

Again, as in the Peruvian case, there are political explana-
tions for the design of excessively expansionary macro-
economic policies. It is clearly difficult to have consistent
economic policies in a context of democratisation, with serious
institutional tensions, with some doubts over the legitimacy of
the President himself, and with crucial elections in November
1986. In this context, the initial success of the Cruzado plan,
and the immense popular support that the governing party and
the President gained as a result, were incorrectly accepted by
the Government as evidence that essential measures of demand
control and adjustment of relative prices was unnecessary. The
Government won the election, but lost the fight against
inflation!

The subordination of economic policy to short-term
political objectives, so frequent in Latin America, led
inevitably in Brazil to unsustainable financial disequilibria,
and to the failure of the unorthodox package. The failure of an
unorthodox package clearly reinforces the attractiveness of
more conventional packages, and the perceived desirability
(within and outside the country) of reaching an agreement on
stabilisation with the IMF, which implies exactly the opposite
result to that desired by the authors of unorthodox macro-
economic packages. An important, though by no means new,
lesson is that if unorthodox stabilisation is to be successfully

implemented, it requires not just a coherent and viable technical package but above all, political consensus on the importance of supporting such a package.

As a result of declining trade surpluses, and foreign exchange reserves, in February 1987, the Brazilian Government declared a unilateral moratorium on all interest payments of its debt to private banks. Whatever its limitations, the unilateral moratorium implied an important step, which clearly marked the beginning of a new stage in debt crisis management. It showed that the largest LDC bank debtor of all, Brazil, when confronted between a choice of restricting growth or unilaterally limited debt servicing chose the latter path. Even though Brazil's unilateral action may well prove to be temporary, it would seem to have posed a far deeper challenge to the multilaterally agreed package framework prevalent since 1982, than for example, Peru's unilateral action since 1985.

There were several problems with the Brazilian moratorium. The declaration of unilateral cessation of interest payments was not part of a clear strategy, but a response to the rapid deterioration in the trade surplus and foreign exchange reserves. In this respect, the timing was very poor; the Brazilian Government declared a moratorium at a time of rapdily increasing inflation and declining foreign exchange reserves. From the point of view of bargaining power, the Brazilian Government's position would have been far stronger if it had taken such action the previous year, when foreign exchange reserves were high, the Cruzado Plan was seen as very successful, etc. (It should, however, be recognised that a moratorium is easier to justify on a 'can't pay, won't pay' argument, which Brazil was far more able to use in early 1987 than it would have been able to in 1986). Second, the Brazilian Government did not, for several months, make explicit its objectives in negotiations with the banks on key aspects such as interest capping, amount of new money required, etc.; thus, the Brazilian Government did not present a concrete alternative proposal on how the debt problem should be managed, which could serve as a base for negotiation of a new type of deal. Unless major innovations are introduced into the agreement that will be reached with creditor banks, the value of the Brazilian unilateral action could be depreciated by the lack of significant improvement or innovation.

In any case, the Brazilian moratorium had two beneficial effects on Latin American economies, by mid–1987. First, it has provided Brazil with some breathing space in the first half of 1987, allowing for higher growth than would have otherwise been possible. Second, other Latin American Governments— such as those of Mexico, Argentina, and Chile—found it far easier to finalise their rescheduling/new money deals more rapidly and somewhat more successfully, due to the wish of bankers to avoid any risk that Brazili's precedent should spread to other fairly large debtors. As Tussie points out very clearly in her paper, the offer of special 'sweeteners' to governments so they do not pursue unilateral action, when such action is taken by another government, also has occurred on previous occasions.

At the time of writing (mid–1987), there seems to be increased agreement within debtor governments that the 1986–7 Mexican deal, successful as it was on its own terms, will in this round—unlike in previous ones—not provide a blueprint for other deals. The difficulty, even for Mexico to receive new money (see paper by Gurria) will be very clearly compounded more for other debtors with less geo-political clout and smaller debts. In this context, the need for a new 'formula' to handle the debt overhang seems increasingly urgent. The outcome of Brazil's negotiations with creditor banks and industrial governments is, thus, important not only for Brazil itself, but also for the future evolution of the management of the debt problem in the rest of Latin America.

b) The hidden agendas

In our workshops, evidence has emerged that in the multilateral negotiations on debt, new lending and adjustment, there were some hidden agendas, often not made explicit in the official documents. As could be expected, political matters and bilateral economic issues, particularly those of interest to the US Government, were high on those agendas in negotiations with Latin American countries. For example, several Central American countries (particularly those not included in our sample) have benefited from more lenient economic conditionality, but have had to accept political and even military conditions. Cross-conditionality, thus, has far more than an economic dimension! Though disturbing the use of economic leverage by major powers to achieve political objectives is a common feature throughout history.

At an economic level, issues such as countries' position on the new GATT round have been made part of the negotiation on debt rescheduling and new money; for example, a senior US Treasury official openly told the Argentinian press before the Uruguay meeting in the GATT that the Argentine Government would not get new credits if it continued to oppose the US GATT position. It would seem that debtor governments have not used sufficiently strongly other agendas (such as access to their own markets, better concessions to foreign investment) in their bargaining on financial flows. It is, however, interesting to point out that on several occasions these hidden agendas were successfully resisted by the Latin America debtors; for example, in one case, the reduction of tariffs posed as a condition of a structural adjustment package was not only negative for the particular country's industry, but also threatened to undermine an existing regional common market agreement; the maximum political authority of that country resisted this condition, and the potential danger to the regional common market agreement was lifted.

As regards agreements with the IMF, often some of the key conditions for approval of a package are not made explicit in the official documents exchanged. This is clearly illustrated by the Brazilian experience, where the importance attached by the IMF to de-indexation of wages is not made explicit in the official documents, but can be clearly deduced from the timing of suspension and renewal of disbursements of IMF credit (see paper by Carneiro).

Another area insufficiently studied until the present, where to some extent there has been a hidden agenda, has been the rescheduling of private non-guaranteed external debt, which has been carried out in a fundamentally different way in the different countries we have analysed. The problem is quantitatively, as well as qualitatively important, as due to both large conversions from private to public debt by several Latin American countries, and the fact that new disbursements of private debt fall below principal repayments, a significant overall fall in private non-guaranteed debt occurred, from US $110 billion to US $99 billion, in 1985 alone.[15]

The most extreme case has been that of Chile, where initially most (around 65 per cent) of the external debt was originally private, *without government guarantee* (a fact on which government had expressed pride, given its belief in the great efficiency of private indebtedness). In this context, it was paradoxical that—when the debt crisis came—*the Chilean Government ex post acted as borrower of last resort*; this is in sharp contrast with the attitude of industrial creditor governments, who have consistently refused to grant *ex post* lender of last resort facilities to the credits held in LDCs by their private banks. Not only did the Chilean Government itself conduct negotiations on debt, a majority of which it had not borrowed or guaranteed; it went further, in giving *ex post* government guarantee to an important part of the private debt, that of the private financial sector. The granting of the *ex post* government guarantee can be partly explained (even though not justified) by the fact that it was the private financial sector whose debts were being bailed out, and that bankruptcy or serious financial distress in an important part of the banking sector would have had potentially very disruptive macro-economic effects. Furthermore, in those cases where it did not grant *ex post* guarantee, the Chilean Government gave different types of subsidies (including a preferential exchange rate) to the private sector, so as to enable it to service its debt; Ffrench-Davis estimates the total cost of this subsidy as reaching roughly one-fifth of one year's GDP!

As Ffrench-Davis points out, the major concession of *ex post* public guarantees and massive subsidies on the private debt were granted by the Chilean Government without this being explicitly used as a bargaining chip to obtain at least some compensatory concessions from the creditor side.

In none of the other countries studied were *ex post* explicit public guarantees granted on private debts. Increasingly, Alvarez reports that in the Venezuelan case, creditor banks did not even demand *ex post* government guarantee for private debt; however, the creditor banks did exert pressure on the Venezuelan Government to grant a preferential exchange rate for private debt servicing, and *linked explicitly* the granting of this concession on the private debt to their willingness to reschedule the public debt. Similarly, as in the case of Chile, Alvarez feels that the Government of Venezuela should have used far more the important concession granted to creditor banks of subsidising servicing of private debt, to obtain far better terms on debt rescheduling or new money. The amount of the subsidy granted by the Venezuelan Government has been fairly substantial. For example, between March 1984 and December 1986, servicing of the private debt was carried out at the preferential exchange rate of Bs 4.30, while most other transactions (except those of essential imports) were made either at the Bs 6.00 exchange rate or at the Bs 7.50 exchange rate, thus, implying a massive subsidy.

Other countries gave less favourable treatment to the servicing of its private debt. Perhaps the most complete and interesting scheme was that developed by the Mexican Government, which established through FICORCA a system that neither granted official *ex post* commercial government guarantee on the private debt, nor gave an explicit exchange rate subsidy (see Gurria's paper). An implicit subsidy may have arisen in periods when, for other economic policy reasons (such as an attempt to control inflation), devaluation has been retarded; however, the magnitude of the implicit subsidy granted seems clearly well below that granted by either the Venezuelan or the Chilean Government.

Within the framework of multilateral negotiations, the Mexican Government seems to have negotiated relatively best on better financial terms (first country to get multi-year arrangement, relatively low spreads, long grace and maturity period and abundant new money in the 1986–7 package) and important degrees of flexibility and heterodoxy in its adjustment package (e.g., growth clause; acceptance of the operational deficit concept). Similarly, the mechanism it has agreed for the private debt has been the least burdensome for the national Treasury, amongst the cases analysed here. The Venezuelan financial package has clearly been less favourable than that obtained by Mexico, particularly as it has implied no money. Similarly, the Venezuelan Government granted large subsidies to the private sector for its servicing of the foreign debt. The most damaging treatment of the private debt (from the point of view of the national interest) has been that accepted by the Chilean Government, which both granted *ex post* guarantee for an important part of the debt and gave large subsidies for its servicing in the rest of it. The Chilean Government's weak bargaining in this aspect coincides with its very weak bargaining on the nature and timing of adjustment. The Chilean Government has obtained slightly better results (or less bad ones) in net transfers between 1982 and 1986, possibly because it has been so willing to make concessions both on the adjustment and treatment of the private debt.

4. A NEW FRAMEWORK

Recent trends
Though important differences exist between debtor nations in the deals on debt, new flows and adjustment between 1982 and 1986, the overall picture is clearly one of continuous negative net transfers from most Latin American nations, insufficient positive net transfers for low-income Africa, and excessive foreign conditionality on policy-making in both regions.

As regards the evolution for Latin America, net negative transfers have declined somewhat in 1986, from their peak of US $32.9 billion in 1985 to US $22.1 billion in 1986; the 1986 outcome, though still *extremely unsatisfactory*, is the least bad of the 1983–6 period. The relative improvement is half due to reduced nominal interest payments (though real interest payments remained high as export prices fell sharply, by over 12 per cent in 1986!) and half due to a small recovery of new net capital flows to Latin America, basically explained by larger new official flows. It can be expected that probably in 1987 negative net transfers will diminish further, as Mexico's new package starts operating and implies a fairly large inflow of new loans, and as Brazil's unilateral stance will have implied a significant reduction in that country's massive interest payments. It should be stressed that such a reduction in 1987 of negative net transfers to an important extent would result from very tough bargaining (within the multilateral framework) by the Mexican Government in 1986 and from explicit, even though possibly temporary, unilateral action by the Brazilian Government in early 1987.

Even somewhat reduced negative net transfers for the next five or ten years, from debtor countries, are clearly unacceptable. Particularly in the context of major changes and the poor prospects in the international environment to which these countries' economies continually have to adjust, developing countries require high levels of productive and social investment to grow and develop. The chapter by Villarreal clearly shows, for the Mexican case, how the imperative of growth and structural adjustment requires levels of investment that can only be achieved if negative net transfers are eliminated and preferably if there is a net inflow of foreign savings from abroad. A similar case is valid for our other case studies. It should be stressed that a reduction or elimination of negative net transfers to creditor banks and institutions will only free domestic resources potentially for domestic investment. However, appropriate policies need to be implemented so as to assure that increased availability of national savings effectively is used in ways that enhance future growth and development. A better 'formula' for dealing with the debt overhang is clearly a necessary but not a sufficient condition for recovery of development.

3. Debtor governments' allies

In their search for a new and more appropriate framework for handling international financial flows from and to them, developing countries may have far more potential allies within industrial countries than they realise. Exporters to indebted developing countries, and foreign investors in them, are perhaps most obvious. There is growing awareness in the US, and increasingly also in Europe, of the large export and job losses that industrial countries have suffered as a result of debt crises in Latin America and Africa. Indeed, alternative 'formulae' for managing the debt problem are increasingly in the US evaluated in terms of the increased level of US exports *and* jobs which they would generate.[16] Producers of goods in industrial countries (e.g. agricultural ones) whose prices are depressed by rapidly increased export volumes from debtor nations may also support measures that reduce negative net transfers and, thus, the pressure on debtor countries to increase export volumes.

Those politicians in industrial nations concerned with political stability in developing countries are also sympathetic to new approaches on the debt issue.[17]

Perhaps less well-known is the fact that many bankers themselves are suffering from 'debt rescheduling fatigue', in a similar, though less painful way, to the 'adjustment fatigue', being suffered by debtor countries, and particularly the poorest and most vulnerable groups in those societies. Such bankers are anxious to overcome the problems of the debt overhang, so as to focus their attention on voluntary new lending or new issuing of securities, either in developing countries *or far more probably, elsewhere*. As pointed out above, many categories of banks have already established large loan-loss provisions on their developing country debt and, therefore, can afford to make concessions without damaging either their stability or solvency.

Perhaps the clearest recognition that a chapter of debt crisis management was closing in May 1987 came from Mr John Reed, the chairman of Citicorp, the bank with the highest exposure in Latin America, when he explicitly recognised that 'the debt problem will be with us into the 1990s and we see nothing in the global economy that would enable these countries to get out of this situation ... The global economy is less solvent today than when the present approach was devised in 1982'.[18]

There is even more 'fatigue' by bankers for 'involuntary new lending', as is reflected in the figures of decling *levels* of bank exposure to all areas of the developing world during the first nine months of 1986! This is partly relaed to the fact that, as John Reed clearly pointed out, world trade volumes and particularly commodity prices have been disappointingly low since 1985. However, the unwillingness of banks to make further new lending (either 'voluntary' or 'involuntary' to heavily-indebted developing countries) has even deeper causes. It is conventional wisdom that private banks consider a ratio of around *200 per cent* between total external debt and value of total exports, as a maximum over which they do not wish to increase their exposure; however, that ratio reached *401 per cent* for Latin America in 1986; it had been systematically *rising since 1982.*[19] It is unlikely on these grounds, that there will be significant new bank lending, especially of a voluntary nature, for at least five or ten years more. The problems caused to all involved by the debt crisis will deter even further for many years the willingness of banks to renew significant new flows. The myth that in the short term, successful adjustment will restore major new private flows is being increasingly disbelieved.

The realisation that there will not be significant new lending from banks lead perceptive observers to the inevitable conclusion that new approaches are needed. A distinguished analyst of the international financial system, John Williamson, concluded in early 1987 that 'in 1985, Fred Bergsten, William Cline and myself had concluded in a study that the best approach was to maintain a flow of concerted new lending packages, but that if that process broke down, it would be necessary to resort to interest capitalisation. Recent events suggest that the time has come to examine what we then conceived as no more than a contingency plan.'[20]

The need for specific proposals

A key conclusion from our project is that debtor governments have achieved better results when they have taken the initiative and put forward clear, specific proposals to the creditors. Though not always all their suggestions have been accepted, *a clear initial position* by the debtor governments can serve as a basis for the package adopted. The Mexican deal signed in 1986–7 seems to illustrate this rather well. On the other hand, the Argentine position in 1984, in which a tough stance *vis-à-vis* creditors was hinted at, but no clear proposals emerged, did not contribute to obtaining an improved deal.

A limitation of the Mexican negotiation in 1986 may have been the complexity of the financial package proposed, even though net financial flows required for the next two or three years were clearly put forward (see paper by Gurria). The package had many interesting and creative innovative elements (e.g. use of exit bonds, linking payments to the relationship between the price of oil and interest rates, etc.); however, in a sense the package contained too many innovative elements at the same time to be easily implemented and, above all, to be acceptable to the banks. The pressure of time to reach an agreement gave bankers an additional (partly legitimate) reason to turn down the Mexican proposal. The package adopted implied a major improvement in the financial deal and incorporated some but not the main new concepts supported by the Mexican authorities.

It would seem best to make proposals, or at least monitor developments, in terms of the variable that affects most centrally debtor developing countries, that is *net transfer of resources*. A drastic reduction or elimination of negative net transfers, for middle income debtors, at least until the end of the eighties, may seem radical in the present context, but in terms of economic development theory or international justice, is a fairly modest target. An elimination of negative net transfers would free an important amount of resources to allow for restructuring of middle income debtor economies, to make feasible their development in the nineties, as well as to start servicing their domestic 'social debt', incurred with the poorer and more vulnerable groups during the years of 'adjustment without growth'. An additional secondary objective would be that the level of total foreign debt in relation to the volume of exports should not continue to rise, as this only postpones the problem into the future.

Of importance in the case of middle income heavily-indebted countries is the proposal of reduction in interest rate payments to a certain level (e.g. 5 or 6 per cent), the excess of which would only be repaid *if and when* interest payments fell below that level during the period of the loan. The difference between the 'market rate' and the fixed rate would be financed by an interest compensatory fund. In November 1986, a concrete proposal along these lines was made by Mr A. Herrhausen, Speaker of the Management Board of the largest German bank, Deutsche Bank; the idea has received an important amount of support in European circles. One of the proposal's interesting features (increasingly relevant after May 1987) is that part of the 'subsidy' would be funded by private banks, drawing on loan-loss provisions they have accumulated.

Another area where specific proposals are important is that of principal payments. Until now the main way of reducing amortization payments has been via rescheduling, which postpones the problem to the future (in the case of 1986–7 Mexican deal, the postponement has been significant). However, the market value of the debt is increasingly recognised to be *below its face value*, as is reflected in the rapidly growing (though rather thin) secondary market and in increasingly widespread loan-loss provisions. It seems absurd that if the market and most of the creditor banks have recognised explicitly that the book value is unrealistic, debtor governments and economies are still obliged to service the debt as if it was worth 100 per cent of this value. To allow the value of the debt being serviced to reflect closer market realities, a number of options can be pursued. Amongst these, *debt equity swaps* are already being implemented in a number of countries; the 1987 Argentine package also includes *exit bonds* used by banks wanting to withdraw from the process of rescheduling/new money, albeit at a loss. A third variety has been suggested, but not yet implemented; these would be so-called *'debt development' swaps*. In that case, part of the debt or debt service would be converted into investment/expenditure *in the domestic economy* for high priority activities, such as exports, import substitution or social expenditure, under the monitoring of an international organisation, such as the World Bank, the corresponding regional development bank, or another specialised agency.[21]

In the Latin American context, the Inter-American Development Bank President, Sr Ortiz Mena has launched an interesting proposal which implies a debt/development swap. Part of the interest on foreign debt incurred would be deposited in local currency by the debtor government in an escrow account, administered by the IDB. The funds would be used for productive expenditure *within* the country monitored by the IDB. In the context of low income countries, mostly, but not only, in Sub-Saharan Africa, UNICEF is launching a somewhat similar proposal, which would imply that part of debt or interest relief would be placed in a national child survival fund. This fund would be used for additional expenditure, in nutrition, health and education for poor children; the programme would be jointly designed, implemented and monitored by the government and UNICEF, as well as another multilateral organisation, such as the World Bank.

Such innovations may require changes in banking and taxation regulations in some or all creditor countries, that would smooth (over the years) and make less costly to creditor banks the partial writing-down and writing-off of debt, and/or some sort of interest relief. Such institutional changes are already beginning to be discussed in the US Congress at the time of writing; institutional changes are actually being carried out in Japan that would make such measures possible. Existing regulations have become too major an obstacle to innovative solutions to the debt crisis; it has often been almost forgotten that regulations are only man-made and can be modified if they do not suit current needs!

As regards new credits, it seems important for debtor governments to focus more on negotiations with governments, institutions and private agents, both willing and able to provide significant net flows. In this sense, far less time should be perhaps spent than at present in negotiations with the US Government and banks, *while* the US economy is itself in such a large current account deficit, and particularly while US financial intermediaries are far less able as well as less willing to provide significant new flows to most developing countries than they were in the seventies. Far greater emphasis, both nationally and collectively needs to be made by debtor governments, to attract flows from the Japanese and West German governments, as well as private institutions. Of great interest in this context is the May 1987 proposal (made by WIDER)[22] that Japan contributes—via different mechanisms and institutions—US $25 billion a year to the financing of developing countries. The Japanese Government has already begun to sharply increase its flows to developing countries, particularly heavily-indebted ones. Again, in this sense the 1986 Mexican financial package was interesting, as it incorporated a major new (US $1bn) loan from Japan.

The focus of dialogue for the creation of appropriate financial mechanisms, and possibly on policy conditions, needs to change somewhat from the traditionally large supplier of new funds—US Government and institutions—to the real and potential providers of new funds, the Japanese and to a lesser extent, the West German ones. Though clearly the US Government and banks will continue to play an important role in financial negotiations in Latin America, due to US importance in geo-political and trade terms, as well as due to the level of its existing financial exposure, there should be an increased shift to bargaining more with the providers of new funds. To some extent, this will mean a new additional source of economic dependence for debtor nations; however, it also implies a diversification of dependency, and a diminishment of its political dimension, given that Japan is an economic but not political superpower.

A third area for concrete proposals is that of contingency arrangements for financial flows, in case of fluctuations in international economic variables, such as the price of countries' main export products. In this sense, new ground has already been broken by the packages described for Venezuela and Mexico. Given the high level of instability in key internationally determined variables, the need for contingency clauses in any long-term debt management becomes increasingly important, for all debtor nations.

As regards low income countries, the case for officially-granted debt relief is very strong, and increasingly accepted; debt relief for those countries also has precedent, in the Retrospective Terms Adjustment, granted since 1978, by several industrial governments, which converted official development assistance loans into grants. As Green points out, much more could be done in that direction. At the time of writing, the UK and the French Government had launched a very important initiative in this direction for Sub-Saharan Africa. An important principle to be established here is that negotiations on Sub-Saharan Africa and more generally on low income countries' debt have no direct linkage and establish no automatic precedents for other categories of debtors. Closer liaison than exists at present between representatives from African debtor governments and representatives of Latin American debtor governments is clearly required for this and other purposes.

The bargaining process
In the Latin America and African context alike, a key pre-condition for successful negotiation on debt/new money deals is the existence of clearly defined and appropriate development strategies as well as consistent short-term macro-economic programme. The existence of such plans clearly strengthens the case for extracting concessions/new flows from creditors, as these concessions/new flows can be more easily justified in the industrial country; the existence of development plans and targets also changes the focus of discussion from a purely financial one to the 'real economy'; if a particular growth rate and income distribution is targeted, as well as certain minimum levels of government expenditure and investment required to achieve such targets, then the external financial flows required are dependent to a far more important extent on those national objectives.

Particularly in cases of governments not wishing to accept upper credit *tranche* conditionality from the IMF, it is essential that foreign creditors and lenders, as well as the citizens of the debtor country, see that the government has its own effective and consistent macro-economic programme, that will avoid major financial disequilibria. The lack of such a clear 'alternative adjustment' package seems to have weakened the position of the Argentine government *via-à-vis* its creditors in 1984, and may also weaken the pursuit by the Brazilian Government in mid-1987 of a far more favourable deal with its creditors. In the case of unilateral action, the need for prudent and careful macro-economic management, as well as a clear development strategy, becomes even more crucial than for multilaterally agreed deals; the task is made somewhat easier by the fact that unilateral action frees additional foreign exchange resources, but more difficult because a higher level of contingency foreign exchange reserves are required, in case unforeseen events generate pressure on the country's balance of payments. The Peruvian government seems to have initially successfully combined unilateral action on the debt front with a fairly clear development strategy and an initially relatively balanced macro-economic programme; however, increasing macro-economic imbalances, reflected in rising inflation and declining foreign exchange reserves, pose a growing threat both to the government's long-term development strategy and its independence *vis-à-vis* its creditors—as well as international financial institutions.

A second element relates to the bargaining itself. The experience studied in this project seems to suggest that, even though unilateral action, by debtor governments is undesirable in itself for all actors involved (as it implies the risk of unquantifiable negative effects), either *such unilateral action or the threat of it, may be necessary for debtor governments to achieve financial deals that are consistent with growth and development in their economies.* It would seem that such tough bargaining positions, or even unilateral action is more effective if it has unified support of all branches and levels of the government and the active support of a large part of the countries' population, political parties, trade unions, etc. It is also very important to establish at all times that the position is *not confrontational,* and wishes to avoid harming the creditor institutions. There seems a clear need for debtor government negotiators to show 'good will' in negotiations with creditor banks and governments, to maintain 'channels of communication' open, to maintain formalities and use conciliatory language, not only when taking a very tough negotiating stance, but even when unilateral action is raised as a possibility or carried out. The successful effect of tough positions or actions and diplomatic behaviour is well-illustrated, for example, by the Mexican experience in 1986-7.

Particularly, if some element of concessionality is being negotiated, it seems essential for the debtor government to show not only that: a) the resources freed are used in a developmental context, leading both to sustained economic growth and increased welfare of the population; b) a significant contribution is made by wealthy citizens of debtor countries toward funding development. The containment of capital flight, as well as an attempt to return capital already fled is a very crucial example, as would be increased taxation on high income groups, restrictions on luxury goods imports, etc.

A third important tactical element is to recognise that important differences exist in the interests, aims and regulatory environment of different creditors, particularly, but not, only, private banks. These differences have tended till now to work against debtors in multilateral negotiations, as the relief or new money granted has tended to be 'the lowest common denominator' acceptable to all creditor banks. For example, banks with large loan-loss provisions, for example, some European ones, may be willing to write-off or postpone some interest payments, but are not keen to lend new money, as this will imply they have immediately to increase their loan-loss provisions; on the other hand, the big US banks are more willing to lend new money, but are unwilling to give any concession or even postponement of interest payments, as this lowers the rating of debt in their books. As a result, it is extremely difficult either to get new money or to get interest rate postponements or concessions.

If debtor governments that have negative net transfers were to fix a target acceptable to them in net transfers, they could then negotiate separately with different types of creditors, for example, banks of different nationalities, on the concrete mechanisms through which this target of net transfers would be achieved. The deals would in this case be equitable amongst creditors, but different. As a result US regulations would not constrain German bank actions, nor would German regulations constrain US bank lending. At the time of writing, the Costa Rican Government was embarked on an attempt to strike such a deal.

It seems that some creditors themselves favour such an approach, given its greater flexibility. However, it should be stressed that dealing with groups of creditors separately could become cumbersome. For this reason, the deals would need to be one-off deals, which would attempt to deal with the problem for an important length of time.

The final issue relates to the appropriate forum for negotiation of new flows and rescheduling. Clearly the steering committees and the IMF provide too narrow an outlook on the problem; the greater involvement of the World Bank, though adding an extra fairly heavy element of conditionality, has the positive element that its perspective is more on the long-term and on development issues. It is necessary that both in national and collective negotiations, financial matters are not left only to financial interests, but that broader interests, representing for example, productive and trading sectors in industrial countries and the poorer groups in developing countries (e.g. via their Industry and Labour Ministries or international institutions, such as UNICEF or ILO) are represented. It is crucial that these latter interests and concerns are represented *at the time* the major financial decisions are being made, and *not* as now, left to 'pick up the pieces' of the productive or social cost of the adjustment, after the adjustment was designed by those with fundamentally financial criteria in mind.

NOTES

1. *Managing Third World Debt*, Report by the Second Working Party established by the All Party Parliamentary Group on Overseas Development, ODI, London 1987.
2. Salomon Brothers, 'Less Developed Countries' Indebtedness: Secular Developments in US Banking are Defusing the Problem', *Bank Weekly*, 20 January, 1987.
3. Holley, *Developing Country Debt, the Role of the Commercial Banks*, Chatham House, Paper 35, 1987.
4. Source: *International Financing Review*, FFIEC Statistical Release, E. 16 (126), 13 February, 1987.
5. For a recent review of different options for solution, see P. Wertman, 'The International Debt Problem: Options for solution' in Hearings before the Sub-Committee on International Finance, Trade and Monetary Policy of the Committee on Banking, Finance and Urban Affairs, House of Representatives, *Banking Committee Provisions of the Trade Bill*, Washington, 1987.
6. These concerns are clearly reflected in the US Banking Committee Provisions of the Trade Bill quoted in (5) in the proposals of US Senator Bradley, Congressman Schumer and other US Congressmen, as well as in the Report by the British All Party Parliamentary Working Party quoted in (1).
7. The proper use of deflator for debtor countries for similar variables is discussed in detail and with rigour in C. Massad and R. Zahler, 'World inflation and foreign debt for the creditor and the debtor', in *Latin America: International Monetary System and External Financing*, UNDP/ECLAC, Santiago de Chile, 1986. I would like to thank Adrian Wood for his useful comments on the issue of an appropriate deflator.
8. For an interesting discussion, see A. McEwan, 'Es posible la moratoria en America Latina?', *Comercio Exterior*, January 1987, vol. 37, no. 1, pp. 60–4; see also paper by C. Fortin, in this volume, for a more detailed discussion.

9. For a very articulate statement of this problem and an empirical review of the evidence, see G. A. Cornia, R. Jolly, and F. Stewart (eds), *Adjustment with a Human Face: Protecting the Vulnerable and Promoting Growth*, Oxford University Press, 1987. Increased concern has also been expressed by the World Bank and by the IMF, in their declarations and in their studies.

10. OECD *Geographical Distribution of Financial Flows to Developing Countries, 1982/5* (Paris, 1987).

11. There is a very clear economic correlation between local real interest rates and capital flight in the Mexican case, though not in other Latin American countries. However, there is also high inverse correlation in Mexico between economic growth and capital flight; thus, high real interest rates, on the one hand discourage capital flight, but to the other extent that they inhibit investment and GDP growth, they also encourage it. For an interesting econometric analysis, see E. R. Gonesa, 'The flight of capital from Latin America: causes and cures', paper presented to the Econometric Society, Universidad de Sao Paulo, Brazil, 4–7 August, 1987. Mimeo, Inter-American Development Bank.

12. The capital flight figures estimates used here are taken from Conesa, *op. cit.*, in (11) and the net transfers are taken from CEPAL, see footnote Table 12.2.

13. For the latter, crucial point, see chapter on Peru by L. Figueroa, in (ed), A. Cornia, R. Jolly, F. Stewart, *Adjustment with a Human Face*, vol. II, Oxford University Press, 1987.

14. For a clear description of the Cruzado plan and its problems, see also Carneiro, D. '*The Cruzado Experience*', Mimeo, PUC, Rio de Janeiro, 1987.

15. Source: World Bank, 'Introduction', *World Debt Tables 1986/7*, Washington DC.

16. See, for example, R. E. Feinberg, 'The Debt Trade Equation', in US Congress Hearings, quoted in (5).

17. For a clear presentation, see for example, statement by Senator Bradley in the US Congress Hearings, quoted in (5).

18. Quoted in A. Kaletsky, 'Banks face the facts at last', *Financial Times*, 21 May, 1987.

19. Source: CEPAL, *op. cit.*

20. J. Williamson, 'The Debt Crisis, the IMF and the US Trade Deficit', in US Congress Hearings, *op. cit.* in (5).

21. This idea was developed first in Latin America, see, for example, O. Sunkel, *America Latina y la Crisis Economica Internacional,* Grupo Editorial Latinomericano, Buenos Aires 1985, and R. Prebisch, 'Statement to the US House of Representatives in July 1985' reproduced in *CEPAL Review* no. 27, Santiago de Chile, December 1985. The idea has increasingly received support in industrial countries, particularly by the UK All Party Parliamentary Report in (1).

22. See *Financial Times*, 11 July 1987; for details, see WIDER, 'Mobilising International Surpluses for World Development: a WIDER Plan for a Japanese Initiative'. Study Group Series, May 1987, WIDER, Helsinki.

Index

adjustment, see structural adjustment
AID 171
ALADI 135, 182
Alfonsin, R. 285 373;
Allied Syndicate 193–5
ANCOM 135
Andean Agreement 135
Andean Development Corporation 182
Andean Reserve Fund 182
Andean Trapezium 179
'arms spending' 172–3
amortization; Chile 127, 132
    Costa Rica 199; Mexico 65–6, 72– 6, 80–4; rescheduling 232, 373; Venezuela 223, 351
Arrelano, J.P. 114, 119
Argentina; capital flight 358; IMF austerity plan 293; moratorium 286, 330
Axelrod, R. 299

Bacha, E. 146, 153
Baker initiative 29, 99, 294–5, 304, 337
Banks; Advisory Group 73–4, 77, 88, 91, 98, 100, 102, 325; Chase Manhatten 228; Deutsche 372; European policy 378; Inter American Development 345, 355, 373; Lloyds 228; of America 228; of England 88; of Mexico 76, 78,

81, 82; United States 341–2, 378; unity of 6;
bargaining models; limitations 309; manipulative approach 315–16
bargaining power; brinkmanship 301–2; of debtors 34–5, 300, 326; pluralist regimes 321; political stability 36, 322–3; see unilateral action
bargaining theory 32–5
Belaunde, President 174–5, 289, 355
Bergsten, F. 371
Bermúdez Morales, 172
BIS Annual Report 4, 78, 149
Bogdanowicz-Bindert, C. 208
Bolivia 290
Botswana 246, 248
Brazil; adjustments before IMF 142–7; comparison with Mexico 327; current account deficits 1979–86; Cruzado Plan 160, 164, 362, 369, debt composition 164; debt servicing 295; external indicators 1979–86 147; IMF solution 163; IMF stalemate 151; import structure 158; inflation 362; 'letter of intent' 151–3; macroeconomic data 143; moratorium 8, 165; New Money Facility Agreement 155; Programme for the External Sector 1983 150; proposals to IMF 150; 'smokescreen' 147–8;